D1526181

William H. Crawford

William H. Crawford

1772-1834

Chase C. Mooney

The University Press of Kentucky

ISBN: 0-8131-1270-2

Library of Congress Catalog Card Number: 70-190534

Copyright © 1974 by The University Press of Kentucky

A statewide cooperative scholarly publishing agency
serving Berea College, Centre College of Kentucky,
Eastern Kentucky University, Georgetown College,
Kentucky Historical Society, Kentucky State University,
Morehead State University, Murray State University,
Northern Kentucky State College, Transylvania University,
University of Kentucky, University of Louisville, and
Western Kentucky University.

Editorial and Sales Offices: Lexington, Kentucky 40506

TO

L B W

B W L

W L B

Contents

Preface

FEW MEN played a more prominent role in the political life of the United States from 1807 to 1825 than William Harris Crawford (1772-1834), and few of such major importance in any period of American history have been accorded so little attention by historians. Senator from Georgia for more than six years, staunch defender of the Bank of the United States, minister to France, secretary of war, secretary of the treasury for the fourth longest period in history, instigator and implementer of important reforms, leading contender for the presidency until his illness in the fall of 1823, and active in the educational, political, and judicial life of his state until his death in 1834, Crawford has been all but forgotten by later generations.

Writers of different periods have attributed this neglect to various factors, but the simple explanation is the absence of a single large collection of Crawford's personal papers. He often did not make a copy of outgoing correspondence and was careless about preserving the letters he received. Much of the material that survived was gathered by Crawford's son-in-law, George M. Dudley, who intended to write a memoir, but this material was lost when Dudley's house burned shortly after the Civil War. Over the years bits of Crawfordiana have found their way into depositories scattered throughout the country, and the examination of hundreds of collections has uncovered information that permits an evaluation not clouded by political jealousy and opposition.

There are still many gaps and unanswered questions. The materials on his pre-Senate years are quite skimpy, and information on his private life is not sufficient to limn the portrait one would wish. Politicians—and others—often revealed their motives and true feelings in correspondence with their wives and families, but not a single letter between Crawford and any member of his large family is known to exist. In other instances, key letters are known by reference only. Even so, the new material does show Crawford to have been something more than a master of intrigue driven by ambition and something less than the paragon portrayed by his partisans.

In monographs, biographies, general histories, and specialized series much of the information on Crawford is incorrect or distorted by a bias in favor of one or more of his political opponents. A considerable number of errors have resulted from relying too heavily on the memoirs of John Quincy Adams; others have stemmed from the unwillingness of authors to mine the less productive and more pedestrian bodies of material. It is not the purpose of this study to correct each of these inaccuracies—or even to indicate them. On a few occasions reference will be made to some especially gross misinterpretation or distortion of the evidence.

In gathering material for this biography I have probably been helped by more people than have most authors. More than one hundred and fifty individuals, from directors to manuscript clerks, in some seventy-five repositories throughout the country have extended kindnesses and assistance that are beyond repayment. To all of them I express my sincere gratitude.

My thanks are extended to the staffs of the following repositories who have graciously granted permission to use and quote from collections in their custody: Boston Public Library; Houghton Library, Harvard University; Massachusetts Historical Society; New-York Historical Society; Research Libraries, The New York Public Library, Astor, Lenox and Tilden Foundations; University of Rochester Library; Historical Society of Pennsylvania; Chicago Historical Society; Newberry Library; University of Chicago Library; J. K. Lilly Library, Indiana University; and Henry E. Huntington Library and Art Museum. The location of the materials will be indicated on first citation.

Special acknowledgments must be made to the late David M. Potter for allowing me to use the Ulrich B. Phillips Papers (then in his possession and now at Yale University), to John A. Munroe of the University of Delaware for extending courtesies in connection with the use of the James A. Bayard and the Louis McLane Papers, to William H. Masterson of the University of Tennessee at Chattanooga for sharing some of his notes, and to Miss Fanny Golding (Columbus, Mississippi) and Mrs. E. E.

(Patty) Gross (Hattiesburg, Mississippi) for permission to use the papers in their possession and for personal kindnesses. Financial aid from the Graduate School of Indiana University and the John Simon Guggenheim Memorial Foundation was most welcome and greatly appreciated.

Abbreviations

ADAH	Alabama Department of Archives and History
ASPF	American State Papers: Finance
ASPFA	American State Papers: Foreign Affairs
ASPIA	American State Papers: Indian Affairs
ASPM	American State Papers: Miscellaneous
ASPMA	American State Papers: Military Affairs
ASPPL	American State Papers: Public Lands
BPL	Boston Public Library
GDAH	Georgia Department of Archives and History
HSP	Historical Society of Pennsylvania
ISH	Illinois State Historical Library
MDLC	Manuscript Division, Library of Congress
MHS	Massachusetts Historical Society
MdHS	Maryland Historical Society
NYH	New-York Historical Society
NYP	New York Public Library
NYS	New York State Library
NCDAH	North Carolina Department of Archives and History
OHS	Ohio Historical Society
OSL	Ohio State Library
UGL	University of Georgia Library
UKy	University of Kentucky Library
UNC	University of North Carolina Library
UVa	University of Virginia Library
VSL	Virginia State Library

1

The Early Georgia Years

SOON AFTER the inauguration of John Quincy Adams in March 1825, an uncommonly large man, emaciated and enfeebled from long illness, left Washington, D.C., for a 600-mile carriage trip to the South. He had traveled the same route many times in the preceding eighteen years, sometimes as senator, others as minister to France, and still others as secretary of war or of the treasury. This time the defeated presidential candidate was making his last journey from the capital to his beloved "Woodlawn," a few miles from Lexington, Georgia. He had seriously thought of retiring from national office ten years earlier; now the time had come, and the expectation of a more leisurely life buoyed his spirit during the arduous ride. William Harris Crawford had served his country with distinction; during seven of his remaining nine years he would play a significant role in the political and judicial life of his state.

Crawford, the sixth of eleven children, was born to Joel and Fanny Harris Crawford on February 24, 1772, in Amherst County, Virginia. He had three older and three younger brothers and two older and two younger sisters. The family was not new to Virginia. Joel's great-grandfather John, Earl of Crawford, was born in Scotland in 1600, emigrated to Virginia in 1643, and was killed while fighting in Bacon's Rebellion in 1676. As a family, the Crawfords have been described as clannish, large of stature, physically powerful, given to a considerable amount of inter-marriage, and not without some distinction.[1]

Financial reverses of an unknown nature induced Joel Crawford in 1779 to move his family to the Edgefield District of South Carolina, where he located on Stevens Creek about thirty miles above Augusta, Georgia. The military operations of the Revolution had placed Augusta in British hands earlier in 1779, and apparently in about a year the Crawford family crossed the Broad River into the Chester District. Joel was among those "rebels" put in the Camden jail while the Tory-Patriot conflict raged in the area, but in the late summer of 1780 he was released through the efforts of some of his loyalist neighbors. Within the next two years he returned to the Edgefield District and then in 1783 moved to Kiokee Creek, near the present site of Appling, Georgia. Already a number of Virginia families lived in the area, and more were soon to come.

Young Crawford had received a little schooling in the Edgefield District, and judging from accounts of his father's zeal for education, it can be assumed that his children attended such schools as existed in the Chester District. It is known that they attended a nearby school in Georgia. Joel Crawford apparently hoped to send William Harris to the University of Edinburgh, which he believed offered the finest education available.[2] These hopes were unrealized, however, and Crawford returned to the old field school. In 1788 resources were insufficient to finance his education at the academy in Augusta, and he became the teacher of the school he had so recently attended. That same year his father died and for the next few years Crawford continued to teach and to help on the farm.

Crawford maintained his interest in formal education. In 1794 —at the age of twenty-two—he enrolled as a pupil at Moses Waddel's Carmel Academy, near Appling. Waddel, a graduate of Hampden-Sydney College and a Presbyterian minister who was to become one of the great schoolmasters of the antebellum South, operated basically a college preparatory school. Latin, Greek, mathematics, and English grammar and literature were stressed; oral reading, declamation, and natural and moral philosophy

1 Crawford's birthplace is now in Nelson County. For accounts of the Crawford family see *Laurus Crawfordiana, Memorials of that Branch of the Crawford Family* (New York, 1883); Lucinda Stephens, comp., *Crawford Genealogy* (Macon, Ga., 1936).

2 J. E. D. Shipp, *Giant Days, or The Life and Times of William H. Crawford* (Americus, Ga., 1909), 25-26; [George W. Dudley], "William H. Crawford," James Herring and James Barton Longacre, *The National Portrait Gallery of Distinguished Americans* (Philadelphia, 1840), 4:1. According to Shipp, the plans for young Crawford to accompany a Scottish merchant of Augusta on a buying trip to Scotland—where arrangements would be made for his schooling—were canceled just before departure when the merchant attempted to cut his own throat. Benjamin F. Perry, *Biographical Sketches of Eminent American Statesmen with Speeches, Addresses and Letters* (Philadelphia, 1887), 272, says the death of Joel and the loss of his property rendered attendance at Edinburgh impractical. The Crawford site on Kiokee Creek was in Richmond County, but in 1790 it became a part of Columbia County.

received considerable attention; history, natural sciences, and the newer, more "practical" subjects were relegated to the bottom of the curriculum. Crawford's two-year attendance coincided with the life of this school. No doubt his previous experience, aptitude, and relative maturity prompted his appointment as usher (assistant or underteacher) during the second year. For this service in a student body that included Thomas W. Cobb (a strong supporter of Crawford in later years) and the headmaster's brother-in-law, John C. Calhoun, Crawford's tuition was remitted by one third.

Waddel was never an easy taskmaster, and his recognition of the abilities of Crawford—only two years his junior—seems to confirm the reports that the transplanted Virginian learned his Latin and Greek quickly. He was especially fond, then and later, of Virgil, Horace, Thucydides, Cicero, and Homer,[3] and his later references to the history of the Greeks show that he did not confine his attention exclusively to literature. He loved books and enjoyed extolling their virtues to others; and his interest in and promotion of the writings of some of his friends and acquaintances bespeak an interest in contemporary literature as well.

Many of Waddel's students at Carmel and at his more famous school at Willington, South Carolina (opened in 1804), later enrolled at various colleges in the Northeast, but Crawford was not so fortunate. He had already taught for several years, and his additional experience at Carmel—plus his admiration for the work of Waddel and the lack of any other marketable skill—probably induced him in July 1796 to accept a $300-a-year position as first English teacher at Richmond Academy in Augusta. The rector of the academy, chosen the previous year, was Charles Tait, and a warm friendship and lifelong political association developed between the two men. The school had financial difficulties. Its two old buildings along the river were decaying and too far from the center of the city to compete with the newer and more conveniently located schools. There were evidences of irregular management by one of the clerks, as well as problems resulting from fluctuating tobacco prices and paper money. Tait resigned at the end of 1797, and for the next year Crawford served as rector and first English teacher at a salary of $500–$300

---

[3] Shipp, *Crawford*, 29; Dudley, "Crawford," 2; Joseph H. Cobb, *Leisure Labors; or, Miscellanies Historical, Literary, and Political* (New York, 1858), 135-36.

less than that of his predecessor. On January 1, 1799, Crawford received his last payment of $125 as a schoolteacher.[4]

The two and a half years at Augusta were significant ones for Crawford. His friendship with Tait promoted the political fortunes of both men. Five years after leaving Augusta the ex-schoolmaster married one of his former pupils. Susanna Gerardin, daughter of Louis Gerardin, a Savannah River Valley planter of French Huguenot descent, became Crawford's wife in 1804, the mother of his three daughters and five sons, and the mistress of a lively, happy household for their thirty years together.[5]

An event of 1798, of only routine interest in Augusta at the time, was to plague Crawford during the presidential campaign of 1824. On July 2, 1798, the "young men of Augusta" addressed a letter—to which Crawford subscribed his name—to President John Adams assuring him of their "unalterable attachment to our country and its government." The communication pointed out the shift in their attitudes as the French government had changed from one of worthy revolutionary aims to one of corruption, and concluded:

> Altho' we are attached to the blessings of peace and deprecate the horrors of war, yet we are sensible, that self-preservation now points out a firm and energetic conduct of government; we view with the highest degree of approbation, those measures which have been pursued by the executive, for the preservation of our national honor.
>
> As we enjoy the supreme felicity of being citizens, of perhaps, the only genuine and well balanced republic, now existing in the world, we feel a just contempt for a nation, who can brand us with the imputation of being a divided people, and who presuming on our division, have left us the only lawful alternative, disgraceful peace, or war.

4 Charles Guy Cordle, "An Ante-Bellum Academy, The Academy of Richmond County, 1783-1863" (M.A. thesis, University of Georgia, 1935), 17-21, citing Minutes of the Trustees of Richmond Academy of appropriate dates. The academy closed in 1800 but reopened in 1802.

5 There is much confusion regarding the spelling of "Gerardin," the spelling I accept. In a beautifully written letter to "Dear Grandpa" on June 2, 1821, the oldest Crawford daughter, Caroline, addressed the communication to "Mr. L. Gerardin." It is rather unlikely that her parents would have permitted the letter to be sent with an incorrect spelling. This letter and several other Crawford items are in the possession of Crawford's great-great-granddaughter, Miss Fanny Golding of Columbus, Mississippi.

With the most unlimited confidence, in the firmness, justice and wisdom of your administration, we pledge ourselves to you and our fellow citizens, that we will be ready at the call of our country to defend what is dearer to us than our lives—her liberty and law.

Adams in his reply of July 20 indicated he differed with his fellow citizens in general about the French Revolution, that he considered American support of it to be an "error of public opinion," and that the expression of confidence from Augusta was "more precious, as it was unexpected."[6]

In the 1820s Crawford's opponents charged him with having approved the oppressive measures of the Adams administration. They overlooked, or ignored, the facts that although the citizens of Augusta may have known of the passage of the Naturalization Act (June 18), they could not have had any knowledge of the Alien Act (June 25), and that the Alien Enemies and Sedition acts were passed after the letter was sent.

Crawford had decided, or been persuaded, that greater opportunities lay open to him in another field. During his last year at Richmond Academy he had studied law, and in the spring of 1799 he moved to Lexington, Oglethorpe County, and began practice. Other than the Augusta letter the only indication of Crawford's participation in public affairs prior to 1799 is his alleged opposition to the Yazoo land sales. Although Georgia laws permitted the head of a family to acquire 1,000 acres of land for "office and surveyor fees," by the 1790s the Indian title to desirable land had been extinguished only along the coast and in most of the area between the Savannah and Ogeechee rivers. The influx of population into Georgia was great during this period, with much land speculation, and Georgia had substantial claims to nearly all the present states of Alabama and Mississippi. The character of much of the unsettled land was little known, but the lands of the Yazoo River area were considered desirable. The Yazoo land companies, consisting of speculators from Georgia and many other states, had failed to meet the requirements of a grant by the Georgia legislature in 1789, but through bribery of

[6] The Augusta communication and Adams' reply are in the *Augusta Chronicle and Gazette of the State*, Aug. 11, 1798. Similar letters of support for Adams' French policy and Adams' replies are in the same paper, July 7, Aug. 18, Dec. 8, 1798. John Clark, soon to be Crawford's bitter and lifelong enemy, was signatory to one of these.

the legislators and other means they succeeded in 1795 in obtaining a grant of more than 30,000,000 acres for $500,000, or one and two thirds cents per acre.

The public outcry was heard even before the legislative grant had been signed, and Crawford is said to have been the moving spirit behind a petition from the citizens of Columbia County urging Governor George Mathews to withhold his signature. The petition failed; the governor signed the bill.[7] James Jackson, Revolutionary hero and United States senator, so opposed the sale that he resigned from the Senate to work for repeal of the act, which was forthcoming in the next session of the legislature. There is no direct evidence of Crawford's role, but later political friendships—with Jackson among others—and personal animosities lend credence to accounts of his opposition to the grant.

Although national concern with the Yazoo land frauds seems to have ended with the Fletcher *v.* Peck decision in 1810 and congressional compensation for "injured" purchasers in 1814, the controversy had a more lasting influence on political parties in Georgia. The Federalists, never very strong, were weakened by the popular belief that they were deeply involved in the frauds, and by 1800 they were no longer an effective political force. In the Republican party, Jackson's actions helped to bring about a split that lasted almost three decades; factional alignments within the Republican party depended largely on social and economic factors and on personalities.

At the time of the Yazoo sale the Federalists were headed by Elijah Clark of Revolutionary reputation, by his sons John and Elijah, Jr., and by Mathews. The Clarks were from North Carolina, and it seems that a vast number of migrants from that state settled in Wilkes County and adhered to the faction soon to be dominated by John Clark. Clark had participated with his father in numerous Indian fights, was rough and ready in politics and personal habits, rather overbearing in disposition, and settled differences preferably by violent means. For many years he was the leader of the Republican group of speculators, small farmers, and transplanted North Carolinians.

---

[7] Shipp, *Crawford,* 33; Ulrich B. Phillips, *Georgia and State Rights,* American Historical Association *Annual Report,* 1901 (Washington, D.C., 1902), 2:31, cites no references. I have been unable to substantiate the references on this point in several secondary accounts or to locate any primary materials linking Crawford with this incident.

English-born James Jackson of Savannah was the leader in the coastal area, but he sought the friendship and support of promising young men from all over the state. More able than Clark, Jackson was almost equally given to violence and could not maintain civil social relations with political opponents. His closest political liaisons in this period were with the Virginians who had settled in large numbers in the Savannah River area, especially in Elbert County. Among these Virginians were Crawford, Tait, the Gilmers, the Barnetts, and William W. Bibb. There was a traditional and persistent rivalry between the North Carolinians and Virginians, and often the causes (other than personal) for factional differences in Georgia were difficult to define.[8]

As Georgia expanded westward from the coastal-Savannah River strip and grew from 82,000 in 1790 to more than a quarter million in 1810, the Jackson mantle fell to George M. Troup of Savannah and Crawford of Lexington. Clark became undisputed head of the other group and a bitter personal rival of Crawford. Both factions were Republican, but the Crawford-Troup alignment continued to draw its strength from the Virginians, the larger landowners, the older settled areas, and the regions with the highest proportion of slaves.

In the clannish, turbulent, violent Savannah-Ogeechee River frontier Crawford had grown to maturity, taken advantage of the best educational training that conditions and finances permitted, taught school, attracted the attention of several of the current and future leaders, and launched his legal-political career. Most of the lawyers at that time rode the court circuit; this mobility offered excellent opportunities for a man with political ambitions. In Georgia the political advantages of this practice were even greater than in some of the other states, since the circuit courts were the highest in the state until 1845.

Crawford fitted well into this world. This ruggedly handsome "giant of a man"—six feet three and well over two hundred pounds—had regular features, "clear blue, mild, though radiant" eyes, and a fair and ruddy complexion. He was very active physically but somewhat awkward in movement, possessed little vanity and not many of the social graces, had a fine, logical mind

---

[8] For an account of the development of these factions see Phillips, *Georgia and State Rights*, 94-102.

and a good command of the English language, but his oratorical skills were not proportionate to his powerful voice. Believing so thoroughly in getting to the heart of the matter quickly and possessing a greater desire to convince than to please, Crawford was sometimes considered blunt.

At twenty-seven Crawford's character was doubtless well formed. His sincerity and accessibility, his excellent memory, his prompt and careful mastery of his cases, a professional zeal that made his clients' causes his own, his wit, and the forceful presentation of his cogent arguments to judge or jury in thirty minutes or less helped to make him an immediate success at the bar. Nor should one overlook Crawford's mental and physical courage, his unpolished but genuine amiability, and hearty sense of humor—he loved to tell anecdotes, told them well, and was a "capital" laugher—as qualities that would attract legal business and win friends.

The first fruits of Crawford's rapidly developing connections in Georgia politics ripened at the end of 1799. In December the legislature authorized the Georgia secretary of state, Horatio Marbury, and two commissioners to prepare a one-volume digest of the Georgia laws.[9] George Watkins and Crawford were chosen as the commissioners. Crawford's choice can probably be attributed to his friendship with James Jackson (now governor), the mutual attachment and admiration that had developed between Crawford and Peter Early of Greene County (the leading upcountry lawyer and later governor, 1813-1815), and his association with Watkins who had served as chairman of the meeting of the "young men of Augusta" in July 1798. The three appointees wrote Jackson on December 9, 1800, asking for a part of the money in advance to help meet expenses.[10] Watkins' participation was short-lived, but Marbury and Crawford pre-

[9] No official action had followed an earlier law authorizing a digest, but Robert and George Watkins undertook the work on their own. In 1799 Governor James Jackson disapproved an appropriation for publication of their volume because it contained the Yazoo Act. The contention that the rescinding act was also included had no effect, and before the matter was concluded Jackson and Robert Watkins had fought three duels. Shipp, *Crawford*, 35-39; Dudley, "Crawford," 6-7. For a brief account of Jackson see Thomas U. P. Charlton, *The Life of Major General James Jackson, Part I* (Augusta, Ga., 1809). The Watkins *Digest* was published by R. Aiken of Philadelphia in 1800.

[10] The three to James Jackson, William H. Crawford Papers (Yale University Library).

sented the results of their work to the governor on March 2, 1801. The digest was printed the following year.[11]

Although this digest did not differ greatly from the unofficial one by George and Robert Watkins, the work of preparation kept Crawford for some time in the capital city of Louisville, permitted him to become better acquainted with the details of the laws of the state, and facilitated contacts that seem not to have injured his law practice or hampered his political career.[12] In 1802 Early, elected to Congress, turned his law practice over to Crawford, who thus became perhaps the most active lawyer in the Western Circuit.[13] His rise in the profession, his associations, and his refusal to serve as counsel for land speculators made him *persona non grata* to the Clark faction, which wished to undermine or destroy him. In 1802, a lesser light of the Clark group was the unfortunate instrumentality of an attempt to ruin Crawford.

Peter Lawrence Van Alen went from New York to Georgia in the mid-1790s and took up residence in Elbert County. He allied himself with the Clark faction and in 1800 became solicitor general of the Western Circuit. Opportunities for land speculation were numerous in rapidly growing Georgia, and apparently Clark, Van Alen, and their associates were interested in acquiring large quantities of land by almost any methods. Crawford not only refused to become their attorney in land suits but was vigorous in opposition to their schemes. They seem to have determined to involve him in an affair of honor, apparently

11 Horatio Marbury and William H. Crawford, *Digest of the Laws of the State of Georgia* . . . (Savannah, Ga., 1802). The errata pages seem to have been prepared by J. Meriwether, Edwin Mounger, and George R. Clayton.

12 While in Louisville, Crawford worked and relaxed at the home of his cousin William Barnett. Barnett's father, Nathaniel, had married Crawford's aunt; his brother Joel married Crawford's older sister Ann. William and Joel were for some time in the Georgia legislature, and William defeated John Forsyth for Congress in 1812. Joel became a wealthy planter in Mississippi. Shipp, *Crawford*, 42-43. While at Barnett's, Crawford became acquainted with the Gilmers who lived immediately opposite. Crawford's promise to young George R. Gilmer, future governor of Georgia, was later acknowledged but modified by the suggestion that Gilmer read law with a Mr. Upson. Crawford felt that his duties in Washington prevented his giving adequate attention to Gilmer's legal training. George R. Gilmer, *Sketches of some of the First Settlers of Upper Georgia, of the Cherokee, and the Author*, rev. ed. (Americus, Ga., 1926), 98. The first edition of Gilmer, with the same title, was published in New York in 1855.

13 See Oglethorpe County Inferior Court Minutes, 1794-1811, and minutes of other courts (microfilm, Georgia Department of Archives and History).

hoping he would refuse to duel and thereby be politically ruined or that he would accept and be killed, since he was not noted for proficiency with pistols. As in many such affairs, the details of the route to the dueling stakes are tortuous. Finally, however, Van Alen challenged Crawford.

Crawford accepted and appeared at the chosen site, Fort Charlotte—twelve miles below Petersburg on the Carolina side— with borrowed pistols. It is said he did not even try them out until the morning of the encounter and that they snapped twice while he was testing them. On the first shot neither party was hit; on the second round Van Alen was mortally wounded, but Crawford was uninjured. Instead of ruining Crawford, the episode seems to have increased his prestige—and to have increased Clark's dislike for him.[14]

In the summer of 1803, Thomas Peter resigned as judge of the superior court of the Western Judicial District and John Griffin, who was married to a sister of Clark's wife, was appointed to the post until the legislature could make its selection. That winter both Clark and Crawford were members of the legislature, the latter for the first time. Clark and his partisans supported Griffin for the appointment, but Charles Tait, favorite of the Crawford group, was chosen to the judgeship.[15] Not for some years had the Clarkites suffered so signal a defeat in filling an important office, and from this incident a duel between Crawford and Clark was to develop. The grand juries of the courts of Clark, Greene, Hancock, Jackson, Franklin, and Lincoln counties had recommended that Griffin be chosen. Crawford charged that Clark had recently practiced before all but one of those courts

14 Details may be found in Shipp, *Crawford*, 44-49; Gilmer, *Sketches*, 98-99. Most writers have used Van Allen instead of Van Alen. Nearly all of the letters in the P. L. Van Alen folder, GDAH, are signed P. Alen and the return address is usually Peter L. Van Alen. In the Oglethorpe County Inferior Court Minutes, 1794-1811, Peter L. V. Alen was listed as practicing attorney in the June 1800 term; in the January 1801 term he was listed as P. Alen. Contrary to the statements of several authors, Van Alen was not a kinsman of Martin Van Buren; it does appear that Van Alen's brother David married a cousin of Van Buren.
15 A letter from James Jackson to John Milledge, Sept. 1, 1801, is not at all clear in its meaning. It is clear that Jackson was engaged in political maneuvering and that he had mentioned Crawford as a candidate for the "C[ircuit?] Judgeship" to "have some [one] from the Westward." Barnett, he noted, and the "whole back country" were "wroth" over the other person recommended. But "Crawford will satisfy them all—Early and a few Yazoo lawyers excepted—and we must take some of those friendly Young Men by the hand." Charlton, *Jackson*, 182-85, esp. 184. Shipp, *Crawford*, 41, citing Charlton, 184, has a somewhat different "translation."

and that he had influenced the actions of the grand juries. He did not say that Clark had bribed, or attempted to bribe, the members of the juries, but he pointed out in his letters that influence took many forms. Newspaper letters and personal correspondence of the two simply worsened the matter, and they agreed to meet on the Carolina side in December 1804. An appeal to Governor John Milledge by "several disinterested gentlemen" resulted in the naming of a court of honor, which reported on December 12. The court thought the basis of the dispute of insufficient consequence to have produced the animosity, unhesitatingly declared both gentlemen "brave and intrepid," and urged them to settle their quarrel. Clark and Crawford acceded to the decision, but the former seems not to have been happy about it.

The matter, however, was not settled. In February 1806 Robert Clary accused Clark of being involved in a land transaction in which payment was made with counterfeit money. Clark charged conspiratorial activity against him; he was convinced that Crawford and Tait (before whom Clary's deposition was made) were determined to destroy him—or perhaps he was still determined to destroy Crawford—and on December 2, 1806, after an unsuccessful attempt to impeach Tait,[16] he sent Crawford a challenge, which was accepted on the same day. Two weeks later the parties met at the "High Shoals of the Appalachee" in the Indian Territory. On the first fire Clark was unharmed; Crawford's left wrist was badly damaged. Clark wished to continue but George Moore, Crawford's second, would not allow further exchange. Clark's subsequent challenge, on July 22, 1807, was declined by Crawford who considered that by the previous meeting the "contest was brought to a final issue and the difference adjusted as far as an interview of that kind is intended or calculated for adjustment. . . ."[17]

16 Manuscript Journal, House of Representatives, June 11, Nov. 10, 29, 1806 (GDAH). Clary, accused of Negro stealing, was a prisoner in custody of Josiah Glass. The deposition was taken after court hours. The report disapproving Clark's charges for impeachment of Tait was carried, 53 to 3.

17 Accounts may be found in John Clark, *Considerations of the Purity of the Principles of William H. Crawford* . . . (Augusta, Ga., 1819), 13-105; Shipp, *Crawford*, 50-75. Neither is completely accurate, but it is not considered worthwhile to correct the numerous errors. It seems that Clark may have written the 1807 challenge letter about the time he caught Tait on Jefferson Street in Milledgeville and gave him thirty or forty lashes with his riding whip. For that assault Clark

Crawford's two duels in four years, Jackson's several encounters, and many others reflect the standards of politics and society in Georgia at that time. The man who would not defend his "sacred honor" with his life could not command the respect and esteem of his fellows. Crawford could live with this: he was part and parcel of the frontier and was known from his early years as self-reliant, forthright, and outspoken, though affable and good-natured. He did not run from difficulty, but it does not appear that he intentionally offended others. He would have been rash deliberately to provoke a duel with Clark, whose long-established reputation indicated physical violence as a favorite method of resolving controversies. It is said that Clark mellowed in old age and grew friendly with all but Crawford. Crawford's dislike for Clark probably was less intense than Clark's for Crawford, but there are indications that Crawford would not have been averse to some other person's engaging Clark in mortal combat. After 1806, however, Crawford renounced physical violence as a means of settling differences between himself and others, and in 1811, as John Randolph's second, he appears to have played an important role in persuading Randolph and John W. Eppes that a duel between them was not required.[18]

Crawford continued as representative from Oglethorpe County in the Georgia assembly through the 1806 session; his committee memberships were numerous, and apparently his work was satisfactory and his political friendships and contacts effective, for he was chosen by his colleagues for the United States Senate. Crawford's efforts to establish free schools and to authorize a lottery to raise $3,000 for books for the state college at Athens reflect his lifelong concern for improving education. He sought to improve the judicial system and the electoral process and to provide funds for bridges and making the rivers more easily

---

was fined $2,000 and placed on security for good conduct for five years. Shortly thereafter Governor Jared Irwin remitted the fine in all its parts. Cobb, *Leisure Labors*, 139, says that Crawford, "naturally awkward, nervous, and every way unqualified for a genuine duellist . . . took his position at the peg with the same carelessness as he was wont to swagger to his seat at the bar of a county court, exposing his left arm in a maner to catch the ball of even the rawest duellist." Dudley, "Crawford," 5, says Crawford looked upon his duels with "deep and poignant regret."

18 Randolph to James M. Garnett, April 28, 1811 (including copy of Crawford to Randolph, March 28, 1811), Correspondence of John Randolph and James M. Garnett, compiled by W. C. Bruce (Virginia State Library, Richmond); Irving Brant, *James Madison*, 6 vols. (Indianapolis, Ind., 1941-1961), 5:263.

navigable. He was also successful in advocating that importation of slaves into Georgia, both from other states and from abroad, be prohibited.[19]

The legislature met at the new capital, Milledgeville, for the first time on November 2, 1807, and five days later the two branches proceeded by separate ballot to elect a successor to the late Abraham Baldwin. From the ballots "it appeared that William Harris Crawford Esq. was elected Senator to the Congress of the United States."[20] Crawford's long opposition to the Clark faction, duels with two of that group, flourishing law practice and wide acquaintance in the state, creditable though not outstanding service in the house, personal popularity and recognized ability, support by key figures of the anti-Clarkites, intimate knowledge of Georgia politics, and the setback administered to Clark in his attempt to impeach Tait help to explain Crawford's rise from beginning lawyer in 1799 to United States senator in eight years. He was to remain in national service for eighteen years, and not until 1827 did he again hold state office.

Crawford had a strong attachment to Georgia and to his farm-plantation; during nearly two decades of national service he visited Georgia in the summer whenever possible. Year by year the desire to lead the life of a country gentleman appeared to strengthen, though he did not permanently return to Woodlawn until the spring of 1825.

It seems that Crawford had just acquired the initial tract of Woodlawn at the time of his marriage in 1804. These 260 acres, located approximately three miles from Lexington, were listed on the tax books of 1805 as "second class" or second quality.[21] He was taxed for only two slaves in 1806 instead of the four of 1805, but he had increased his landholdings to 300 acres. Crawford had by then acquired a two-wheeled carriage, a bequest of Francis Meson. The taxable acreage dropped back to 260 in 1807 and remained steady until 1811 when an additional 736 acres, second class, was listed from Jackson County. He had owned and

[19] Manuscript Journal, esp. Nov. 15, 25, Dec. 1, 2, 1803; Nov. 19, 24, 1804; Nov. 12, Dec. 2, 1805; Nov. 15, 19, 1806.

[20] Ibid., Nov. 7, 1807.

[21] It is probable that the William H. Crafford listed in John C. Evans' district in 1799 was Crawford. He was taxed for one Negro, but no land. All information on Crawford's property is taken from "Tax Digest—Oglethorpe County" (microfilm, GDAH). Land in Georgia at the time was classed as first, second, or third quality, and "Pine Land."

apparently disposed of a lot in Athens but held two lots in Jefferson. A four-wheeled carriage was added to the tax list in 1809,
and by 1811 the slaves had increased to sixteen.

The year 1811 seems to have been a turning point in Crawford's
finances, for then he, George Phillips, and Robert Allison filed
their final report with the Court of Ordinary in Lexington on
the administration of the will of Francis Meson. Meson, a
merchant of Lexington, had made his will on August 30, 1806,
and died eight days later. He stipulated that $8,000 be used to
establish an academy, bequeathed to Crawford a carriage and
two carriage horses, and gave equal parts of the remainder of
his estate (after the satisfaction of some express money bequests)
to the three executors. Oglethorpe County had no academy but
did have academy commissioners in 1806; Crawford and Phillips
were two of the five. Action on the academy was rapid, and
Crawford was on the first board of trustees. The portion of the
estate divided among the three executors was "no less than
$30,000."[22] It is probably safe to assume that Crawford had
been Meson's attorney, that the relationship of the two men had
been cordial, and that Crawford used some of the bequest from
Meson for the purchase of land, for Woodlawn increased from
300 acres in 1811 to 800 in 1812 and to 1,100 the following year.

Between 1804 and 1813 Crawford's landholdings had grown
from farmer to planter proportions, but his slaveholdings would
not justify designating him a planter until the 1820s. He was
one of the largest landholders in Oglethorpe County, a reasonably
fertile area of the Georgia Piedmont. Little is known of his
agricultural production beyond the facts that he did raise cotton,
corn, and hogs and had rather extensive orchards. He trusted
only himself and his older children to tend the fruit trees, which
suffered from neglect during his stay in France. Crawford also
experimented with different fertilizing and nitrogen-fixing agents,
but his major innovative efforts were devoted to the introduction
of new seeds, grasses, vines, and fruits. He often asked friends to
experiment by sharing the imports with them. Thomas Jefferson,
James Madison, John Randolph, Nathaniel Macon, and Henry

22 E. Merton Coulter, "Francis Meson, An Early Georgia Merchant and Philan-
thropist," *Georgia Historical Quarterly* 42 (March 1958):26-43; "Meson Academy,
Lexington, Georgia," ibid. (June 1958):125-62. Coulter says that the words on the
marble slab on Meson's grave were probably chosen by Crawford and that it has
been generally assumed that Crawford wrote Meson's will.

Clay were among those who tested seeds and plants that Crawford hoped would prove profitably adaptable to the climate and soil of the southern United States.

The house at Woodlawn was said to boast no "artificial embellishments of taste"; rather it portrayed the "simplicity and unostentatious habits of its illustrious owner." Between the house and the main road was a "magnificent forest of oaks" through which wound an avenue just wide enough for vehicles to pass. To the rear of the house was the extensive plantation clearing, dotted with apple and peach orchards. A spring only a few yards from the house was the source of a clear little brook that meandered through the open area. The garden contained an abundance of flowering shrubs, choice fruit trees, and numerous flowerbeds. On the front lawn, under a large oak, the entire family frequently gathered on summer evenings.[23] There was no affectation in Crawford's manner or dress—and Mrs. Crawford was said to be as unaffected as he—but he was charitable, seldom asked the price of anything, and considered nothing expensive if it contributed to the comfort of himself or his family.

There was little or nothing in the Crawford household to support the image of the stern authoritarian family of the early nineteenth century; Woodlawn was often referred to as "Liberty Hall." Crawford had a great respect for human dignity, sought the development of individuals as free spirits, and was unflagging in his zeal to promote the education of his children. Every child, from the oldest to the youngest, was free to express his or her opinion on the topic of the moment; if an opinion or assertion was combated, it was in such a way as to demonstrate how a more correct judgment might be reached. Each person was encouraged to be himself, and the actions of each were open to praise or adverse criticism by the others. The father was subject to the same treatment as all the others and is said to have admitted his errors or argued his defense in the "same kind spirit and good temper" as everyone else. Free speech, equal rights, and equal suffrage—the trinity of democracy—began at home. Misfortunes and joys were borne or shared in common. Indoor amusements included chess, drafts, and other games of calculation and judgment as well as games that called for "rapid thought, quick perception, and ready answers." Outdoors, games of cour-

23 Cobb, *Leisure Labors*, 233-34.

age and agility were played. Though robbed of much of his physical power by his illness, Crawford often participated in these activities throughout his life.

Crawford's espousal of the techniques and the freedom of the Pestalozzian school was in perfect keeping with his general philosophy of rearing children, and he and William W. Bibb (doctor, senator, and Crawford partisan) established and sustained a Pestalozzian school in Georgia for several years. But much of the education of the Crawford children took place in the capital city. They were sent to the best schools and Crawford personally examined the children daily to satisfy himself about their progress and the methods of instruction. He would often have them read with him. The Bible was the chief classbook for these sessions, and Job and the Psalms were Crawford's favorite books. All during his cabinet service—except for the period of his severe illness—he held these extrainstructional meetings, and after his return to Georgia he continued the practice with his younger children. Though Crawford frequently read the Bible, he thought formal sectarian religion often hypocritical; he never made a profession of religion but believed in Christianity and was a life member of the American Bible Society.[24]

When Crawford left Woodlawn in 1807 it was a farm of only three hundred acres, and this man who had risen so rapidly was thirty-five, the father of Caroline and John, and in his manners showed few traces of his frontier background. His intimate and detailed knowledge of Georgia political activities dimmed with the years away from home, but his zest for the game quickly revived when he returned to his beloved estate in 1825.

[24] Ibid., 234; Dudley, "Crawford," 2-5, 7; Gilmer, *Sketches,* 129.

2

In the Senate:
Defender of the Bank

WHEN CRAWFORD became a senator in late 1807, both the United States and the Republican party were divided. Beset by persisting commercial and diplomatic difficulties which periodically reached crisis proportions in the succeeding five years, Congress reflected acute sectional differences, interparty struggle, and intraparty strife. The war among the European powers—especially between England and France—had permitted the American shipping interests to engage in a lucrative wartime, or mushroom, commerce with the colonies of those countries, but the normal commerce of the United States—particularly in cotton and other heavy products—had suffered a great decline because it was less rewarding to the shippers. The shipping areas of the country took a jaundiced view of any attempt to curtail or interdict the wartime commerce, while the areas producing the heavy goods were ardent in the defense of neutral rights as a protector of the normal commerce which was essential to their economic well-being. Generally, the Federalists supported the shipping interests and the Republicans the producing, but there were significant exceptions.

Resolution of the problems facing the nation was made more difficult by the growing factionalism in the party in power, the Jeffersonian Republicans. The President's recall of James Monroe after his abortive effort to negotiate a satisfactory commercial agreement with England placed Monroe temporarily in opposition to the administration, though not in alliance with the eccentric John Randolph and his followers, who since the impeachment trial of Associate Justice Samuel Chase had tended to go their own way. Republican ranks were further rent by the activities of Aaron Burr, whose trial for treason had recently closed at Richmond. Also, the Republicans had come to differ among themselves about the proper role and function of the national government almost as sharply as they had differed with the Federalists a few years before.

Crawford's public experience had been confined to the state level, and there is no evidence that he had really grappled with national issues or had reached any firm conclusions about the role of the central government. As a freshman senator—arriving six weeks after the session began—he spoke infrequently, but his attack on the statements of William Branch Giles, senator from Virginia and long a national figure and Republican factionalist, indicated an unwillingness to be bound by any party considerations. Generally, during the 1807-1808 session Crawford seemed to be acquainting himself with some of the problems and fulfilling a number of committee assignments creditably.[1]

Soon after the adjournment of Congress Crawford returned to Georgia in company with congressmen William W. Bibb, George M. Troup, and Thomas W. Cobb, all of whom were to play important roles in his political career. They traveled with John Randolph and were guests at his plantation, "Bizarre." They must have discussed James Monroe's chances for gaining the presidency that year because Randolph thought they would reach Georgia with a "greater zeal for the election of Colonel M[onroe] than possessed them" when they left Washington. Three weeks later Randolph wrote that Bibb, Cobb, Crawford, and Joseph Bryan (a Georgia senator at the time) were zealous in the cause of the election of Monroe. Monroe's candidacy brought a temporary break in a long friendship with Madison, and Bryan's support of Monroe hurt the state senator "greatly." Other Georgia supporters of Monroe, Bryan said, had been "destroyed" politically by their opposition to the successful Madison.[2]

One can only guess how zealous Crawford was in Monroe's cause, but whatever his role it apparently had no adverse effects on his career. Perhaps a letter of March 23, 25, and 26 to a "friend in Hancock County" was intended to persuade some of his fellow Georgians to support Monroe rather than Madison. Crawford

---

1 *The Debates and Proceedings of the Congress of the United States* . . . (Washington, D.C., 1852), 10th Cong., 1st sess., 1:47, 55, 64, 79, 86, 98-99, 106, 131, 177, 313-17, 375, 381-82. Hereafter cited as *Annals*.

2 John Randolph to James M. Garnett, May 8, 27, 1808, Randolph-Garnett; Joseph Bryan to Randolph, Jan. 31, Feb. 3, 1808, Jan. 4, 1810, Joseph Bryan Papers (Virginia State Library).

said some favorable things about Monroe's communication of the previous month on his activities in England, thought a full view of the negotiations would justify Monroe's and William Pinkney's signing of the treaty with England, and believed that the former minister had acted the part of an "honest upright Republican."[3] A certain independence—or even recalcitrance— on the part of Monroe may have attracted Crawford, but there is no evidence to indicate a close friendship between these two until after Monroe began his service as secretary of state in 1811.

In the fall of 1808, Crawford staked his claim to recognition and leadership by his discussion of the embargo, but he was little involved in strictly domestic matters either in that session of Congress or the special session of the following summer. In 1809 he was keenly interested in the gubernatorial contest in Georgia; he made two trips to the state, visited several counties, and corresponded and conferred with the successful candidate, David B. Mitchell. Crawford must have been pleased late in 1809 when his friend of many years, Charles Tait, was chosen as his colleague in the Senate.[4]

Crawford's claim for national stature was strengthened in early 1810 by his speech against the frigate bill during which he sharply criticized President Madison's message to Congress,[5] but it was in February 1811 that he definitely established that stature —and gained a position of preeminence in the Senate—by his able and vigorous advocacy of the renewal of the charter of the First Bank of the United States.[6] Henry Clay, later ardent supporter of the bank, was the most vocal opponent of renewal.

The establishment of the bank in 1791 had been part of the ideology and power struggle between Alexander Hamilton and Thomas Jefferson, but the Jeffersonian Republicans had come to recognize the beneficial effects of the institution and had actually strengthened and expanded it. The bank played a vital

3 *Georgia Argus,* April 12, 1808 (Tuesday morning extra). The original letter has not been located.

4 Crawford to General [David B. Mitchell], May 1, 1809, Miscellaneous, MSS C (New-York Historical Society); Crawford to Mitchell, Oct. 15, 1809, Miscellaneous Collection (Historical Society of Pennsylvania); *Annals,* 11th Cong., 2d sess., 519.

5 For Crawford's routine activities and committee assignments see *Annals,* 11th Cong., 2d sess., 473, 479, 483, 484, 511-12, 525, 530, 550, 577, 587, 634, 664, 671-72, 674. See chapter 3 for a discussion of the frigate bill.

6 Action on the renewal bill had been postponed during the preceding session. Ibid., 598, 625, 661, 669.

role as fiscal agent of the government and acted as a stabilizing influence on the economy and a restraining force on state banks whose notes often were not backed by specie. Some Republican opponents of the bank, particularly from the South, believed the bank an unconstitutional manifestation of federal power dangerous to democratic institutions, while others professed to fear the evil influence which British stockholders might exercise. Still others (such as Samuel and Robert Smith of Maryland, Michael Leib of Pennsylvania, and Giles) appeared more concerned about the influence of Albert Gallatin, secretary of the treasury and long a supporter of the bank.

During 1810 the state banks waged a campaign to arouse public opinion against the bank. The campaign was most successful in the larger states, and several legislatures, including those of Virginia, Massachusetts, and Pennsylvania, had instructed their senators and requested their representatives to vote against recharter. In the smaller states the efforts of the state banks met with indifferent success, and many thought the imminence of war made the time inauspicious for disrupting the fiscal system of the government.

On December 10, 1810, a petition from the directors of the bank seeking renewal of the charter was referred to a five-man committee, with Crawford as chairman. Secretary of Treasury Gallatin, who in 1809 had recommended renewal of the charter, told the committee that continuation of the bank would greatly facilitate the collection of revenue and promote the public welfare; he cautioned that serious shock to commercial, banking, and national credit could come from ceasing the operations of an institution which circulated $13 million and to which the merchants owed $14 million in addition to the $10 million or $12 million they owed the United States for duties. On February 5, 1811, Crawford presented a bill to extend the life of the bank to March 4, 1831.[7] He made no remarks in favor of the bill, nor did he explain the committee's recommendations, though Gallatin's letter was submitted with the bill.

The showdown began in the committee of the whole on February 11, when Joseph Anderson of Tennessee (who, with

---

[7] *Annals*, 11th Cong., 3d sess., 21, 22-25 passim, 122; Crawford to Gallatin, Jan. 29, 1811; Gallatin to Crawford, Jan. 30, 1811, ibid., 122-23, 123-25. On February 1 Crawford's credentials, showing he had been elected for the six-year term beginning in March, were presented to the Senate. Ibid., 114.

Crawford, had also been on the bank committee of the previous session) moved to strike the establishing clause of the renewal bill. He said every citizen had made up his mind on the issue— as had perhaps every member of the Senate—so he would not discuss the matter. Crawford, as closemouthed in presenting the bill as Anderson in his proposal for defeat of the measure, was astonished by the Tennessean's approach to the renewal issue: the good effects of the bank had for twenty years been universally experienced, and no reason was assigned for not continuing the bank other than public opinion. Admittedly, the public will should play a great role in a democracy, but Crawford questioned the magnanimity and fairness of Anderson's procedure. He hoped someone would give reasons for opposition to the bank's re-charter.[8] Samuel Smith, powerful in business as well as political circles, saw nothing novel in Anderson's action, thought Craw-ford knew the state legislatures had taken up the issue, and maintained the burden of proof rested with the introducer of a measure. Crawford had expected to delay his defense of the measure, but the fear of a vote being taken without debate impelled him to explain the reasoning of the committee[9]—or perhaps his reasons for supporting the bill.

As chief spokesman for the renewal of the bank charter, Craw-ford ran counter to the majority of the Republican party and to public opinion in general, and his use of the doctrine of implied powers to "prove" the constitutionality of the bank places him outside the fold of Old Republicanism. His reliance on the necessary and proper clause was less offensive to Old Republicans, but his contention that this clause, together with the express authority to collect taxes, duties, imposts, and excises, "fairly invests Congress with the power to create a bank" did not prove persuasive. Congressional authorization of a lighthouse, he said, was no more a law to regulate commerce than establishing a bank was a law to collect taxes, imposts, and duties. Yet the erection of a lighthouse tends to facilitate and promote the security and prosperity of commerce just as the creation of a bank tends to facilitate and insure the collection, safekeeping, and transmission of the revenue.[10]

8 Ibid., 132-33.

9 Ibid., 133-34; Macon to Joseph Nicholson, Feb. 11, 1811, Joseph Nicholson Papers (Manuscript Division, Library of Congress).

10 *Annals*, 11th Cong., 3d sess., 134-40.

Crawford would not say that the government absolutely depended upon the existence of a bank; he did insist that the bank
enabled the government to manage more advantageously its fiscal
concerns. The present imperative must not be subordinated to
tradition and precedent: "We are, when acting to-day, not to
inquire what means were necessary and proper twenty years ago,
not what were necessary and proper at the organization of the
Government, but our inquiry must be, what means are necessary
and proper this day. The Constitution, in relation to the means
by which its powers are to be executed, is one eternal *now*. The
state of things now, the precise point of time we are called upon
to act, must determine our choice in the selection of means to
execute the delegated powers."[11]

In denouncing the larger states that sought destruction of
the bank, Crawford charged their actions were motivated by the
desire to dominate and by avarice: they hoped to compel the
United States to use their banks as places of deposit and thus
increase their dividends. He reminded his colleagues of the
equality of the states and questioned whether the already excessive influence of the great states should be increased at the expense
of the country as a whole.[12] Still focusing his remarks primarily
on the large states, he sharply criticized the newspapers, which
had "teemed with the most scurrilous abuse against any member
of Congress who has dared to utter a syllable" in favor of recharter of the bank. Should the senators "tamely act under the
lash of this tyranny of the press? . . . Instead of reasoning to
prove the unconstitutionality of the law, they charge members
of Congress with being bribed and corrupted. And this is what
they call liberty of the press. To tyranny, under whatever form
it may be exercised, I declare open and interminable war. To
me it is perfectly indifferent whether the tyrant is an irrespon-
sible editor or a despotic monarch."[13]

He denied the charge that the bank had been established by

11 Ibid., 141-42.
12 Ibid., 143-44. Henry Adams, *History of the United States of America . . .,*
9 vols. (New York, 1909-1911), 5:335 (hereafter cited as Adams, *History*), says that
when Crawford "flung so freely" his charge of avarice and ambition about the
Senate he had Samuel Smith "directly in his eye." In 1824 Smith strongly supported
Crawford's presidential candidacy.
13 *Annals*, 11th Cong., 3d sess., 145. Crawford stressed that the first bank had
not been created in the "hard unconstitutional times which produced the Sedition
Law." Ibid., 144.

the opponents of the present party of administration, noted that under Jefferson the Congress had not only supported the bank but had even extended it into the Louisiana Territory, and reminded his colleagues that the current session of Congress had incorporated additional banks for the District of Columbia. The entire banking system, he contended, was "too long and too deeply rooted, to be frowned out of existence by Congress."[14] And the objection to the bank because of the large number of British stockholders he thought of little consequence; the United States could at any moment seize such investments and thus be able to exert more influence on the conduct of investors than investors could possibly exert upon affairs of the United States. Crawford asked those senators who might be bothered by supporting an institution strongly favored by their political opponents to sacrifice their pride at the "shrine of public good."[15]

During the next nine days Crawford occasionally addressed himself to a point of clarification when some other senator made reference to his remarks, and on February 20, the last day of debate on the bill, he again made a major speech. He disagreed with Samuel Smith that the bank in its origin had been a party question; the vote would show many distinguished Republicans for and many distinguished Federalists against the original charter. The point was pursued into the area of "correct apportionment," which if it had existed would have brought a heavier vote for the bank, not against, as the opponents of renewal asserted. Crawford returned to the matter of state influence, noting that the central government could do no more than withdraw deposits from state banks, but the very life of the Bank of the United States depended on the will of Congress. Further, he said, the disposition of state banks to control the operation of the central government would "increase with every increase of the means of annoyance, which the folly and improvidence of Congress may throw into their hands."[16]

Crawford discussed at some length credit and revenue bonds, the discounting of bonds that had an additional endorser and were on deposit in the bank at Philadelphia, the bank's responsibility for the collection of such bonds, and the resulting increase

14 Ibid., 146.
15 Ibid., 147-50.
16 Ibid., 331-34.

of credit and collection of large sums without any possibility of loss by the government. Credit, he said, was the true basis of commerce and the bank the "most powerful engine in the collection of revenue which human ingenuity can devise." Yet, the opponents of the bank had contended that it had nothing to do with the collection of the revenue.[17]

In his earlier speech Crawford had expressed uncertainty as to the constitutionality of state banks, but on February 20 he picked up the argument of Henry Clay and other antibank senators regarding state taxation and turned it in a rather novel direction:

> It has been said . . . that the right of the States to tax bank stock is inconsistent with the right of Congress to create a bank. That the right of taxation destroys the right to create, because the States, by immoderate taxation, could drive the bank out of their limits. All arguments drawn from the abuse of a right ought to be received with great caution; but, if it is entitled to any weight in this case, it equally proves the unconstitutionality of the State banks, because the right of Congress to lay and collect taxes is subject to but two restrictions: that they shall be uniform, and that direct taxation shall be according to population.[18]

He ridiculed the fears of some of the senators by saying that the Constitution had given the government unlimited power over taxes, unlimited power to raise armies and navies, unlimited power to make war and peace, but some of his colleagues were alarmed at the incidental power to create a bank to aid in the management of its fiscal operations.[19]

The recharter of the bank was not a partisan question, and Crawford would not be troubled by party conformity; he would advance with a "firm, undeviating step, unappalled by the howling of party rage, more terrific than the yell of the aboriginal savage."[20] Not only had a number of the Republicans voted for the bank in 1791, but the Republicans, he again noted, had extended it into the territories. Furthermore, they had taken action in 1807 (as had the Federalists in 1798) against counterfeiting, and these precedents should have some weight. If the

17 Ibid., 334-35.
18 Ibid., 342.
19 Ibid.
20 Ibid., 331, 338.

Republicans had thought the bank unconstitutional, it was their duty to have amended the Constitution, either by expressly giving or taking away that power. To decide that the bank was unconstitutional was to disturb what had been settled for twenty years. Ten years later others might decide that it was constitutional and recharter it for twenty years. The bank would then have been constitutional for twenty years, unconstitutional for ten years, and constitutional for twenty years. "Are we to go on in this unsettled, miserable, halting manner? God forbid!" If he preferred political standing in his state to the public welfare, Crawford said he would rejoice in the success of Anderson's motion, but since he believed the public welfare infinitely more important than any "fleeting popularity which an individual like myself can expect to enjoy," he would sincerely regret success of the motion. He concluded by saying that support for and success of the bank might uphold the tottering credit of the commercial class until the storm had passed; failure to recharter might draw down to "undistinguished ruin thousands of your unfortunate and unoffending fellow-citizens."[21]

Maybe Anderson was right when he said on February 11 that perhaps every member of the Senate had made up his mind on the bank, and on that day Nathaniel Macon—then a representative and later senator from North Carolina—had correctly predicted a tie vote in the Senate. Nine of its members from the free states voted for renewal and nine against; eight from the slave states were for recharter and eight against. The vote of Vice President George Clinton killed the measure.[22]

Although Madison remained aloof and a number of administration men had opposed recharter, the bank seems to have gone down—as Gallatin recounted years later—because of the personal opposition of the Clintons, the Smiths, Leib, and Giles to the President and to Gallatin. Soon after the defeat of the bank bill, Gallatin—weary of factional quarrels and perhaps resentful of Madison's failure to give active support to the measure—submitted his resignation. Crawford and other Gallatin friends called on the President to remonstrate against the secretary's leaving office. Madison declined to accept Gallatin's resignation; instead

---

21 Ibid., 344-46.
22 Macon to Joseph Nicholson, Feb. 11, 1811, Nicholson. In the House the bill for recharter had earlier been indefinitely postponed by a 65-to-64 vote.

he dismissed Secretary of State Robert Smith, who for some time had given less than full support to the President's policies.[23]

The odds against Crawford's winning the fight for the bank were too great, but his efforts won the admiration of many and raised him to preeminence in the Senate. His distinguished speech of February 11, partially if not wholly extemporaneous, clearly signaled his ideas of constitutional powers and his conviction that individual, sectional, and party interests must not be allowed to threaten national measures and goals. It displayed his independence of spirit and action, his frankness and fearlessness, his ability of clear and logical exposition, and his composure in the heat of debate. Further, he had ridiculed party rigidity, declared war on special interests and tyranny, and appealed for action in the name of the public welfare.

Among Crawford's contemporaries, Gallatin was especially attracted to Crawford's qualities, and the recharter fight probably was the beginning of a close friendship between the two men. Several years later, after indicating to a lifelong friend how various men had failed to meet his standards in a search for a successor to Jefferson, Gallatin said: "One man at last appeared who filled my expectations . . . Crawford, who united to a powerful mind a most correct judgment and an inflexible integrity—which last quality, not sufficiently tempered by indulgence and civility, has prevented his acquiring general popularity."[24]

Much later, historian Henry Adams, while noting that Crawford was a "crude Georgian, with abilities not yet tried in administration," indicates that the defense of the bank made Crawford the representative of the Madison administration in the Senate and the favorite of the "Jeffersonian triumvirate" for succession to the presidency. At another place Adams says that Crawford's speech of February 11 was "remarkable for the severity of its truths," but the Georgian showed the "faults of a strong nature— he was overbearing, high-tempered, and his ambition did not spurn what his enemies called intrigue; but he possessed the courage of Henry Clay, with more than Clay's intelligence, though far less than his charm. Crawford was never weak, rarely rhetor-

---

[23] Gallatin to Nicholas Biddle, Aug. 14, 1830 (confidential), Albert Gallatin Papers (NYH): Adams, *History*, 5:434-35; Brant, *Madison*, 5:278; Crawford to Joseph Nicholson, March 1, 1811, Nicholson.

[24] Gallatin to John Badollet, July 29, 1824, Gallatin.

ical; and if he was ever emotional he reserved his emotion for other places than the Senate." Crawford, under Gallatin's teaching, bade fair—in Adams' opinion—to make himself what the South desperately needed, a statesman who understood its interests. He, however, was far in advance of his people, who were more correctly represented by Giles of Virginia.[25]

Whatever might be one's definition of civility and crudeness, or agreement or disagreement with these estimates, it seems clear that by the spring of 1811 Crawford had achieved an enviable position among the Republicans. It is not clear that Crawford was the representative of the Madison administration; he was the most effective opponent of antiadministration forces in the Senate, but he, too, was on several occasions sharply critical of, and even opposed to, the administration. Nor is it certain that Crawford was "favored" for succession to the presidency; if this were true, the "favor" was short-lived. The breach between Madison and Monroe was healed just at this time, and Monroe became secretary of state in April 1811. Monroe was soon the favorite, and a close friendship developed between the new secretary and Crawford. Certainly, Crawford had become a major force in national politics by early 1811.

In the fall of 1811 Crawford was reappointed to most of the important committees on which he had previously served. Illness kept him from the Senate from December 20, 1811, to January 28, 1812, and limited his activity for almost another month. His committee work seems to have taken a sharp upturn during the first three weeks of March, but he was soon removed from the active participant's role. On March 23 the Senate adjourned because of the indisposition of the Vice President; the following day Crawford was elected president pro tempore on the first ballot. It is highly probable that Crawford's subordination of partisan politics to issues and the impartiality of his criticism were significant factors in his being chosen as the first "permanent" presiding officer (other than the Vice Presidents) of the Senate, though it is also possible that his opposition wished to neutralize his influence.[26]

25 Henry Adams, *The Life of Albert Gallatin* (Philadelphia, 1880), 428, 433 (hereafter cited as Adams, *Gallatin*); Adams, *History*, 5:332-33.

26 *Annals*, 12th Cong., 1st sess., 177 passim; ibid., 2d sess., passim: Nathaniel Macon to [Bartlett Yancey], Jan. 2, 1812, Personal Miscellany, AC2548 (MDLC).

Steps were taken to grant Crawford the same compensation, during his period of service, as was allowed the speakers of the House. In May 1812 Crawford was one of seventeen senators attending the caucus which renominated Madison for the presidency and chose John Langdon of New Hampshire as his running mate. The latter declined the nomination, and on June 6 Crawford read his letter to another meeting, which then chose Elbridge Gerry.[27]

Clinton had died within a month of his indisposition, and Crawford was reelected president pro tempore at the next session. He seems not to have used his position to make partisan appointments or confer personal favors, but the use of his influence as presiding officer—and perhaps now as leader of the administration forces—may be inferred from the voting on a few occasions.[28] By this time the United States had been several months at war, and Crawford had played a major role in the congressional events leading to the country's involvement in that conflict.

[27] *Niles' Weekly Register* 2 (May 23, 1812):192-93; (June 27, 1812):276; *National Intelligencer*, June 9, 11, 1812. Gerry died before the end of 1814.

[28] For example, see the action on the bill for the regulation of seamen. *Annals*, 12th Cong., 2d sess., 107-8, 111.

3

In the Senate:
Embargo or War

WHEN CRAWFORD took his seat in the Senate on December 9, 1807, the United States was sharply divided over response to the violations by France and Great Britain of her neutral rights and national honor. Napoleon's Berlin decree of 1806 and Milan decree of 1807 declared the British Isles blockaded and subjected merchant ships bound to or from England to seizure and confiscation by French warships and privateers; British orders in council authorized the same treatment for vessels of any nation at war with Britain or vessels trading with any port under Napoleon's domination. That same year, 1807, the commercial provisions of the Jay Treaty expired. William Pinkney, bearing with him the yet inoperative Non-Importation Act of 1806, had been sent to England to help Minister James Monroe negotiate a new agreement. The failure of these negotiations left American commerce completely at the mercy of both belligerents. Boardings, searches, seizures, condemnations, confiscations of vessels and cargoes, and impressment of seamen were carried out by both France and England. But what many thought the ultimate outrage had occurred in June 1807 when a contingent from the British *Leopard* boarded and seized four crewmen from the frigate *Chesapeake,* a national ship and thus an extension of national territory. War sentiment ran high, but President Thomas Jefferson's determination to avoid war helped to keep an uneasy peace for five years more.

Jefferson's substitute for armed conflict was economic warfare, an embargo on all American shipping. Crawford, as a freshman senator, had little time to improve his understanding of the issues involved in this controversy, for nine days after he arrived in the capital a vote on the embargo act was called for. He requested additional time to study the measure; his motion for temporary postponement was defeated 16 to 12, and on that same day

Crawford was among the minority of six opposed to passage. The majority counted twenty-two votes.[1] It probably would have been more appropriate for Crawford to abstain, but this was a tactic he rarely adopted; he was inclined to vote against measures he had not studied. Before the end of the session, however, he opposed a move to repeal the embargo.

Though Crawford said little on foreign affairs during his first session in Congress, a letter of March 1808 to his friend in Hancock County, Georgia, foreshadowed his later conviction that war was the only honorable alternative to the embargo. The choices open to the United States were not happy ones: if she stayed out of the conflict and Napoleon should destroy England, he might destroy the United States also; if she acceded to the British, she would have to give up all national rights. Continuation of the embargo would mean inconvenience, privation, and the sacrifice of personal gain to the public good, but these he considered minor compared to the devastation and death of war.[2]

By late 1808 Crawford was a staunch defender of the embargo. Much discussion had followed the introduction on November 11 by James Hillhouse of Connecticut of a bill for repeal, and on November 23 Crawford spoke at length against this measure. He again emphasized the importance of public opinion in a republic, noted that the people had suffered privation because of the embargo, and expressed awareness of some discontent, but he stressed that in his area of the country the embargo was viewed as the only alternative to war, was applauded, and cheerfully submitted to. And no region was more immediately affected than the South because of the loss of the cotton market, a loss considered temporary since England must always buy raw materials from those who buy her manufactures.[3]

He believed the embargo had vitally affected the British and ridiculed the argument that unemployment of 50,000 British "mechanics" had simply strengthened the British army and navy; the only conclusion to which this argument could lead was that the destruction of British manufactures would make Britain more powerful. Certainly, the United States should not continue this act of self-denial unless there was a probability of its pro-

---

[1] *Annals*, 10th Cong., 1st sess., 51. Later, when Crawford was accused of Federalist leanings because of this vote, John Quincy Adams came to his defense.

[2] *Georgia Argus*, April 12, 1808 (Tuesday morning extra).

[3] *Annals*, 10th Cong., 2d sess., 63-65.

ducing some adverse effect on those who made it necessary. Continuance would hurt the southern states, which must have foreign markets, more than the commercial states of the North, since the commercial states were also the manufacturing states. If the influence of the embargo were to be counteracted by the Spanish revolt against the French and the recent British victories in the Peninsular War, Crawford would abandon it—"but its substitute should be war, and no ordinary war."

Nor should the embargo be continued if it could not be enforced, but the ease with which this law was said to be evaded simply proved to Crawford that the morals of the evaders could not have been very sound when the measure was passed. And the sentiment that the United States had no just cause of conflict against Great Britain and that "all our complaints are a mere pretext for war"—expressed in petitions introduced in the House of Representatives and in resolutions of one of the state legislatures—made him "blush for the disgrace they reflect on my country . . . blush that any man belonging to the great American family should be so debased, so degraded, so lost to every generous and national feeling, as to make a declaration of this kind. It is debasing to the national character." Complaints are not pretext: it is the undeniable right of an independent nation to trade with the whole world, except in absolutely blockaded ports or in contraband of war, and no nation has previously attempted to control another in such trade. Nor could he see the difference between a tacit acquiescence in the British orders in council and paying tribute, for if the embargo was raised Britain would require the shipment of produce to England and the payment of an arbitrary sum before it could be shipped elsewhere. It mattered little to Crawford whether the United States suffered more from England or France; he was long convinced that both intended to do all the evil they could, and a difference in the amount of injury resulted only from an "inability in the least mischievous to do more."[4]

Repeal of the embargo would result in war or the abandonment of neutral rights. The idea of arming merchant vessels to create a force to oppose the British navy he thought impossible and absurd. To permit vessels to go to sea in the face of orders in council, blockading decrees, and proclamations would expose the

4 Ibid., 66, 67-69, 70-71.

country to new insults and aggressions. It was useless to talk of the magnanimity of nations.

Usually even tempered in discussion, Crawford seemed angered by the argument of Timothy Pickering of Massachusetts and of Hillhouse that perseverance in a measure opposed to the interest of a people may lead to insurrection and revolution:

> If the nation be satisfied that any course is proper, it would be base and degrading to be driven from it by the murmurs of a minority. We are cautioned to beware how we execute a measure with which the feelings of a people are at war. I should be the last to persist in a measure which injuriously affects the interests of the United States, but no man feels more imperiously the duty of persevering in a course which is right, notwithstanding the contrary opinions of a few; and though I may regret and respect the feelings of those few, I will persist in the course I believe to be right, at the expense even of the Government itself.[5]

The repeal motion was defeated by a 25-to-6 vote on December 2.

On the last day of 1808 Crawford expressed even more firmly, in a letter, his conviction that war was the only real alternative to the embargo, for repeal without the adoption of stronger measures to him meant abandonment of the independence of the nation. However, the growing Federalist control in the New England states and the rising voices of discord led him to believe that measures of war—or measures that would lead to war—would be as unpopular as the embargo. Perhaps more so. In the event of war, the intensity of the feelings of the "Yankee Federalists" might drive them into union with Canada, Nova Scotia, and New Brunswick. If the war spirit developed among the people as it was mounting in Congress, only a change of course by Britain and France could prevent conflict. Crawford had little hope for such a change, but he opposed a special session for the following May—the decision for war could be made on March 1 as well as on May 1.[6]

By February 1809 Crawford was greatly disturbed by the turn of events. The House seemed determined to replace the embargo and had refused to allow the issue of letters of marque and

5 Ibid., 73.
6 Crawford to Thomas Carr, Dec. 31, 1808, Henry Jackson Papers (University of Georgia Library, Athens).

reprisal, which would have permitted the arming of merchant vessels. Since such letters were the "lowest stage of war," he could only conclude the House had decided to submit, after insisting throughout most of the session that the nation would resist. Opposed to all substitutes that had been offered for the embargo, Crawford wished to see an end to the humiliation of the nation by either war or peace. His distaste for the dissident Yankee had indeed become intense: "If we can get out of this scrape, I for one, will suffer them [the British] to impress every Yankee in the nation if found upon the high seas, & to interpolate new principles into the law of nations as often as they please. The Yankees have brought the nation into the scrape, & have in Congress en masse deserted it in the hour of trial. . . . We have gone too far to recede, and are so frightened with dissention at home that we dare not advance."[7]

The embargo issue, in one form or another, was almost constantly before that session of Congress. Crawford voted for amendments for its more effective enforcement, but on February 4 Giles moved to repeal the embargo on March 4—except in its application to England, France, and their dependencies. Although Crawford was on the committee for the bill, there is no evidence that he spoke further on the measure. He did vote with a majority (14 to 11) against striking the provision permitting the issue of letters of marque and reprisal, but this section was later struck by the House and in the Senate concurrence Crawford did not vote. On the final passage of the bill Crawford and eleven others voted in the minority while twenty-one cast votes for the Non-Intercourse Act, which became law on March 1, 1809.[8] The law repealed the embargo and provided that the United States would restore commercial relations with the first power (England or France) to lift its offensive trade restrictions—or, as Crawford had said, the measure put up the "warlike services of the nation at auction, not to the highest, but first bidder."

The experiment with total economic coercion had ended, and, as Crawford had predicted, great numbers of American ships were soon seized by both England and France. Apparently feeling that the new act represented submission, Crawford, as well as

7 Crawford to Carr, Feb. 20, 1809, ibid.
8 *Annals*, 10th Cong., 2d sess., 230, 241-56, 298, 310-11, 318-19, 345, 353-83, 409, 413, 415, 436, 1830.

fellow senator John Milledge and four other senators, cast his vote on March 1 against the appropriation bills for the Treasury, War, and Navy departments, and the support of the military establishment. The following day he voted with the majority against imposing additional duties.[9]

The British plenipotentiary, David Erskine, moved quickly, and in April 1809 negotiated an agreement settling the *Chesapeake* affair and providing for repeal of the orders in council. James Madison, only a month in the presidency and doubtless hoping to add to his prestige by resolution of some of the commercial-diplomatic difficulties he had long unsuccessfully grappled with as secretary of state, did not wait for British ratification of the agreement. He reopened trade with Britain. The "conciliatory" mood of the President was reflected in the special session of Congress (which began in May) by the postponement of a bill which would have excluded the armed vessels of other nations from the ports of the United States. The five-man committee, including Crawford, recommended the delay because it believed the British moves were made in good faith and that agreements could be reached that would "guard our flag from insult, our jurisdiction from aggression, our citizens from violation, and our mercantile property from spoliation." The committee expectations were not realized, and at the next session Crawford was one of twenty-six passing the bill.[10]

The British government repudiated the Erskine agreement, maintaining that their envoy had exceeded his powers. Madison's precipitate action raised questions about his judgment, and his prestige suffered severely; he did not recover the lost ground by his ambiguous message to Congress on January 3, 1810. The hand of the opposition forces was strengthened, and Macon Bill No. 1, permitting the importation of French and British goods in American ships only, was defeated.

Crawford, again in this 1809-1810 session a member of the committee on intercourse with Great Britain, thought by late January 1810 that Macon Bill No. 2 would be passed. He suspected easterners of trying to delay passage so they might buy southern cotton at the existing low prices, but he believed their estimates of profits from this activity too sanguine. Crawford was one of the Senate managers who went into conference with House counterparts on May 1, 1810—the day of passage of this Macon bill and the day of adjournment.[11]

Macon Bill No. 2, which pleased neither Macon nor the President, repealed the Non-Intercourse Act and provided that if either England or France withdrew her trade restrictions and the other did not follow suit, the United States would reestablish nonintercourse with the noncomplying nation. Later in the year Madison foolishly accepted the Cadore letter—saying the Berlin and Milan (though not the Rambouillet) decrees were revoked—to the American minister in France as official action. Nonintercourse against Britain was revived, and Napoleon, having accomplished his purpose of getting cargoes within reach, revived spoliation of American commerce. Madison's political opponents had additional ammunition, the loyalty of Secretary of State Robert Smith became an open question, the criticism of Gallatin (the staunchest supporter of the administration) increased, but it was not until the spring of 1811 that Madison could bring himself to dismiss Smith and appoint Monroe in his place.[12]

Crawford, too, had become critical of Madison's leadership and the ambiguity of the President's position. It is, however, difficult to define precisely Crawford's position during 1810 and 1811: he had favored war if the embargo was repealed; war did not come, and he seems to have earnestly desired an honorable peace but opposed "warlike" proposals as totally inadequate to meet the situation. His major speech of the 1809-1810 session was made in opposition to the bill authorizing the fitting out, officering, and manning of frigates belonging to the United States. More than two weeks before his remarks in the Senate he had expressed in a letter his displeasure with the President's stance. Madison's cautiously worded message, he said, had pleased almost every man in Congress because every man interpreted it as he pleased:

> One says it is a war message—another, it is for peace. One says it was intended to support Mr. Macon's bill—another, it was sent to knock that bill in the head. And all of these declare that they

[11] Ibid., 2d sess., 550, 554, 578, 583, 585, 664, 673, 674, 678-79; Crawford to Thomas Carr, Jan. 29, 1810, Henry Jackson. See also Macon to Joseph H. Nicholson, March 26, 1812, Nicholson.

[12] For brief accounts of the divisions in the government, see Adams, *History*, 5:180ff.; Dice Robins Anderson, *William Branch Giles* . . . (Menasha, Wis., 1914), 146-70.

are right if they understand the English language—& if they are not right they will give up Madison for ever. Poor man I believe they would give him up if he had not the distribution of the loaves & fishes, but as long as he holds this magic wand, so long will he be the object of their adulation.[13]

Giles, who so often opposed the President, was the leading spokesman for the frigate bill, which, he said, stemmed from the President's recommendation of a system of preparatory measures to "meet any exigencies that may await the country." Two evident purposes of the measure were preservation of the frigates by repairing them and employment of the vessels as instruments of protection. Repair was justified on grounds of expense, time, and superiority of the seasoned over the green timbers that would be used in new vessels. Admitting the frigates were not capable of resisting even a small squadron of the British fleet, Giles contended they would be useful in defense of a town under attack and should be considered a part of the "combined system of forces." By being prepared for war, the United States would contribute to the maintenance of peace. The issue, he asserted, was whether Great Britain or the United States should regulate the commerce of the United States.[14]

Moving to postpone consideration of the bill, Crawford said the senator from Virginia had convinced him that the additional naval force was either to protect commerce in time of peace or to prepare the nation for a declaration of war, which "we intend to issue, or expect to be issued against us, by one or both of the great belligerent nations." The means, however, were not adequate to the object; the inadequacy of the navy to protect commerce was glaring. Even if $100 million were spent over the next four years, commerce would still be unprotected or the nation would be involved in war. So apparent was the inadequacy of the proposal to provide protection for commerce that Crawford thought it reasonable to suppose it was intended to prepare for a declaration of war which the United States planned to issue.

Crawford briefly reviewed the history of the embargo and the refusal to allow letters of marque and reprisal; if the country ever intended to declare war before she was invaded, March 1809

---

13 Crawford to Dear Capt. [James Hamilton, Wrightsboro, Ga.], Jan. 8, 1810, copy in Ulrich B. Phillips Papers (Yale).
14 *Annals*, 11th Cong., 2d sess., 532-35, 536-38.

was the time. Then, he said, there was "cause, and more than cause for war, if war would have produced redress. . . . Our ships were then in our ports—our seamen were at home—the property of the nation had been gathered in from the winds of heaven, and we were prepared to strike where the enemy was vulnerable." Though Crawford had been sensibly affected by the insulting conduct of Britain's minister (the notoriously ill-tempered Francis James Jackson), he did not think it proper to merge the aggravations and accumulated wrongs of the nation in the quarrel between the negotiators of the two countries and said, "Let it . . . be the wisdom of this nation to remain at peace, so long as peace is within its option."[15]

It was not to France's interest, Crawford asserted, to declare war on the United States, for the British fleet would in effect be on the side of the United States. Britain would gain little by war, since she gets all she wants by purchase and capture. If the frigates are in port, they cannot protect the commerce; if they go out to prey on commerce, few if any will ever return to port. At this point, Crawford turned to an attack on President Madison's message of January 3, 1810, which, he said,

in point of obscurity, comes nearer my idea of a Delphic oracle than any State paper which has come under my inspection. It is so cautiously expressed that every man puts what construction on it he pleases. Is he for war? The Message breathes nothing but destruction and bloodshed. Is he for peace? The Message is mere milk-and-water, and wholly pacific. Is he for the bill before you? The Message calls for its passage. Is he a friend of a large standing army? Why then the Message means 20,000 regular troops. Is he friendly to the militia? The Message does not call for regular troops—it means militia. Thus, sir, the Message means anything or nothing, at the will of the commentator. If the Message is oracular in its meaning, it was no less miraculous in its promulgation. The newspapers to the east of this, stated that such a message would be delivered, and stated its contents nearly one week before it reached the two Houses of Congress. To account for this phenomenon, is neither within my power or province.[16]

The Georgian believed it was vain for the United States to contend upon the ocean with a nation that spent $300 million

15 Ibid., 541-43.
16 Ibid., 544-45.

annually, or six times the total exports of the United States. He agreed with Giles that the Republicans had reduced the navy to a "Peace Establishment," but they had stopped short of their duty: "they should have amputated the fungus of the body politic. . . ." Indeed, the nation had spent $12 million on a navy built only for the purpose of patronage. He could see no reason for the enormous expense and cautioned that armies and fleets must be employed in war activities to justify their exorbitant costs. If the nation becomes involved in war, the conflict should be prosecuted with vigor, both offensively and defensively, and the "energies and resources of the nation ought to be put in requisition." Until that time Crawford was opposed to measures that would exhaust the treasury without adding to the substantial defense of the country.[17]

Crawford was still puzzled about the motives of the backers of the frigate bill even after it had been overwhelmingly passed. The expenditure for the navy would be increased to at least $3.5 million, and since the supporters acknowledged they neither expected to declare war nor to have war declared by another nation he could not understand why they would incur this expense when the treasury was empty but had refused such an expenditure when there was a surplus of revenue and the danger of war was as great or greater than at the present time. Three months later he perhaps saw the political nature of their position, for John Randolph (whose remarks in the House on the frigate bill were similar to but more spectacular than Crawford's) believed Crawford, Bibb, and John Taylor would leave Washington with a thorough "detestation of the Cabal [i.e., the Smith brothers-Leib-Giles group] who have been permitted to disgrace . . . our country."[18] At this time, and later, the cabal—aided and abetted by the Federalists—seemed more interested in embarrassing the President than in defending the nation's honor and rights. Measures requiring more expenditure than those recommended by the executive would help to increase general discontent with the administration.

17 Ibid., 545-47. Only five senators voted with Crawford on this issue: Joseph Anderson and George Washington Campbell (Tenn.), James Turner (N.C.), and John Condit and John Lambert (N.J.). The statement by Anderson, *Giles*, 157, that Crawford's views, with the exception of the criticism of the message, no doubt came direct from Gallatin appears to be without substantiation.

18 Crawford to Carr, Jan. 29, 1819, Henry Jackson; Randolph to Joseph H. Nicholson, April 29, 1810, Randolph-Garnett.

During 1810 and 1811 Crawford actively promoted the territorial interests of the United States and supported an increased effectiveness of the army, but he retained his dislike and distrust of the naval establishment until some time after war had been declared against England. After an illness of about six weeks, he James Lloyd, and Joseph Bradley were—on February 21, 1812—designated the committee to consider the report of the secretary of the navy. Six days later Lloyd offered an amendment to a bill on the naval establishment authorizing construction of several new frigates, and he and Giles spoke for the proposal.[19] On March 2 Crawford opposed the measure in his last major speech in the Senate.

Replying to Lloyd, Crawford said it was incorrect to state that commerce had paid into the treasury the sum of $200 million and that the government had done nothing for commerce while commerce had done everything for the government. Imposts and duties were not paid by commerce but by the consumer—the money was "collected immediately from the merchant but ultimately from the nation." If demand exceeded supply, the consumer paid; if supply exceeded demand, the grower paid in the form of a reduction in price equal to the duty imposed.[20] The only money that came to the treasury which could justly be credited to commerce was that retained by the government on debentures: this amounted to 0.7 percent upon goods paying a duty of 20 percent ad valorem and had never amounted to more than $400,000 in any one year.

The charge (by Senator Obadiah German of New York) that the people of the southern and western states were hostile to commerce and that opposition to building the frigates was rooted in that hostility resulted, Crawford maintained, either from ignorance or from prejudice. He pointed out that cotton comprised approximately one fourth of the country's exports and insisted that the grower was not less interested in commerce than the merchant and shipholder, because the price of the product was determined by the market and the cost of transportation. Consequently, every circumstance that tended to destroy competition and reduce the number of markets directly affected the grower. But the landholders, country people, and most agriculturists in

19 *Annals,* 12th Cong., 1st sess., 127, 131-47.
20 Ibid., 149-51.

the United States never had, and never could have, any direct interest in the "mushroom commerce" which was carried on chiefly with the French and Spanish colonies. As a neutral the United States had a right to prosecute that trade no matter how it affected the belligerents, and, as a result of the drawback system (a substantial refund of duties when imported goods were re-exported), the shippers of the United States had been able to undersell the British in the foreign markets. But by contending for the right to engage in a trade not open to them during peace-time, the United States had jeopardized the general commerce of the nation and "sacrificed that which is essential to the growth and improvement, and to the comfort and happiness of the people." How could anyone contend that nothing had been done for commerce and that steps had been taken to ruin commerce?[21]

In commercial matters, Crawford said, the United States wanted only a good market for the surplus production of the country. Britain furnished the most suitable and extensive market, and the benefits of commerce, conducted on just and liberal principles, were strictly reciprocal. The "contest" about to be entered was a result either of dispute over the colonial trade or of commercial jealousy of Great Britain. It was rendered necessary by the in-justice of Britain, but if it was "dishonorably abandoned" the fault for abandonment and total exclusion from the carrying trade must rest with the "Eastern gentlemen."

Crawford believed that Lloyd's estimates of the cost of naval expansion were about one half what they should be. Besides, the frigates would have no real effect by preying on British commerce, and the idea of protecting American commerce with them was "worse than visionary." Only annihilation of the adversary's naval force would provide such protection. He maintained, how-ever, that "Individual enterprise, directed by individual interest, will more effectively destroy the commerce of the enemy, than any number of frigates in the power of the Government to build and employ." How this was to be done Crawford did not say, but perhaps he was referring to the issuance of letters of marque and reprisal.

He reminded his colleagues that every additional expense involved the possibility of additional taxes. Expense should not be a determinant, for if war was thought necessary,

21 Ibid., 152-55.

We ought not to doubt for a moment that the people will willingly furnish the means necessary for its vigorous and successful prosecution. If there is not a sufficiency of good sense and patriotism in the nation to submit to the impositions necessary for the successful execution of those measures which have been adopted pursuant to their wishes, and for the protection of their rights, then indeed our rights and liberty are but empty names—the idea of our free and happy Government, an idle phantom! Whenever the fact shall be demonstrated, the preservation of our Constitution, and the integrity of the Union, will not be worth a struggle. But until it is demonstrated, its possibility ought not to be admitted, and will not be admitted by the National Legislature.[22]

The Lloyd amendment was defeated 19 to 13 on March 6, and in the final act the funds for repairs—reduced from $480,000 to $300,000—were to be used only to ready the *Chesapeake, Constellation,* and *Adams* for active service. The measure authorized officers and men for these three ships and permitted an annual expenditure of $200,000 for three years to purchase materials for repairing the *Philadelphia, General Greene, New York,* and *Boston.*[23]

Crawford continued to oppose expansion of the navy after the declaration of war against Britain; in December 1812 he was one of two senators voting against the building of more ships. The brilliant achievements of the navy in the conflict changed his attitude, and he heartily approved the large appropriations for the navy in the postwar years.

The war sentiment of the country had increased steadily during the winter of 1811 and the spring of 1812, but Madison did little or nothing either to check the fever or to encourage it. The President did believe, however, that Congress should declare war on Britain before adjourning—if there was no "accommodation" with that country. At least this is what Monroe, on March 31, told the House Committee on Foreign Affairs, which committee was then more powerful than its Senate counterpart.[24] The next day Madison sent a secret one-sentence message to Congress asking for a sixty-day embargo on all vessels in port and on all arriving thereafter—a step intended as a prelude to war, though not so

---

22 Ibid., 156-59, 160.
23 Ibid., 164; 2 *Stat.* 699.
24 Harry Ammon, *James Monroe: The Quest for National Identity* (New York, 1971), 305. Hereafter cited as Ammon, *Monroe.*

publicized at the time. Controversy over the secrecy of the Senate discussion, defeat of a resolution calling for information from the President, and consideration of placing a communication from Jonathan Russell (then in Paris) before the Senate were followed by the defeat of attempts to repeal the acts governing intercourse between the United States and Britain and France by the extension of the embargo to ninety days, and the President's signing of the measure on April 4.[25] Memorials and petitions to repeal or modify this restriction on commerce, generally considered a concession to the more moderate Republicans, began to appear almost as soon as the law was enacted.

Crawford, removed from active participation by virtue of his position as presiding officer, voted consistently with the war party. He opposed the reduction of the term of military service from six months to three, favored the bill for raising an additional military force, voted against all emasculating amendments to the act declaring war, and favored the measure authorizing issuance of treasury notes for financing war preparations.[26]

The declaration of war was to come almost as soon as Crawford had expected; early in May he had felt that unless a change took place in the sentiments of the representatives from the East hostilities would come by the middle of June. The Federalists had made gains in Massachusetts and the merchants were making every effort to procure repeal of the nonimportation act and to prevent adoption of measures of hostility by presenting petitions and memorials and by refusing to subscribe to the loans. The last, Crawford thought, would certainly tend to prolong the war or bring it to a disgraceful issue. The rise of anti-Madison sentiment in New York indicated to the Georgian that New Yorkers—Republicans and Federalists—were more interested in promoting DeWitt Clinton for the presidency than in promoting the public good. He realized that a nation such as the United States could never be as well prepared for war as a nation where the power of declaring war rested in the executive. Men of energy and talent in key positions would help, but this happy condition did not prevail. It was widely believed that Secretary of War

25 Crawford to Monroe, April 2, 1812, James Monroe Papers (MDLC); *Annals*, 12th Cong., 1st sess., 189-91.
26 *Annals*, 12th Cong., 1st sess., 191-93, 209, 267, 270, 286-87, 296-98, 300, 305, 308-9, 311.

William Eustis (whom Crawford thought a tool of Samuel Smith and Giles) and Secretary of the Navy Paul Hamilton were incapable of handling their duties, but since Madison was almost the only exception to this opinion they were retained in office.[27]

The paucity of evidence—and the ambiguity of some extant material—makes it impossible to determine precisely the role Crawford played immediately prior to and following Madison's war message of June 1. A fragment of a communication from Monroe to Gallatin asked Gallatin to see Crawford and "explain to him the policy of the plan preferred" before he came to the President's on the morning of June 1. This explanation hopefully would avoid difficulty in the Senate committee, but it is not clear whether Gallatin, Crawford, or both of them were going to confer with Madison. The fragment does seem to say that Monroe thought only a naval war should be attempted at the moment, and Madison's chief biographer holds this view. Monroe's most recent biographer disagrees, noting that such a stance would be inconsistent with Monroe's earlier and later positions. Certainly, in light of Crawford's attitude toward the navy he could scarcely be expected to support such a limited declaration.[28] Had Monroe held such a view of the war, he would have become political bedfellow of Smith, Leib, and Giles who sought unsuccessfully to limit the war to naval operations and then to require measures against France unless proof of the repeal of the decrees was soon received. The opposition to war was strong, but the declaration of June 18 was plenary. Smith, Leib, and Giles joined Crawford and fifteen others in carrying the measure, 19 to 13.

For more than two years before the declaration of war, Crawford had been periodically involved as agent of the President or as intermediary in activities and negotiations—some semisecret, some official—that he and others hoped would make both East and West Florida parts of the United States. On June 10, 1810, Secretary of State Robert Smith informed Crawford that Madison wished him to select a "gentleman of honor and discretion" to execute a trust of "interest and delicacy."[29] Crawford chose

27 Crawford to John Milledge, May 9, 1812, Crawford, MDLC; Crawford to Charles Yancey, July 3, 1812, Keith Read Collection (UGL).

28 Monroe to Gallatin, June 1, 1812, Gallatin; Brant, *Madison*, 5:476-77; Ammon, *Monroe*, 309, 632 n 60.

29 See Clarence E. Carter, ed., *The Territory of Orleans, 1803-1812* (Washington, D.C., 1940), 885.

George Mathews, former governor of Georgia who had signed the Yazoo land bill, to try to arrange with Vizente Folch, commandante proprietario (though generally referred to as governor) of the Floridas for a peaceable and mutually satisfactory transfer of the Spanish possessions to the control of the United States. The exact relationship between the Mathews-Folch interview at Mobile and Folch's proposal to treat directly with the President for the transfer of his province (carried to Washington by John McKee) is not at all clear,[30] but Madison's proclamation of October 27, 1810, directing the seizure of West Florida and the disavowal of Folch's intent by his superiors brought failure to this phase of activity by Mathews and others.

However, Folch's offer and Mathews' report—relayed by Crawford to Smith—that he and the Spanish official had agreed it was to the "joint interest of the United States and the Spanish provinces to prevent any European nation from obtaining a footing in the new world" raised Madison's hopes that prompt action might bring acquisition of both West and East Florida.[31] Congress took only twelve days to respond favorably to Madison's request of January 3, 1811, for a declaration that the United States "could not see, without serious inquietude, any part of a neighboring territory, in which they have, in different respects, so deep and so just a concern, pass from the hands of Spain into those of any other foreign power." The President was authorized to take possession of all or any part of the Floridas east of the Perdido River if local authorities agreed to such action. Folch was informed of acceptance of his offer, and Mathews and McKee were appointed commissioners to carry it out.[32]

[30] Nor is it clear exactly when Crawford appointed Mathews. A delay in the transmission of letters, or the failure of Crawford to write—maybe because he had not yet engaged Mathews—seems to have resulted in Washington's remaining uninformed until early fall. Mathews seems to have become active in September 1810.

[31] *American State Papers: Foreign Relations*, 3:395; Crawford to Robert Smith, Nov. 1, 1810, Miscellaneous Letters (National Archives). Also in the fall of 1810 Crawford served as intermediary between Buckner Harris and the government on East Florida matters. See B. Harris to Crawford, Nov. 21, 1810, ibid. Almost nothing is known about Crawford's role here, but some intriguing references in this Harris letter lead to the speculation that his role was greater than the direct evidence indicates.

[32] *Annals*, 11th Cong., 3d sess., 370, 371-80, 1251-63, 1273-74. The West Florida question is thoroughly treated in Isaac Joslin Cox, *The West Florida Controversy, 1798-1813* (Baltimore, Md., 1918). For Mathews' activities, see esp. 463, 481, 488, 522-23, 526-28, and I. J. Cox, "The Border Missions of General George Mathews," *Mississippi Valley Historical Review* 12 (Dec. 1925):309-33. Paul Kruse, "A Secret

This so-called agreement with Folch did not come to fruition, and many of the later maneuverings and machinations, especially in East Florida, seemed to hinge on interpretation of the term "local authority." Quite often the United States seemed to have a hand in establishing a "local authority" which then expressed a desire for attachment to the United States. The short, thick, red-headed, seventy-four-year-old Mathews, who wore a three-cornered cocked hat, top boots, and a shirt full-ruffled at the bosom and wrists, and who acknowledged only George Washington as his superior, apparently kept in close touch with Crawford, communicating his plans by mail and personal contacts and requesting the senator to explain them to the government. Crawford, in early November 1811, informed Madison that as soon as the Senate was organized he would relay what Mathews had told him.[33] The President certainly knew of Mathews' intent to seize Amelia Island and seemed not displeased that he did so. But the use of agents in territory of another nation and seizure of a portion of that territory was highly embarrassing, following so closely on the Senate consideration of, and wide publicity given to, the John Henry letters. These letters, at most, showed that the British had paid an agent to promote subversion in the New England area, but the administration righteously used them to stir up anti-British feeling. Madison resolved his dilemma by having Monroe disavow Mathews' action on April 4, 1812.[34]

Crawford, extremely mortified by the disavowal, informed an angry and disgusted Mathews that the gentlemen at his boarding house had generally been in favor of supporting Mathews but had been overruled by the cabinet. He had feared the situation would not be acceptable to the President, for Crawford's reading of the patriotic manifesto indicated to him that an arrangement made

Agent in East Florida: General George Mathews and the Patriot War," *Journal of Southern History* 18 (May 1952):193-217, is primarily concerned with the secret aspect of events and makes little mention of Crawford. Rembert W. Patrick, *Florida Fiasco: Rampant Rebels on the Georgia-Florida Border, 1810-1815* (Athens, Ga., 1954), focuses a large part of his story on Mathews, but Crawford's role in late 1812 is not mentioned. Nor are some of the earlier Crawford materials in any of these items. Mathews and McKee were in Washington the first part of January 1811 when they received instructions from Robert Smith, and Mathews talked with Madison.

33 Mathews to Crawford, Oct. 11, 1811, Golding; Mathews to Monroe, Oct. 14, 1811, Monroe, MDLC; Crawford to Monroe, Nov. 5, 1811, Miscellaneous Letters (National Archives); Gilmer, *Sketches* (1855), 78.

34 Adams, *History*, 6:176ff.; *Niles' Weekly Register* 2 (March 14, 1812):19-29, 31; (March 21, 1812):44-45.

by an agent of the United States had produced the revolution, rather than the revolution producing the arrangement. Governor David B. Mitchell of Georgia had been directed to return the area, but Crawford expected war by June 1, and then he presumed there would be agreement on the propriety of holding East Florida. Further, if Mathews should get possession of Augustine before he received news (supposedly official) of the disavowal, it was hoped he would hold it—and Crawford did not think Mitchell would be in a hurry to hand it over to the Spanish. If the province should be retained, or taken later, he saw little difficulty in obtaining the government of it for Mathews.[35]

Three months later—about seven weeks after the declaration of war on Britain—Mathews came directly from Augustine, which he had taken, and spent two days with Crawford in Georgia. The patriots, with Mathews' consent, had formed a government, and Crawford thought Mathews more concerned about them than about himself. If they could be secured from loss and injury— and especially if the country should be taken and retained—the old general would be reconciled to the mortification resulting from the disavowal of his seizure of Amelia Island. Crawford's comments on the term "local authority" as used in the act of January 1811 seem to offer justification for the actions of the patriots. Public feeling in Georgia was high on the Florida matter; much dissatisfaction would arise if the troops were withdrawn, the country given up, and the patriots abandoned, but Crawford would endeavor to reconcile public opinion to whatever course the President should adopt. Apparently Mathews was not completely satisfied with his conversations with Crawford: he set out for Washington to deal directly with the President—one author says to "thrash" him—but he died at Augusta on August 30.[36]

Crawford continued to hope that Florida could be acquired without direct official force, and he informed Monroe of his willingness to receive it for the United States. If the Spanish governor, by sanction of the Spanish minister to the United States, could officially cede the area, such action would be within the

35 Crawford to Mathews, May 4, 1812, Read. The last part of this letter is badly mutilated, but the sense of it seems to be that the government would be anxious to soothe Mathews' feelings.

36 Crawford to Monroe, Aug. 6, Sept. 9, 1812, Monroe, MDLC; Gilmer, *Sketches* (1855), 78.

letter of the law of January 1811 and would "compel our mal-contents in the senate to support it." Or perhaps the province could be placed in the custody of the United States as indemnity for Spanish spoliations on American commerce—the conditions of delivery mattered not to the Georgia senator. He was not to have the pleasure of accepting the area for his country, but toward the end of 1812 he believed the Spanish minister had written to the Cortes requesting power to cede Florida in full satisfaction of all spoliation claims.[37]

After the coming of war with England, sentiment for military action against Spain (England's ally) increased. In November and December 1812 and early January 1813 Crawford corresponded with Brigadier General Thomas Flournoy, in command of United States troops in the Southeast, cautioning him that he would have to take military action soon against the Spanish in Florida, expressing apprehension that Flournoy did not have the necessary equipment, and hoping military activities in the South would dispel the gloom which had hung over the troops in the North and East. Flournoy said he had done all he could to get ready to act, but he did not have the required materials. Georgia had not delivered on her promises, and he asked Crawford to file his application for resignation rather than permit him to be ordered to attack Augustine with the "few naked troops" under his command.[38] Flournoy was not ordered to move; Crawford could get only thirteen other senators to support his motion to make the seizure of East Florida contingent upon hostilities with Spain; but he was with the majority (22 to 11) in approving the West Florida possession measure.[39] The acquisition of East Florida had to wait for the Adams-Onis treaty of 1819-1821.

Crawford had not hesitated to criticize ineffectiveness in the executive branch prior to the war with Britain, and this ineffec-tiveness was less tolerable to him during the conflict. Incompe-tency of the men who would have principal management of the

[37] Crawford to Monroe, Sept. 9, 1812; Crawford to David B. Mitchell, Dec. 4, 1812, Crawford, MDLC. Crawford said he could not blame Onis if he took such action merely to gain time.

[38] Crawford to Flournoy, Nov. 19, 21, Dec. 26, 1812; Flournoy to Crawford, Jan. 5, 1812 [1813], Thomas Flournoy Papers (MDLC); Crawford to Flournoy, Nov. 30, 1812, Flournoy Papers (Clements Library, Ann Arbor); Crawford to John Milledge, Dec. 26, 1812, Crawford, MDLC.

[39] *Annals*, 12th Cong., 2d sess., 127-33. The measure was signed on February 13, 1813. As secretary of treasury Crawford strongly urged the acquisition of Florida.

war had caused him misgivings about entering the conflict, and he feared continuation of the war would only lead to other defeats such as Detroit. He wrote scathingly of Eustis' and Hamilton's preoccupation with trivia; if Madison could not bring himself to dismiss unfaithful or incompetent officers, he must be "content with defeat and disgrace in all his efforts during the war. So far as he may suffer from this cause, he deserves no commiseration, but his accountability to the nation will be great indeed."[40]

Continued defeat and criticism brought change by year's end. On December 3 Monroe sent Crawford a note saying he wished a conference with him. Monroe wanted to avoid attention, stated in confidence that Eustis had resigned, and said that he might be offered the secretaryship of war. He wished to talk about the circumstances connected with, and public reaction to, this appointment.[41]

There is no record of this interview, but apparently Crawford informed Monroe (who had become acting secretary when Eustis resigned) that Senate confirmation as permanent secretary was by no means certain. Opposition stemmed primarily from the fact that Monroe was a Virginian, and resentment of the Virginia influence mounted with every year one of the dynasty occupied the presidential chair. Rejection by the Senate would injure Monroe's chances of succession, as would the placing of a rival in the state department. Monroe declined to be nominated as permanent secretary, and Madison continued his search.[42]

Crawford was asked (whether by Monroe or Madison or both is not clear) to give his opinion about John Armstrong, Henry Dearborn, Daniel Tompkins, and William Henry Harrison, the leading candidates for the position. He had no personal knowledge of the last three; Armstrong, he thought, did not possess the confidence of the nation.[43] Major General Dearborn refused the post, as did Crawford, who said his training and experience did not qualify him for the position when the nation was at war. It is not clear when the offer was made to Crawford; apparently the

40 Crawford to Monroe, Sept. 9, 1812, Monroe, MDLC. Adams, *History*, 6:395-96, incorrectly gives the date of this letter as September 27, and his quotations from it contain several inaccuracies, without, however, changing the meaning of the communication.
41 Monroe to Crawford, Dec. 3, 1812, Monroe, MDLC.
42 Ammon, *Monroe*, 314-15.
43 Crawford to David B. Mitchell, Dec. 4, 1812, Crawford, MDLC.

entire matter was handled through personal contacts, and some-time between December 3, 1812, and January 4, 1813, Crawford declined the offer. Some of the friends of the administration thought Crawford would be more valuable in the Senate; this may have been a factor in Crawford's decision.[44] The position went to Armstrong, former minister to France and at the time of his appointment a brigadier general in the United States Army. William Jones replaced Hamilton as secretary of the navy.[45]

The cabinet reorganization—delayed by the President until after the November election—did not end Crawford's dissatisfaction with Madison's administration. Everything, he wrote Monroe, depended upon the vigilance, promptitude, and energy displayed by the chief of the nation, and if he could not bring himself to believe that examples must be made of public delinquents then it would be better to repeal the declaration of war and submit without further expense to the violation of rights and degradation consequent to such submission. Madison's power over the army was as great as that of Frederick the Great or Napoleon; if he failed to act, subordinates could not be expected to exercise vigilance, promptitude, and energy. Crawford considered examples of severity necessary to give life and vigor to the military enterprises, surrounded as the United States was by both internal and external enemies. Madison was in an excellent position safely to make the necessary examples because most of the nation believed him to be honest, intelligent, patriotic, mild, and unambitious. Thus every act of severity, every dismissal from office, would be "ruling the people as a sacrifice of his good nature to a sense of his duty to the nation. . . . The fate of the Republic, and of Republican government is now committed to Madison's

[44] Hard evidence on this cabinet reorganization is scarce. Adams, *Gallatin*, 469-70, says that as far as can now be guessed Monroe and Gallatin wished to have Monroe as secretary of war, Gallatin as secretary of state, and possibly Crawford as secretary of treasury. Such an arrangement "would have given strength to the government and eliminated many causes of weakness." Brant, *Madison*, 6:127, probably has the best account concerning the secretaryship of war, but of necessity much of the evidence is circumstantial and inferential. See also *Richmond Enquirer*, Aug. 6, 1824; Charles Tait to Crawford, April 22, 1813 (copy), Charles Tait Papers (Alabama Department of Archives and History).

[45] The nominations were submitted to the Senate on January 8; Jones was approved on January 12 (no vote was given) and Armstrong on the following day, 18 to 15. *Journal of Executive Proceedings of the Senate*, 2:315, 316. Hereafter cited as Senate *Executive Journal*. Crawford, who voted for both men, said the vote for Jones was unanimous. Crawford to [?], Jan. 16, 1813, Crawford, MDLC.

hands. If the powers invested in him shall be feebly executed, we are lost, perhaps forever."[46]

Apparently a closer personal relationship was developing between Crawford and Madison; in early March he wrote the President a completely frank letter giving him some seemingly unsolicited advice about General James Wilkinson. It was necessary to move Wilkinson from the New Orleans station: the general's character was not above suspicion and a great majority of the people of Louisiana opposed his remaining in New Orleans. Crawford indicated the possibility of moving Wilkinson to Norfolk, New York, or Philadelphia where he might be less obnoxious to the inhabitants—if the vote of the senators on Wilkinson's recent promotion reflected the wishes of the people. Crawford hoped Wilkinson would not be sent to the Southeast and sincerely regretted that the cabinet felt it necessary to employ him anywhere.[47] Wilkinson was transferred to the Northern theater.

Crawford's work in the Senate was done; on the very day of this letter Congress adjourned, and apparently at about this time Crawford agreed to become the successor to Joel Barlow, minister to France, who had died near Cracow the preceding December 26. Barlow had made the unusual move of leaving Paris—not departing his carriage until reaching Berlin—to go eastward to meet the French officials, retreating from Russia, and had just completed his conversations toward an agreement that proved totally unacceptable to the United States. On May 28 Crawford was commissioned minister plenipotentiary to the court of the Emperor of the French and King of Italy.[48] For most of the next two years he was absorbed in diplomatic matters.

---

[46] Crawford to Monroe, Jan. 24, 1813, Monroe, NYP.

[47] Crawford to Madison, March 3, 1813, Madison Papers (MDLC). On March 1 the Senate had confirmed, 16 to 12, Wilkinson's promotion to major general. Crawford voted with the minority. On the same day he cast one of the majority votes in the 23-to-4 confirmation of Harrison to the same rank. Senate *Executive Journal*, 2:329-30.

[48] The original of the commission is in the Golding Collection. Crawford had been approved (no vote given) by the Senate on May 28. Senate *Executive Journal*, 2:346. He resigned his Senate seat on March 23, 1813; William H. Bulloch replaced him in the session which began on May 24, but on December 6, 1813, William W. Bibb was seated to serve the remainder of Crawford's term. The choice of Crawford's successor was not an easy matter for the party in Georgia; several declined to stand for his seat, and one of Crawford's friends noted that the Republicans "had slept at the posts til the helm was well nigh grasped from their hands." Thomas W. Cobb to Charles Harris, Oct. 21, 1813, Read.

The new minister was his own man. In five and a half years he had risen from state prominence to near preeminence on the national scene, a rise that involved no truckling to any man or group and no discoverable political bargains. As a senator he had forcefully expressed his position on the major issues before the nation. He had believed that war should come when the embargo was repealed; he had become the champion of the bank after only two years in the upper house; he staunchly defended the rights of his state, but he was an ardent nationalist and expansionist; he submitted to no party discipline and severely criticized inefficiency and ambiguity—even in the chief executive; by 1812 he was a close personal friend of Secretary Monroe and Secretary of the Treasury Gallatin and sometimes spokesman for them and for Madison in the Senate; he had declined the secretaryship of war. He was an able senator, considered by many to be qualified to assume the presidential office. There is no evidence that he had presidential ambitions at that time, and apparently he wished to remain in the Senate. However, he was persuaded that he might perform valuable ministerial services for his country. At forty-one Crawford began his only trip abroad.

4

Minister to France

MARCH AND APRIL 1813 were busy months of preparation for Crawford: a fatiguing nineteen-day trip to Woodlawn, resignation from his Senate seat, selection of Henry Jackson, a professor at Athens, as secretary of legation, attention to his personal affairs, and taking leave of friends and family. About the first of May he began the trip back to Washington, and early on June 4 he and Jackson set out for New York. To lessen the possibility of capture on the ocean voyage, his departure time from the capital had been kept secret, and to protect his anonymity Crawford did not register at the inns or add his name to the window sills—as did Jackson—in a dining room in Pennsylvania. A week in New York, involving social engagements with Mrs. Albert Gallatin, John Jacob Astor, the Russian consul at Philadelphia, and Robert Fulton, brought some relief from the arduous carriage and stage trip.[1]

A favorable wind sprang up on June 18, and the next day the brig *Argus* under Captain William H. Allen (age twenty-nine) was put to sea. The voyage was not particularly pleasant for Crawford. He stayed on deck the first day until he was soaked with rain, and he "cascaded copiously." Since the deck was no defense against attack, he retired to his berth where he was free from violent retching. By June 27 he was almost over his seasickness, but his stomach felt as if it were the receptacle for the grease and tar the ship carried. A storm struck on June 30; the deck was awash, the brig made eleven knots with only the main foresail up, and Crawford feared she might be swallowed up. The next morning the storm increased, the main foresail was taken in and the ship allowed to roll. Crawford rolled until he was "quite sore and exhausted"; he was very sick during the storm, and even two days later the best Madeira tasted like salt and weak vinegar. He had not been much impressed by the sunset on June 22, but the storm was "grand and magnificent." The weathering of the thirty-six-hour disturbance let him view with tranquillity and composure the "grandeur and sublimity of the scene," and he "felt, deeply felt, the insignificance of things, which under other circumstances, were of the highest importance." Allen, under orders to avoid engagement if possible, sighted several ships during the voyage: one—an American vessel that had been captured by the British—Allen burned after she struck colors; two other British ships, a brig and a frigate, did not engage.

Crawford landed at L'Orient on July 11. He noted that he was in a country where the rulers were "everything, and the people nothing," while in the United States one was "insensible of the existence of governments but in the granting of benefits."[2] His twenty-one-month stay in France seemed to deepen his devotion to the principles of republicanism. Sickness delayed his departure from the port, but on July 19 he, Jackson, and two servants began the journey to Paris where they arrived at the "Hotel D'Étrangèr" on July 24.

When Crawford arrived in France, that nation had known only about one year of uneasy peace in the preceding twenty years, and the European War of Liberation against the domination of Napoleon was in a state of high preparation. A month earlier, the English had concluded a subsidy treaty with Prussia and Russia, and approximately one month after Crawford reached Paris Napoleon won his last great victory, Dresden, on German soil. Before the end of October he had suffered decisive defeat at Leipzig. His empire fell in on itself; on April 12, 1814, he abdicated and was exiled to Elba.

Difficulties of various kinds had arisen between the United States and France from the early 1790s, but the Convention of 1800 again placed the two nations in an amicable relationship— at least temporarily. The institution of the Continental System and subsequent highhanded and illegal actions of the emperor and his minions strained that relation. Until the time of the

1 Crawford to David B. Mitchell, March 23, 1813, Telemon Cuyler Collection (UGL); Crawford to Monroe, March 20, 1813, Records of the Department of State, Diplomatic Despatches, France, Volume 14 (National Archives). Hereafter cited as DD France 14. Information on the trip from Washington to France is taken from Crawford's manuscript journal, kept at the suggestion of Charles Tait. It contains entries from June to November 1813 and is a part of the Crawford Letterbook (MDLC).
2 Journal, July 11, 1813.

embargo the offenses of the French had differed little from those of the English (except for impressment), but in April 1808 the Bayonne decree ordered seizure of all American vessels then in French ports. Slightly less than two years later the Rambouillet decree commanded seizure and sale of all American shipping that had entered French ports since the effective date of the Non-Intercourse Act of 1809. Ships and cargoes—contraband or not— were captured and burned on the high seas or seized and sold in the ports, a licensing system which violated all principles of a free commerce was instituted, interminable delays were imposed, return cargoes were required, and France steadfastly refused to pay—or even to recognize responsibility for—indemnity for her illegal actions. Napoleon needed the articles of commerce; he took them whenever it suited his purpose. The Cadore letter and the falsely dated St. Cloud decree further convinced the United States of the perfidy and complete lack of scruple of the French government. The injuries inflicted by France were less than those of the English, but—as Crawford had said several years before— the difference resulted only from the inability of the French to commit greater depredations. The diplomatic bargaining power of the United States vis-à-vis France was probably lessened by the declaration of war on England; committed to war against the greatest naval power, the United States could ill afford a complete rupture with France. The dismal performance of the American military establishment prior to Crawford's arrival in France scarcely permitted him to negotiate from a position of strength. His assignment was indeed a difficult one.

Monroe told Crawford he was to be governed by the careful initial and subsequent instructions to his predecessor which he would find in the embassy files. He was to seek indemnity for illegal captures at sea and for spoliations on the commerce of the United States in French ports and to try to place commercial relations with France on a footing of reciprocal advantage, that is, eliminate the return cargo requirement and abandon the license system.[3] The United States could not relinquish claims

---

[3] Napoleon used the license system to undercut Russian commerce, and this action helped to bring Russia's defection from the Continental System. England also used it, and some American ships—flying the English, then the French, then the English flag—traded between France and England. Under the license system only the holders of licenses could trade, they were subject to the restrictions imposed, and Napoleon changed the rules when whim and advantage dictated.

for a just reparation for spoliations under the Bayonne and Rambouillet decrees; if these claims were refused, Crawford was to decline any arrangement whatever with the French government. However, Barlow had indicated that an agreement had been reached on some matters of spoliation and commerce; if Crawford thought the terms satisfactory, he should sign and forward the treaty. If he did not approve them, he should notify the French government and try to obtain alterations.

Indemnity was also to be demanded for spoliations on the United States commerce with Lisbon and Cadiz, and this French obligation might be discharged in stock or negotiable paper if France was not able to make payment in specie. Crawford should negotiate only on injuries resulting from violations of neutral rights; the attitude to be taken toward France if an accommodation was made with England would be decided at the proper time. On that point, Crawford was cautioned in his communications to the French government not to compromit the United States.

No arrangement was to be entered into unless there were just reparations for damages under the two most obnoxious decrees, but Crawford was informed that relations with France might be improved by restoring to their owners American vessels still detained under the decrees and by placing commercial relations with France on a just and stable foundation. The violations had come as a result of edict; normal relations might be restored in the same manner, and the President wished Crawford to follow that course if unable to negotiate a treaty. Madison had been greatly dissatisfied with the conduct of the French government since the beginning of the Barlow mission; failure to correct the situation before the emperor's expedition to Russia was a new offense to the United States, and the lack of success of the Barlow negotiations at Vilna had simply added to the offense.[4]

Crawford, the only United States minister in western Europe, was given superintendence of all consuls of the United States in France, her European dependencies, and Italy and was instructed to adopt appropriate measures to keep them in strict performance of their duties. Because of the delay in the sailing of the *Argus,*

---

[4] Monroe to Barlow, July 26, 1811; Monroe to Crawford, May 29, 1813, Records of the Department of State, Diplomatic Instructions, All Countries, Volume 7 (National Archives). Hereafter cited as DI 7.

Crawford received Monroe's long communication on consular difficulties before he left New York. David Bailie Warden, William Lee, and Isaac Cox Barnet (consuls at Paris, Bordeaux, and commercial agent at Le Havre, respectively), had all moved to assume varying degrees of control of United States diplomatic relations since the death of Barlow. Warden, a favorite of some of the French functionaries, assumed the title of consul general, acted the role of a chargé d'affaires, and took supervision of some of the embassy papers, which should have remained with the secretary of the legation, Barlow's nephew Thomas. The effrontery of the other two appeared less serious, but Crawford was to relay the President's displeasure with their conduct and to communicate their explanations to Monroe. Crawford gave the matter the early attention he promised and severely reprimanded Warden and Lee for publicly disputing and quarreling over the handling of prize vessels and commissions on the sale of such vessels. Warden continued to deal with French officials and refused to recognize his dismissal on May 31, 1814, until Crawford should give him a legalized copy of Monroe's communication authorizing the action. He received no such document and had to accept his dismissal, but he refused to turn over many embassy papers until informed that the settlement of his account depended on their delivery. The matter was finally resolved in August 1814.[5]

Diplomatic exchanges with the French government were also slow paced. In reply to Crawford's letter announcing his appointment and arrival, the Duke of Bassano (Maret), said that he would be glad to receive communications from Crawford. Receiving this letter on August 8, Crawford decided to communicate

[5] Monroe to Crawford, June 10, 1813, Crawford Papers (Duke University Library); Crawford to Monroe, June 15, 1813, Monroe, MDLC; Crawford to Warden, July 25, 1813; May 31, June 8, Aug. 4, 1814, David Bailie Warden Papers (Maryland Historical Society); Lee to Warden, June 29, July 10, 12, 17, 1813, ibid.; Crawford to Monroe, Aug. 15, Sept. 3, 20, 1813; Jan. 16, 1814, DD France 14; Monroe to Crawford, Feb. 8, 1814, DI 7; Journal, passim. More detailed information may be found in DD France 15; Consular Instructions, 1801-1817; Despatches from Consuls, Bordeaux, III; Despatches from Consuls, Paris, IV, V (National Archives). In correspondence on this matter Crawford commented favorably on several people who had been helpful in various ways. Among these were Asbury Dickins, who later served as one of Crawford's clerks in the treasury and as "campaign manager" in 1824, and George W. Erving (later minister to Spain) who for many years was to write long and gossipy letters to Crawford. Erving numbered his letters, but only a few of them have been located.

with Bassano, but then changed his mind. He did not think the correspondence could be brought to a conclusion before Napoleon reached Paris—Crawford did not intend to go to Dresden—and he doubted that Bassano could act without the authority of the emperor. Then, too, he thought it most important that his first communication be "dressed up entirely to the palate" of Napoleon, who might otherwise stop the correspondence by saying Crawford was not the accredited minister of the United States. Another reason for delay was the belief in Paris that the emperor did not like the Russian offer to mediate the American-British conflict.[6]

The legation files contained no copy of the agreement Barlow had drawn with the French government; but if the copy Crawford secured from the office of exterior relations and sent with his letter of August 15 was accurate, the minister understood how Barlow could be considered a tool of the French government. This document, which gave sanction to the license system and placed arbitrary power in the hands of French officials, he proposed to lay aside unless it could be used as evidence of France's admission of the principle of indemnity. Crawford was probably most troubled by two secret articles which were to be made patent only by mutual consent. According to these, the French government was to deliver eighty licenses to the American minister who could dispose of them as he thought proper. Each license was for one cargo of not less than 300 tons and not more than 400 tons, with eight months allowed for execution. Any flag except the English could be flown, no hindrance or impediment would be placed in the way of the vessels, and no other license for similar cargo would be granted within the eight months. In return for these licenses, the minister of the United States agreed to cause to be exported from France within an unspecified number of years either French or Italian produce to the value of that imported under the licenses. Money, up to

---

[6] Crawford to Bassano, July 27, 1813; Bassano to Crawford, Aug. 1, 1813; Crawford to Monroe, Aug. 15, 1813 (no. 3). Most of Crawford's communications to the French government are in the Crawford Letterbook, as well as in DD France 14, which also contains many of the letters from Crawford to Monroe. In addition, communications from American officials to the French government may be found in Archives des Affaires Étrangères, Correspondance Politique, États-Unis, Vols. 69 (part IV), 70, 72, 78, 79, and Supplement, Vol. 5 (photostats, MDLC). For some reason these volumes contain only a small amount of the Crawford correspondence of 1814.

$6 million, from this arrangement was to be used to satisfy indemnity claims.[7] Certainly this was not an agreement which Crawford's instructions would allow him to sign and forward for State Department approval.

While trying to decide whether to communicate with the French government on the major purpose of his mission before being officially received, Crawford wrestled with the consular problem, became acquainted with many Americans and a number of Frenchmen (including Barbé Marbois, Dupont de Nemours, and Lafayette), observed and commented on several facets of French life and culture, moved the American ministry to Hôtel Le Grand Batellière, began the study of French, and engaged a coach, horses, and coachman for 500 francs per month. The coach apparently was much more useful for social purposes and pleasure than for performing any functions connected with the solution of spoliation claims, and nondiplomatic occasions seemed sufficiently numerous. Among other places, he visited the gallery of statues and paintings where the only "drawback" he found was the continued "recurrence of the crucifixion in glowing colors." He thought the Venus de Medici and Apollo Belvidere beautiful statues, but his sensations were not "glowing" when he went through the gallery. A little later he considered the vocal and instrumental music of the opera good, but his senses were not "hurried away as most people represent theirs to be." Of the nude statues in the Luxemburg Gardens and the "Thuelleries," he remarks, "I am not pleased with their nudity. If I was supreme legislator of the United States I would prohibit the importation and even the manufacture, of naked people, in marble, plaster, or paper."

On one occasion Crawford dined with Mrs. Barlow, her family, and George W. Erving (sensible and well informed but eccentric in manner and dress) at Dravel, the 1,200-acre seat of Daniel Parker, who had been viewed by many Parisians as the American minister for the last ten years. With Parker lived Mrs. Henry

7 In DD France 14. Irving Brant, "Joel Barlow, Madison's Stubborn Minister," *William and Mary Quarterly* 15 (Oct. 1958):447-48, says that Barlow proposed the money for indemnity be raised in this manner and that Bassano knew this was unauthorized and contrary to American policy. Vernon G. Setser, *The Commercial Reciprocity Policy of the United States, 1774-1829* (Philadelphia, 1937), 178-80, briefly describes the commercial convention, says nothing about any recognition of indemnity claims by France, and makes no mention of the articles Crawford transmitted.

Preble (sister-in-law of the late Commodore Edward Preble) and her three children. Even in Paris, said Crawford, this arrangement produced some slanderous tales, not very honorable to Preble, his wife, or Parker. It was understood that Preble was an occasional visitor but had no "ostensible, or as is believed, covert connections with Mrs. Preble." As the minister noted in connection with another relationship, "They order these things well in France."[8]

On September 8 Crawford received Bassano's reply to his letter of August 16. Crawford's uncertainty as to how to comply with Bassano's wish that the minister's credentials be presented to the emperor stemmed from the Parisians' belief that Bassano and the emperor would be absent from Paris all winter. He was embarrassed by his position: he had not been received officially and felt he could not comply with the requests that came every day from American citizens for him to help with their cases before French tribunals. He told Monroe he had not then determined what course he should take.[9]

Crawford was not completely honest here, for his journal indicates he had determined on September 6 to discuss the indemnity claims. The next day he began working on a communication to the French government; he continued that activity on September 9 and 10 and was "much relieved" when he sent his statement of the American case to Bassano. Carefully expressing dissatisfaction with the long and indefinite delay in his recognition as minister, Crawford indicated that the interest of the United States required him to avail himself of the offer of August 1 to communicate directly with Bassano. The duke, he noted, was well informed on the nature of the United States claims for acts committed in "violation of principles consecrated by the usage and practice of all civilized states." The causes of delay had not been within the control of the United States, her arguments had not been answered, and yet her efforts had not been attended with success.

The deep solicitude the American Government has constantly manifested to obtain just reparation for these acts of violence and injustice had not been so much the result of the magnitude of the interest in an abstract point of view, as of the magnitude

8 See Journal, esp. July 28, 30, Aug. 1, 3, 6, 8, 15, 17, 18, 19, 25, 26, Sept. 1, 1813.
9 Crawford to Monroe, Sept. 8, 1813, DD France 14.

of the consequences which will probably flow from the rejection of this just and equitable claim. It is not necessary for me to enter into a long and labored train of reasoning to prove that the acts of which the United States complain are in open hostility with the principles of moral justice and have no other foundation than that of force. This has already been proven in a most irrefragable manner by my predecessor in his letter of 5th June 1812 to the Duke d'Albe.

But, said the minister, the condemnation and subsequent confiscation of vessels and cargoes under regulations adopted after the arrival of the vessels in ports of the empire, followed by the ultimate rejection of the claim for indemnity, "would inflict a deadly wound upon the commerce of the nation which the utmost exertions of the government would be unable to heal as long as the victims of its injustice should be able to give publicity to the history of their wrongs."

Even though France had recognized the principle of indemnity in the agreement negotiated with Barlow, French action was still irreconcilable with their contention that the long and destructive wars of Napoleon were fought for the "obtainment" of the rights of neutrals. The lawless and wanton depredations continued daily: cargoes were taken and ships seized and burned while bound to the ports of Spain and Portugal which were neither besieged nor blockaded. And these "atrocious outrages" were justified by orders issued under the long-revoked Berlin and Milan decrees. These actions could not be attributed to neglect, for Barlow had called attention to this last December. The President had instructed that reparation be demanded for all wrongs committed on American commerce since the revocation of the Berlin and Milan decrees—and that orders be given immediately to prevent all such depredations in the future.[10]

This state paper brought no worthy results. Five days later the minister protested the referral to the emperor of the favorable decision by the council of prizes in the *Nancy* case—because the minister of marine opposed that decision. This vessel, which left the United States on January 20, 1813, for nonbesieged and nonblockaded Lisbon with a cargo containing no contraband, was burned at sea on February 4 by the French frigates *Elbe* and

[10] Crawford to Bassano, Sept. 11, 1813 (triplicate), ibid. The Journal says the note was sent on Sept. 10, but all Crawford's later references are to Sept. 11.

Hortense. Every writer of celebrity said the vessels of nations in amity with France were not subject to French capture in the prosecution of this trade, and whether it could have been captured under the Berlin and Milan decrees would not even be asked—the United States had never admitted, and would never admit, the justice or legitimacy of those decrees. Besides, they were no longer in force. In addition, the owner of the *Nancy,* on representation of the captors, was imprisoned for fifty days. Crawford's hopes for an early decision, an inquiry, and the most exemplary punishment for those who had so unjustly administered the laws of the emperor were not to be realized.[11] The *Nancy* case was not settled until February 1815.

Crawford was well aware of the influence of European and American events on his negotiations and thought the outcome of the Russian mediation offer would have a decided bearing on his efforts. He wanted John Quincy Adams (the American minister to Russia) to be successful, even though Adams' success would "greatly embarrass" Crawford's own diplomatic activities. He suggested that the two keep each other informed of developments. Shortly thereafter he wrote Gallatin (who had been sent to seek Russian mediation of the war and who was soon appointed, with Adams and three others, to negotiate with the British) that he could not make any progress toward the claim for indemnity—"if I ever do." The major part of this letter was concerned with the American armies where he saw "so little talent for command . . . that it requires no insurmountable obstacle to stop their advances." He especially lambasted William Henry Harrison and expected no success for American arms so long as they were under the command of such men. He entreated Gallatin: "For God's sakes when you return, endeavor to rid the army of old women, & blockheads, at least in the genl staff."[12] Certainly the records of the American military had not strengthened Crawford's position.

Throughout his ministry Crawford wrote long, informative, and quite accurate letters to Monroe on the military and political situation in France and the rest of Europe. In late September he indicated that many Parisians rejoiced at the emperor's

11 Crawford to Bassano, Sept. 16, 1813, DD France 14.
12 Crawford to Adams, Sept. 13, 1813, Crawford Letterbook; Crawford to Gallatin, Sept. 22, 1813, Gallatin.

humiliations; he was astonished at the freedom and asperity of comments against the emperor, and he believed there would be no lasting peace until France was reduced within the Rhine. More important perhaps to Monroe was Crawford's belief that the probable expulsion of France from Spain would permit the English to use a large body of veterans in the defense of Canada and thus prevent the United States from taking that country. Or these troops could be used against some vulnerable point of the United States. Next to a numerous and well-disciplined army, Crawford believed prohibition of export of provisions of all kinds would be the most effective means of defeating a British move against the United States the following year. In November he wrote that if Canada were not acquired by the end of the European campaign, the United States might be invaded in the spring.[13]

On Sunday, November 14, nearly four months after his arrival, Crawford was received by Napoleon. The minister made his speech, and the translation was read to Napoleon by M. de Cabre. In answer to a few observations which Crawford made in presenting his credentials, Napoleon (whose countenance was "serene and frank") said he had great regard for the United States and would do everything in his power to make the relations between the two countries as friendly and beneficial as possible.[14]

Almost immediately there were changes in the government: Bassano became secretary of state and Vicence (Caulaincourt) minister of foreign relations. On November 23 Crawford wrote to Vicence expressing the desire that the long pending discussions be "conducted to a prompt and equitable termination."[15] In a conference four days later Crawford was informed that the emperor was disposed to adjust every cause of controversy but thought the United States had done wrong to mingle the matter of indemnity with the speculations of the merchants of Paris and Bordeaux. This would cause France to pay more than she should and the speculators would profit. The United States, said Crawford, had never been disposed to make such a connection; rather,

---

[13] Crawford to Monroe, Sept. 28, Oct. 9, 15, Nov. 10, 1813, DD France 14.

[14] Journal, Nov. 11, 13, 14, 1813; Crawford to Monroe, Nov. 19, 1813, DD France 14. For some of the stories connected with this official occasion see Cobb, *Leisure Labors*, 186; Eugene Vail, "Reminiscences of Wm. H. Crawford," *Southern Literary Messenger* 5 (1839):362. The last entry in Crawford's Journal was on November 14, the day of his recognition.

[15] Crawford to Vicence, Nov. 23, 1813, Crawford Letterbook.

it had uniformly insisted that the French government repair the injuries it had inflicted upon Americans without the United States being a party to that reparation. Clarification of the emperor's point of view revealed that he had reference to the plan of indemnity discussed with Barlow, whereupon Vicence was told that the United States had been decidedly opposed to the license system in every possible form and that no arrangement connected with that system would be acceptable. Vicence spoke no English and Crawford no French, so M. de Cabre was designated as the future conferee with Crawford. Crawford thought, however, that everything had been said that needed to be said; he would await the decision of the emperor.[16]

Four weeks later Crawford learned that Vicence had, according to his promise, made a detailed report to Napoleon; the moment a decision was reached Crawford would be notified. Spurred by the newspaper announcement of January 15 that Napoleon was to place himself at the head of the troops, Crawford determined to write Vicence urging more strongly the necessity of immediate decision. On the day Crawford was to present the note, Vicence set out for the emperor's headquarters at four in the morning, and the impression prevailed that Napoleon would leave immediately for Metz. Crawford thought this departure would render his note useless and decided not to send it; he regretted that decision since Napoleon was still in Paris the next day. Though his patience was exhausted and he was becoming apprehensive of accomplishing anything beneficial, on January 18 Crawford pressed upon Vicence the necessity of an immediate conclusion of the problem. He thought that before the end of the year Britain and the United States would be the only contestants, and the cause of the United States would be the cause of the civilized world. Should a "concurrence of untoward circumstances" compel the United States to quit the war and acknowledge the legality of the principles insisted upon by Great Britain before the nations of Europe were awakened to the sense of danger, the principles of maritime law for the world would be "dictated from the deck of a British ship of war and promulgated

16 Crawford to Monroe, Dec. 1, 1813, DD France 14. At this meeting Crawford brought up the matter of the communication of the St. Cloud decree, falsely dated April 28, 1811, which the French never chose to explain. See Bradford Perkins, *Prologue to War: England and the United States, 1805-1812* (Berkeley, Cal., 1961), 247, 250, 336; Brant, "Joel Barlow, Madison's Stubborn Minister," 439-52.

by the thunder of its artillery." Crawford did not think this would happen, but it was his duty to labor with indefatigable zeal to prevent even its possibility. Settlement of differences between the United States and France would dispel the possibility of United States withdrawal and might shorten the connection of some of the continental powers with England. The strongest reason for settlement, however, was the justice of the claim. Further delay by France would simply add to the original injury and indirectly advance the interests of the common enemy.[17] The French felt no such urgency about spoliation claims—allied armies were on French soil and pressing toward Paris.

Official Washington was less discouraged than Crawford. Monroe relayed Madison's approval of the minister's course and thought the accounts of the audience with the emperor and the interview with the minister of foreign affairs indicated a disposition to accommodate the differences of the two nations. He suggested it might be advantageous to the United States, in relation to French and British affairs, for a regular correspondence to be maintained between Crawford and United States commissioners soon to be negotiating with England at Göteburg. Long before this letter reached him, Crawford expressed serious doubts about the success of the negotiations and conveyed his expectation that the Bourbons would be restored if the allies reached Paris.[18]

The allies continued to advance toward Paris, a provisional government was set up, and near the end of March Louis XVIII returned to France. At about this time Dupont de Nemours, secretary of the provisional government, remarked that France would pay for all the illegal confiscations which had been committed on American commerce; this suggested that the change in government had brightened the prospects for remuneration. Crawford requested new credentials and permission to return home as soon as he had made a fair experiment with the restored Bourbon government. He did not despair of success, but the

17 Crawford to Monroe, Jan. 16, 1814; Crawford to Vicence, Jan. 18, 1814, DD France 14.

18 Monroe to Crawford, Feb. 8, 1814, DI 7; Crawford to Monroe, Feb. 15, 1814, DD France 14. Madison considered appointing Crawford to the peace commission (which met with the British at Ghent), but the French minister to the United States said such action would retard the negotiations in France. Brant, *Madison*, 6:239-40. The correspondence between Crawford and the commissioners is discussed briefly below.

longer he remained the stronger became his desire to return—he had found nothing in France in unison with his feelings and sentiments.[19]

Monroe was pleased with the turn of events, for he thought the French under Louis XVIII might assume a less imposing attitude, that France might suffer injuries from other powers, and that it might be to her interest to cultivate the friendship of the United States. If such were the case, Crawford might obtain from the Bourbons redress for the wrongs committed by the previous government. He sent a letter of credence in blank which Crawford filled in. Crawford was presented again on August 16, but the incidents of this public audience furnished him no data from which he could draw any rational conclusions. Rather, he thought that any act of justice or apparent friendship on the part of the existing government would result from the conviction that the interest of France required it.[20] The presence of Talleyrand (the Prince of Benevent) as secretary of state for foreign affairs in the new government would afford some justification for Crawford's estimate.

In opening negotiations with the new government Crawford pointed out to Talleyrand some of the violations of neutral rights that had taken place during the war between France and England (now over), denied the legality of a paper blockade, and emphasized that England had established a paper blockade of the coast of the United States. The United States, when neutral, adhered "inviolably to the principles of public law recognized by civilized nations"; as a belligerent she wished to give the maritime states of Europe the "strongest evidence" of her respect for these principles. To that end the President had issued a proclamation strictly forbidding the commanders of public vessels of the United States to interrupt, detain, molest, or vex any vessel belonging to any neutral or friendly power and directing that such vessels as

[19] Crawford to Monroe, Feb. 28, March 1, 16, 26, April 11, 12, 18, 1814, DD France 14. Monroe indicated to Crawford (June 1814, Golding) that he must allow a little time for the choice of his successor and for the "difficulties of the moment." Crawford recommended Clay as his successor; Clay thanked Crawford but decided two months later to accept his election to Congress, which had already taken place. Europe held no attractions for him, Clay said. Crawford to Monroe, Aug. 17, 1814, DD France 14; Clay to Crawford, Aug. 22, Oct. 17, 1814, James F. Hopkins, ed., Mary W. M. Hargreaves, assoc. ed., *The Papers of Henry Clay*, 3 vols. (Lexington, Ky., 1959-), 1:971-72, 990. Cited hereafter as *Clay Papers*.

[20] Monroe to Crawford, June 25, 1814, Crawford, Duke; Monroe to Crawford, June 27, 1814; Crawford to Monroe, Aug. 17, 1814, DD France 14.

were actually bound for American ports be rendered all the aid they might require. Further, the President was determined to favor by every means in his power the commerce of France with the United States. Talleyrand replied that all American vessels sailing into French ports would be received in a friendly manner.[21] Many were received in the same "friendly" manner as during Napoleon's time; Crawford's success was neither greater nor less than with the Napoleonic government.

Crawford communicated the President's proclamation to the ministers, in Paris, of all neutral nations at whose courts the United States had no ministers. Convinced that the best informed Europeans he had been in contact with were either wholly unacquainted with the causes of the war or had received all their information from English newspapers, he sent along with the proclamation a brief statement reviewing the English claims for continuing the war, the American contentions on neutral rights, the desirability of dropping or postponing the issue of impressment, and the reasonableness of a *status quo ante bellum* (though more advantageous to Britain than to the United States) as the major premise of a peace treaty.[22]

Crawford did not hurry to bring up again the general indemnity claims: Talleyrand was at the European congress in Vienna, the French internal situation was explosive (with the possibility that the Bourbons might be replaced during the winter), and he was trying to settle some current cases, which he did not want to connect with the general claim. Among the current cases was that of the *Decatur*.[23]

The *Decatur,* a letter of marque, had been seized and held from the security of port for forty-five days. The French first justified their action on the ground that the vessel was armed; later they used the pretext that she was a privateer by virtue of having captured during her voyage a British merchant vessel (which had been ordered to a port in the United States) and carried prize cargo. Action against the *Decatur* did not conform to the French regulations of May 22 governing commerce between France, now neutral, and the United States and Great Britain, the only remain-

21 Crawford to Benevent, Aug. 22, 1814; Benevent to Crawford, Sept. 2, 1814, ibid., 15.

22 Crawford to Monroe, Sept. 10, 1814 (two letters); "Reflections upon the War between the US and England," by Wm. H. Cr., ibid.

23 Crawford to Monroe, Sept. 26, 1814, ibid. There are five letters of this date.

ing belligerents. Those regulations contained only two prohibitions: no belligerent ship could arm in the ports of France and the sale of American prizes was provisionally suspended.

In his communications on the *Decatur* Crawford vigorously, almost heatedly, presented the American case to Jaucourt, with whom he dealt while Talleyrand was in Vienna. Among the many points he made were: France's actions as a neutral were very different from those of the United States when she was neutral; England's failure to remonstrate against the French regulations was an admission of their conformity to the laws of neutrality; conditions dictated that American commerce be armed, and the French action raised doubts about the "friendly disposition" of France toward that commerce; France was applying her regulations unevenly, for three fully armed British letters of marque (according to the declaration of one of their captains) had entered Bordeaux after the *Decatur* had been detained; the sole object of a privateer was capture of enemy vessels, while the taking of prizes was incidental to the commercial purpose of a letter of marque; the character of a vessel cannot depend upon incidental circumstances; and a neutral can take no cognizance of acts between belligerents unless those acts occur within the jurisdiction of the neutral. Crawford considered the French action so flagrant that he wondered whether the United States could keep a minister at the French court unless the matter was settled; certainly he could not stay. It was near the end of March 1815 before all the troublesome and unreasonable restrictions were removed and the *Decatur* was allowed to proceed with reloading.[24]

By that time Napoleon had returned to France, the United States and England were at peace, and Crawford had not only completed his interchanges with the Ghent commissioners but had served as their host and guide during a visit to Paris. A regular correspondence between Crawford and the commissioners, suggested by Monroe for their mutual advantage, began about the middle of April 1814 and ended the day before the treaty was signed, with letters to and from each of the commissioners and to them collectively. Crawford played an active role and

[24] Crawford to Jaucourt, Sept. 30, Nov. 3, 30, 1814; Crawford to Monroe, Oct. 21, Nov. 5, Dec. 12, 16, 21, 1814; Jaucourt to Crawford, Dec. 14, 1814, ibid.; Crawford to Jaucourt, March 7, 1815; Crawford to Monroe, March 16, 28, 1815; Jaucourt to Crawford, March 7, 1815; Vicence to Crawford, March 24, 1815, ibid. 16.

one of substantial importance, but most accounts of the making of the Treaty of Ghent do not even mention him.[25]

Crawford, in Paris, was more advantageously located than the commissioners for learning about the attitudes and positions of the various European powers. He soon informed them that they should not count on the influence of any allied powers on their deliberations, examined the possibility of any fruitful results of the tsar's interesting himself in mediating the war, told of placing before Alexander I (via Lafayette) a short statement of the reciprocal causes of complaint between the United States and Britain, and correctly expected no beneficial results from Alexander's proposed visit to London.[26]

Original instructions to the commissioners called upon them to resolve the issue of impressment, but before negotiations really began the allies had achieved victory over Napoleon, thus greatly curtailing England's need for seamen. The changed situation was quickly realized by those in Europe: Bayard and Gallatin wrote Monroe on May 6 and 10 that Britain would not officially give up the right to impress, and Crawford wrote on May 11 urging Monroe to change the instructions on that issue. On May 13, in the same letter in which he reviewed the tsar's role, Crawford told of his letter to Monroe and discussed the relation of impressment to the negotiations. He did not expect the British to relinquish the principle by treaty, but he was confident that peace could be made without "admitting the legality of their claim.— This is all we can expect in the present state of the world. This will leave us free to apply the proper remedy when the evil shall be felt." Crawford believed negotiations should not be jeopardized by waiting for new instructions; there were occasions when a public officer should not "hesitate to jeopardize his own reputa-

25 Philip Jackson Green, *The Life of William Harris Crawford* [Charlotte, N.C., 1965], 95-112, details Crawford's relations with the commissioners, but he did not use several important sources. Fred L. Engelman, *The Peace of Christmas Eve* (New York, 1962), devotes little space to Crawford's activity in this area.

26 Crawford to Monroe, April 20, 1814, DD France 14; Crawford to Commissioners, May 13, 28, 1814; Crawford to Gallatin, May 24, 1814, Gallatin. Most of the Crawford communications are in DD France 14 and those to Clay and the commissioners at the appropriate chronological places in *Clay Papers*, 1, 2. Some appear in the *American State Papers: Foreign Relations*, 3, and "Letters Relating to the Negotiations at Ghent," *American Historical Review* 20 (Oct. 1914):108-29, is useful. Henry Adams, ed., *The Writings of Albert Gallatin*, 3 vols. (Philadelphia, 1879), does not include a number of the letters, and by shortening others Adams has minimized or eliminated Crawford's role. This work is hereafter cited as Adams, *Gallatin Writings*.

tion" rather than the national interest. Clay thought their instructions would not permit them to take the action Crawford suggested, but if continuation of the war hinged on that single point, the United States government would not persist in demanding the "abandonment of what is now a mere theoretic pretension, the practical evil having for the present ceased; and if I were persuaded that the interests of our Country demanded of me the personal risk of a violation of instructions I should not hesitate to incur it."[27] James A. Bayard, in Paris from May 31 to June 15, 1814, agreed with Crawford on every question relative to the peace.[28]

It was June 27 before Monroe sent new instructions authorizing the commissioners to omit "any stipulation on the subject of impressment, if found indispensably necessary to terminate" the war. Monroe mentioned having received the Gallatin and Bayard letters but said nothing of Crawford's letter of May 11, so it is possibly safe to conclude that Crawford had no immediate influence on changing the instructions. His insistence, however, was that the commissioners proceed without waiting for the change.[29] Throughout the summer and early fall Crawford expressed some distrust of the British and rather despaired of success of the negotiations. All but Clay, among the commissioners, shared this pessimistic attitude.

Bayard and Jonathan Russell kept Crawford posted on the negotiations which actually began in August, and toward the end of that month the commissioners seriously considered Adams' return to St. Petersburg via Vienna where he would personally inform Alexander of what was happening at Ghent—that is, the delaying tactics and uncompromising position of the British, who said American recognition of an Indian buffer state was absolutely prerequisite to discussion of other matters. By early October Crawford "anxiously wished" the negotiations might be closed.

27 Crawford to Commissioners, May 13, 1814; Clay to Crawford, July 2, 1814, *Clay Papers*, 1:904-9, 937-39. Adams' version of Crawford's letter, *Gallatin Writings*, 1:614-17, contains none of the material in the text above.

28 Elizabeth Donnan, ed., *Papers of James A. Bayard, 1796-1815*, American Historical Association, *Annual Report*, 1913, 2 vols. (Washington, D.C., 1915) 2:509-10; Crawford to Clay (via Bayard), June 10, 1814, *Clay Papers*, 1:932-36. During the stay in Paris, Bayard and Crawford visited the underground caverns, the Louvre, Versailles, and other points of interest, and dined with Lafayette, Marbois, LaForest, and others.

29 Monroe to Commissioners, June 27, 1814; Monroe to Crawford, June 27, 1814, DI 7.

He thought, however, they would be continued until Castlereagh was satisfied that the Congress of Vienna would terminate amicably; England would then be free to play whatever hand she wished. Though Crawford had sent his statement on the war and peace to the European powers after the defeat of Napoleon, he felt the true state of the negotiations should be made known to the principal powers by either Adams or Gallatin—and directly to the emperor of Russia or Talleyrand. However, it might be unsafe to trust the latter.[30] The idea of Adams or Gallatin going to Vienna persisted until the middle of October when the meetings began to turn toward meaningful discussions.

The unanimous opposition of the commissioners to the British-proposed Indian state forced that item into the background, but some difference of opinion developed—and sharp and heated controversy came a few years later—over the fisheries-Mississippi River proposal. Apparently Russell's letter of November 4 gave Crawford his first news of the British position that if the United States were to retain the fishing rights acquired by the treaty of 1783 Britain should have the right to navigate the Mississippi River. This letter caused Crawford "much uneasiness," and he could not think of a "solitary reason which offers itself in favor of proposing a free navigation of the Mississippi River as an equivalent of taking fish within the British jurisdiction and of drying them on their uninhabited shores." This privilege was advantageous to the United States, but, said Crawford, it ought not to be purchased at the "expense of an equivalent" of "value to the enemy only as it is directly injurious to us." Since American ports were all free and British vessels could enter them without difficulty with cargoes that were not prohibited, why should Britain be permitted to navigate the river? And what is the "object of their solicitude in accepting this as an equivalent?" Certainly it would make it easier to smuggle prohibited articles and to embroil the United States with the Indians. He hoped this offer had not been made; if it had been, it no doubt was accepted unless everything that had been done at Ghent was a farce.[31]

30 Crawford to Gallatin, Oct. 6, 1814, Gallatin, NYH: Charles Francis Adams, ed., *Memoirs of John Quincy Adams . . .*, 12 vols. (Philadelphia, 1874-1877), 3:23, 53. Hereafter cited as Adams, *Memoirs.*
31 Crawford to Gallatin, Nov. 10, 1814, Gallatin. Earlier Crawford had expressed a similar view regarding introduction of manufactures into the United States

Clay (with support from Russell) bitterly opposed any mention of the fisheries-river issue in the American projet and declared he would not sign any treaty that restored to the British the right to navigate the river. After several votes, the group left the question unnoticed in their proposal. On December 23 Russell detailed the differences of opinion in general, noted that the British had been told a *status quo ante bellum* was required, and indicated a treaty was close. It was signed the next day, and two days later the Duke of Wellington informed Crawford of this action.[32] The "major premise," as Crawford had several times suggested, was the *status quo ante bellum*.

During his ministership Crawford also carried out his assigned duties as supervisor of all the American consuls in western Europe. In addition to the problems of prize ships and cargoes he also had to administer through the consuls and vice consuls the activities concerning distressed seamen and prisoners of war. These sometimes involved citizenship, alleged acts of barbarity, inhumanity, and cruelty by captains of American vessels, and the always troublesome problems of finance. But these matters seem to have been resolved with little more than the anticipated difficulties.[33] At the end of the war with England Crawford devoted some attention to the appointment of consuls in Europe, detailing for Monroe those who then held posts and were appointed by the President, and noting that a number of those listed in the almanac for 1814 (which Monroe had sent to him) were either dead or had returned to the United States some years before.[34]

should Britain secure control of Louisiana in her upcoming invasion attempt. Crawford to Monroe, Aug. 17, 1814, DD France 14.

[32] Adams to Crawford, Nov. 17, 1814; Clay to Crawford, Nov. 24, 1814; Russell to Crawford, Dec. 2, 1814, Golding; Russell to Crawford, Dec. 23, 1814; Wellington to Crawford, Dec. 26, 1814, Letters to Crawford; Samuel Flagg Bemis, *John Quincy Adams and the Foundations of American Foreign Policy* (New York, 1949), 209, 213, 214. In his discussion of Ghent, 196-220, Bemis does not mention Crawford and cites only two Clay letters to Crawford. Available evidence indicates that Russell eight years later, in supporting Clay for the presidency but perhaps concerned more with discrediting Adams, distorted the events at Ghent. Ibid., 498-509; *House Documents*, No. 75 (serial 67), 17th Cong., 1st sess. Hereafter cited as *House Doc.*

[33] See, for example, Crawford to Bassano, Oct. 16, 1813; Crawford to LaForest, April 21, 1814, Crawford Letterbook; Crawford to Bassano, Oct. 15, 1813; Crawford to Monroe, March 10, April 20, June 8, 1814; Circular to Consuls, Sept. 23, 1813, Jan. 24, 1814, DD France 14; Crawford to Monroe, Dec. 30, 1814, ibid. 15; Monroe to Crawford, Aug. 30, 1813, Feb. 13, 1814, DI 7.

[34] Crawford to Monroe, Dec. 28, 1814, DD France 15; Crawford to Monroe, Feb. 15, 1815, Monroe, MDLC.

Nearly a year after leaving Europe Crawford recommended an increase in the pay of some of the ministers and thought some changes in the consular system might be desirable. Most of the consuls (in reality perhaps more representative of business than of the government) were not on salary, but they were usually able to enter into partnership with the "most respectable" mercantile houses in the various ports by investing only the "advantage of their position." Because such associations might subordinate their official acts to their economic interests, it might be preferable to give them an annual salary and prohibit their trading activities. The salary, Crawford said, would have to be considerable or it would not be equivalent, and it would need to be given to all consuls, not just those at the capital cities. He also thought it might be beneficial to appoint a consul general (with a competent salary) to each of the principal commercial states with the power to superintend the conduct of and make general regulations for the other consuls in that country. To help raise money for the consular salaries a small tonnage duty might be levied on all American vessels entering foreign ports; when the duty collected in a port exceeded the salary of the consul stationed there, the surplus could be used toward the salary of another consul in the same state where the fees had not been equal to the salary.[35] The merits of the proposal seem obvious, but not until 1856 did Congress systematize the consular service.

While Crawford was bringing the *Decatur* case toward a satisfactory resolution, encountering occasional difficulty in meeting the financial requirements of distressed seamen, and serving as host and guide for some of the Ghent commissioners who were still in Paris,[36] he was informed that Napoleon had escaped from Elba, had landed in France, and was advancing toward Paris. Crawford would not predict whether the Bourbons would be overthrown, but he detected little enthusiasm for them and

[35] Crawford to Monroe, April 5, 1816, Gallatin.

[36] Adams arrived during the first week of February; the others had come in early January and had been presented to the king two weeks after arrival. All but Bayard, who was dangerously ill, were again presented on February 7, at which time Crawford—in reply to the king's question—identified Adams as the son of the "celebrated Mr. Adams." Clay left for London on March 17 and Gallatin followed a few days later. Adams, *Memoirs*, 3:151, 185-86; *Clay Papers*, 2:3-9; Crawford to Monroe, March 21, 1815, Monroe, MDLC; Bayard to [Isaac Cox Barnet?], April 23, 1815, Donnan, ed., *Bayard Papers*, 380.

thought the sovereign who in the nineteenth century presumed to rule by divine right "must not expect any enthusiasm in support of his pretensions."[37] Three days later, March 19, the royal family had left the Tuileries, and Napoleon occupied it the next morning. The papers of that morning displayed an entirely changed tone, but since his departure for the United States was near, Crawford thought he could avoid any connection with the court without giving offense or in any way committing the interests of the United States. He was now convinced that if the Bourbons ever regained the throne it must be by the same means Napoleon's restoration was effected, for the great mass of talent, wealth, and enterprise were opposed to the Bourbons and the principles upon which they were willing to rest their right to the throne.[38]

The corps diplomatique had been meeting every day since Napoleon had landed on French soil, but only on March 20 did Crawford hear of these meetings. Since he had not been informed, he would not attend, and he now felt war more than probable—it would start between England and France and then spread to a general conflict. Within a week the foreign ministers had applied for their passports, and many had left Paris. Crawford was the only remaining minister who did not represent a nation at war with France at the time of the abdication of Napoleon, and he planned to leave soon.[39]

But he did not get away as soon as he expected, and he had one more interview with Vicence. On April 3 he reviewed the situation of prizes brought in by American ships and the provisional suspension of sales by the king. When Vicence was reminded of the claim for indemnity and was asked the sentiment of Napoleon on the matter, his countenance immediately changed —he had supposed a solution had been arranged by the last government. To Vicence's statement that since the United States and Britain were at peace and the issue ought to be considered settled, Crawford retorted that the wrongs committed by France could not possibly have been arranged in a treaty between the

<hr>

37 Jaucourt to Crawford, March 7, 1815; Crawford to Monroe, March 8, 16, 1815, DD France 16; Crawford to Monroe, March 16, 1815, Monroe, MDLC. Crawford noted that he had been ill for four weeks but was considerably improved in the past few days.

38 Crawford to Monroe, March 21, 1815, DD France 16.

39 Crawford to Monroe, March 21, 28, 1815, ibid.

United States and England. Whereupon Vicence said he would examine it as soon as "other pressing avocations would permit." Crawford, who had decided to let the temper of this discussion determine his relations with the new government, presently informed the duke of his imminent return to the United States.[40]

Having determined there was no possibility of settling the indemnity claims, Crawford made preparations to leave. On April 24, at Grignon's in the Rue Neuve des Petits Champs, forty-five people attended a farewell dinner for him, and two days later Crawford left for England. He did not expect to be there more than ten days, and on May 9 he wrote Bayard that he, Clay, and Gallatin (the last two negotiating a commercial treaty with England) would arrive at Plymouth on May 16 or 17.[41] But negotiations did not go as rapidly as expected, departure dates were several times postponed, and finally Crawford was informed that Gallatin had written the *Neptune* captain for a sailing date of June 25.[42]

Bayard, too ill to attend the dinner for Crawford in Paris, was now in a "debilitated" condition. At the end of May Crawford had told Clay that in determining the sailing date of the *Neptune* Bayard's condition and feelings ought to be considered "without any regard to my convenience."[43] Apparently fearful that further delay in sailing might result in Bayard's death before he got home, Crawford did not wait for Clay and Gallatin. He ordered the *Neptune* to sail on June 18, leaving Clay and Gallatin (and Adams who arrived soon after) to complete the negotiations on July 2. Crawford and Bayard arrived at Wilmington, Delaware, on August 1 and Bayard died six days later.[44]

---

[40] Crawford to Monroe, April 15, 1815, ibid.

[41] Crawford to Bayard, May 9, 1815, Simon Gratz Collection (HSP). Henry Jackson had been left as chargé in Paris; Russell returned to Sweden; Adams, the new minister to England, did not reach London until after Crawford left that place; and Gallatin, after a brief visit to the United States, took up his post as minister to France.

[42] Clay to Crawford, June 10, 12, 1815, Letters to Crawford.

[43] Crawford to Clay, May 31, 1815, *Clay Papers*, 2:39-40. Clay's letter of May 27, referred to by Crawford, has not been located.

[44] Bayard and his friends felt the "warmest gratitude" to Crawford for his attentions, and Crawford explained to Mrs. Gallatin the reasons her husband had been left in England. Donnan, ed., *Bayard Papers*, 348n; G. B. Milligan to Crawford, Aug. 4, 1815, Golding; Crawford to Hannah Nicholson Gallatin, Aug. 16, 1815, Gallatin. In a long fragment draft to Clay (n.d., Golding), which probably was not sent, Crawford stressed the importance of Clay and Gallatin remaining until the treaty was concluded, examined the reasons the *Neptune* should no longer delay

While in France Crawford frequently was distressed by the continued inefficiency of the administrators of the war effort, the inadequacy and failure of the military leaders, and the division and discontent the war had brought among the people of the United States.[45] He also speculated on how the United States might avoid war in the future, concerning himself with the depredations belligerent maritime powers would commit on the commerce of a neutral nation. To him only two ways seemed open: diminish the inducement to depredate or counteract that inducement by a constant state of preparation. The first could be done by repealing the system of drawbacks and thus keeping commerce near its peacetime level; achievement of the second would mean maintaining a war establishment—and taxes—from the beginning to the close of every war between the principal maritime states of Europe. The earlier policy of becoming the carriers of the weaker belligerents and at the same time trying to avoid war would subject the commerce to depredations of the stronger belligerent. But to form a correct judgment of the merits of the two policies the profits of one ought to be compared with the costs of the other, and the possibility of having to enter war no matter what policy had been followed, as well as the subsequent loss of the profit of the carrying trade and of the direct commerce, ought to enter into the evaluation. But to insist upon the exercise of national rights and permit the habitual violation of those rights degraded the national character and invited aggression of a more general and vital nature.

However, he thought the problem would resolve itself when the United States reached a population of thirty million; then the country could venture upon the enjoyment of the trade of the weaker belligerent without the danger of being forced into war. Meantime, no agreement should be made to abstain from such trade. The commerce of the United States could be controlled by changes in the revenue laws, changes made at the pleasure of the United States without offense to others. He did not believe the report that Trinidad had been exchanged for the Floridas;

---

sailing, and regretted not having gone immediately from Plymouth to Liverpool, thus avoiding the unpleasant situation he was then in.

45 See, for example, Crawford to Gallatin, Sept. 22, 1813, Gallatin; Crawford to Monroe, Jan. 16, May 11, Sept. 10, 1814, DD France 14; Crawford to Charles Tait, Oct. 12, 1814, Tait. Several letters Crawford had asked Gallatin to pass on to the addressees are in the Gallatin Papers.

even if this were true, the English control of Florida during peacetime could not be very injurious to the United States. He concluded that when "our population shall double that of the British Isles, her possessions in our neighborhood may be considered more in the nature of security for her good behavior than as endangering our peace, or injurious to our interests."[46]

There is no doubt that Crawford did not accomplish the major purpose of his mission, but the later accusation of his political foes that his appointment was strictly political and that failure resulted from Crawford's deficiencies does not seem justified. Crawford was well regarded by his contemporaries, and Bayard, a staunch Federalist, thought him the ablest and most influential man in the Senate at the time of his appointment. Henry Adams later described him as the "only vigorous Republican leader in the Senate" but thought Crawford's manners and temper "little suited to the very delicate situation" in which he was placed.[47] Crawford's letters to Monroe and communications to the French government indicate abilities of a high order, and though he disliked the court etiquette and thought he might have made "many blunders" there is no intimation that his manners and his alleged temper in any way affected negotiations. He was brusque and harsh only in preventing the Russians from violating the diplomatic immunity of his mission grounds and quarters. His advice to and consultation with the Ghent commissioners reveal a thorough comprehension of the European situation and helped those commissioners to arrive at new positions or gave support to positions which they had independently reached. It seems reasonable to assume that no one could have settled the issues with the French government at that time, and in all fairness it should be noted that these problems did not yield to solution for almost twenty years.

Crawford must have been happy to return to his own country; he had felt rather useless in France, and though he had made some warm and lasting personal friendships he felt no particular attachment to the French nation.[48] Indeed, his French experience

---

[46] Crawford to Jonathan Fisk, Dec. 8, 1814, Jefferson Papers (MDLC); Crawford to Monroe, Feb. 21, 1815, Monroe, MDLC. See also Jefferson to Crawford, May 31, 1816, Jefferson.

[47] Adams, *Memoirs*, 2:519; Adams, *History*, 7:49; Adams, *Gallatin Life*, 510.

[48] The acquaintance with Lafayette ripened into a strong friendship, and Crawford kept Lafayette's letters with "more than usual care." Dudley, "Crawford," 9;

strengthened his already strong devotion to republicanism. He was not, as he had expected when he asked permission to come home, to return to the service of his state as a United States senator; for almost ten years he would be a member of Madison's and Monroe's cabinets.

several letters from Lafayette to Crawford are in the Lafayette Papers at the University of Chicago.

5

Secretary of War

WHILE THE UNITED STATES and England remained at war, Crawford anticipated resuming an elective office when he returned home. But, in February 1815, shortly after the war ended, he seemed to have little expectation of remaining in public service; the needs of his family and of his farm would determine whether he returned to the practice of law.[1] Exactly one week after Crawford expressed these sentiments, the Senate confirmed him as secretary of war, replacing Monroe who had resigned.[2] Before he left Paris, Crawford received unofficial news of this action from Gallatin in London, but no one in Washington wrote him on the matter. Madison, who had made the nomination without consulting Crawford, did not write because he "had taken it for granted" that Crawford would leave Europe by early April; even so, as late as May 18 the President was wondering whether Crawford would return soon or remain in France to pursue the purpose of his mission under the changed conditions.[3]

Crawford had been in England some days before he learned from newspapers—not from the expected dispatches—brought by the *Neptune* that he had been appointed to head the War Department. From Plymouth, before sailing for home, he expressed an indebtedness to the President for his continued confidence in him after the total failure of the mission to France, but he regretted the appointment. Crawford said his services were entirely at the command of the government so long as the war continued, but when peace was made he had decided to devote his time to his domestic interests. He had no expectation of a new position and would make no decision until he reached the United States and talked with Monroe and Madison. Perhaps, he mused, the appointment had not been made; he had no official notification of it. In fact, since the middle of December 1814 he had received from the United States only a letter of introduction.[4]

The *Neptune* arrived at Baltimore on August 2, and Crawford went to Washington by steamer that afternoon and evening. The following day he was handed letters from Monroe and Madison and a commission as secretary of war. On August 4 Crawford accepted the appointment, noting that the harmony he presumed to exist in the cabinet was a factor in his decision. He would endeavor to promote that harmony, promised exertion in the discharge of his duties, and expressed the desire to extend the reputation of Madison's administration and to strengthen and perpetuate the republican institutions.[5] Though he had thought himself unqualified to handle the department during wartime, Crawford seemed to have no such misgivings concerning administering the office during peace. By Tuesday, August 8, the new secretary had assumed his duties; two weeks later he left the capital for Woodlawn,[6] spent five weeks in Georgia, and—with his family—was again in Washington on November 14. The Crawfords were not to return permanently to Georgia for nearly ten years. In that time the promise of a bright political career had been fulfilled, though the final goal of the presidency was never attained.

Crawford's tenure as secretary of war ended in October 1816, but in the short time he held that office he effected some notable innovations, began several programs that were carried to fruition by his successors, laid the bases for some disastrous enmities, and made a thoughtful report on the Indians which was almost brutally distorted in 1816 and revived in 1824 to assist in Crawford's political assassination. All seem to attest to Crawford's

1 Crawford to Charles Tait, Feb. 22, 1815, Tait.

2 Previously Henry Dearborn had been rejected, but the Senate consented to erase this record from its journal. There was no roll call vote on Crawford's approval. Senate *Executive Journal*, 2:625, 626, 627; *National Intelligencer*, March 4, 1815; Adams, *History*, 9:89. Alexander J. Dallas carried the duties of secretary of war and secretary of treasury during many months of 1815.

3 Gallatin to Crawford, April 15, 1815, Letters to Crawford; Madison to Monroe, May 18, 1815, Monroe, MDLC.

4 Crawford to Monroe, June 14, 1815, DD France 16.

5 Crawford to Monroe, Aug. 4, 1815, ibid.; Madison to Crawford, July 18, 1815; Crawford to Madison, Aug. 4, 1815, Golding. The original commission, dated Aug. 1, 1815, is in ibid.

6 War Office, Military Book No. 8 (National Archives); *National Intelligencer*, Aug. 26, 1815. The first item is hereafter cited as MB 8. Crawford received something of a hero's welcome in Georgia and was the honored guest at a ball in Lexington and at a public dinner in Athens. A partisan described him as the "most imposing gentleman who had ever been seen in Georgia." *Athens Journal*, Sept. 14, 1815; *Athens Gazette*, Sept. 14, Oct. 12, 1815; Gilmer, *Sketches* (1855), 127.

devotion to duty and his capacity for work, but it has been fashionable to detract from his abilities and achievements. In reality, Crawford as secretary of war (and secretary of treasury) was reasonably imaginative, practical, efficient, administratively competent, and ethically sound.[7]

The early months of the War of 1812 had demonstrated the inefficiencies of the War Department and the ineffectiveness of the army commanders. Crawford and others thought poorly of the head of the department and a number of the generals, but deficiencies were not due entirely to personal shortcomings—improper organization lay at the base of some of the difficulties. Some reorganization was effected by the act of March 3, 1813, but exactly two years later the law fixing the peacetime military establishment at 7,950 officers and men all but destroyed those administrative gains. The postwar legislation greatly reduced the adjutant general and topographical departments and replaced the departments of the inspector general and quartermaster with four brigade inspectors and quartermasters. The President saved some of the wartime gains by deciding the more recent measure did not apply to the ordnance and purchasing departments or to judge advocates and chaplains. Further, he ordered the provisional retention of an adjutant and inspector general, two adjutants general, a quartermaster general, a paymaster of the army, an apothecary general, five hospital surgeons, and a number of assistants for each of these staff officers.[8]

Crawford definitely did not approve of the postwar changes made by Congress. He maintained that the evidence furnished by the first two campaigns of the late war "incontestably established" the expediency and necessity of having a peacetime organization of the military that would make it efficient in time of war. Further, a complete organization of the staff would contribute as much to economy as to efficiency. The stationary staff should be organized without reference to the number and

7 For an especially laudatory view see L. D. Ingersoll, *A History of the War Department of the United States* (Washington, D.C., 1879), 75-76, 455, 457.

8 For an account of the wartime and immediate postwar organization of the War Department see Lloyd Milton Short, *The Development of National Administrative Organization in the United States* (Baltimore, Md., 1923), 125-29. The officers mentioned above were referred to as the general staff, but it should be noted that these military and civilian officials were concerned with housekeeping functions of the army, not with overall general military planning.

distribution of troops, and he urged that a general staff be established for each of the two military divisions (northern and southern) set up by the general order of May 17, 1815. Congress responded favorably to Crawford's recommendations with the act of April 24, 1816, which completely reorganized the general staff and made permanent the provisional actions of President Madison. In December 1818 Calhoun told Congress that the staff organization of 1816 combined simplicity with efficiency; he made only a few changes.[9]

The War of 1812 had also clearly shown that systematic protection of the coast and interior was essential to the defense of the country. Early in 1816 Crawford emphasized the necessity of coastal fortifications, indicated the intention of the government to complete those that had been started and to establish others as rapidly as appropriations would permit, and asked the governors to use their good offices in securing cession to the United States of the sites of the fortifications.[10] In the winter and spring of 1816 correspondence among Jacob Brown (commanding the northern division), Joseph G. Swift (senior officer of the corps of engineers), and Crawford led to agreement on most of the details concerning repairs to be made, new works to be undertaken, surveys of canals and bridges to be conducted, number of officers needed in the corps, and pay of troops to be used in construction work. Congress responded favorably to Crawford's request with the act of April 29, 1816, which provided an appropriation of $838,000 for the launching of a major program of fortifications.[11] One phase of the program—doubtless triggered by the British activity in the Chesapeake Bay and the easy invasion of Washington—called for a joint survey by the army and navy to determine what fortifications were necessary to prevent the entry of a hostile fleet into the bay, and to defend points within the bay should such an entry occur.[12]

Contractual problems, personal interests, sectional and regional

9 Crawford to Richard M. Johnson, Dec. 27, 1815, MB 8; *American State Papers: Military Affairs*, 1:636, 780; 3 *Stat.* 297.

10 Crawford to various governors, Jan. 16, 1816, MB 8.

11 Crawford to Jacob Brown, April 3, May 7, 1816; Brown to Crawford, April 26, May 31, 1816; Brown to Swift, April 27, 1816, Jacob Brown Letter Book, Jan. 1, 1816–Feb. 5, 1828 (MDLC); Swift to Crawford, Jan. 9, 1816; Crawford to James Barbour, April 9, 1816, James Barbour Papers (NYP).

12 See Crawford to George Bomford, May 31, 1816, MB 9.

wishes, and spheres of jurisdiction sometimes caused vexing delays in carrying out the program, but these yielded to administrative patience and judicious compromise. And so did the shortage of supervisory personnel. Swift had indicated he needed sixty more officers in the corps of engineers. Crawford used this expressed need to revive his recommendation—made while in France—that French engineers be employed in the United States when they became available. Especially did he mention the illustrious Simon Bernard. He thought Swift might not want to recommend a Frenchman for a major generalcy, but suggested that Bernard's value to the United States might be apparent in light of the number and importance of the fortifications to be built in the next four years at an expenditure of about $4 million. The employment of Bernard might also produce the promotion of several other men in the corps—and this would be desirable.[13]

Congress did authorize the President to employ a foreign engineer; Henry Jackson in Paris was directed to communicate with Bernard, and Crawford wrote directly to him, indicating the prospect of permanent employment in one of the academies expected to be established. With the permission of the French minister of war Bernard came to the United States, where he took on responsibility for the construction of Fortress Monroe and several fortifications around New York City and for much of the civil engineering connected with the Chesapeake and Ohio Canal and the Delaware Breakwater.[14] The fortification program was moving smoothly when John C. Calhoun became secretary of war.

Meanwhile Crawford was moving to stop violations of regulations and to improve the quality of education at West Point, which was under the supervision of the secretary of war. Some young men, admitted as cadets in 1813, had never appeared at the academy; some instructors thought some of the cadets unqualified and indicated that the required admissions examinations

---

13 Crawford to Monroe, May 11, Aug. 17, 1814, DD France 14; Crawford to Gentlemen, Oct. 14, 1814 (copy); Commissioners to Crawford, Oct. 19, Dec. 2, 1814, Gallatin Letter Book, 2:250-51, 252-53; Crawford to Barbour, April 9, 1816.

14 Crawford to Gallatin, May 6, 1816, Gallatin; Crawford to Bernard, May 6, 1816, MB 9; Gallatin to Crawford, Aug. 6, 1816, Gallatin Letter Book, 4:18-19. Bernard returned to France after the revolution of 1830, was made a lieutenant general by Louis Philippe, and served as minister of war in 1836. Reports to Congress on the fortifications program may be conveniently located in *Niles' Weekly Register*.

were not being given to all prospective students. Crawford requested General Swift (superintendent of West Point by virtue of his seniority in the corps of engineers) to forward without delay the names of those not properly qualified. Recommendation of unqualified young men made it necessary for the academic staff to give an admission examination, the act of 1812 defining qualifications would be the guideline, and the letter of appointment would be delivered only after successful completion of the examination.[15] The bluntness of Crawford's last letter seems to have settled this matter.

Crawford made slight changes in the course of study which had been in effect since June 1810, answered complaints by altering some eating and mess-house regulations and demanding compliance with others, and made arrangements for purchase abroad of books, maps, and instruments that would be useful in the academy's instructional program. He also had friends send him muskets, rifles, and pistols of European manufacture that exhibited interesting or advanced features, and thus might be of value to the American military.[16]

Congress had not acceded to the request to provide for a complete topographical survey of the interior of the United States, but limited activity in this area was possible. Crawford detailed Major Stephen Long (from General Jackson's command) to make a survey of the Upper Mississippi Valley as far west as Prairie du Chien. Long's publication of his observations was followed by Jackson's order of April 1817 forbidding officers under his command to obey any order of the War Department that had not been transmitted through him. Crawford thought this incident one of the causes of Jackson's hostility to him.[17]

Perhaps more basic to that decade-long hostility were the differences of opinion between the two men on Indian lands and Indian treaties. From time to time, Crawford—in conformity with his duties and with national law—instructed the commanding generals to remove intruders and squatters from Indian (and

15 Andrew Ellicott to Jacob Brown, Feb. 8, 1816, Jacob Brown Papers (MHS); Crawford to Swift, May 2, 10, 1816, MB 9.

16 Crawford to Swift, July 1, 1816, NB 9; Contract: Crawford to George Boyd, Oct. 9, 1816, George Boyd Papers (Huntington Library); Crawford to Gallatin, Oct. 10, 1816, Gallatin; Jonathan Russell to Crawford, June 22, 1816, Jonathan Russell Papers (Brown University Library).

17 Crawford to Stephen Long, June 18, 1816, MB 9; Crawford to Charles Jared Ingersoll, Aug. 17, 1822, Ingersoll Papers (HSP).

public) lands and to destroy their habitations and improvements,[18] and in March 1817 he ordered renegotiation of the
Treaty of Fort Jackson. This treaty, concluded by the general
with the Creek, was protested by the Cherokee who contended
some of their lands were included in the cession. Jackson, in
Washington when the Cherokee chieftains arrived, defended the
treaty, and urged Madison and Crawford not to receive the
deputation. Crawford did see the chieftains, believed their claims
just, and with Madison's approval ordered renegotiation. Jackson,
far from pleased, believed the facts did not support the Cherokee
claims; he could not understand what led the President to
surrender the best portion of the country ceded by the Creek and
maintained that the security of the lower country had been given
up with the five million acres. The people complained loudly,
he said, of the government action.[19]

On the very day Jackson expressed the above sentiments, he,
David Meriwether, and Jesse Franklin were appointed with full
power and authority to adjust all differences between the Chickasaw and the United States. The instructions of July 3, 1816,
were followed two days later by a few admonitions from Crawford, probably prompted by the Chickasaw deputation's strong
complaint against the "menacing stile" of a Jackson letter. It
was expected, the secretary said, that the conduct of the three
would be conciliatory and calculated to "inspire the nation with
a just sense of the equity and magnanimity of the conduct of the
government toward them." He thought the wants of the Indians
and conflicting claims of the Chickasaw and Cherokee would
make the commissioners' task easier, and he advised that they
"press or relax according to the disposition of the Indians."[20]

Jackson was probably infuriated by this advice on behavior,

18 See, for example, Crawford to Edmund Gaines and Jacob Brown, Jan. 27, 1816;
Crawford to Andrew Jackson and Alexander Macomb, Jan. 29, 1816, MB 8. For a
discussion of this problem see Francis Paul Prucha, *American Indian Policy in the
Formative Years: The Indian Trade and Intercourse Acts, 1790-1834* (Cambridge,
Mass., 1962), 139-87.

19 James Parton, *Life of Andrew Jackson*, 3 vols. (Boston, 1883), 2:355-56; Crawford
to Jackson, March 8, 1816, MB 8; Jackson to Crawford, June 4, 1816, Andrew Jackson
Papers (Duke).

20 Crawford to Jesse Franklin, June 4, 1816; Crawford to Franklin, Meriwether,
Jackson, July 5, 1816, Miscellaneous Papers, Series I, Vol. II (North Carolina Department of Archives and History); Madison to Crawford, June 29, 1816; Gross;
Crawford to Madison, June 11, 1816, Adrian Hoffman Joline Collection (Huntington Library). Other commissioners were appointed to treat with the Choctaw and
the Cherokee.

but there is no record of reply or comment from him. The treaties were soon concluded, and Crawford was well aware that he was not the most popular man in the West: he had been denounced and burned in effigy in Tennessee because of the Cherokee convention and in the Mississippi Territory for being disposed to remove the intruders from the public lands. He expected the distemper of Tennesseans soon to disappear because lands ceded by the Cherokee and Chickasaw treaties connected the settlement in Tennessee with the Gulf of Florida. Crawford was pleased with this important cession but felt it "scandalously violated" the 1802 agreement between the United States and Georgia by which the central government agreed to remove the Indians from Georgia in return for the Georgia cession of the Alabama-Mississippi region. Treaties with the Sac and Fox extended the Illinois purchase to the shores of Lake Michigan, and Crawford thought if the Choctaw claims east of the Tombigbee River could be satisfactorily adjusted "we have nothing further to desire in the West for many years."[21] Like many Americans of the period, he apparently believed it would be years, maybe generations, before the land already held by the United States would be populated.

While the matters of Indians and public lands were not without excitement and permanent effects, something of a national furor was created by Crawford's report on Indian affairs. Submitted on March 3, 1816, in answer to a Senate resolution, this lengthy report and extensive accompanying documents and statements constitute an important survey of the Indian "problem." The documents dealt with annuities due and the sums actually paid to the Indian tribes within the United States, the presents made to them, and the general expenses of the Indian service during the four years preceding March 3, 1815. The War of 1812 had prevented payment of some annuities; on the other hand, the amounts shown as presents included a great quantity of provisions furnished friendly tribes that had taken refuge within American settlements. These presents had swelled to unreasonable amounts; Crawford thought it necessary to discontinue the practice or to devise some checks to prevent recurrence of the existing situation.[22]

---

21 Crawford to Gallatin, Oct. 9, 1816, Gallatin; Adams, *Gallatin Writings*, 2:12-13.
22 *American State Papers: Indian Affairs*, 2:26-28; the accompanying materials are on pages 29-88.

Some statements indicated that the Indian trade, conducted through the factor system, showed an annual profit of $15,000; but the annual support from the treasury exceeded $20,000, resulting in an annual loss of $5,000. Better management, more intimate acquaintance with the trade, more skillful selection of goods and of agents vending them, and a considerable increase in the capital invested would produce a small and increasing profit. But profits could not be any inducement for continuing the system; justification could be found only in the influence gained by the government over the tribes. By disallowing all intercourse between the tribes and the whites—except those who have the permission of the government and over whose conduct a direct control is exerted—peace between the Indians and the government had been greatly promoted.

If civilization of the tribes was considered more important than acquisition of the Indian lands, the secretary would continue the present system. Modifications were needed, and success depended on exercising all the influence that went with annuities and presents. He believed that skillful direction of the program would bring the tribes "distinct ideas of separate property," first in things personal and then in relation to lands. More attention must be given to Indian habitations and to the increase of distinct settlements: a portion of the land should be preserved to an individual, who should acquire full title after a stipulated number of years of residence on and cultivation of the land. Such a policy and a liberal commerce with the Indians might bring complete success, but commerce on the contract scale and profit basis would tend only to diminish the influence of the government and alienate the Indians. Trade must be greatly extended or abandoned to individual enterprise. Crawford would greatly expand it, for to keep the trade in the hands of the government and only partially supply the wants of the Indians would make them feel the influence of the government only in their "privations and wretchedness."[23]

Under existing laws the governors of the territories were required to grant trading licenses to all who gave security. Craw-

[23] Ibid., 27. Crawford would permit British merchants from Canada to participate in the trade with some of the Indians until the United States was in a position to know about and meet their wants. Gradually all foreign participation should be ended.

ford believed the governors should have power to refuse licenses for reasons of character, and that requiring an oath to obey the laws governing the trade—especially in connection with the sale of spirituous liquors—might improve the quality of the traders. He supported the proposal of Governor Ninian Edwards of Illinois Territory and the superintendent of Indian affairs for the development of a depot (in the St. Louis area) that could supply the regular and established trading houses and make advances of goods up to $10,000 value to persons of good moral character.

In answer to a portion of the resolution, Crawford thought it would be highly proper to place the management of Indian affairs in a separate and independent department if the government was to retain control of commerce with those nations. The small military force required at the various trading posts could be furnished by the War Department no matter who supervised the trade. This constituted no burden, but the accounts and accounting procedures heavily taxed the time of the secretary of war. Accounts of the Indian trade were returned to the Treasury Department; those of the agents to the several tribes were returned to and settled in the War Department. The determination and payment of annuities were particularly troublesome and time-consuming. Crawford detailed the elaborate procedure for deducting amounts for robberies, thefts, and depredations; the hearing of the extrajudicial evidence; and the necessity for the secretary to approve almost every disbursement of money connected with the Indian service. The year-by-year accumulation of accounts had become so great that legislative aid was required to correct it: a separate department to handle the Indian accounts was not the answer; the accounting office must be reorganized. If a new department were formed, many of the miscellaneous duties of the State Department should be transferred to it; such transfers would be brought to the attention of the Senate when reorganization was under discussion.

Although Crawford could think of a plan of trade with the Indians that would be less expensive to the government, he believed the existing system with the suggested modifications would be of greatest advantage to the Indians. He emphasized that capital in the area where people were knowledgeable in the Indian trade was not sufficient for commerce among the citizens.

This capital was exposed to no risks, and the profit was great; consequently it would not be employed in the Indian trade. Those in the commercial cities who had capital would not supply the money because of the risks and the "casual want of integrity" of the traders. The proposed St. Louis depot would be highly beneficial in supplying this capital and skilled persons and would eventually justify relinquishing the trade, under judicious regulations, entirely to individual enterprise.

All his views, Crawford said, were founded on the conviction that it was the true policy and earnest desire of the government "to draw its savage neighbors within the pale of civilization." If he was mistaken, and the primary object of the government was to extinguish the Indian titles and take their lands as rapidly as possible, then commerce with them ought to be abandoned to individual enterprise with no government regulation. This would bring continual warfare and the extermination or expulsion of the Indians to more distant and less hospitable regions.

> The correctness of this policy cannot, for a moment, be admitted. The utter extinction of the Indian race, must be abhorrent to the feelings of an enlightened and benevolent nation. The idea is directly opposed to every act of the government, from the declaration of independence to the present day. If the system already devised, has not produced all the effects which are expected from it, new experiments ought to be made. When every effort to introduce among them the ideas of separate property, as well in things real as personal, should fail, let intermarriages between them and the whites be encouraged by the government. This cannot fail to preserve the race, with the modification necessary to the enjoyment of civil liberty and social happiness. It is believed, that the principles of humanity in this instance, are in harmonious concert with the true interests of the nation. It will redound more to the national honor, to incorporate, by humane and benevolent policy, the natives of our forests in the great American family of freemen, than to receive, with open arms, the fugitives of the old world, whether this flight has been the effect of their crimes or their virtues.[24]

24 Ibid., 28. Lewis Cass seems to have drawn rather heavily on Crawford's report for his thirty-seven-page "Proposals of Organizing the Indian Department" [1816], Edward E. Ayer Collection (Newberry Library). See also Francis Paul Prucha and Donald F. Carmony, eds., "A Memorandum of Lewis Cass: Concerning a System for the Regulation of Indian Affairs," *Wisconsin Magazine of History* 52 (Autumn 1968):35-50. John C. Calhoun later paralleled many of Crawford's suggestions,

Three days after this report was sent to the Senate the Republican caucus met and nominated James Monroe for the presidency. Crawford received only eleven fewer votes than Monroe; the placing of his name before the caucus in opposition to Monroe's brought forth a torrent of ridicule and abuse centering on the intermarriage proposal and the last sentence of the above quotation, which, it was asserted, slandered and derogated a vast majority of the population of the country. The harsh criticism, sarcasm, and irony revived when Crawford was a candidate for the presidency eight years later, but before then he had explained that he was not the first to advance the idea of civilizing the Indians by intermarriage, that the idea had gained some acceptance among the Creek, Cherokee, and Chickasaw, and that he had no intention of casting an unjust reflection on foreigners. Perhaps the expressions used were not "best calculated" to convey his meaning, but he said he had just entered the department, was extremely pressed by business, and was severely afflicted with rheumatism. The idea he intended to convey was that "we had acquired reputation by the reception we gave to foreigners without enquiring into the cause of their emigration, & by facilitating their incorporation into the mass of our citizens, & that we would acquire still more reputation by civilizing the children of the forest & incorporating them into the great body of the nation."[25] Had he put it this way in 1816, he probably would have had only the intermarriage proposal to haunt him.

Criticism did not cause Crawford to slacken his efforts to improve the condition of the Indians and the management of the government operations among them. He took steps to gain as much reliable information on the tribes as possible; to ensure that reports were properly made in connection with the law of May 7, 1816, which embodied his recommendations on foreign participation in the trade and some other matters; to gather information on all sub-agents, interpreters, and other persons connected with Indian relations; to explore the matter of the use among Indians of persons skilled in the mechanical arts; to approve a "pilot" school among the Cherokee who would be fur-

including division of the land among individual families and the factor system, but on May 6, 1822, the licensed traders and managed trading houses were abolished. Report of the Secretary of War, Dec. 5, 1818, *ASPIA*, 2:181-85; 3 *Stat.* 679-80.

25 Crawford to Charles Jared Ingersoll, July 4, 1822, Ingersoll.

nished plows, hoes, and axes for the purpose of introducing the "art of cultivation" among the pupils (if there was a female teacher of sufficient skill to teach the women spinning and weaving, the necessary materials would be furnished); to grant permission for groups to move; and in general to handle the multifarious duties with understanding, efficiency, and some degree of imagination.[26]

In the spring of 1816 the announced intention of Alexander J. Dallas to quit as secretary of treasury in September—or sooner if his successor could be found—gave Madison the desired opportunity to try to make his cabinet more national in character by appointing a westerner to head one of the departments. He wanted Henry Clay to become secretary of war; this meant, then, that Crawford would have to assume another position. But Crawford was content with his position and gave Madison a decided negative when the President "pressed" him to succeed Dallas. There were "reasons" for not putting Clay in the treasury post, Crawford said, and for these he would yield to the President's wishes had he not expected to retire in March 1817. Later he said he also opposed transfer because he might be charged—by the papers which delighted in assailing him—with being influenced by the "foolish vanity of wishing to fill all the major departments."[27]

In early July, when Crawford left for Georgia, he called Madison's attention to the serious opposition being made to Clay's reelection to the House; a communication indicating Madison's intention to offer Clay a cabinet post might be helpful to Clay. From Wilkes County, Georgia, a month later, Crawford wrote that his views and wishes had not changed, but a desire to enable Madison to form a cabinet according to the President's views of general policy imposed on him the duty of complying

26 See, for example, Crawford to David Holmes, Sept. 2, 23, Oct. 4, 1816, Territorial Archives, Governors' Records, Series A, Vol. 16 (Mississippi Department of Archives and History); Crawford to Ninian Edwards, May 8, 1816, Ninian Edwards Papers (Chicago Historical Society); Crawford to Erastus Granger, Sept. 2, 1816, Erastus Granger Papers (Buffalo Historical Society); Crawford to Brothers of the Six Nations, Feb. 12, 1816; Crawford to David Holmes, May 10, 1816, Ayer Collection; Crawford to Rev. G. Kingsbury, May 14, 1816, MB 9; several letters to Crawford in 1815 and 1816, William Clark Papers (Missouri Historical Society). See also Prucha, *American Indian Policy*, 215-24.

27 Crawford to Gallatin, May 6, 1816; Crawford to G. W. Erving, May 14, 1816, Gallatin; Adams, *Gallatin Writings*, 1:699-700; Crawford to Thomas Worthington, Nov. 23, 1816, Thomas Worthington Papers (Ohio State Library).

with Madison's wishes. However, should Clay decline the appointment and the selection of another person not make the change necessary, Crawford preferred to remain in the War Department.[28] Apparently Crawford and Madison discussed the transfer when Crawford stopped at Montpelier on his return trip to Washington, and at the end of September Madison had communicated Clay's refusal of the secretaryship of war. Crawford felt he should not be pressed further on the subject—his conditional acceptance of transfer was limited to Clay's acceptance. But the President had written Crawford and Dallas that the post had been offered to William Lowndes of South Carolina; he told Dallas he had informed Crawford of this step "with an intimation of the expediency of his assuming the Treasury Department as soon as he can make it convenient to do so."[29] Extant materials do not tell the whole story; additional conversations must have occurred to remove Crawford's objections to transfer, stated as late as October 9. Lowndes also declined the appointment, but Crawford became secretary of treasury on October 22, 1816. He served the remainder of Madison's term, was reappointed by Monroe and served under him for eight years, and declined appointment by John Quincy Adams to the same post.[30]

In his administration of the War Department Crawford appears to have been governed by his belief in the tripartite division of powers, harmony between and among the branches of the government (with no increase of the executive power and influence vis-à-vis the legislative), rather wide legislative discretion, rather narrow jurisdiction—but absolute within its limits—for the judiciary, minimum government regulation of the relations between individuals, and gaining approval for one's position by

28 Crawford to Madison, July 9, Aug. 8, 1816, Madison, MDLC.
29 Madison to Crawford, Sept. 30, 1816, Gross: Madison to Alexander J. Dallas, Sept. [30?], 1816, George M. Dallas, *Life and Writings of Alexander J. Dallas* (Philadelphia, 1871), 477; Crawford to Gallatin, Oct. 9, 1816, Gallatin. Brant, *Madison*, 6:412, has no information to bridge the gap on Crawford's transfer. Raymond Walters, Jr., *Albert Gallatin: Jeffersonian Financier and Diplomat* (New York, 1957), 302, says that Crawford took the treasury as "consolation." Further, he states, "Hopeful that Gallatin might fit into his future plans, Crawford showered him with gossipy letters on political and economic subjects, local and national." This is an unrealistic estimate and unfair judgment; Crawford and Gallatin had been close friends since 1810 and often corresponded on matters of common interest.
30 George Graham, chief clerk under Crawford, served as acting secretary of war until the appointment of Calhoun. Crawford's commissions as secretary of the treasury, dated Oct. 22, 1816, and March 4, 1817, are in the Golding Collection.

appeal to reason and judgment only. He expected his subordinates to follow his example of devotion to duty; they should also function efficiently and economically. He expressed strong disapproval of dishonesty and any actions which might encourage that characteristic.[31] He displayed these same beliefs and ethics as secretary of treasury.

[31] See, for example, Crawford (from Woodlawn) to Gentlemen, Sept. 22, 1815, Crawford, Duke; Crawford to G. W. Erving, May 14, 1816, Gallatin.

6

The Treasury:
Organization and Administration

CRAWFORD had resisted transferring to the treasury, and he was not happy with the organization and distribution of functions in the largest of the departments in Washington. His duties as secretary of war had been numerous, but those of secretary of treasury were myriad. The department was a potpourri of agencies, commissions, organizations, services, and institutions over which the chief officer exercised direct, indirect, intermediate, joint, or only nominal supervision. Among these were the customs service (with its collectors, inspectors, weighers, gaugers, and other functionaries), the land offices (under the register and the receiver of the public monies, but with the General Land Office a Washington-based administrative and clerical agency), the internal revenue service, the post office, lighthouse service, coastal survey, Marine Hospital Service, the sinking fund, the mint, and the office of the commissioner of claims. The secretary had other responsibilities, especially in connection with audits of accounts, to say nothing of the important relations between the treasury and the newly established Second Bank of the United States and his advisory and consultative role as a cabinet member.[1]

The personnel of the department in Washington far exceeded that of any other, but the multiplicity of duties, cumbersome procedures, and division of responsibilities contributed to ineffective if not inefficient operation. Settlement of public accounts and making individuals accountable for the collection and expenditure of public money presented perhaps the greatest difficulty. The never-strong accounting system had broken down under the impact of claims during the War of 1812. Until 1817 the problem was accentuated by the army and navy accountants serving as auditors, and final settlements were often not made for years. Crawford had called attention to some of these problems in his report on Indian affairs in early 1816, and as secretary of treasury one of his first objectives seems to have been an increased effectiveness of the headquarters office.

Stimulated by Crawford's report, the Senate required—by a resolution of April 20, 1816—the four secretaries to report jointly a plan to ensure the annual settlement of accounts and a "more certain accountability" of public expenditures. Their report of December 1816, sometimes called the "first essay in administrative reorganization," was developed by Crawford and signed by him, Monroe (secretary of state), Benjamin Crowninshield (secretary of navy), and George Graham (acting secretary of war). It recommended the placing of a miscellany of functions—supervision of the territorial governments, construction and maintenance of national highways and canals, the post office, the patent office, and the Indian department—in a home department and some reorganization of other offices as well as an increase of personnel.[2]

Part of the delay in the settlement of accounts,[3] the secretaries said, was due to excessive loads imposed on the heads of the departments; part resulted from procedures. In keeping with the intention of the original organizers of the department, the primary and final settlement of accounts should rest with the treasury; the office of superintendent general of military supplies and army and navy accountants should be abolished; four additional auditors and another comptroller should be added, and a solicitor responsible for the prosecution of delinquent officials should be authorized. The secretaries recommended that the cumbersome, slow, and ineffective process of settling accounts be replaced by a summary process permitting seizure and sale of the real and personal properties of the delinquents and their sureties.

Congress did not act favorably upon the home department,[4]

---

[1] For a discussion of the accretion and shifting of duties and offices in the Treasury Department see Short, *National Administrative Organization*, 143, 150-58, 169, 201-2. See also J. H. Powell, *Richard Rush: Republican Diplomat, 1780-1859* (Philadelphia, 1942), 14-15, 20-21.

[2] *ASP: Miscellaneous*, 2:417-18. Crawford and Monroe had had experience in two departments; Graham, chief clerk when Crawford was secretary of war, was later to head the General Land Office.

[3] Arrearages in War Department accounts went back to 1798; no post office accounts after 1810 and no Treasury Department accounts after June 1815 had been settled at the end of 1816.

[4] A Senate bill to create a home department, proposed several times before 1816,

summary process, and solicitor proposals, but it approved the abolition of the office of the superintendent general of military supplies and the army and navy accountants and the appointment of another comptroller and four more auditors. It stipulated that the annual published list of individuals whose accounts had not been settled should be continued, but the comptroller was authorized to stop publication of three-year delinquents after three listings and was allowed to distinguish cases where arrearage was a matter of form.[5] All accounts were to be settled within a year; how the secretary was to accomplish this is not clear, for he was given no additional authority. In the actual reorganization the work among the auditors and the comptrollers was so divided as to separate completely military and civil accounts. With minor modifications, this system of accountability endured in principle until 1921.[6]

Extant materials do not reveal whether Crawford actively sought congressional approval of the recommendations concerning the treasury, but he definitely contributed to passage of the measure by refusing to remain as secretary unless changes were made in the department and Georgia was granted some compensation for the claims connected with cession of her western lands to the central government. On January 28 he met with Peter Hagner, who later became the third auditor, to discuss the bill before the Senate for a better organization of the departments.[7] Further, a copy of the bill to regulate the hire and compensation

was defeated on January 29, 1817. See Short, *National Administrative Organization*, 98, 205-8; Leonard D. White, *The Jeffersonians: A Study in Administrative History, 1801-1829* (New York, 1951), 171. The Department of the Interior was established in 1849.

[5] 3 *Stat.* 366-68 (March 3, 1817). The earlier lists, published and republished until the accounts were settled, had wrongfully placed many individuals in an unfavorable light: when accounts were not settled, names were published even though the claim might be against the government rather than the individual.

[6] White, *Jeffersonians*, 11. Crawford pointed out nearly four years later that the act of March 3, 1817, had added only one government employee, the fifth auditor; persons appointed to the other new positions held offices abolished by the act. Crawford to Samuel Dana, Jan. 9, 1821, Treasury Department, Series E, Vol. 6. This series, Letters and Reports to Congress, ends in February 1821, and there is a gap in these books from 1812 to Dec. 16, 1816, when Volume 6 was started. All Treasury Department records, unless otherwise indicated, are in the National Archives.

[7] Crawford to Gallatin, March 12, 1817, Adams, *Gallatin Writings*, 2:23-25; Monroe to James Barbour, March 3, 1817, Barbour; Monroe to Crawford, March 4, 1817, Golding; Invitation, Jan. 28, 1817, Peter Hagner Papers (University of North Carolina Library).

of clerks and messengers was sent to Crawford, and he was asked for suggestions of changes that might be necessary if the measure for the prompt settlement of accounts was passed. Crawford, in turn, asked the register and other officers of the treasury to make an estimate and specifically requested the comptroller to confer with the accountants of the War and Navy departments.[8]

Within the year after reorganization Crawford's chief subordinates reported to him, and he to the Senate, on the operation of the new set-up. First comptroller Joseph Anderson said that more clerks were needed to deal with such matters as the new tariff levies, the convention with Great Britain, recent acts relative to tonnage, and the extensive correspondence with the district attorneys and marshals. Others echoed this need, while a small minority were satisfied with the existing situation.[9] Crawford reported good progress in some offices and stressed the great amount of work still to be done in others. He called attention to the increase in amount and complexity of work caused by the internal and direct taxes, the greater number of government depositories after the failure to recharter the first Bank of the United States, and the subdivision of the revenue into cash, special deposits, small treasury notes, and treasury notes bearing interest. The greatest backlog of work was in the office of the third auditor, where a mass of the old accounts of the War Department remained unsettled. He said remedies of the "most energetic character" were required.

The lack of power to compel delinquent officers to render their accounts was seriously felt. Crawford detailed and criticized the existing methods; his views of December 1816 had been strengthened by his experience of the last twelve months. As long as a person held office, threat of removal might be sufficient to bring settlement of his account, but means of compelling settlement were "extremely defective" after he was out of office. The gov-

8 Samuel D. Ingham to Crawford, Feb. 11, 1817, Crawford, Duke. Newspapers paid little attention to the recommendations of the secretaries, but the *Georgetown Messenger*, Jan. 16, 18, 1817, regretted congressional indifference toward the proposals and opposed the adoption of a summary process. The actual procedures of reporting on collection, disbursement, and the auditing and settling of accounts prior to 1817 are in White, *Jeffersonians*, 163-64.

9 These letters are in *Senate Doc.*, No. 74 (serial 2), 15th Cong., 1st sess., 12-21. Richard Cutts, former superintendent general of military supplies, had been appointed second comptroller. The third auditor, Peter Hagner, said there were more than 5,000 accounts on the books of his office.

ernment could lose, by continued delay in making changes, the whole amount of the many still unsettled accounts from the War of 1812. He suggested the rejection of all vouchers not presented to the accounting officer of the treasury before commencement of an action for recovery and the appointment of an officer charged exclusively with instituting and superintending such suits brought by the United States. He was fully convinced that the duties now required of the first comptroller "cannot be performed by any officer whatever."

Crawford then expressed what might be considered the first principles of administrative supervision. It is not expected, he said, that the principal officers in the primary or secondary departments of government will be able minutely to examine every case they decide; but unless it is understood that a certain portion will be so examined, "a degree of negligence and laxity on the part of the subordinate officers in those departments, whether principal, or secondary, may be reasonably expected." Further, the "gradation from unintentional error, to willful negligence, and from the latter to deception, is gentle and almost imperceptible." The principal officer is responsible to the nation for the correct discharge of his official duties. If his duties are so great and multifarious as to prevent his adequate examination of the acts of his subordinates, "there is imposed upon him the highest responsibility without the adequate means of acting up to that responsibility." This he believed to be the situation with the first comptroller. The appointment of a solicitor was essential, whether or not Congress enacted the proposed changes concerning the collection of debts. Crawford's additional comments on the changes made the year before, the failure to provide some relief to the secretary of war, and the complications resulting from transferring the Indian accounts to the fifth auditor indicate that he was not entirely pleased with what Congress did do and was clearly displeased about the lack of action on other parts of the four secretaries' proposals.[10]

Congress, however, wanted a fuller accounting of the executive departments. Crawford transmitted the letter to his subordinates, but in addition he requested a detailing of the duties of each clerk, information on those who presided over independent

10 Ibid., 5-9. See also *ASPM,* 2:460-66.

branches of the service with those subordinate to them, and information on those who performed a service independent of any control other than that of the principal officer of the department, either directly or through the chief clerk. It was desirable, he said, that the statement should show the relative importance of the different branches and the degree of responsibility attached to the discharge of the duties respectively required in those branches. In effect, he called for full job descriptions for all positions.[11]

The collected information was submitted by the secretaries of state, war, treasury, and navy, but only the jobs of the clerks of the Treasury Department were described in detail.[12] Congress took no action on Crawford's recommendations, and during the next session Crawford returned to the expediency of appointing a solicitor and to the desirability of adopting a summary process for the recovery of public monies. He noted that such a process had been adopted in cases of less urgency, and all objections to it should be removed by making its operation "entirely prospective." Without the solicitor, aided by the summary process, it was "hardly practicable" to secure the prompt settlement of accounts and efficiently protect the public interest against those defaulting officers who embezzle the public money and "degrade the government by which they are employed."[13] More than a year later Congress finally authorized the President to appoint a treasury official as agent for recovery of sums due the United States and sanctioned a summary process to be used against all officers of collection. The transfer of the prosecuting power from the first comptroller to the agent and the pressure brought by Congress for more vigorous action produced favorable results.[14]

Whether requests from Congress for information were initiated by the departments in order to instigate or stimulate discussion of legislation they thought desirable is generally impossible to determine, but on several occasions such was doubtless the case.[15]

11 Crawford to Richard Cutts, Jan. 29, 1818, Letters Received, Second Comptroller's Office, Aug. 16, 1817 to Dec. 30, 1820. Letters to other subordinates may be found in the appropriate places in the National Archives.

12 *House Doc.*, No. 194 (serial 11), 15th Cong., 1st sess. The 152 Treasury Department clerks, including thirteen in the General Land Office, were paid an annual total of $134,046.58, with very few receiving more than $1,000.

13 Crawford to Samuel Smith, Jan. 14, 1819, Series E, Vol. 6.

14 3 *Stat.* 592-96 (May 15, 1820). Stephen Pleasonton, fifth auditor, was designated the agent.

Then, too, in this period Congress was reacting to the strong leadership in the departments and asserting its own control over certain government operations, especially expenditures. And having no aid or staff of their own, congressmen could best secure information by requiring reports from the executive branch. Whatever the case, the Treasury Department in the 1820s made as many reports to the House as the other three major departments combined. Annually the secretary was required to make seventeen, the first comptroller three, the treasurer one, and the secretary (as chairman of the sinking fund commission) one.[16]

The reports on the balances and settlement of accounts were among the more elaborate and important, and some of those showed that accounts remained unsettled twenty years after judgment had been rendered. Rarely, however, did the government lose large amounts of money. Peter Hagner, the third auditor, found the accounts transferred from the War Department the most troublesome. In almost all cases, additional vouchers were necessary before final settlement; some accounts had not even been entered on the books; it was necessary to have correspondence with every receiver of public money—which correspondence in three and a half years filled twenty-three letterbooks. But Hagner reported substantial progress. Although he would have nine fewer clerks (as required by law) after January 1, 1821, he thought he could continue to reduce the number of unsettled accounts.[17]

As the accounts were audited, reviewed, and "settled," those who were delinquent in their payments were soon dismissed from office, but no law would permit the comptroller to clear from his

15 Crawford was quite active in drafting bills for congressional consideration; discussions on this activity sometimes took place in cabinet meetings, references dot his letters and correspondence, and within ten days in January 1819 he sent four draft bills to congressional committees. Adams, *Memoirs*, passim; Series E, Vol. 6.

16 White, *Jeffersonians*, 94; *House Doc.*, No. 1 (serial 76), 17th Cong., 2d sess. The secretary of war made eight; the secretaries of state and navy, seven each; and the secretaries of navy, war, and treasury (as commissioners of the naval hospitals), one.

17 *Senate Doc.*, No. 101 (serial 15), 15th Cong., 2d sess.; *House Doc.*, No. 80 (serial 36), 16th Cong., 1st sess.; ibid., No. 10 (serial 50), 16th Cong., 2d sess. At the time the indefatigable Hagner began work on these accounts they amounted to more than $40 million, "distributed in the hands of several thousand persons." Hagner to Joseph Anderson, Nov. 20, 1820, ibid. On accounts and balances also see *House Doc.*, No. 68 (serial 67) 17th Cong., 1st sess.; ibid., Nos. 148, 149 (serial 102), 18th Cong., 1st sess.

files the accounts of persons deceased or insolvent. Such legislation was urged in February 1825.[18]

Crawford's strong recommendations for effecting amelioration,
the devoted efforts of his subordinates, and increased congressional
concern had brought remarkable improvement in the state of
the accounts by 1821. The failure to recharter the first Bank
of the United States, new duties resulting from postwar legislation
and international agreements, problems attending the first years
of the operation of the Second BUS, the enormity of land purchases, the Panic of 1819 and subsequent retrenchment, and the
slowness of congressional action could not be completely offset
by even the most vigilant supervision and indefatigable efforts.
Then, too, the prevailing concept that public officials were
gentlemen had its influence; one outstanding student of government administration has noted: "when one gentleman had to
deal with another in a business disagreeable to both there was
a wide margin of tolerance . . . some debts remained uncollected
pending improvement in the fortunes of the debtor—always to
be hoped for, if not always achieved."[19]

Crawford was careful that all operations of the department be
kept within established legal bounds, and efforts to catch up
and to improve the operation of the office never ceased. The
annual survey of the department in the fall of 1822 showed that
most employees had no remunerative activity other than their
clerical jobs, that personnel had increased about 10 percent in
five years, and that salaries totaled nearly $174,000, or about
$4,000 less than the appropriation for that year. The existing
organization of the offices was termed simple, and no change
was contemplated. Economy could be effected by reducing
salaries or the number of employees; the first, Crawford thought,
would be impolitic, but he believed that a reduction of personnel
would be found "practicable" in some of the offices. Indicating a
thorough understanding of the human being, Crawford said
such reduction "will depend more upon the character and conduct of the principal officers of the Department, than upon legis-

---

18 *House Doc.*, No. 149 (serial 102), 18th Cong., 1st sess.; ibid., No. 107 (serial
118), 18th Cong., 2d sess. The report to the second session of the Eighteenth
Congress showed the accounts of approximately five hundred individuals amounting
to several million dollars had remained on the books for more than three years
prior to 1824.
19 White, *Jeffersonians*, 182.

lative enactments."[20] The Washington office underwent no further significant changes before the end of Crawford's term.

Effective operation of the Washington office of the treasury depended to a considerable extent upon the timeliness, exactness, and comparability of reports from its field officials charged with collecting the money due the government. These were principally the collectors of the customs and receivers of the public monies at the land offices; their accounts were returnable directly to the treasury and were not the source of as many difficulties as were the accounts over which the treasury had no initial control. But with the customhouses spread from Maine to the Gulf of Mexico, the land offices deep in the interior, and the slowness of the communication system—or the absence of a system—it is little wonder that treasury officials spent much time informing and directing the collectors and receivers and not surprising that some should be far behind in reports and payments before negligence, laxness, or fraud became apparent to their superiors.

Contact between Washington and the field was maintained through regular reports on imported goods, collection of imposts and tonnage duties, registration of vessels, amounts of bonds posted and suits for collection of defaulted bonds, land sales, deposits of monies, and other activities; correspondence on particular problems as they developed; circulars of instructions interpreting revenue and trading laws, treaties, and general duties of officers; and particularized directions dealing with specified problems. Regular or routine reports and much of the correspondence went to or from the commissioner of the revenue or the first comptroller. The latter official also issued over his signature many of the circulars to the collectors, naval officers, and surveyors of the customs. Some of these directions were very lengthy and on occasion contained court opinions and were accompanied by the tariff and other pertinent laws. Though

20 Adams, *Memoirs,* 6:143-44 (June 11, 1823); *House Doc.,* No. 4 (serial 76), 17th Cong., 2d sess. In a similar vein is Crawford's one-sentence reply to a query on safety regulations for steamboats: "I am of opinion, that legislative enactments are calculated to do mischief, rather than prevent it, except such as subject the owners and managers of those boats to suitable penalties in case of disasters, which cannot fail to render the masters and engineers more attentive, and the owners more particular in the selection of those officers." *House Doc.,* No. 69 (serial 116), 18th Cong., 2d sess. The increase from thirteen to twenty-nine clerks in the General Land Office accounted for the total increase in the Treasury Department. The ninety-seven clerks in the State, War, Navy, and Post Office departments were paid approximately $100,000. *Niles' Weekly Register* 22 (March 30, 1822):70-71.

authorization for action was delegated, the secretary bore the responsibility, and his name is to be found on practically every known type of communication and directive.[21]

Required reports might be weekly, monthly, or at longer intervals, but Crawford seems to have maintained a continuing review of their periodicity and form in order to make them more reasonable and informative and at the same time more helpful in protecting the interest of the government by ensuring a stricter accountability of the reporting officials.[22]

Almost immediately upon taking office he told the collector at Philadelphia to take the necessary measures to deposit in the BUS, for collection purposes, all the customhouse bonds outstanding on January 1, 1817, and the following spring he informed all collectors of new procedures resulting from the agreement between the treasury and the BUS by which the latter assumed responsibility for collection of the bonds for import duties. The weekly returns of money deposited in the several offices of the BUS and in state banks to the credit of the treasurer of the United States were thereafter to be made to the cashier of the BUS rather than to the Treasury Department.[23] Crawford thought it advisable to recapitulate the regulations which were not altered by the agreement and to add such as "are thereby indispensable." Every receipt for public money must show whether the money came from customs, internal revenue, direct taxes, postage, or other sources, and weekly statements made to the BUS must "strictly correspond" with those receipts. All deposits must be entered to the credit of the BUS for use of the treasury, and all treasury drafts would be drawn upon the cashier of the BUS and would designate the office of discount and deposit —or state bank employed as such—at which it was to be paid. These drafts would be returned to the treasury by the BUS. In addition, monthly returns to the treasury on the state of the

21 These materials, vast in quantity but with some serious gaps, are in the Treasury Department Records, National Archives. And, of course, those dealing with the collectors and receivers—even when one includes Hagner's twenty-three letterbooks of special correspondence with the receivers—constitute only a small portion of the total. An account of the normal operations of the treasury at any given time would be a monograph in itself; here only a smattering of activity concerning customs, lands, and personnel will be given to indicate method of operation and some special problems.

22 See, for example, Treasury Circulars, Feb. 3, April 29, 1817: June 3, 1819.

23 Crawford to John Steele, Oct. 30, 1816, uncat. letter, HSP; Treasury Circular, April 29, 1817. The BUS, in turn, reported to the treasury.

receiving offices and the state banks in which public money had been deposited must be made on the previously prescribed forms.[24]

But the treasury was left without a clear picture of its available resources because the collectors made deposits on whatever day of the week suited their whims. To bring uniformity and regularity the BUS was requested to issue on each Monday a certificate of deposit (bearing the date of the last day of the preceding week) for sums received during the preceding week and to forward to the treasury each Monday returns showing the amount of these receipts. The collectors were told to apply on Mondays for the certificates and to forward them with their returns to the department.[25] Thus the treasury would have a double check on the collectors and on the places of deposit.

The monthly schedule of bonds liquidated for duties was designed to give the treasury the earliest information on the amount of duties accrued monthly on imports and tonnage. But seemingly some reports were rendered long after the end of the month, while others detailed information on bonds accrued months before—thus defeating the purpose of the reports. The treasury requested that the schedule for each month be forwarded as early as practicable—at the latest within thirty days—and as far as practicable that it be concerned only with the bonds for duties accrued within the month reported on.[26]

When examination of monthly returns revealed that a receiver of public monies had retained a considerable quantity, the treasury asked to be "informed why the same has not been deposited . . . in conformity with the instructions heretofore given by this department." Or, when the treasury was hard pressed for money (as during the period after 1819), the collectors were asked to deposit all except the amount absolutely necessary to defray the current expenses of the office.[27]

24 Treasury Circular, April 29, 1817.
25 Ibid., June 3, 1819.
26 Ibid., June 22, 1822. To ensure uniformity of weekly reporting on bonds put in suit for collection, a new form was prescribed by the treasury circular of July 3, 1819. In 1823 every accountable officer was required to make quarterly returns within three months after the end of each quarter (six months if the officer were out of the country). Any failure was to be reported to the President, and the offender was to be dismissed, unless he could make his peace with the chief executive. 3 Stat. 723-24 (Jan. 31, 1823).
27 See, for example, Crawford to Samuel Quinby, Aug. 21, 1819, Series N, Vol. "O"; William Jones to James Mauney, Oct. 4, 1820, Treasury Circulars.

From time to time special reports were required of the collectors, receivers, and others connected with the revenue. By these the department officials sought information for a report to one of the houses of Congress, secured data on the functioning of a particular law or regulation, or gained evidence that would enable the President to decide whether to modify the bonds of certain officials. Regular and special reports were means to an administrative end and Crawford—as the agent of the chief executive—sought as many and as efficient checks as were reasonable under the circumstances.[28]

But no matter what continuing supervisory efforts were made, losses to the government did occur. Duties were not paid when articles were imported; bonds, payable from six to twelve months from their dates, were posted. In effect, this meant that slightly less than one fourth of the revenue was collected the first year, nearly three fourths the second year, and the remainder the year following.[29] When payment was not made at the designated time, bonds were placed in suit by the district attorney—acting after he had been notified by the collector. Delay by that official, deceitful practices, insolvency, flight, death, and other factors resulted in a loss of about 5 percent of the import duties. The summary process, sanctioned in 1820, seems to have helped in reducing government losses.[30]

There were, of course, other ways by which the government might be deprived of its legitimate income. In the spring of 1817 Crawford wrote to James H. McCulloch of Baltimore of the general impression that frauds upon the revenue were being committed by invoicing merchandise (subject to ad valorem duty) which cost less than twenty-five cents per yard with that which cost more in order to produce an average above twenty-five cents and thereby introducing coarse and cheap fabrics without paying the duty contemplated by the tariff.[31] Also, articles not described in the invoice had been imported. A more rigid in-

28 See Treasury Circulars, Nov. 11, 1817; May 25, 29, June 22, Sept. 1, 1818; Crawford to Monroe, July 14, 1820, Gratz.

29 Revenue from import duties by no means reflected the existing state of trade, and this method of securing government revenue was sharply criticized because of the uncertainty and fluctuation of the source.

30 For an especially full report on this matter see Crawford to president pro tem of the Senate, Feb. 25, 1822, *Senate Doc.*, No. 83 (serial 60), 17th Cong., 1st sess. The task of the district attorney was not made easier by the uncertainty and the division of supervisory authority among the attorney general and the secretaries of state and treasury. See *House Doc.*, No. 123 (serial 387), 26th Cong., 2d sess., 195-96.

spection system was ordered, but five months later Crawford concluded, from communications from the collectors, that continuance of the new inspection practices would produce more inconvenience to the fair and honorable importer than advantage to the treasury. Therefore, they no longer formed a general rule for the collector, but they could be enforced when that official thought circumstances warranted—especially in cases of importation upon consignment.[32]

The Baltimore situation, in customs and in banking matters, was especially troublesome. The district attorney had told Crawford that the inspectors there were in the habit of receiving bribes from the importing merchants, but the "informers" were unwilling to testify publicly. Indignant letters from Crawford to McCulloch were answered with the retort that all the inspectors were honest men. On numerous occasions the cabinet discussed conditions in Baltimore, including action that should be taken against "privateers" and "pirates" in the area.[33] But the climate produced by the illegal activities during the War of 1812 persisted and only gradually yielded to improvement and correction.

Smuggling was also carried on without the connivance of officials. At times duties were thought to be a contributing factor, and on other occasions a modification of rules governing certain trade might have increased the illicit introduction of goods.[34] But no matter what the cause, the treasury was to be informed of every violation of the revenue laws resulting in the illegal introduction of foreign merchandise. Weekly reports were to be made whenever violations occurred, and in all cases of smuggling the species and value of merchandise were to be described and the names of the parties concerned or interested in the transaction were to be given.[35]

The enforcement of the laws against illegal importation and smuggling depended to a considerable degree upon the efficiency of the revenue cutters. In the summer of 1819 the secretary told

31 Under the minimums system cotton goods valued at less than twenty-five cents per yard were dutiable at twenty-five cents a yard.

32 Treasury Circulars, May 7, Oct. 8, 1817.

33 See Adams, *Memoirs*, 4:318-19, 401, 415, 445 (March 29, July 16, Aug. 21, Nov. 22, 1819); 5:64-66, 146-47, 154-55 (April 11, 12, June 9, 19, 1820). Crawford thought McCulloch should have been removed "long ago." Ibid., 5:154.

34 See Treasury Circulars, Jan. 18, 1819, and Sept. 7, 1821, allowing certain discretionary action in reference to the law of April 20, 1818, and seeking information concerning the effects of the law of March 2, 1819.

35 Ibid., June 22, 1822.

the captains of the cutters that the effectiveness of their vessels would be greatly diminished if they remained relatively stationary. If the captains were uncertain of their authority as officers of the customs, they should consult the collectors under whom they were placed—though they could determine most of their duties from copies of the acts of 1793, 1799, 1818, and two of 1819 which he enclosed. He cautioned them about the nature of the illicit trade and recommended that they keep logs, a copy of which should be forwarded to the treasury each month.

The conduct of the officers was the subject of a long paragraph:

> While I recommend, in the strongest terms, to the respective officers, activity, vigilance, and firmness, I feel no less solicitude that their deportment may be marked with prudence, moderation, and good temper. Upon these last qualities, not less than the former, must depend the success, usefulness, and, consequently, the *continuance* of the establishment, in which they are included. They will always remember to keep in mind, that their countrymen are freemen, and, as such, are impatient of every thing that bears the mark of the domineering spirit. They will, therefore, refrain, with the most guarded circumspection, from whatever has the semblance of haughtiness, rudeness, or insult. . . . They will endeavor to overcome difficulties, if any are experienced, by a cool and temperate perseverance in their duty—by address and moderation rather than by vehemence or violence.

The remainder of the communication underlined the idea that even the capture of a smuggler must be done in a gentlemanly manner![36]

Inadequacy of the cutter force and other difficulties bedeviled the customs service, but the problems of Addin Lewis, collector at Mobile, were probably as numerous as those of any other. In early 1817 his funds had been so depleted by drafts and the receipts were so small he could not meet the expenses of the office. One of his inspectors was about to leave with $600 due him, so Lewis asked the New Orleans collector to meet the

[36] Ibid., July 13, 1819. The personnel complement of cutters had not been changed with the return of peace, but the distressed state of the revenue brought action in the spring of 1821. Thereafter, the maximum complement was a captain, first and second mates, four seamen, and two boys, with only the officers receiving wages higher than those of an able-bodied seaman. Collectors were cautioned to exercise the greatest economy and to allow the captains no expenditure of any description without previous permission and the presentation of satisfactory vouchers. Ibid., March 19, 1821.

obligation if he could. The revenue boat, in use for several years, was too small and defective to be used beyond the waters of the bay. He needed a strong boat to deal with the smugglers of slaves and goods who operated under the Mexican or any other flag that best suited them, plundering the slaves and goods from Spanish ships or receiving them from privateers at sea. But he had only the *Alabama,* a four-ton sailboat with four oarsmen and an inspector, to "oppose the whole confederacy of smugglers and pirates." In September 1817 he first asked for a better cutter. Six years later some repair work had been done, but Lewis got no new or more effective vessel. Meanwhile, he had discussed his boat problems while in Washington, and against his wishes, Captain F. J. Costigan had become the new commander. He spent three pages telling how useless the cutter had been under Costigan and how inefficient and incompetent an officer Costigan had been. Lewis concluded this commentary with, "I should mention that he has a wife & children at the extreme part of Bon Succours Bay, which may account for his beating about that bay so often with the cutter, a place where she is not at all wanted."[37]

Lewis also had his problems with the certificates on wine, tea, and distilled spirits, for he said that the certificates—which were to be delivered by the seller to the purchaser—were not examined and compared with the marks on the casks, boxes, and chests when shipped coastwise. He noted that some customhouses permitted masters of vessels to use figures to indicate the number of boxes of goods in their manifests rather than "expressing the same in words at length." This, he said, struck at the "root of the whole system" for "1 may be made 10, & 10-100" with the same pen and ink five minutes after clearance. In addition, some slaves seized on board the schooner *Constitution* "were stolen away from the neighborhood of this town" and would probably be conveyed to New Orleans. These were not the first slaves to be introduced illegally; perhaps more than a hundred had been smuggled in during the six months prior to March 1818.[38] Lewis'

37 Lewis to Beverly Chew, April 17, 1817; Lewis to Crawford, Sept. 23, 1817; Feb. 23, June 2, Nov. 15, 1818; Feb. 27, Aug. 1, 1819; Nov. 6, 1820; Oct. 22, 1822; Lewis to Joseph Anderson, Oct. 3, 1821; April 17, 1823, Crawford, Yale.

38 Lewis to Anderson, Nov. 13, Dec. 9, 1817; Lewis to Chew, Aug. 10, 1818; Lewis to Anderson, Feb. 23, 1818; Lewis to Joseph Nourse, Oct. 16, 1821, ibid. Lewis thought the act of March 2, 1819, had unquestionably contributed to smuggling in the area, and he felt the entire measure should be repealed.

difficulties were accentuated by the nature of the coast and the piracy, privateering, and other activities accompanying the revolt of the South American colonies, but they were by no means peculiar to him.

Abuses in the importation of tea took a different turn with importer Edward Thomson, who surreptitiously moved large quantities from the customhouse at Philadelphia before duties had been paid or secured. Several inspectors either would lend their keys to the storer or would take the key from the surveyor's office, attend to a delivery, lock up, and then return the key. About 15,000 chests of tea were involved and the malpractices extended from 1822 to 1825. Because Thomson had become insolvent, the government would probably sustain a heavy loss.[39]

There were other defaulters or defrauders: the collector at Wilmington, North Carolina, absconded with some loss to the government; there were troubles with the accounts of the collector at St. Mary's, Georgia; the collector at Savannah apparently "shorted" the government of more than $100,000; and there were reports that owners of vessels occasionally employed in mackerel fishing sought to obtain the legal allowances for vessels engaged in the Banks and cod fishing.[40]

In sharp contrast to Philadelphia and some of the other larger ports were such customs districts as Champlain and Vermont where the incomes of the collectors were meager. If smuggled goods were seized the officers of the customs might be "rewarded" by having their compensation further reduced—they were asked to pay the difference between the costs and what the smuggled goods were sold for. In addition they were "out of pocket" the amount paid to informers.[41]

Crawford was from the beginning of his treasury position aware of the vast differences in compensation of the collectors and of the pressures that might be exerted to create new collection districts or to designate additional places as ports of entry. There was also the possibility of decreasing the ports of entry, but most

[39] *House Doc.*, No. 137 (serial 138), 19th Cong., 1st sess.

[40] Crawford to Joseph Anderson, May 4, 1821, Letters Received from the Secretary of Treasury—First Comptroller; Anderson to Crawford, May 5, 1821, Revenue Letters, No. 33; Anderson to Crawford, July 26, 28, 1823, ibid., No. 36; Anderson to Crawford, Feb. 16, 1824, ibid., No. 37; Crawford to Samuel A. Morse (collector at Machias, Me.), Dec. 8, 1820, Treasury Circulars.

[41] Crawford to Thomas Newton, Feb. 24, 1817, Crawford, NYH; *Senate Doc.*, No. 22 (serial 109), 18th Cong., 2d sess.

of Crawford's recommendations to this end seem to have failed to convince Congress. His answer to the first query from the House on the expediency of increasing or diminishing the ports of entry said that his predecessors had not made a practice of collecting information necessary to such a decision.[42] That fall Crawford recommended some changes in the salaries and emoluments of customs officers, but he had no suggestions on the number of districts and ports of entry. He admitted all his information was not yet exact, but he had determined that the emoluments of the naval officers and surveyors of the customs should be increased by 25 percent. He proposed that the fees received by the collectors be divided equally with the naval officers and surveyors, who in turn should pay a portion of the expenses of office rent, fuel, and stationery. In the larger ports— where there was no salary—the collector sometimes received as much as $30,000 net from the commission fees; in the small interior ports Crawford proposed raising some of the salaries from $250 to $500, whereas in others they should be allowed to remain at the $150-$250 level. He recommended an increase in the commission rate for several places.[43] Congress did not respond favorably, and soon the Panic of 1819 resulted in action decreasing considerably the fees of the collectors, naval officers, and surveyors. Crawford again recommended a 25 percent increase in the fees for the naval officers and surveyors. He pointed out that the "disposition which is inherent in human nature to acts of benevolence, and to the exercise of patronage, requires that the commissions and emoluments assigned to the collectors of the principal ports should be regulated so as to render the practice of economy necessary to secure to the officer the maximum to which he is limited." He used the expenses and the balances of the ports of New York and Boston to illustrate his point.[44]

In December 1818 Crawford submitted to the Senate a list, compiled from letters from the various collectors, of eighteen collectors and twenty-six surveyors who might be discharged from the public service at a saving of almost $10,000. Some of the districts were recommended for elimination—they were unpro-

42 Crawford to Newton, Feb. 17, 1817, Series E, Vol. 6.
43 *House Doc.*, No. 131 (serial 10), 15th Cong., 1st sess. Crawford stressed the "strong temptation" to smuggling along the "whole extent of the inland frontier."
44 Crawford to Speaker of the House, Dec. 8, 1820, *House Doc.*, No. 26 (serial 48), 16th Cong., 2d sess.

ductive—and many of the surveyors would have no duties because of the recommendation for the abolition of that office in several ports.[45] Two years later he sent the same list to the House, noting that the saving to the government would now amount to only $8,000 per year. Crawford said that another saving—of at least $100,000 per year—could be effected by repealing that part of the law of March 2, 1799, which provided fees for weighers, measurers, gaugers, and markers. He considered the inspectors competent to perform those duties.[46] Apparently Crawford's interest in economy and retrenchment was greater than that of Congress and extended to places other than the military.

Earlier in 1820 he had indicated that the refusal of credit at the customhouse to any one whose revenue bond was due would ensure payment of the debt, but Congress took no action and allowed the old procedure of placing the bonds in suit to continue. It was not until 1822 that a rider to the appropriations bill forbade any payment as compensation for services to a person in arrears in his payments to the United States, and the comptroller was instructed to disallow all disbursements when pay had been advanced to such persons and to forward to disbursing officers the list of those indebted to the United States. And three weeks later Crawford took steps to fix compensation and limit the number of clerks in those collection districts where emoluments exceeded the sums to which the officers were limited. He noted that the "public interest requires that the concerns of the nation, and especially the collection of the revenue, should be managed with the same view to economy as the affairs of an individual."[47]

Monroe's cabinet was one of first-rate executive ability. Under the direction of his department heads and "largely at their initiative the administrative machine, now over a quarter century in motion, had its first overhauling."[48] Crawford was among the

45 Proposed abolition of the office of surveyor in some Massachusetts ports involved eleven of the surveyors. *Senate Doc.*, No. 27 (serial 14), 15th Cong., 2d sess.

46 *House Doc.*, No. 25 (serial 48), 16th Cong., 2d sess. For additional information on consolidation of functions and economies in the customs service see *Senate Doc.*, No. 82 (serial 60), 17th Cong., 1st sess.; *House Doc.*, No. 112 (serial 56), 16th Cong., 1st sess.; Revenue Letters on Accounts, passim, begun in 1821.

47 Crawford to Speaker of the House, Feb. 11, 1820, *House Doc.*, No. 73 (serial 35), 16th Cong., 1st sess.; Crawford to Anderson, May 4, 1822, Letters Received from the Secretary of Treasury—First Comptroller; Treasury Circular, May 24, 1822; 3 *Stat.* 668. It should be recalled that congressional approval in 1820 of a summary process for settling accounts did help.

most active of those overhaulers and doubtless could have achieved more had Congress been more interested in the process. But political consideration, patronage, and almost unbelievably long tenure in many offices—notably collectors of the larger ports—prevented further improvement. Crawford could report just before leaving office that the accounts of all active officers of the customs were current, and not a single one was indebted to the government. Actually, all had balances in their favor.[49] But the accounts did not tell the whole story. The wonder is that there was so little loss to the government, for there was no inspection of the customs service until the Jackson administration. There were precedents for the use of this administrative device in the War Department and in the land offices, and it was in connection with the latter that Crawford introduced most of the elements of modern inspection.

Public lands were second only to the customs as a producer of revenue for the central government. In 1812 duties connected with the public lands, formerly performed by the secretary and the register of the treasury and the secretaries of state and war, were consolidated in the General Land Office, whose commissioner was in charge of all land matters but operated under the general direction of the secretary of treasury. The General Land Office, primarily a clerical office, held a unique position in financial matters, since it settled the accounts of the land offices on its own responsibility and reported directly to the comptroller without the preliminary inspection of an auditor. In 1824 there were thirty-nine land offices in the country, each in charge of a register who was the "public broker for the sale of lands" and each having a fiscal agent, or receiver of public monies.[50] Exactly what constituted general supervision by the secretary of treasury

---

48 White, *Jeffersonians*, 12.

49 Crawford to Speaker of the House, March 1, 1825, *House Doc.*, No. 106 (serial 118), 18th Cong., 2d sess.

50 White, *Jeffersonians*, 519-22. Josiah Meigs was commissioner from 1814 until his death in 1822; John McLean held the office until his appointment as postmaster general in 1823; George Graham succeeded McLean and held the position until his death in 1830. The land offices were always subordinate to Washington, but the relation of the surveyor general to the General Land Office was obscure and sometimes inharmonious. It was not until 1836 that he definitely was subordinated to the land commissioner. Ibid., 523. See also Malcolm J. Rohrbough, *The Land Office Business: The Settlement and Administration of American Public Lands, 1789-1837* (New York, 1968). It should be noted that in two years of Crawford's tenure other sources brought more to the treasury than did land sales: internal duties in 1816 and 1817 and direct taxes in 1816.

varied greatly: it could take the form of consultation with the commissioner; it could be direct instructions to the receivers and registers; it could be the appointment of special representatives to try to secure to the government the deposits in certain banks; or it could be a suggestion that the commissioner exercise the "most vigilant superintendence" over and confide as little in the judgment of one of his clerks as the situation would permit.

The treasury's major concern, however, was with proper reporting, handling of monies, and the strict accountability of the receivers. Crawford did not always see the instructions given the receivers by the commissioner, but he presumed they were directed to make monthly returns to the treasury as well as to the federal land office of the amount and price of lands sold. The receiver should enclose receipts and vouchers showing the amount carried to the credit of the United States.[51] But the registers had not been in the habit of balancing their books, though legally required to do so annually. The monthly reports of lands sold and monies entered showed no balances, and it was not until October 1818 that the commissioner realized the nonfeasance of the registers. Monthly returns enabled the General Land Office to catch any errors in the accounts of the receivers, but Crawford was asked to decide whether the labor of balancing the books of the registers for the last eighteen years should be undertaken. The commissioner had notified the receivers that the balances must be regularly transferred from quarter to quarter and their books posted so that an examiner might see the balances of the quarter preceding his investigation.[52]

Crawford apparently thought Josiah Meigs' action adequate for the time being, but soon he decided that the monthly reports of the receivers were not sufficiently revealing. In September 1819 he notified the receivers of a change in the reporting forms so that the sum received for lands entered or intended to be entered during the month could be distinguished from those sums received for earlier entries. Also all accounts were henceforth to be countersigned by the registers. The secretary believed that the intimation that money received had in some cases been exchanged for less valuable money, which was subsequently deposited, was

[51] Crawford to John Taylor and Alex Pope, Oct. 10, 1817, Series N, Vol. "O".

[52] General Land Office to Crawford, Oct. 10, 1818, GLO, Miscellaneous Letters, Vol. 8. The land office accounts were then in much the same condition as those of other government agencies.

"generally unfounded," but means of repelling these intimations should at all times exist. On the back of the receipts the kind of money received should be described, and only during the public sale of land—when this practice might be found impracticable—could this procedure be temporarily delayed. Further, the receivers were told that it would be necessary for them to indicate upon all receipts for money paid by them—excluding their deposits but including their own commissions and salaries—the kinds of money paid out and to furnish a statement containing this information to the register of the land office.[53]

The lot of the land office officials was not an easy one. The multiplication of paper money during and after the War of 1812 made it virtually impossible for the receiver to know what to accept, and the credit system contributed to enormous sales in the postwar period. Had payments been made—as legally required—at the end of the second, third, and fourth years after purchase, the receivers might have found it easier to keep their books posted and the treasury could have more accurately estimated receipts. But there was an interest penalty only before the fifth year, and numerous relief acts had been passed since 1809. There was no strong inducement to punctuality since failure to pay did not deprive the buyers of credit, and Crawford thought the "abolition of the credits now allowed to purchasers, or the refusal of credit, in all cases where an installment is not paid when it becomes due, will be necessary to secure the collection of that portion of the revenue which is derived from the national domain."[54]

Crawford played a large role in devising the act of April 24, 1820, which abandoned the credit system of land purchase, and in framing the relief act of March 2, 1821. Several provisions of the latter, as well as earlier relief laws, required administrative

[53] Crawford to Receivers of Public Monies, Treasury Circulars.
[54] Crawford to Speaker of the House, Feb. 11, 1820, *House Doc.*, No. 73 (serial 35), 16th Cong., 1st sess. Crawford noted that sections 8 and 9 of the act of April 20, 1818, were intended to provide a remedy against banks that failed to discharge their notes on demand, but in some states a corporation could not be brought into court. He suggested that the cashiers and presidents of the banks be made responsible and that a service consist merely of leaving a notice at the banking house. The indebtedness of public land purchasers at that time was approximately $20 million. In 1818 Crawford had favored an extension of two years for the redemption of lands sold for direct taxes and bought in by the United States, but interest of 10 percent should be charged from June 1, 1818. Crawford to William Lowndes, Feb. 2, 1818, *House Doc.*, No. 137 (serial 10), 15th Cong., 1st sess.

interpretation before they could be carried out. This often took the form of questions by the commissioner of the General Land Office to Crawford, who then made the decisions on the meaning of the law, sometimes after discussion with other members of the cabinet and of Congress.[55]

The reentry of the BUS into the picture, the resumption of specie payment, the mismanagement of the BUS, the wild speculation, the Panic of 1819, and the new land law of 1820 meant, of course, rapidly changing circumstances for the receivers. At times they were permitted to take only specie and bills of the BUS and its branches, but in August 1820 Crawford—to equalize and to increase the facilities for making payments for the public lands—authorized them to accept the notes of the incorporated banks of Boston, New York, Philadelphia, Baltimore (except the city bank), Richmond, South Carolina, and Georgia, and those specie-paying banks in the state in which the land office was situated. Previous instructions were superseded, except the one which prohibited the receipt of paper money of any bank which did not discharge its notes on demand in specie; "that prohibition must, in every case, be rigidly adhered to."[56]

Herein, of course, lay much of the problem. Banks might for a short time meet the demands for specie, and then through overissue, speculation, peculation, or other causes cease to function. The government could then be—and sometimes was—the loser. The secretary spelled out the procedure for the receivers: they were to give notice to the various banks of the amounts of their notes contained in each deposit; if informed by the cashier of the bank of deposit that any bank in the state had failed to redeem its deposited notes in specie, no more notes of that bank were to be received. "It may be proper," he said, "for you to take the first occasion to intimate, in respectful terms, to each of those banks, the consequence that will result from a want of punctuality in paying its notes on presentation." The procedure did not differ materially from that in practice before the economic collapse.

[55] Thomas Hart Benton, *Thirty Years View* . . ., 2 vols. (New York, 1856), 1:12; Secretary of Treasury to Speaker of the House, *House Doc.*, No. 73 (serial 35), 16th Cong., 1st sess.; *Niles' Weekly Register* 17 (Feb. 12, 1820):419-20; GLO to Secretary of Treasury, May 20, July 11, 17, 1820, GLO, Miscellaneous Letters, Vol. 10; Crawford to Meigs, July 11, 1820, May 17, 1822, Series N, Vol. "O".

[56] Crawford to Receivers of Public Monies, Aug. 1, 1820, Treasury Circulars.

Problems had long before appeared in several places, and some were quite persistent. On March 1, 1817, Crawford informed Meigs that the information in the enclosed letters indicated it was necessary to institute an examination of the books and the accounts of the receiver at Vincennes. Two days later the commissioner said he had requested Benjamin Parke to make the examination, and the receiver had been directed to afford Parke every facility to carry out his task. Several banks, as well as receivers, were to be involved in the next few years, but every effort was made to take full cognizance of, and give consideration to, the economic conditions in which the westerners were caught and, at the same time, keep the government losses to a minimum.[57]

Some of the cases of dishonesty which even the "most vigilant superintendence" could not prevent were resolved with dispatch, but others lingered for years. Early in 1817 Monroe removed the receiver of lands east of the Pearl River for "incontestable evidence of mal-feasance";[58] the dismissal of John Brahan, receiver at the Huntsville, Alabama, office, occurred only after seventeen months of correspondence—and two years later it was determined the government had lost rather heavily. Crawford's communications to Brahan are not subject to misinterpretation, and in his letter of March 1819 the secretary stated what might be termed his code of ethics for the public servant:

It is extremely desirable that the conduct of the officers of the government, especially those who have charge of the public money, should not only be correct, but there should be no possible cause of suspecting them to be incorrect. If there should exist any peculiarity in the situation of an officer which is calculated to excite suspicion, it is more imperiously to his interest and duty to exert more than ordinary diligence in the discharge of his official duties.[59]

To secure direct and accurate information for the use of the government, special inspectors or representatives were employed in the Vincennes, Brahan, and other cases, but general inspectors

[57] Crawford to Meigs, March 1, 1817, Series N, Vol. "O"; GLO to Secretary of Treasury, March 3, 1817, GLO, Miscellaneous Letters, Vol. 7.

[58] Crawford to Meigs, April 14, 1817, Series N, Vol. "O". William Crawford, no relation to the secretary, was the new appointee.

[59] All materials dealing with the Brahan default are in *House Doc.*, No. 130 (serial 69), 17th Cong., 1st sess. and ibid., No. 149 (serial 102), 18th Cong., 1st sess.

or examiners had been used since 1804 when Congress mandated the secretary of treasury to cause the books of the land offices to be examined and their balances ascertained once a year. For several years inspections were made by persons, selected by the treasury, who resided in the vicinity of the land offices, but—as Crawford later reported—the annual inspections were made in compliance with the injunctions of the law rather than from a "conviction that the information obtained was of any intrinsic value to the public service." In 1816 Secretary Alexander J. Dallas changed the procedure by directing that Nicholas B. Van Zandt, a clerk in the General Land Office, examine the offices in Ohio and farther to the west. His period of inspection was short, the report went to the secretary of treasury, and the commissioner of the General Land Office sent out the letters of instruction and correction.[60]

Regular annual inspections by individuals from headquarters became standard procedure, but Crawford's concept of the purposes of inspection differed from that of his predecessors. In instructing Meigs to direct a thorough examination of the books and accounts of the receivers and registers in Ohio, Indiana, and the Illinois Territory—with Van Zandt as the inspector—he indicated his desire that Van Zandt be told to obtain all the information he could on the general character and standing of the officers, "with due regard to propriety and a proper respect for their feelings." The officers, especially the receivers, should sign the statement the examiner drew at the end of his scrutiny. The commentary upon the facts which the examiner might feel it his duty to make would be distinct from the statement and should not, of course, be submitted to the officers. It was expected that the banks in which the deposits had been made would give the inspector "every facility necessary to enable him to discharge the trust beneficially to the government."[61]

This procedure seemed to bring no controversy or political repercussions during the inspection of Van Zandt, those of John Dickins in 1818 and 1819, and of Dickins and Richard B. Lee in 1820. In 1821 two westerners were sent on a general commission: Alexander Anderson of Tennessee to the offices in Mississippi and

60 White, *Jeffersonians*, 523-24. A number of special examinations of particular offices followed the first headquarters inspection. See GLO, Miscellaneous Letters, Vols. 6, 7, passim.
61 Crawford to Meigs, May 27, 1817, Series N, Vol. "O".

Alabama, and Jesse B. Thomas, senator from Illinois and member of the Committee on Public Lands, to Ohio, Indiana, Illinois, Missouri, and Detroit. In addition to the usual examination of the offices, Thomas was authorized to enter into any agreement with the Bank of Vincennes that would secure the debt owed to the United States—any agreement that he might consider to be in the interest of the nation provided it did not stipulate payment of a sum less than the amount actually due.[62]

Thomas was highly successful in his negotiations at Vincennes, and he inspected all the offices except Detroit. But his and Crawford's political opponents sought to make political capital of the appointment. Late in December 1821 Daniel P. Cook (member of the House from Illinois and son-in-law of Ninian Edwards, the other senator) hoped the editor of the Detroit paper could say something derogatory about Thomas' failure to visit that place and accused Crawford of promoting intrigue and buying support through patronage in a manner that subverted the party and violated the Constitution. Early in January 1822 Cook introduced a resolution concerning Thomas' employment, and the next month Crawford submitted the requested information to the House. The report of a select committee under the chairmanship of Louis McLane of Delaware gave a brief history of the inspection process, pointing out that increased receipts of the land offices had added to the importance of inspection at the time Dallas changed the procedure in 1816. It emphasized that Thomas secured to the United States a large amount of public money in the Vincennes bank and for that service he neither received nor asked any compensation. The committee did not think the appointment (it was not an office) a violation of the Constitution; senators and representatives had been given various appointments since 1800. Nor did it see anything in the case indicating that Crawford or Thomas had any intention of violating the law or abusing or disregarding the "spirit and policy of our institutions." The employment of Thomas originated in the desire

62 Crawford to Thomas, April 6, 1821, Jesse B. Thomas Papers (Illinois State Historical Library). In 1821 there were thirty-nine banks holding paper—to the government credit—which was irredeemable or only partially redeemable. For a concise statement on this matter see Crawford to Speaker of the House, Feb. 12, 1821, *Niles' Weekly Register* 20 (March 17, 1821):36-37. See also Crawford to Speaker of the House, April 27, 1822, *House Doc.*, No. 119 (serial 69), 17th Cong., 1st sess.; *American State Papers: Finance*, 3:718-82; *American State Papers: Public Lands*, vols. 3, 4.

honestly to discharge an important public duty; the peculiar importance of the trust and the character and status of the person employed "calculated rather to invite than forbid his selection"; and there was no reason to believe that the duty was not faithfully performed in a manner conducive to the public good.[63]

Of more basic significance than the brief political furor was Crawford's defense of the post-1815 method of examination as decidedly preferable to that used before:

> When a different person is employed to examine each office, the judgment which is formed of the manner and style in which the books are kept will depend upon the intelligence, the prejudices, or partialities, of the different examiners: but, when the same person examines a number of offices, the same intelligence is exercised in each case, exempt, too, from partiality or prejudice, when the examiner is not a neighbor or connexion of the officer. . . . An examination now is not a matter of form. The time the examiner is to arrive is unknown. When he does arrive, the examination commences, and is continued without relaxation until it is completed. . . . It is also an object of some importance that the examiner should communicate, confidentially, many things that he would not be willing to incorporate in his report, and which it would be improper to incorporate. The value of such communications will depend entirely upon the knowledge which the head of the Department has of the character of the person who makes them.[64]

Here is perhaps the first statement by a high-ranking government official that includes most of the essentials of a sound inspection system.

There were many other duties connected with the sale and management of the public lands, some even touched with a bit of humor. In sending Monroe a proclamation announcing the public sale of land in Alabama—and each time there was a sale

[63] Cook to William Woodbridge, Dec. 28, 1821, William Woodbridge Papers (Burton Historical Collection, Detroit Public Library); Crawford to Speaker of the House, Feb. 18, 1822, *House Doc.*, No. 71 (serial 67), 17th Cong., 1st sess.; *Niles' Weekly Register* 22 (April 13, 1822):102-5. In his letter to Woodbridge Cook said that "all fair means" must be adopted or "that Rascal" will be the next President. A Crawford partisan thought the committee report "completely *cooks* Mr. Cook—the little serpent wreathed & twisted in its perusal—it is a statement of facts & reasoning highly satisfactory to the friends of Mr. Crawford." R. M. Saunders to Bartlett Yancey, April 3, 1822, Walter Clark Papers (NCDAH).
[64] *ASPPL*, 3:512 (Jan. 28, 1822); White, *Jeffersonians*, 525-26.

such a proclamation had to be issued—Crawford sent along a letter from General Abner Lacock relative to compensation for assistants in the surveying process. Crawford commented to the effect that he thought a cook and baggage handler were necessary, but he did not think that horses would in "any stretch" fall under the term assistant. But the compensation was low and everything ought to be allowed that could be.[65]

The vast majority of the officials connected with the land offices were scrupulously honest and by 1824 grossly underpaid. Shortly before leaving office Crawford noted that not only had the compensation of the registers and receivers fallen below the allowable maximum of $2,000 per annum but that it averaged only about $850. This he considered inadequate and recommended that the commission of those officers be increased by one half percent of the public money received, thus restoring the rate to the pre-1818 level. The receiver should also be allowed something for transporting the public money to distant places of deposit. Such an allowance might be regulated by the secretary of treasury, but it should in no case exceed one half percent of the amount deposited. The pay of the receivers and registers was the same; all thirty-nine offices had reported. At only nine places did they receive more than $1,000; the one at St. Stephens received $2,131, while at Lexington, Missouri, the pay was only $278.80. All others were paid between $500 and $955.42.[66]

No matter what the organization, the procedures, and inspection method, or the degree of supervision, efficient and effective performance depended in the final analysis upon personnel. Crawford, who had said in late 1822 that reduction of personnel in an office would "depend more upon the character and conduct of the principal officers . . . than upon legislative enactments," indicated by his actions in connection with strict accountability and organizational reform, as well as by his remarks of earlier

[65] Crawford to Monroe, June 13, 1820, Monroe, NYP. There seem to have been inequities in the salaries and allowances of the surveyors and their help. For especially pertinent information on some of the problems of administering and leasing the lead mines and the salines, as well as on an interesting experiment in the "encouragement of the vine and olive," see GLO to Secretary of Treasury, Dec. 19, 1816, Jan. 2, 1817, GLO, Miscellaneous Letters, Vol. 7; *Senate Doc.*, Nos. 143, 144 (serial 3), 15th Cong., 1st sess.; ibid., No. 70 (serial 60), 17th Cong., 1st sess.

[66] *House Doc.*, No. 92 (serial 118) 18th Cong., 2d sess. In early 1818 the maximum salary for receivers and registers was $3,000.

years, that competence, honesty, and performance of duty were prerequisites to appointment and continuance in office. This is not to say that he did not appoint to, or recommend keeping in, office some individuals whose records would not bear close scrutiny in all three categories; "blemishes" may be found on the record of every person in an important administrative role for any substantial period of time. That Crawford sought to appoint friends to vacancies resulting from deaths, resignations, removals, or new positions seems only natural, but to charge that he used the patronage to build an electioneering engine does injustice to his professed and practiced concepts of the public service and ignores the realities of the existing situation.

The personnel of the Treasury Department in Washington and in the field was far greater than that of any other department, and appointments were primarily political. But until 1820 almost every employee had unspecified tenure; only the marshals had been placed on a four-year term by the Federalists. Many of the public employees had grown old in the service; several had already served large segments of forty-year careers, and removals were few.[67]

There were additional appointments during Monroe's administration, and the multifarious activities of the Treasury Department meant that Crawford might be consulted on a number of appointments—or he might not be. Monroe sometimes acted entirely on his own, sometimes he consulted others, but never did he have any intention of relinquishing his presidential prerogative in this area. After the summer of 1822 Crawford and Adams both confessed to having little or no favorable influence on appointments, and Monroe, keenly aware of the scramble for favor, said he pursued his own course by appointing those he knew and confided in. Had he distributed the "offices among the friends of the candidates, to guard myself against the imputation of favoritism . . . the office in my hands, for two or three years of the latter term, would have sunk to nothing."[68]

[67] Madison and Monroe removed a total of only fifty-four civil officers in sixteen years. More than thirty of these were collectors. Adams, who thought Monroe too lenient about removals, rarely admitted any kind of inferiority, but he did note that "At this game [appointments] I have a perfect demonstration that Crawford is an overmatch for me." *Memoirs*, 5:158 (June 23, 1820), 89 (May 2, 1820). Monroe was the only public figure of prominence who did not suffer from Adams' pen.

Monroe's determination to control appointments, even prior to 1822, is well revealed in choosing four officials for the land offices in Illinois in 1820-1821. The roles of the President, the cabinet officer under whose supervision the individuals would work, and of the senators of the state were all involved. Monroe was embarrassed by disagreement and conflicts between Senators Edwards and Thomas, thought the appointments should be made in such a way as to "put it out of the power of either to say that we are in any degree partial to the other," and indicated a division of the offices might be proper. Edwards complained of not getting proper consideration of his recommendations, apparently suggested that he and Thomas each choose two persons, and denied that he was trying to transfer the appointive power from the President to the senators. A troubled Monroe twice had Attorney General William Wirt write his friend Edwards. Wirt emphasized that if the President were bound by the nominations of the senators, the appointment would not be that of the chief executive, who still must bear the responsibility. The President asked no sacrifice of the rights of the senators in opposing or rejecting nominations; why should they seek to narrow his freedom in making such? Further, Wirt thought Edwards took an improper view of the nominations and would impair his dignity and place Monroe in a "degraded light" by bringing the President into party conflicts within a state. Even the most successful politician could "buy his triumphs too dear." In this, as in most other decisions, Monroe had his way.[69]

The public service was still small, and transactions and appointments were widely known and talked about. There were few defaulters and little peculation. Monroe, Crawford, and other members of the administration generally held high standards, and when deceived about the qualities of a person whom

[68] Crawford to Van Buren, May 9, 1823, Martin Van Buren Papers (MDLC); Crawford to Thomas Worthington, June 10, 1823, Worthington; Adams, *Memoirs,* vols. 7, 8, passim; Monroe to Jefferson, March 22, 1824, Stanislaus Murray Hamilton, ed., *The Writings of James Monroe,* 7 vols. (New York, 1898-1903), 7:11-12. Hereafter cited as Hamilton, *Monroe Writings.*

[69] The most pertinent materials on this episode are: Monroe to Crawford, July 24, 1820, Golding: Edwards to Monroe, Dec. 22, 1820; Wirt to Edwards, Jan. 11, 15, 1821, E. B. Washburne, ed., *The Edwards Papers . . .* (Chicago, Ill., 1884), 166-67, 167-68n, 186-89 (hereafter cited as Washburne, *Edwards*): Edwards to Crawford, Jan. 1, 11, 1821; Crawford "note verbale," Jan. 2, 1821; Crawford to Edwards, Jan. 10, 1821, Edwards. As a young man Wirt had lived for some time in the Edwards home; he and Ninian were "almost" brothers.

they had been persuaded to recommend they showed considerable vexation. Crawford maintained that he was influenced by two considerations only: the qualifications of the individuals and the desire to give strength and popularity to Monroe's administration. If he had failed in any case, in either of these respects, he said it had been because he himself had been deceived.[70]

It seems that Crawford really did not like to choose individuals for office and said he found this selection "always disagreeable." It was, however, a "highly important duty which must be performed"; his duty was to aid the President in the solution of the affairs of the Treasury Department as far as he was able—and that duty he would discharge with "rectitude, if not with wisdom."[71] Under pressure from individuals and his own ambition, Crawford must have found this a difficult rule to follow, but he seems to have done as well as any of the other members of the administration. Extant materials indicate that he would not recommend some of his long-standing friends because of some of their actions, that others were not happy with their appointments (feeling they deserved better), that he was well aware of the resentment that might be engendered by a Georgian interfering in the appointments in another state, that he was successful in some of his recommendations and not in others, that he did not differentiate sharply between Federalists and Republicans, that he was on occasion mortified by the loss of a letter of recommendation, and that very few of his appointees were guilty of violating the code of ethics to which Crawford subscribed.[72]

The greatest criticism and condemnation of Crawford's role in appointments has come in connection with the Tenure Act of

[70] Monroe to Crawford, Oct. 17, 1817, Crawford, MDLC; Crawford to Monroe, Aug. 17, 1821, Gratz. If anyone was ever conscientious about appointments or recommendations for appointment, that person was John Quincy Adams. But even Adams was "deceived" by his intimate friend, Dr. Tobias Watkins. White, *Jeffersonians*, 420-21; Adams, *Memoirs*, 8:141 (April 21, 1829).

[71] Crawford to Worthington, May 18, 1819, Worthington.

[72] See, for example, Crawford to Charles Tait, Nov. 7, 29, 1819; J. W. Walker to Tait, Dec. 20, 1819, Tait; Tait to Thomas W. Cobb, Feb. 29, 1820, J. W. Walker Papers (ADAH); Monroe to Crawford, June 30, July 7, 1820; Crawford to T. U. P. Charlton, March 13, 1819, Crawford, MDLC; Crawford to John M. O'Connor, April 27, May 16, 1818, Crawford Papers (Rice University Library); Crawford to Jacob Brown, Jan. 26, Aug. 4, 1819; Brown to Crawford, Nov. 28, 1819; Brown to John Armstrong, March 2, 1820; Ambrose Spencer to Brown, Nov. 15, 1819, Brown, MHS; Crawford to John E. Howard and others, Aug. 25, 1819, James Bayard Papers (MdHS); Crawford to Monroe, Aug. 25, 26, 1823, Monroe, MDLC; Monroe to Crawford, Aug. 15, 1821, Golding.

May 15, 1820, which provided that the principal officers concerned with the collection and disbursement of money should
thereafter be appointed for fixed terms of four years (though
removal could take place at the pleasure of the appointive power)
and that the terms of the incumbents should expire at stated
intervals, but not earlier than four years from time of appointment. This applied to the district attorneys, collectors of the
customs, naval officers and surveyors of the customs, navy agents,
receivers and registers of the land offices, paymasters in the
army, the apothecary general and his assistants, and the commis-
sary general of purchases. It did not apply to clerical help of
those officers nor did it affect the pursers, Indian agents, post-
masters, or any accounting or clerical officers and employees
in Washington.[73]

Crawford and Congress had for at least four years been deeply
concerned about a stricter accountability of those persons handling the public monies, and this seems nothing more than
another step in that direction. There is evidence, in Adams'
diary and in other materials contemporary with the actions, that
Crawford was the author and drafter of bills for consideration
by Congress, but none supports the charge that he was father
of this one—and only an occasional partisan asserted that he
intended to use it to advance his political ambitions.[74] There is
some important evidence that Crawford was not the author
of the measure. On June 12, 1820, Crawford wrote Monroe
that Vice President Daniel D. Tompkins had been with him
that day and wanted to know if any decision had been made
concerning David Gelston, collector at New York. Crawford
told him that nothing had been said on the subject. Tompkins,
indicating public opinion called for a new incumbent and that

73 3 Stat. 582.
74 Carl Russell Fish, "The Crime of W. H. Crawford," American Historical Review
21 (April 1916):545-46, finds no proof that the act was the origin of the spoils
system or that Crawford was its conscious author. He believes Crawford had no
intention of using the law to secure his election and that the act had some justification as an administrative measure. Edward Channing, A History of the United
States, 6 vols. (New York, 1912-1925), 5:353-54, rather timidly follows Fish. Theodore
Roosevelt, Life of Thomas Hart Benton (New York, 1887), 79-80, makes several
incorrect statements and insupportable judgments about the act. John Quincy
Adams' charge concerning authorship and Crawford's use—or intended use, for
Adams says Crawford's illness prevented such use—was not made until 1828. The
remark about Crawford's illness in relation to use of the act is patently absurd:
the measure had been in effect for well over three years before Crawford was
stricken in late 1823.

much dissatisfaction would develop if a change were not made, said Gelston was eighty years of age, rich, crabbed and peevish with persons with whom he had to deal, and that it was time for him to be withdrawn from the laborious duties of collector. The Vice President insisted that Gelston's case was the one which gave rise to the law and that Senators Mahlon Dickerson (New Jersey) and Nathan Sanford (New York)—the principal supporters of the law—had his case particularly in view. Crawford further detailed Tompkins' comments on possible successors to Gelston; he thought he should communicate this information to Monroe since it was "highly probable" the subject would be presented to him by others.[75]

In another communication to Monroe on the same day Crawford expressed his feelings about the new act. He said:

The law changing the tenure of office of certain officers, certainly was not intended to disqualify the present, or future incumbents. I presume that reappointment will not take place, where there are any reasonable grounds of dissatisfaction. To remove an officer is supposed to fix some stain upon his character. To omit to re-appoint, is nothing more, than an implied declaration that the person selected, has higher qualification, or stronger claims upon the justice and liberality of the nation, than the former incumbent. If an officer has discharged his duty with such intelligence & integrity that the public interest cannot be promoted by substituting another in his place, it is presumed he will be continued; unless some person having stronger claims upon the justice of the nation cannot be otherwise provided for. These views I have communicated to Col° McLane, as those which would probably regulate your conduct under the act. I am happy to find that they are in accord with those expressed.[76]

[75] Crawford to Monroe, June 12, 1820 (fragment), Gratz. Gelston was farther behind in balancing his accounts than any other collector of the public monies. *House Doc.*, No. 148 (serial 102), 18th Cong., 1st sess. Sanford had been active in bringing about passage of the "reorganization" law of March 3, 1817. Crawford's detractors point to Dickerson's introduction of the bill in the Senate as another indication of the secretary's connection with the measure. Dickerson was a Crawford supporter in 1824, but extant materials do not indicate a close relationship between the two until considerably later than 1820.
[76] Crawford to Monroe, June 12, 1820, Monroe, MDLC. Monroe, in a letter from Oak Hill, presumed the law was not intended to preclude renomination if the officer should be thought to merit it. He felt the enclosures relative to Col. McLane (probably Allen McLane of Wilmington, Del.) might furnish a "suitable occasion for giving a practical construction" to the law. Monroe to Crawford, June 8, 1812, Crawford, MDLC.

The only papers that have been discovered which deal with large numbers of appointments do not indicate that the act of 1820 was being used to create a political machine for anyone. On December 14, 1820, Crawford sent to Dickerson, of the Senate Committee on Commerce and Manufactures, a list of twenty-four individuals who were collectors of customs, surveyors and inspectors, and naval officers—spread geographically from Maine to Mississippi. All were renominations. The collectors of Vienna and St. Mary's in Maryland had scarcely any duties to perform, and there was no known opposition to their appointment. Their names were not on the list, for in consonance with the resolution of the Senate it was being recommended that the offices be abolished.[77] The following month the two individuals were renominated. In February 1821 Crawford wrote that the accounts of those persons specified in the enclosed resolution of the Senate had been regularly rendered and settled and the money received promptly paid over. All were renominations. The following year a list of nominations sent by Dickerson was returned with a statement of their accounts; nine of these were new appointments, but Crawford requested that two of these be held up because the persons had not yet gone to their posts. The conduct of two of the renominees was not approved. Charges had been brought against them, an investigation was underway, and delay in the decision of the Senate was requested until the result of the examination had been received. In April 1822 Crawford noted that some misunderstanding had occurred relative to the accounts of one person and he would request the President to withdraw the nomination the following day.[78] Crawford's massive electioneering engine seems to have been under the close scrutiny of the Senate and the President!

The report of a Senate committee, chaired by Thomas Hart Benton, in May 1826 was sharply critical of the great amount of patronage in the hands of the executive branch—specifically the President. But the remedy was not sought in reduction or in a merit system but by a recommendation for repeal of the

[77] It should be noted that the Senate *Executive Journals* do not differentiate between reappointments and new appointments. By checking through them one could determine such in many instances, but without other materials the information gained would not be especially meaningful.

[78] Crawford to Dickerson, Dec. 14, 1820; Jan. 5, Feb. 7, 1821; Jan. 15, April 4, 1822, Mahlon Dickerson Papers (New Jersey Historical Society).

May 1820 act and transfer of the power of appointment to the legislative branch.[79] There seems little doubt that this report was a part of the anti-Adams campaign of the Jackson supporters.

However the act of 1820 may be interpreted—as a means of enforcing stricter accountability by providing a periodic review of all handlers of public money, as a way of replacing super-annuated individuals without fixing stains upon their characters, or as a device to create a political machine—there is inconclusive evidence connecting Crawford with its authorship, and available materials do not even insinuate his use of the act to promote his political fortunes. Had the secretary of treasury—or any other department head—been inclined to use the measure for that purpose, Monroe would effectively have prevented such. Perhaps no President has had a more able cabinet, and perhaps none has more efficiently utilized his advisers. But the decisions and the responsibility were Monroe's.

Contemporary estimates of Crawford's administration of the Treasury Department varied according to political inclinations and partisanship, but it can safely be said that he was a leader in overhauling and reorganizing the government machine, he was an able and intensely honest administrator who expected his subordinates to adhere to a high code of ethical behavior, he introduced modern inspectional methods into government operations and persistently sought strict accountability of those who received and disbursed the public money, he was interested in honorably advancing his own and Monroe's reputation, and by continuing and improving the Republican policy of vigilance he left the treasury with fewer employees (who were doing far more work) and a smaller payroll than it had in 1801.[80]

[79] Senate Doc., No. 88 (serial 128), 19th Cong., 1st sess. See also White, Jeffersonians, 390-93.

[80] ASPM, 1:260-319; Senate Doc., No. 88, 19th Cong., 1st sess. Headquarters and customs service personnel had increased by 103 and 187, respectively, to a total of 1,075, but the internal revenue service had been liquidated. Crawford exercised the same careful supervision over the seamen's or marine hospitals, the lighthouses, and the purchase and erection of government warehouses as he did over other operations of the department. See, for example, Treasury Circulars, Sept. 28, 1818, April 16, 1821; Crawford to Joseph Wingate, Nov. 5, 1821, Autograph File (Houghton Library); Crawford to John Gaillard, Dec. 9, 1818, Senate Doc., No. 52 (serial 14), 15th Cong., 1st sess.; Richard Rush to Speaker of the House, Feb. 13, 1826, House Doc., No. 93 (serial 135), 19th Cong., 1st sess. Practically all the government warehouses had been purchased or built during Crawford's tenure as secretary.

7

The Second Bank
and the Currency

SOME OF THE problems with which Crawford had to deal would never have been present—or certainly would have been less severe—had his efforts for rechartering the first Bank of the United States been successful in 1811. War heightened the financial chaos resulting from the removal of the restraining influence of the national bank: wildcat banks and worthless paper money increased with amazing rapidity and specie payment was suspended in most parts of the country by late summer of 1814. A first recharter attempt failed in 1815, but under John C. Calhoun's guidance the Second Bank of the United States was chartered on April 10, 1816. Passage of Daniel Webster's resolution twenty days later required that all payments to the United States after February 20, 1817, be in gold or silver, treasury notes, notes of the BUS, or notes of banks payable and paid on demand in specie. Secretary Alexander J. Dallas had made several attempts to work out an agreement among the banks for resumption of specie payment but had not been successful at the time he relinquished the office to Crawford.[1] The task was not an easy one, for there were legitimate interests of the government, the BUS, the state banks, and the individual that needed to be protected and served. Improperly done, resumption might contribute to, rather than ameliorate, the existing financial disorder.

The relationships of the secretary of the treasury and the president of the BUS and their respective roles in currency matters were not explicitly defined; the influence of the secretary seemed to vary with economic conditions and with the faith the treasury head and the president of the BUS had in one another. The operations of the BUS have been well depicted in other places,[2] but the relations between Crawford and the bank presidents have not been detailed sufficiently to show the secretary's concept of the function of the bank, his willingness to "bend"—if government interests were not injured—his inflexibility if government interests were threatened, and his ideas on money and currency.

Crawford, one month after taking office in October 1816, wrote to William Jones, president of the new BUS, on the resumption question. He felt the principal state banks, by saying they would not resume until July 1, 1817, had in effect declared they would not bear any part of the sacrifice required to restore order to the currency nor forgo any of the advantages of a return to financial stability. But should the government refuse to accept the bills of those banks, the great mass of unoffending citizens would be the sufferers—unless the government was prepared to furnish sufficient legal currency to meet indispensable demands. He wished to know the bank's potential for supplying a national currency without the aid of the state banks. Treasury notes, he thought, should be withdrawn from circulation, for the government (with a large surplus) would be pursuing an unjust and unsound policy by permitting paper, which might be funded at 6 percent, to remain a part of the currency. If the government were to assume the principal burden for resumption, part of the profit should go to the national treasury. Noninterest-bearing government paper, receivable for all payments to the United States and not fundable at more than 5 percent, might be put into circulation through the agency of the BUS; the BUS could reissue and pay a stipulated interest to the government. Other possible methods were mentioned. Whatever plan was followed, the issue and reissue of government bills would cease when a sufficient amount of currency had been put into circulation. If issued, the amount of government paper would be limited to the estimated surplus revenue during 1817, but the secretary "ardently desired" that this type of currency would not have to be used. Crawford emphasized he was taking "soundings" and not discussing any decisions which had been reached.[3]

[1] Ralph C. H. Catterall, *The Second Bank of the United States* (Chicago, 1903), 4, 23.

[2] See Catterall, *Second Bank;* Bray Hammond, *Banks and Banking in America from the Revolution to the Civil War* (Princeton, N.J., 1957).

The next month Crawford tried to convince the state banks that it would be to their advantage to resume on February 20, 1817. If they did so, government money in their vaults (more than $11 million) would not be transferred to the BUS, and the treasury would draw from them only the minimum required in its transactions. Since receipts would probably exceed current demands, a pay-as-you-go policy would be followed. After July 1 the government would draw as needed, but money would be transferred from the state banks to the BUS only to "sustain it against any pressures" which might be made upon it or its branches. However, if the banks persevered in their decision not to resume until July 1, the transfer of funds from the state banks would be ordered with as "little delay as the interest of the community will admit." Crawford pointed out that the interests of the banks and the community were not in opposition and said that any sacrifice the banks might incur by resuming on February 20 "will be compensated by the advantages and facilities which it is in the power of the treasury to afford them."[4]

The state banks still refused to change their date for resumption, and Crawford turned the matter over to Jones. Jones met on February 1 with representatives of the larger eastern banks; the resulting agreement to resume on February 20, highly favorable to the state banks and to the treasury, set the BUS on the road to near disaster. The BUS became responsible to the government for public deposits held by the state banks but agreed not to use or transfer those funds before July 1. At the same time it pledged itself to meet government demands on those deposits. The article guaranteeing mutual protection meant that the BUS had for all practical purposes assumed a unilateral obligation.[5]

---

3 Crawford to Jones, Nov. 29, 1816, *Niles' Weekly Register* 15 (Feb. 6, 1819): 437-38.

4 Treasury Circular, Dec. 20, 1817, *ASPF*, 4:283. The demand for money had been heavy in the postwar period and the calling in of debts (so that specie payment might be resumed) by even the soundest of state banks might contribute to serious economic disorder. See, for example, William Ward (State Bank of Boston) to Crawford, Jan. 1, 1817, Frank M. Etting Papers (HSP).

5 *ASPF*, 4:496, 974-80; Catterall, *Second Bank*, 24-26. See also *ASPF*, 3:231-32. The agreement also provided that the BUS was not to call for other balances against the state banks until it had discounted for individuals (exclusive of those with duties to pay) $6 million and that it sustain "with its unbroken credit and whole capital" every bank that subscribed to the arrangement. Thus the BUS extended its credit while the state banks contracted theirs before the reckoning day of specie resumption.

Crawford approved the agreement, but he thought it important for a larger proportion of the state banks to be a party to resumption. He suggested more might be persuaded to this policy if the BUS allowed the state banks to retain existing deposits interest free until April 1. If this would result in harmonious action, the beneficial consequences would be cheaply obtained.[6] No general policy was adopted in this regard, and the inexactness of the arrangement between the BUS and several of the state banks troubled Crawford. However, the action of the BUS and the eastern banks was generally "forcing" on the other state banks, and specie payment was resumed with "no inconvenience in any part of the country."[7]

But the western banks held rather large sums of notes as special deposits to the credit of the government. The convertibility of many of these notes was a matter of great uncertainty, and Crawford was anxious that new depositories for the public funds be designated as quickly as possible. The charter of the BUS required that public money be deposited in the bank or its branches (except where there were urgent reasons for not doing so) in places where those offices existed. In states where no branches existed, the treasury would determine the number of depositories and leave to the BUS the right of selection and arrangements for the transfer of funds. There was no obligation to transfer public funds from an area with no branch bank to a branch in another area, but the government desired that the BUS "should be immediately or mediately the sole depository of the public money in every part of the Union." As soon as the branches of the BUS were established, the treasury would transmit drafts in favor of the BUS on all banks in the western country which distinguished between special deposits and cash.[8]

These banks of the interior, Crawford thought, might be entitled to some special consideration. Pursuant to the agreement

---

[6] Crawford to Jones, Feb. 7, 1817, AC5303, U.S. Finance (MDLC). Crawford emphasized that relieving the banks of interest for the six weeks after February 20 would more than compensate them for any premium they might have paid for specie beyond what they would have paid independent of engagements with the treasury.

[7] Crawford to Gallatin, April 23, 1817, Adams, *Gallatin Writings*, 2:37. See also Hammond, *Banks and Banking*, 246-50.

[8] Crawford to Jones, Feb. 28, 1817, Etting; Crawford to Jones, March 17, 1817, Gratz. For relationships of the treasury, the BUS, and the state banks concerning special deposits see Catterall, *Second Bank*, 453-74, esp. 453-64.

of early February with the eastern state banks, the issue of bills
and discounts made by the BUS had enabled those powerful banks
to curtail their discounts without producing a pressure upon the
community. In the interior this curtailment had not been so
easily effected. While Crawford was an "enemy to the principle of
scattering banks profusely over the whole surface of the interior,"
the treasury had "too deep an interest in their credit at this
moment to be willing to see them sunk." Once again he suggested
that the "country banks," especially with respect to special
deposits, not be required to pay interest before April 1; in Kentucky and Ohio interest should not be insisted upon until the
branch banks began operation in those states. Arrangements
between the BUS and the state banks should be more specific
than earlier ones; the places of intermediate deposit must continue to make weekly returns to the treasury, and money deposited
in them would be drawn out by treasury drafts in conformity
with the terms agreed upon by those banks and the BUS. This
was the procedure during the existence of the first BUS; if Jones
thought some other mode preferable, his ideas would receive
the "most respectful consideration."[9]

Without question Crawford wished the BUS to be the dominant force in banking and currency circles. He viewed the
multiplication of state banks as a "great evil" and believed it
to be in the interest of the BUS and the country to prevent
the creation of more of those banks—and perhaps to put down
many of those already existing. If the BUS would complete its
arrangements with the banks of the interior of Pennsylvania and
the western country, measures would be taken immediately to
exclude the receipt of bills the BUS would not consider as cash.
Crawford had not wished the BUS to assume responsibility for
the mass of paper that had been collected in the interior; he
had always calculated upon some loss when the final adjustments
of those accounts were made and thought it unreasonable to
throw any part of this loss on the BUS. However, he was
anxious to be rid of the special deposits arising from the current
receipts and wished to avoid employing more banks as places
of intermediate deposit.[10]

9 Crawford to Jones, March 17, 1817, Gratz; Crawford to Jones, March 23, 1817,
Library Company of Philadelphia.
10 Crawford to Jones, July 19, Aug. 1, 1817, William Jones Papers (HSP). For
extensive materials relative to public deposits, see *ASPF*, 4:495-1077.

The BUS was soon in trouble; it expanded its business too rapidly and brought ruin to many state banks through demand payment of their notes; loans increased incredibly fast; fraud and speculation in bank stock were quite widespread; declining trade hurt; and neither Jones nor the board of directors seemed to understand the business and the function of the bank. Government pressure to set the house in order contributed to the injury inflicted on the state banks, and the treasury's redemption in July 1817 of more than $13 million of the public stock in possession of the bank led to further extension of the discounts.[11]

Within a little more than a year after beginning operations the BUS was on the verge of bankruptcy. Crawford did not wish to place additional burdens on the bank, but he did not want that institution to shirk any of its legal responsibilities. In reply to Jones' letter of May 29, 1818, presenting difficulties and embarrassments of the bank, Crawford admitted the BUS could not legally be required to become responsible for public money when deposited in banks over which it had no control or to use state banks as places of deposit merely for the purpose of creating depositories of public money. But in states where there was no branch bank, it was required that a state bank be employed for "transacting the duty of commissioners of loans and of agent for the payment of pensions." For monies deposited in those banks the BUS was responsible "without any special assumption of that responsibility." And the BUS, on its own proposal, "incurred a complete responsibility for the money heretofore deposited in the state banks selected by it for that purpose." At the same time, money in those banks was subject to any disposition the bank thought proper.

The BUS, Crawford said, could terminate its liability for deposits in those banks by relinquishing control over the money. This the bank had suggested, but the proposal that money deposited in the state banks, as places of intermediate deposit, be transferred to the BUS or its nearest office was "liable to objection." In such a transfer the state bank would be paying

11 For problems and difficulties of the BUS during Jones' presidency, see Catterall, *Second Bank*, 26-50. Crawford rejected the idea that the power of the BUS to sell the stock subscribed to it (section 5 of the charter) was intended to or could operate as a qualification or limitation of the right of the government to redeem that stock at its pleasure. Crawford to Jones, June 18, 1817, Etting. On other occasions Crawford thought Jones' interpretations of some of the articles of charter were "novel" and not "contemplated" by the people who helped to reestablish the bank.

THE SECOND BANK 133

over public money—a duty which in the first instance might have been exacted from the collector. Further, such a transfer would abridge the right of the government to tender to any of the bank offices the bills of the BUS (without reference to the place of issue) which had been received as payment for taxes and debts. The treasury was not prepared to accept "any proposition which by implication may affect the rights of the government in a point so essential" and noted that transactions between the treasury and the BUS must not be viewed as having a commercial character.

He opposed a change in the relations between the BUS and the banks selected as depositories only because it destroyed the simplicity of the arrangement, which had not been in operation long enough to "develop its true character." However, he re- luctantly consented that the existing arrangement be terminated but emphasized that the bills of the BUS and its branches, regardless of place of issue, and other bills that the bank or its officers ordinarily received from individuals should be received when and where tendered by the treasury. Soon after, Crawford decided that all monies deposited in the selected banks after June 30 were not subject to drafts of the BUS. The banks would be so informed, and money would be drawn from them by treasury drafts in favor of the BUS or of individuals having demands against the treasury.[12] Obviously Crawford had decided to keep in the hands of the treasury all possible control of the public funds.

Strenuous efforts to save the BUS began in July 1818; a con- traction policy was initiated, and on August 28 the offices of the BUS were forbidden to take any notes but their own—even on deposit.[13] Some improvement took place—or at least the rate of deterioration was slowed. Rumors of fraud and improper operations spread; the enemies of the BUS continued to increase, but Crawford was convinced that the bank must be kept in operation to fulfill its vital role in connection with the public revenue. He did not slack, however, in determination that the bank operate according to the provisions of the charter. In the fall of 1818 the bank notified Crawford that it would sell about

[12] Crawford to Jones, June 3, 1818, Gratz; Crawford to Jones, July 2, 1818, Crawford, MDLC.
[13] Catterall, *Second Bank*, 54. At the time this restriction was applicable only to private accounts.

$400,000 worth of government stock unless it was taken within fifteen days for the account of the United States. Crawford said that if the BUS sold the stock to individuals, the United States still had the right to redeem the stock on the same terms as if the stock had remained in possession of the bank. He did not wish to drain the treasury of $400,000, but he did agree to take the 3 percent certificates (about $90,000), the only part of the stock it seemed important for the public to retain.[14]

Congressional opponents of the bank sought to destroy it, and both the House and the Senate in the fall of 1818 and early 1819 collected information about its activities. Crawford was somewhat handicapped in meeting the demands of the House investigating committee, headed by John C. Spencer of New York (by no means a Crawford partisan), because Jones did not always supply him with information sufficiently precise to pass on. The committee report of January 16, 1819, was harshly critical of the administration of the BUS, pointed to speculation by bank officials and to several violations of the charter, and urged that the abuses be corrected.[15] Crawford said he had neither official nor unofficial knowledge of the "highly censurable" actions of the BUS until the report was made. Fairly presented, these actions deserved the "severest animadversion," but he thought the Spencer report had presented them in a most unfair manner. Monroe "forced" the resignation of Jones, an action Crawford considered "indispensable, not only as a propitiary offering upon the altar of public opinion, but for the preservation of the bank itself."[16]

Langdon Cheves, the new president, informed Crawford of the critical situation of the bank, which was "badly prepared" to sustain specie payments and to reinvigorate itself for future

14 Adams, *Memoirs*, 4:139-40 (Oct. 19, 1818). In 1817 Crawford had "compelled" the bank—by giving notice of the treasury's intention to redeem it—to purchase $2 million worth of stock to replace a like amount which it had sold.

15 Crawford to Jones, Nov. 27, 1818, C. W. Conarroe Collection (HSP); Catterall, *Second Bank*, 58-60; *ASPF*, 3:306-15, 315-91 (documents); *Niles' Weekly Register* 15 (Jan. 23, 1819):402-13, 436-63, 465-75.

16 Crawford to Cheves, April 6, 1819, Langdon Cheves Papers (South Carolina Historical Society); Crawford to Gallatin, July 24, 1819, Adams, *Gallatin Writings*, 2:112-14. James G. Fisher, president pro tempore of the BUS, mentioned Crawford and Cheves as possible successors to Jones. He hoped harsh measures would not be taken because of the speculative actions revealed by the report and warned that the bank needed all the aid the government could give it. Fisher to Rufus King, Jan. 25, 1819, Charles R. King, ed., *The Life and Correspondence of Rufus King*, 6 vols. (New York, 1894-1900), 6:198. Hereafter cited as King, *King*.

profitable and useful operations. He agreed with Crawford—whose public actions had "abundantly shown" his attitude—that at least the parent BUS should continue to meet the demands for gold and silver. But the bank had only about $720,000 in its vaults, little other specie under its control, and credit only with the Barings abroad. He asked several questions about the revenue, drafts, trade, and the debt, but said he sought only such information as Crawford was at liberty to confide.[17] Crawford found Cheves' views deeply interesting to the government, noted that the bank must take the lead in correcting the derangement of the currency and the embarrassment of all the fiscal transactions of the government, questioned the expediency of the BUS continuing to import specie but indicated that naval vessels would help as much as possible in this matter, and said that not more than $3 million of the Louisiana debt would be redeemed ($2 million of which would be foreign-held). To help prevent exhausting the public funds in the Atlantic cities he had induced the secretary of war to spend a larger amount of the War Department funds in the western states than formerly. Crawford promised to help the bank in every way possible in support of specie payment.[18]

Cheves indicated it would be "utterly impossible" to support specie payment to June 1. Nor would it be possible, without a loan in Europe, to pay the $2 million of the Louisiana debt receivable by foreign stockholders. The bank found itself under the necessity of paying where appropriate funds had not accumulated, and time was needed to get money to those places. The problem was further complicated by a traffic in notes and bills which made them cash for all other purposes but at the same time kept them in reserve for the payment of public demands. The notes of the western and southern offices of the bank were running constantly to the East and North in payment of government dues, and capital was thus shifting to the West and South. This exchange could be controlled by the government declining to receive the branch notes in payment of dues except where the notes were made payable or by the BUS stopping the issue of western notes and greatly diminishing the issue of

[17] Cheves to Crawford, March 20, 1819, Monroe, NYP. This ten-page letter is marked private and confidential as are many others between these two individuals.
[18] Crawford to Cheves, March 27, 1819. Six pages of this letter are in the Monroe Papers, NYP; pages one and four are in the Cheves Papers.

southern notes. He asked the government to stop receiving branch notes in the eastern cities.[19]

This request triggered a lengthy discussion on section 14 of the charter, which stated "That the bills or notes of the said corporation originally made payable, or which shall become payable on demand, shall be receivable in all payments to the United States, unless otherwise directed by Congress." Crawford sent the letter from Cheves, and a copy of his reply, to Monroe, and in the covering letter he said there was no "necessary, much less legal relation between the limits within which the notes of one of the offices circulate, & the boundaries of a state." If the interpretation of the bank were accepted, the notes of the bank and its branches circulating in a state where there was no branch would not be receivable for government dues. He thought specie payment would be suspended before the end of the summer and wondered what course could be adopted during the recess of Congress to preserve the public faith. It was more important to know whether the bills of the BUS could be refused in payment to the government because they are not payable at the place where they are tendered. He asked the attorney general for an opinion, sought the President's views, and believed that Calhoun might be able to give the ideas that prevailed at the time Congress chartered the BUS.[20]

In the reply to Cheves—a well-reasoned twelve-page communication—Crawford said no difficulty would result from permitting time for the transfer of funds to meet the payment of treasury drafts, since decision on this matter rested entirely in his department, but he doubted that the BUS—in spite of all the exertions—would be able to continue specie payment throughout the year. The safety of the bank could be effected only by withdrawing nearly all its paper from circulation, and he believed this action would compel all other solvent banks to do the same. Gold and silver would then be introduced and banking institutions could gradually resume their accustomed operations. During this process the community in all its operations would be "greatly distressed," but it was highly desirable that some good

---

19 Cheves to Crawford, April 2, 1819, Monroe, NYP. For further information on Cheves' administration of the bank see Catterall, *Second Bank*, 68-92. The loan in Europe was negotiated, and Cheves did curtail the notes of the southern and western branches.

20 Crawford to Monroe, April 7, 1819, Monroe, MDLC.

come from the suffering which had already been experienced. Crawford saw no middle course and felt that palliatives might prolong the existing embarrassments and aggravate the existing evils by exciting the hopes and fears of the community—but they could not influence the final result.

He would not consider the legality of government receipt of bills of the bank and its branches at any place other than where they were payable; rather he would examine the consequences of the adoption of such a measure. Much clamor against the BUS and the government would be raised, receipts would be insufficient to meet current expenses, the vital interests of the nation would be sacrificed, and complete fiscal derangement would result. The BUS would gain nothing but a little time for transporting specie from one place to another, and the measure would have the effect of confining the circulation of the paper of the bank and its offices to the districts in which it is issued—much as that of the state institutions. Pressure on particular offices would be reduced while that on others would be increased. The measure would be "simply palliative" and furnished nothing like a "radical remedy." Probably the treasury would be obliged to receive the bills of the bank and its offices without regard to the place where they were payable.[21]

Another long letter went to Cheves on April 9. Crawford noted that Horace Binney's opinion that the bills of the bank and its branches were everywhere receivable corresponded in every respect with his own, and he proceeded to bolster with additional arguments the position he had taken in his earlier letter. Cheves, he felt, had connected too closely the obligation of the government to receive with its obligation to deposit the public money where received in the bank and its offices. The obligation to receive depends in no degree upon the proximity of the bank or its offices to the place of receipt. The sites of the bank and its offices are "mathematical points," but there is no connection between the bank and its offices and the limit of the state in which they are located. The limit of the circulation of their paper is determined by the "commercial intercourse between the place of its establishment and the surrounding country, not by state boundaries." If the bills of the banks are considered as

21 Crawford to Cheves, April 6, 1819, Cheves. See also Crawford to Cheves, n.d. (fragment), Library Company of Philadelphia.

current money—and section 14 of the charter binds the government to this view—the proposal that the bank notes are receivable only where payable is untenable. "Current money must be current co-extensively as to place, with the authority which makes it current." He contended in this particular case that it may be "current beyond the jurisdiction of the law," and that a contract with the stipulation that the bills should not be received would be void, for it would be a contract against law.

Crawford had not received the opinion of the attorney general, but even if Wirt thought it correct, he doubted whether he would feel authorized to adopt the rule Cheves believed necessary to the security of the bank.[22] He felt sure, however, that the action of the board of directors would be dictated by honorable motives, and the Treasury Department would not oppose it unless "imperious interest" required it. Expediency of the measure, said Crawford, and not its legality should be the principal concern of the directors. He reiterated his conviction that continuance of specie payment required the amount of notes in circulation be reduced to the amount of specie held by the bank.[23] The BUS, however, decided to adopt the proposed rule, and when its bills and those of its branches were tendered at places other than where payable they were termed special deposits until the BUS could transfer the specie from the issuing to the receiving office.

The financial position of the government seemed to become more difficult with each passing day, but Crawford never wavered in his desire to protect the interests of the bank and the government—as a matter of fact he seemed to feel they were inseparable. In writing and in person he suggested exempting the Washington office of the bank, insofar as it was the agent of the treasury,

22 Binney, a director of the first BUS, was one of the finest legal minds of the first half of the nineteenth century. Wirt, maintaining his duty was to "construe" not to "make" the law, agreed with Binney and Crawford. Wirt to Secretary of Treasury, April 15, 1819, *House Doc.*, No. 123 (serial 387), 26th Cong., 2d sess., 195. Diplomat, famous constitutional lawyer, and former attorney general of the United States William Pinkney, whose opinion Crawford also requested, held the same view. Adams, *Memoirs*, 4:344-45 (April 20, 1819).

23 Crawford to Cheves, April 9, 1819, Cheves. Crawford emphasized to Gallatin that great distress had been caused by the export of specie to the East Indies and China and that the redemption of $5 million of the Louisiana debt (four fifths of which was held by foreigners) the preceding October 21 had contributed to the distress. Crawford to Gallatin, April 24, 1819, Gallatin; Crawford to Gallatin, April 26, 1819, Adams, *Gallatin Writings*, 2:98. Samuel Smith, Baltimore merchant and senator from Maryland, was one of the largest exporters of specie to the Far East.

from the general rules prescribed for the conduct of the offices. The new rule on payment of notes might produce more embarrassment than utility to the bank; the treasury, however, would try to "get along with it and give it a fair trial," for if it is "essential to the safety of the bank the public interest is intimately connected with it." Crawford could not see that the Washington bank would suffer by being permitted to issue its bills *ad libitum* in discharge of the checks of the treasury and could not understand how the BUS gained by the restriction on the Washington branch.[24]

Crawford was criticized for permitting the bank regulation regarding receipt of its bills in violation of the charter, and opposition to the BUS was heightened by the revelation of fraud and mismanagement in some of the branches. Crawford was well aware that section 14 of the charter was not being honored, but strict legality could be temporarily abandoned to prevent the return of the earlier economic chaos.[25]

Cheves wished Congress to sanction the April ruling of the BUS board by changing section 14 so that bank bills would be receivable by the government only where they were payable—except in states or territories where no office existed. Crawford maintained such a change would destroy the bank notes as bills of exchange by making their circulation local, but it would secure to the western states a sound local currency. It would relieve the bank of certain expenses of transferring the public money and provide a better control over the bank officers and the issue of notes. Also it would enable the BUS to do more business and to circulate more notes on the same amount of specie—especially expanding their business in the cities of the middle and eastern states. On the other hand, the mercantile class would have to bear the burden of exchange, and travelers would have to carry specie or be shaved by the brokers in every state through which their pleasure or business carried them. He thought the first was not an evil, but the second objection was a serious one.[26]

24 Crawford to Cheves, May 17, 1819, Etting; Crawford to Cheves, May 24, June 11, 1819, Cheves.
25 For a representative, if not typical, criticism see *Niles' Weekly Register* 16 (Aug. 21, 1819):416-18. On several other occasions Crawford disapproved or took exception to bank actions or proposed actions. See, for example, Crawford to Cheves, Aug. 31, 1819, Etting; Cheves Papers, passim.
26 Crawford to James Barbour, Sept. 18, 1819, Barbour.

By the spring of 1820 several members of Congress were convinced that the requested charter change was necessary to the well-being of the bank but injurious to the government. With the suggested exemption of the bills of the parent bank and of the Washington branch Crawford thought there would be no objection to the measure—if it were not for the radical opposition in Congress to the institution. The entire Virginia delegation opposed the bank and the western members seized every opportunity to attack it. Crawford analyzed the opinion in other parts of the country and concluded it would be imprudent to bring any proposition having as its object the interest or advantage of the bank before the present session of Congress. However, something might be done at the next session.[27]

The treasury remained in dire straits in 1820 and continued to borrow. Cheves, believing he had a solution to the government's problems, presented to Crawford a proposal for "deficit" financing: the government should permit the purchasers of public lands to pay their obligations in installments, with the first payments coming due on January 1, 1822. Each annual payment, he said, should include interest and would amount to 10 percent of the original debt; sixteen payments would be necessary. The government should meet its needs by borrowing against this fund and with the proceeds from it cancel the debt created by the loan. He thought the plan feasible, and in his "poor opinion, you could not adopt a measure which would more truly promote the best interests of the Country or make you more friends." The plan, Cheves said, would in effect create no debt, taxes would not be necessary, the payment of a doubtful debt (for the land purchases) would be secured, the western country would be relieved, aid in restoring a sound currency to the western states would be provided, the law requiring cash for future land purchases would be sustained, the government would make a profit because it would get a premium on a loan which would bear the same rate of interest which the debtors would pay, dilapidating retrenchments would be avoided in the military and naval establishments, and the "elevated tone of feeling" (among the country's most valuable possessions) would be promoted.[28] While there is a faint

[27] Crawford to Cheves, April 11, 1820, Cheves.
[28] Cheves to Crawford, Oct. 16, 1820, Monroe, MDLC. The "plan," which was

similarity between the plan and the relief act of 1821, the latter made no connection between land payments and government borrowing. And Cheves was much too sanguine about the collection of money owed by land purchasers.

Crawford and Cheves corresponded on many other matters of mutual interest, including the government directors of the BUS, possible stock conversions, the dividend which the bank paid to the government, and bank loans to the government during the period of its financial distress.[29] The BUS provided all the government loans authorized by Congress, and though objected to by some this policy did not result in a "holy alliance" between treasury and bank.

Crawford and Cheves worked closely together,[30] and their cooperation seems to have been beneficial in the long run to both bank and government. Cheves' contraction policy (which had been begun by Jones and which Crawford repeatedly advocated) produced some hardship and ill will, but it placed the bank on a sound footing and helped to achieve a currency of some stability. The ruling of the bank board on section 14 caused temporary inconvenience to the government; its ultimate effect was beneficial. By the time of Cheves' resignation the BUS was administratively and financially sound, and the government was no longer bedeviled by scarcity of revenue. The routines of reporting, transfer, payment, and all other functions of the BUS as a "government agency" were well established.[31] The relationship between Crawford and the new BUS president, Nicholas Biddle, was strictly a business one and contrasted sharply with that between Crawford and Cheves.

---

originally enclosed with the letter, is in the Golding Collection. The fact that several of the letters from Cheves to Crawford are in the Monroe papers seems to indicate close consultation between Crawford and Monroe on bank matters.

[29] See, for example, Crawford to Cheves, April 20, 24, 1819; April 13, 25, Nov. 7, 17, 1820; March 12, 23, June 8, Dec. 12, 1821; Jan. 2, 1822, Cheves; Crawford to Cheves, June 21, 1820, Crawford, MDLC. On several occasions Crawford thought the government interest was adversely affected by the composition of the boards of some of the branch banks.

[30] Cheves' confidential revelation that he would resign in late 1822 was followed by Crawford's suggestion that Gallatin consider the presidency of the BUS; Gallatin was not interested. Cheves' intention to resign was made public in *Niles' Weekly Register* 22 (July 1, 1822):291.

[31] Crawford asked Cheves to correct some inaccuracies in materials that Cheves planned to submit to the stockholders at the time of his resignation. This "Exposition," or account of Cheves' presidency, is in *Niles' Weekly Register* 23 (Oct. 12, 1822):89-96. It was also published as a pamphlet by William Fry of Philadelphia in 1822.

The adequacy of the legal tender in circulation was a subject of much discussion in this period, and the directors of the bank in 1818 requested the charter be changed so that notes other than those signed by the president and cashier could be issued. Crawford agreed, but he felt that all the larger bills should be signed by the authorized officials and opposed the issuing of bills by the cashier and president of the branches.[32] Had the privilege been granted and the branch banks been refused the right to issue and overissue notes, the flow of specie to the West and South might have been prevented and a uniform national currency established. However, certain other early practices of the bank might well have prevented such a desirable development.

The investigation of the bank in early 1819 was followed by a House resolution of March 1 calling on the secretary of treasury to report, among other things, on the amount of capital, notes, and deposits, and requesting that he also report "such measures as in his opinion may be expedient to procure and retain a sufficient quantity of gold and silver coin in the United States, or to supply a circulating medium in place of specie, adapted to the exigencies of the country, and within the power of the Government."[33] In response to this resolution Crawford's so-called Currency Report was sent to the speaker of the House on February 12, 1820.[34]

[32] Crawford to Chairman, Senate Committee on Finance, April 7, 1818, *Senate Doc.*, No. 182 (serial 3), 15th Cong., 1st sess., 3-7. This privilege, several times requested, was never granted. Catterall, *Second Bank,* 116.

[33] *Annals,* 15th Cong., 2d sess., 1426. Adams thought the resolution had an "insidious aspect"; it was introduced by John C. Spencer, "shrewd and warm partisan" of DeWitt Clinton, who hoped to ensnare Crawford into disclosing some doctrine that would affect his popularity. But he thought the report showed awareness of the design, for it avoided commitment on every important aspect of the subject. The only merit Adams found in the report was its discouragement of paper money. Crawford expressed awareness of the political nature of the resolution. Adams, *Memoirs,* 4:396 (June 24, 1819); 5:36-37 (March 25, 1820); Crawford to James Barbour, Sept. 18, 1819, Barbour.

[34] The original manuscript is in Series E, Vol. 6, pp. 253-305; printed "official" versions are in *House Doc.*, No. 86 (serial 36), 16th Cong., 1st sess. and *ASPF,* 3:494-508. It may be more conveniently consulted in *Niles' Weekly Register* 18 (March 11, 18, 25, 1820):34-40, 41-45, 70-79, and citations below are to this source. It may also be found in the *National Intelligencer,* March 4, 7, 1820. Several newspapers commented on the report, and some pamphlets appeared. On this and related matters, see Murray N. Rothbard, *The Panic of 1819: Reactions and Policies* (New York, 1962), esp. 112-35. An interesting undated document headed "Honble/ Henry Clay/Mr Laws System/& observations/WHC" is in the Golding Collection. Seven pages are devoted to the management mechanism ("metropolitan board" of

The report gave the condition of the BUS and its offices as of September 30, 1819, the amount of bank capital authorized by law for various years, the active bank capital of the United States (estimated at not more than $75 million), the conditions of the state banks from which returns had been received, a comparison of the amount of circulating bank notes and bank capital, and Crawford's analyses, opinions, and recommendations. He set the amount of specie in the hands of the state banks at $12,250,000, with an additional $3,250,000 in the BUS. In circulation he thought there was not more than $4,500,000, bringing the whole "metallurgic" currency to $20,000,000. Notes in circulation were estimated at $40,000,000, making a total circulating medium of about $45,000,000—down from $110,000,-000 in 1815.[35]

This great decrease in the currency had produced much distress, checked the ardor of enterprise, and seriously affected the productive energies of the nation. However, Crawford thought there must be further reduction before the currency became sound, and the nation would "continue to suffer until this is effected."[36] He described the exhilarating economic effects of credit and paper money in a period of prosperity and noted the inevitability of contraction in a time of adversity. If the public's confidence in the ability to redeem declined, there was an immediate demand for specie. If this demand was not promptly met, a depreciation would result. In the "circle" of specie and paper money thus established, Crawford said a "just proportion" between the paper circulation and the specie necessary to support it could be obtained only by reducing the amount of paper.

Crawford believed that if the existence of banks depended upon the authority which regulated the currency, it might be "practicable to impose salutary checks upon excessive issues of

five to seven members) of controlling and introducing small coins and $20 million of United States paper currency into the circulating medium. The paper would provide a substitute for specie and deprive the BUS of every excuse for not "meeting" their notes with specie or government notes. The proposal contains some elements of the National Banking System and some of the Federal Reserve System. There are nine pages of observations on the proposal. The paper might well be Crawford's version of some of the proposals of Thomas Law, advocate of a national inconvertible paper money. For information on Law see Rothbard, *Panic of 1819*, 114-20.

35 *Niles' Weekly Register* 18:34-36, 77-78. Considerable attention was given to the relationship of bank capital and bank notes.

36 Ibid., 36-37.

paper during suspension: and in some degree to guard against an excessive issue of the currency." Such was not the case in the United States, and he found it impossible to imagine a currency "more vicious than that which depends upon the will of nearly four hundred banks, entirely independent of each other, when released from all restraint against excessive issue."[37] These banks, through the credit system, have produced a "fictitious state of things, extremely adverse to the sober, frugal, and industrious habits, which ought to be cherished in a republic." The government was not without fault, for it had contributed to extravagance, idleness, and the spirit of gambling adventure through its credit system of land purchase.

The secretary discussed several reasons for the inadequate supply of gold and silver in the United States, offered some mild criticisms of Congress, and thought it important that the mint ratio of silver and gold be changed from 15 to 1 to 15.75 to 1— the approximate market ratio. This would cause the importation and retention of gold but would not cause silver to be exported unless the state of the foreign trade warranted it. In addition, the copper coinage of the country could definitely be improved. Copper alone was too massive; coins of copper and silver from one- to ten-cent denominations would be "much more suitable." Change, or the fractional parts of the dollar, he considered "so indispensable to the community, that its applicability to manufactures, and its exemption to exportation, instead of forming objections, are recommendations in its favor."[38]

Crawford did not take kindly to the idea of issuing $5 million in treasury notes to relieve the distress: if these were receivable by the government, the revenue would be paid in them and the

[37] Ibid., 38-40.
[38] Ibid., 41-43. Apparently Crawford's coins were similar to the "billion pieces" or silver-center cents of France, which had caught Alexander Hamilton's fancy, and he clearly intended the pieces to be fiduciary. His proposals, says Carothers, represented both sound principles and antiquated theory. Neil Carothers, *Fractional Money: A History of the Small Coins and Fractional Paper Currency of the United States* (New York, 1930), 65-66, 85-86; A. Barton Hepburn, *History of Coinage and Currency in the United States and the Perennial Contest for Sound Money* (New York, 1903), 29. The mint, operating under the nominal supervision of Crawford, did not produce a sufficient number of gold, silver, and copper coins to meet the demand. See *Senate Doc.*, Nos. 67, 68 (serial 15), 15th Cong., 2d sess. A statement of the director of the mint accompanied the secretary's annual report to Congress.

United States would not have the specie to meet its obligations on the public debt. If section 14 of the charter were changed so that the notes of the BUS and its branches were receivable only at the point of issue, a small amount of treasury notes might be issued without depreciation. They would be used—and in constant demand—for the transmission of money. If they were redeemable at the treasury for specie, the amount put in circulation would probably exceed the sum demanded for the facile transmission of money; if not receivable, but redeemable at a fixed period, they would immediately depreciate unless they bore 6 percent interest. Unless advanced as a loan, they would afford no substantial relief where the distress was greatest. He could justify the issue of treasury notes as a financial resource only where the deficiency they were intended to overcome was small and temporary. However, issue under the existing circumstances "would tend to increase this unnatural and forced state of things, and give it a duration which it would otherwise never obtain."[39]

The last "member" of the resolution, said Crawford, assumes by implication the practicability of substituting a paper currency for that which now exists. Paper currency, whether issued by the governments, employed as a financial resource, or made the instrument of cupidity, had been a failure, and no one had attempted to determine the principles upon which a stable paper currency must be founded. He explored these and said to ensure the possibility of such a currency being used to advantage it was necessary that the power of the government over the currency be absolutely sovereign; the stability of the government be above suspicion; its justice, morality, and intelligence be unquestioned; the issue of the currency be made not only to depend upon the demand for it but that an equivalent be actually received; an equivalent could be found only in the delivery of an equal amount of gold, silver, or public stock; and whenever from any cause the currency might become redundant, it might be funded at an interest rate a fraction below that surrendered at its issue.

In discussing these points Crawford restated some of the positions he had taken in his correspondence with Cheves, and above all he made it clear that he believed in a national currency

39 *Niles' Weekly Register* 18:43-44.

of gold and silver over which he thought the government had absolute power. He was not certain that the Constitution gave the central government the power to create a national inconvertible paper currency. Some, but not many, treasury notes might be beneficial. The full cooperation of the central and state governments was essential to the success of any paper currency; such a currency should be put into circulation only upon receipt of "articles in exchange of equal value," and an uncontrolled, unregulated paper currency, issuing from many banks, was to be avoided at all costs. The large amount of this nonredeemable currency that had been in circulation had deeply wounded the worthy characteristics of good republicans, and the body economic must suffer to recovery by continued withdrawal of the inflationary opiate. The report contains several assertions, assumptions, and allegations used by bullionists and non-bullionists seventy-five years later, but Crawford was reasonably noncommittal except in his opposition to unsupported and unlimited paper money.[40]

The following year a select committee indicated general agreement with the report and pointed out that a gold coinage of approximately $6 million had practically disappeared from use—the difference between the market and the mint ratios being about sixty cents for every fifteen dollars. But no action was taken. Nor was there acceptance of the baser coinage proposal. Almost annually Congress passed laws to permit the continued circulation of foreign coins, the mint ratio of gold and silver was not changed until 1834, subsidiary coinage was not established until 1853, and the copper-nickel cent was not created until 1857, when all foreign coins were withdrawn as legal tender.[41]

The currency report was made in answer to a special resolution of the House. More central to the duty of the secretary of treasury was the annual report on expenditures and receipts of the government.

[40] Ibid., 71-76. For some other materials of the time on the currency see Crawford to John W. Eppes, Dec. 29, 1818; Report of Senate Committee on Finance, *Senate Doc.*, No. 68 (serial 15), 15th Cong., 2d sess.; Crawford to Speaker of the House, Dec. 1, 1820, *House Doc.*, No. 9 (serial 48), 16th Cong., 2d sess.

[41] Hepburn, *Coinage*, 26, 27, 30; Carothers, *Fractional Money*, 83. Carothers, 84, believes that at any time from 1792 to 1834 the application of the subsidiary coinage principle to quarters, dimes, and half-dimes would have revolutionized the currency situation.

8

The Treasury Secretary
and the Budget

ANNUALLY THE secretary of treasury reported directly to Congress on the receipts and expenditures of the government and on the estimated income and expenses for the coming year, making such remarks as he saw fit on the tax structure, the economic conditions of the country, government proposals for reducing or increasing the revenue, and such other matters as he deemed pertinent. In preparation for the report, the register of the treasury gathered projected expenditures and other materials for the secretary, who then furnished a brief statement for the President's annual message. Soon thereafter the treasury report (without general cabinet consideration) was sent to Congress. The secretary had virtually no control over expenditures, and in the early years only Albert Gallatin (with Jefferson's help) seemed able to bring any effective reductions in the estimates and to achieve considerable support for a balanced budget. The situation was to change little during Monroe's presidency, except that after 1820-1821 the annual report received cabinet scrutiny prior to submittal to Congress.[1]

During most of Crawford's tenure the budget consisted of two parts, the so-called permanent and temporary allocations. The former included the sinking fund for the retirement of the debt, money for the gradual increase of the navy, and appropriations for the militia and Indian annuities. The temporary portion can be conveniently grouped into three main categories: civil list, miscellaneous, and foreign intercourse; military department, including the Indian department and military pensions; and navy, including the Marine Corps. The military department received approximately twice the amount of the other two combined, and after 1817 the sinking fund of $10,000,000 annually was the major item in the permanent appropriations. But the decreasing revenue and the depression called for retrenchment which seriously affected the sinking fund and brought a decrease in military expenditures and an increase in political conflict.[2]

At the time Crawford assumed the secretaryship of treasury the government was embarrassed by its surplus revenue. The public debt of about $75,000,000 in 1791 had been reduced to approximately $65,000,000 in 1812, in spite of the $15,000,000 obligation for the Louisiana Purchase. The War of 1812 had boosted the funded debt to a little less than $116,000,000 by 1816. Revenue for the preceding year had been just under $50,000,000 and expenditures $38,000,000. But approximately three fourths of the income was derived from customs duties and thus subject to drastic fluctuations; proceeds from that source decreased from $36,000,000 in 1815 to $17,000,000 in 1817 but rose to nearly $20,000,000 in 1818. Government expenditures were running about $20,000,000 per year.

Crawford's first report of December 20, 1816, noted that the treasury was affluent; income had been almost $39,000,000 in the first three quarters of the year and the estimated total was $46,900,000. The secretary pointed out the difficulty of making any reliable estimate of income with customs as the major source, but using the average of several years and assuming expenditures of $24,000,000 per year he predicted an annual excess of $8,400,000 for 1818, 1819, and 1820. He estimated temporary expenditures at $12,750,000 but reduced these by $300,000 in a message to the House early the next month.[3]

The President's message and the secretary's report stressed the need to restore a uniform circulating medium[4] and to have available additional funds for the retirement of the national debt. Congress, by the act of March 3, 1817, authorized the secretary to add $9,000,000 to the sinking fund, and—if it was

1 White, *Jeffersonians*, 68-69, 141-46. See also Lucius Wilmerding, Jr., *The Spending Power: A History of the Efforts of Congress to Control Expenditures* (New Haven, Conn., 1943).

2 This, of course, is a great simplification of the report, which contained detailed information of all types of income, the public debt, and financial and economic conditions.

3 *ASPF*, 3:140-44; Crawford to Speaker of the House, Jan. 4, 1817, ibid., 148. The reduction was all from the military estimates. The report of the secretary was always accompanied by several statistical documents, the most important of which was from the register of the treasury. Page references for those are not included in the citations. All figures in this chapter are to the nearest thousand.

4 Resumption of specie payment and efforts to establish a uniform currency are discussed in the preceding chapter.

thought expedient—to add another $4,000,000 which would be considered an advance on the 1818 payment. And after 1817, whenever at any time after the adjournment of Congress there was a surplus of more than $2,000,000 above the sums appropriated, all above the $2,000,000 should go into the sinking fund. The commissioners of the fund were authorized—if the President approved—to apply any surplus beyond the amount of interest and principal that was actually due and payable to purchase of the debt.[5]

Few believed that the happy financial situation of 1816-1817 was permanent, but it was considered unwise to add to the large surplus. With the defeat of the Bonus Bill (which committed to internal improvements the money paid to the government by the BUS for its privileges) at the end of Madison's term and Monroe's known scruples against the use of central government funds for internal improvement purposes, with the army and the navy already spending nearly half the total government outlay, there seemed no solution to the overabundance of funds other than the reduction of taxes. Congressional sentiment favored the repeal of the internal taxes in March 1817, but legislation for this purpose was initiated so late in the session that congressmen decided to postpone the measure until the fall. Then, too, Crawford thought the great number of new members at the next session might vote money with a "lavish hand" and greatly diminish the source of revenue. Only the strong hand of the President could prevent this action, he said.[6]

During Monroe's administration the secretary of treasury did not operate as independently of the President as many writers have indicated. As a matter of fact, Monroe kept a rather tight rein on all his department heads—no mean feat when one considers the caliber of his cabinet. The secretary did not work in

5 Annually, $10,000,000 from revenue from imports and tonnage duties, internal duties, and western lands were to go to the fund. The secretary of treasury was given some discretion as to the date of payment so long as it was made in time to meet obligations. Ceilings were set on the prices that could be paid when the various stocks were purchased with the surplus, and the commissioners should prescribe the manner of cancellation or destruction of the purchased stock. 3 *Stat.* 379-80.

6 Crawford to Gallatin, March 17, 1817, Adams, *Gallatin Writings*, 2:23-29, esp. 27-28. The Compensation Act of 1816, substituting salaries for the per diem allowances of representatives and senators, had brought defeat in the fall of that year to many members of the Congress passing the act.

splendid isolation on his report and in preparing a statement for the President's message. For example, in October 1817 Crawford detailed for Monroe the favorable condition of the revenue and treasury and noted that unless there were greatly increased demands by the War and Navy departments or for expenditures for a system of internal improvements, revenue would exceed the demands of the government. If the increased demands did not materialize, how should the revenue be reduced? Should the system of internal revenue be retained and the reduction effected in the customs? Should both systems be reduced and retained? Internal taxes, he observed, were already as low as was reasonable in relation to expenses of collection. If reduced—and the expenses of collection could not be—the impression might be created that such taxes were kept for the sake of patronage and not for revenue purposes. Crawford firmly believed these taxes must be wholly retained or abolished completely. When the President returned to Washington, Crawford hoped to be able to furnish him the facts necessary to a "correct decision of this delicate question."[7]

Monroe endorsed Crawford's recommendation that the internal taxes be abolished. The treasury report was made on December 5, the House Committee on Ways and Means reacted favorably, and the measure repealing the act of March 3, 1815, became law on December 23, 1817. The taxes were discontinued on December 31, 1817.[8] The internal revenue "establishment" did not immediately disappear; it exhibited the usual government tendency to creeping demise. Crawford took action in early 1819 to speed final settlements,[9] and a year later the office of commissioner of the revenue was abolished and the duties were transferred to one of the auditors.

Before the ending of the internal duties the House had requested Crawford's opinion on the expediency of repealing the

7 Crawford to Monroe, Oct. 11, 1817, Monroe, MDLC.

8 Monroe to Madison, Nov. 24, 1817, Hamilton, *Monroe Writings,* 6:33; 3 *Stat.* 401-3. The treasury had more than $11,000,000 at the beginning of 1817, and with an estimated expenditure for 1818 of $38,370,000 (including $10,000,000 on the debt) a balance of $8,500,000 was anticipated for Jan. 1, 1819. *ASPF,* 3:220-23.

9 Joseph Anderson to Crawford, Jan. 19, 1819, Excise Letters, No. 5; Crawford to Samuel Smith, Jan. 21, 1819, Series E, Vol. 6. Internal duties, exclusive of the direct tax, brought in more than $17,000,000 from January 1, 1814, to December 31, 1817, but the cost of collection was more than 5 percent greater than the cost of collecting import duties.

law laying a duty on imported salt, granting a bounty on exported pickled fish, and giving allowances to certain vessels employed in the fisheries. Crawford did not reply until after the internal duties were abolished; he then pointed out that for the three preceding years the duty on salt had amounted annually to slightly more than $900,000 and the bounty and allowances a little less than $100,000. Repeal of the internal taxes would reduce the revenue for 1818 from the estimated $24,500,000 to just over $22,000,000, or within $78,000 of the estimated expenses. If the salt duty were eliminated, there would be a deficit of more than $700,000, until the proceeds of the sale of lands in Mississippi and Alabama became available. He thought a "reduction of the balance in the Treasury, so as to prevent its application to this object [retiring the debt], ought to be carefully guarded against."[10]

While Crawford wrestled with the bank and currency problems, a decline in revenue soon relieved the government of its burdensome surplus. The $26,000,000 income for 1818 was slightly less than payments from the treasury; while this presented no problems for that year, Crawford thought it might be necessary to resort to temporary loans or the issue of treasury notes in 1819 rather than impose new taxes. Loans, it appeared, would not be required for the year following.[11] By then, however, the full force of the panic was felt.

In his report of December 10, 1819, Crawford gave the receipts and expenditures for several preceding years and estimated the

[10] Crawford to William Lowndes, Jan. 5, 1818, *House Doc.*, No. 13 (serial 10), 15th Cong., 1st sess.; *ASPF*, 3:260-61. The estimates for 1818 expenditures had been submitted to the House on December 17, 1817. Congress appropriated $5,083,000 for the military establishment and $2,509,000 for the navy, not including the annual $1,000,000 for the gradual increase of that arm. 3 *Stat.* 407-8, 463, 411.

[11] The treasury report was made in late November 1818. *ASPF*, 3:273-75. Estimated income was a little more than $24,000,000 and probable demands about $25,500,000. Income actually was $21,435,000. Ibid., 548. The military establishment appropriation for 1819 rose to $6,850,000, including more than $2,000,000 for pensions and half pensions—making the nonpension money available about the same as that of the year before. The navy was voted $2,835,000. 3 *Stat.* 480-81, 483-84, 540. The department heads were well aware in the spring of 1819 of the economic distress which was at that time confined chiefly to the South and West. Because of the nature of the system of revenue (the posting of bonds for future payment) government receipts had not been sensibly affected; upward or downward trends in the economy were reflected about six months later by the treasury receipts. See Adams' report of conversation with Crawford, *Memoirs*, 4:375 (May 27, 1819), and periodic reports of treasury receipts which accompanied the annual reports of the secretary.

receipts of 1820 applicable to ordinary and current demands at just more than $22,000,000. The 1820 expense estimates were not yet complete, but those that had been received indicated not less than $27,000,000 would be required. The deficit of $5,000,000 could not be supplied by ordinary sources. After legal obligations were discharged, there would be about $2,500,000 in the sinking fund which could not be used if the price of public stocks remained above the price at which the commissioners were authorized to purchase. During 1821, 1822, and 1823 an average of $5,000,000 would be in the fund if the existing price of the stocks continued. If legal, the use of this money would postpone the imposition of additional burdens to meet the public expenditures, but such use "would have the effect of ultimately retarding the redemption of the public debt."

Public interest, said Crawford, required that the revenue be augmented or expenditures be decreased. Some import duties might be increased, but it was thought improbable that any modification of the tariff—which might result in a temporary decline of revenue—could prevent the necessity of internal taxes, unless expenses were reduced. Crawford maintained that

Should Congress deem it expedient to modify the present rate of duties, with a view to afford that protection to our cotton, woollen, and iron manufactures, which is necessary to secure to them the domestic market, the necessity of resorting to a system of internal taxation will be augmented. It is believed that the present is a favorable moment for affording efficient protection to that increasing and important interest, if it can be done consistent with the general interest of the nation. The situation of the countries from whence our foreign manufactures have been principally drawn authorizes the expectation that, in the event of a monopoly of the home market being secured to our cotton and woollen manufactures, a considerable portion of the manufacturing skill and capital of those countries will be promptly transferred to the United States, and incorporated into the domestic capital of the Union. Should this expectation be realized, the disadvantage resulting from such a monopoly would quickly disappear. In the mean time, it is believed that a system of internal taxation would be severely felt by the great mass of our citizens.

The secretary certainly was not inflexibly committed, but he was firm in his conviction that neither the increase of the revenue nor the diminution of expenses could be accomplished in time to prevent the necessity of a loan. Since the 6 percent stock was considerably above par, he thought the sum required for government operations could be advantageously and conveniently raised by the sale of that stock or the issue of treasury notes. If the revenue and expenses were equalized, the issue of noninterest-bearing treasury notes rather than the sale of stock was recommended, for in those circumstances the loan would be small and temporary.[12]

The next month, January 1820, the House asked Crawford how much reduction in the revenue would result if the importation of cotton and woolen goods and iron manufactures were prohibited and how any resulting deficit would be supplied. Fluctuations in duties on imports made it difficult to say how great the loss of revenue would be, but Crawford thought it would average $6,000,000 for several years. If an increase in duty rates would bring a proportionate increase in revenue, the deficiency might be easily supplied. But reason and experience denied this direct relationship; the importation of foreign merchandise was regulated by the capacity of the importing country to pay an equivalent; when duties are raised to an "extreme," importation may cease. When the duty "equals" the risk incurred by illicit introduction of the article, smuggling upon an extensive and systematic scale begins. He believed that the existing rates were contributing to increased smuggling. Small increases might be made in the duties on linens, coffee, brown sugar, teas, wines, molasses, spices, and other small articles. Deficiencies of revenue would have to be supplied by internal or direct taxes. If internal taxes were thought advisable, the importation of ardent spirits might be prohibited without material injury to the revenue and with "manifest advantage to the agricultural interest." Taxes on domestically produced spirits could replace the revenues collected from the importation of foreign spirits.[13]

Meantime, the direct submittal to Congress of the secretary's

12 *ASPF*, 3:423-26 (quotation on p. 426). In his communication to the speaker of the House on December 23, 1819, Crawford estimated the temporary and permanent expenses of 1820 at $15,418,000 and $11,857,000, respectively.

13 Ibid., 468-69; *House Doc.*, No. 62 (serial 35), 16th Cong., 1st sess. Accompanying statistics showed that the net revenue on merchandise (25 percent ad valorem), mostly woolens and cottons, had been $17,600,000 in 1815, $10,000,000 in 1816, $4,300,000 in 1817, and $6,200,000 in 1818. The revenue from duties on iron was just under $400,000 in 1818.

report had come under discussion; Monroe seemed not to like the practice; John Quincy Adams thought it against the spirit of the Constitution and felt the report should always be under cabinet and presidential scrutiny before being submitted. There was, however, no administrative agreement on what should be done to meet the financial needs of the government. Monroe and Adams believed use of the money in the sinking fund would be the best solution, but Samuel Smith of the Committee on Ways and Means had said his motion to that end had been rejected on January 7. The members of the House thought retrenchment the proper means, but retrenchment could not be carried out if the sinking fund were used to supply the deficiency. Adams thought retrenchment would be "fallacious."[14]

But the House had asked for an accounting of expenses since the beginning of the government, and this was submitted by Crawford on February 7, 1820. Up to June 30, 1819, total receipts had been $517,704,000, including foreign and domestic loans of $143,315,000. Customs duties had brought in $318,-738,000 of the remaining $374,389,000. Of the $513,567,000 expended, $136,000,000 was chargeable to the military establishment, $66,000,000 to the navy, $19,382,000 to the civil list, and $16,353,000 to miscellaneous activities. Perhaps a review of these figures helped Congress to decide where retrenchment should be effected. However, it would appear that the retrenchment of 1820 was not absolute in relation to the appropriations of the preceding year; it seems to have been a reduction of the estimated expenditures rather than of the money actually voted by Congress. The military appropriation for 1820 was $7,841,000 ($3,108,000 for pensions); an earlier appropriation amounted to $276,000, and an unexpended balance of $338,000 ($85,000 for pensions) was made available. Exclusive of pension money, the army had at least $310,000 more than for the year before. The navy was reduced $285,000 to $2,550,000.[15]

Congress decided also that $2,000,000 from the sinking fund should be applied to normal expenditures and that $3,000,000

14 Adams, *Memoirs*, 4:500-501 (Jan. 8, 1820). It seems that the treasury report was thereafter discussed by the cabinet before it went to Congress. Adams had recorded on April 5, 1819 (ibid., 324), that Smith had written Crawford saying the military establishment would certainly be reduced at the next session of Congress.

15 *ASPF*, 3:485-90; 3 *Stat*. 562-63, 553-54. The "item" figures which Crawford gave to the House included only the temporary, not the permanent, expenditures.

might be borrowed. The BUS offer for the $2,000,000 loan in late June—6 percent at 102 for 100 (a 2 percent premium)—was considered the best and was accepted. The premium of $40,000 was $10,000 above the next best offer; some thought it might have been larger but for the uncertainty of the term of the loan; others felt a "little more frankness and precision" might have brought twice the premium since there was "so much money seeking a safe investment."[16]

It was the cutback in the military establishment and appropriations for 1821 that brought a sharpening of political differences and the furor over appointments in 1822 that led to a near rupture of the long friendship between Crawford and Monroe. Perhaps this story will never really be told satisfactorily, partly because of a lack of evidence on many points and partly because of a conflict of evidence. Then, too, the matter of historians' preferences cannot be discounted. There was no question that something needed to be done—as Crawford said, either increase the revenue or cut the expenditures. If expenditures were to be cut, the military and naval establishments, which consumed such a large part of the budget, were the logical places for substantial savings. If the revenue was to be increased, internal taxes seemed the reasonable answer. But that system had just been liquidated, and the economic condition of the country boded ill for much success from this tack.[17] No panacea was in sight, and many seemed to share the sentiments expressed in Crawford's currency report of February 12, 1820, that the economic malaise would just have to wear itself out. At any rate, congressional politicians thought economy and borrowing preferable to increased taxation.

The senators and representatives who advocated retrenchment

16 Crawford to Monroe, June 23, 1820, Monroe, NYP; 3 *Stat.*, 582-83; *National Intelligencer*, June 23, 1820; *Niles' Weekly Register* 18:314, 315-16. The other $1,000,000 authorized by Congress was not borrowed. The BUS, by arrangement with the government, also met the October 1820 payment on the debt. For information on treasury loans during Crawford's tenure see William F. DeKnight, *History of the Currency of the Country and the Loans of the United States from the earliest period to June 30, 1896* (Washington, D.C., 1897), 57-62; Rafael A. Bayley, *The National Loans of the United States, from July 4, 1776 to June 30, 1880* (Washington, D.C., 1881), 61-66. The public debt at the beginning of 1820 was $89,000,000.

17 Crawford regretted the repeal of the internal taxes; he thought in 1817 he "saw years" before commerce would fail as a source of revenue, but he would not advocate reestablishment of the internal revenue system until it became indispensable. Crawford to Tait, May 20, 1820, Tait.

came to be known as radicals and partisans of Crawford. No-
where is this group defined—and they probably cannot be—but
they are generally pictured, possibly unjustly, as negative ob-
structionists. There is no point in denying that political position
was involved in the legislative process; it is inherent in it.
Crawford as head of the treasury and the leading contender as
Monroe's successor was the cabinet member most likely to be
attacked by other contenders—or their partisans. But the word
radical had a variety of meanings depending on circumstances;
it is a term of the period, stereotyped by later commentators.
Excess attention to the word breeds difficulty as well as over-
simplification while obscuring the reality of events. There simply
was no fixed coalition, no coalescing of forces behind or for one
individual. Partisans of Crawford, Clay, DeWitt Clinton, Jackson, and Adams are to be found in the retrenchment and non-
retrenchment camps. Crawford had the largest number of
followers among congressmen—retrenchment or not—but they
could not carry measures by themselves. Moreover, in 1820-1821
there was no real political motive for Crawford partisans to
"urge war" on Calhoun, who at that time was running a very
distant second to William Lowndes, friend and sometime
supporter of Crawford. That there was a fight for the "right
to succeed" seems all too obvious (and hardly to be denounced
unless one condemns the entire political system), but the troops
united under subalterns, skirmished, fell back, regrouped,
deserted, went awol, were cashiered by their constituents, were
broken, or rose to officerdom as a result of the depletion of the
ranks. The infighting of personal and one-party politics was
probably as severe as in any period of United States history. A
detailed accounting of congressional alignments on various
measures is profitless; it leads one into a jungle of tortuous trails
and covered switchbacks.[18]

Whether blame should be attached to anyone in particular

[18] The term "radical" has, of course, been used at many other times in United
States history—and with just as little justification. It has even less validity and
meaning in the 1820s than it has when applied to the Republicans in the recon-
struction era. Adams and Ninian Edwards talked, in March 1821, about the
"systematic" attack on the War Department and Calhoun in the two preceding
sessions of Congress and seemed to conclude that most of the major leaders were
anti-Jacksonians, that the partisans of Crawford and Clinton had "concurred," and
so had those of Clay to some degree. Adams decided the views of the principals
were discordant and Clay was too impatient to brook the delay incident to a full
coalition with Crawford. *Memoirs*, 5:327 (March 10, 1821).

is debatable, but Samuel Smith of the House ways and means committee said in late 1819 that Calhoun had assured Crawford the War Department would require no greater appropriation for 1820 than it had in 1819. Estimates were prepared accordingly, and when Calhoun's figures came in on December 9—the day before Crawford submitted his annual report—they were $2,000,000 above those for the previous year. This increase completely "disjointed" the system of the preceding three years which had been based on an annual expenditure of $24,000,000. Crawford was in "great distress," thought internal taxes might have to be levied, and hinted that Richard M. Johnson (senator from Kentucky) and his brother had pressured Calhoun into the increased spending.[19]

The decrease in the army appropriations involved the estimates, not the actual amount appropriated. But during the congressional debates some Crawford partisans, among them Thomas W. Cobb of Georgia, had attacked the War Department, and Eldred Simpkins, South Carolina representative and Calhoun follower, in speeches and letters to the papers accused Crawford of exaggerating the depleted state of the treasury and tried to convince the army that Crawford purposely sought to injure it. Crawford thought that both Simpkins and Calhoun knew Cobb well enough to realize that he permitted no one to influence him—and Cobb sought retrenchment in all departments.[20]

Actually Crawford had been too optimistic about the state of the treasury, but a mistake of nearly $3,000,000 in his report in the fall of 1820 opened the gates for further attacks. Pressures of office had kept Crawford in Washington in the summer of 1819, so in 1820 he left for Georgia in early August and did not return until October 22. From Georgia he wrote his chief

[19] Smith to J. Spear Smith, Dec. 9, 1819, Carter-Smith Papers (University of Virginia). John W. Taylor of New York, discussing the speakership with Adams in late 1822, had said that he favored the reduction of the army and "understood" that Crawford did. He thought Calhoun had been unjust and ungrateful, for it was through Taylor's influence that Calhoun's plan was substituted for that of the House committee. Adams, *Memoirs,* 6:113-15 (Nov. 30, 1822). Taylor had also said he favored a northern man for the presidency, but if there was no chance of electing a northerner he "should perhaps incline to favor" Crawford. By 1824 Taylor was an Adams supporter.

[20] Crawford to Moses Waddel, Jan. 27, 1821, Gratz; Crawford to Allen Daniel, May 2, 1821, Crawford Letterbook. Crawford understood that Simpkins acted against Calhoun's wishes and advice, but the two secretaries had not talked about the matter. Crawford was probably right in his estimate of Cobb, who on several occasions was sharply critical of Crawford.

clerk to ask the register and others to have the statements necessary to preparation of the report ready when he arrived. Two days after returning Crawford was stricken with influenza; he was confined to bed for a week and "affected by the illness" during all the month of November. He relied on the statements furnished by the register and warrant and appropriation clerks without "scrutinizing them with rigidity."[21]

The report was submitted on December 1; estimated receipts were $16,550,000 (of which not more than $1,600,000 would be from land); the total appropriation chargeable to the military was an expected $7,445,000 and that to the navy, $5,171,000. But other anticipated expenditures (including money for interest only on the debt) would bring the total to $21,363,000. This deficit added to the $2,638,000 expected "balance against" the treasury on January 1, 1821, would leave an unfavorable balance of $7,452,000 at the end of 1821. The condition of the country made it inexpedient to add new taxes.[22] Crawford discovered the error and on December 21, 1820, explained it to the speaker of the House. The mistake resulted principally, he said, from the different manner of keeping the warrant and appropriation accounts in the treasury. He meticulously detailed the discrepancies and indicated the deficit at the end of 1821 would be $4,658,000, or $2,794,000 less than shown in the annual report. He still asked for $7,000,000 in loans, for he thought the treasury should keep a favorable balance of at least $1,000,000.[23]

The major controversy in early 1821 concerned the reduction of the army from 10,000 to 6,000 men, though the number is given only in terms of regiments in the law of March 2. Generally the advocates of reduction pointed to the rapid increase of army posts in the preceding three years, the distressed state of the revenue, the poor prospects for improved economic conditions, and the undesirability of continuing deficits. The

[21] Crawford to Edward Jones, Sept. 20, 1820, Gratz; Crawford to Tait, April 1, 1821, Tait.

[22] *ASPF*, 3:547-53, esp. 550.

[23] Crawford to Speaker of the House, Dec. 21, 1820, ibid., 580-81; *House Doc.,* No. 32 (serial 48), 16th Cong., 2d sess. The military and naval totals showed $6,798,000 and $3,428,000 in the "corrected" estimates. Crawford noted that after he had made the correction the original error was seized upon for the purpose of "producing mistrust of all the treasury statements." His opponents, he said, would "produce as many discords as skill goaded on by malignity can possibly effect." Crawford to Tait, April 1, 1821, Tait.

necessity for a standing army was recognized, and *ad hominem* arguments were avoided. In the House the vote on engrossing for a third reading was 109-47, and the measure passed, 109-48, on January 23. There is no recorded vote on Senate passage.[24] The reduction of the army by 40 percent would result in a considerable saving.

While the army reduction bill was under consideration the House ways and means committee seemed as confused as everyone else about the government income and expenditures for 1821. In reports of February 6 and 28 it indicated incomes of slightly more than $17,000,000 and $16,355,000; expenses were estimated at $17,000,000 and then set at $15,457,000. Its recommendation for a $4,500,000 loan was later raised to $5,000,000. The committee stressed retrenchments of $2,130,000 in 1820, and $2,317,000 for 1821, or $4,447,000 for the Sixteenth Congress. The effect of the reduction of the army would continue to be felt; the saving in 1821 of $561,000 was expected to reach $1,000,000 by 1822. The 1821 cut in the civil list was given as $116,508; in the military, $1,481,000; in the naval, $720,000 including $500,000 of the gradual increase fund.[25]

The actual appropriation for the military establishment was $4,272,000 plus an earlier appropriated $320,000 and an unexpended balance of $450,000—a total of $5,042,000. The pension appropriation of $1,200,000 was also unexpended for the previous year, but when that was deducted the military establishment had only $3,842,000 for ordinary expenses. This was a cut of $1,318,000 from the previous year. The naval appropriation was reduced $334,000 (not counting the gradual increase item) to $2,215,000.[26]

24 *Annals,* 16th Cong., 2d sess., 933, 936-37, passim; 3 *Stat.* 615-16. The peacetime military establishment had been set at 10,000 by the act of March 3, 1815; important organizational changes had been made on April 24, 1816, and other minor ones on April 14, 1818. Ibid., 224-25, 297-99, 426-27.

25 *ASPF,* 3:677-78. The act of April 29, 1816, providing $1,000,000 per year for the gradual increase of the navy, was repealed on March 3, 1821. 3 *Stat.* 642. See also *Niles' Weekly Register* 20 (March 17, 1821):34-35, 37-38.

26 3 *Stat.* 633-34, 634-35. These figures do not agree with the ones given above from the House ways and means committee report, and both differ from the figures given in *House Doc.,* No. 33 (serial 48), 16th Cong., 2d sess. which purports to give the appropriations for 1821. One encounters a comparable situation for almost every year: additional appropriations were sometimes made after the regular appropriation bills were passed; obligations against departments had not always been met by the first of the year, so that some expenditures would show in the secretary's report of the following year; retrenchment sometimes seems to have been

Crawford had asked for $7,000,000 in loans to cover the deficit of the budget, but with the retrenchments of about $2,300,000 (including the elimination of the gradual increase fund for the navy) and the $5,000,000 borrowing authorization, the treasury would have at least $300,000 more than required—if the ways and means committee was correct in its estimates. Crawford suspected the retrenchment was in fact less than $2,000,000, and thus the authorized loan would not meet the authorized expenditures. He hoped there would not be any considerable deficit for the year; if that were the case, there was good ground to believe no further retrenchment in the civil, military, or naval departments would be required or effected.[27] About three months later he expressed the opinion that the defense establishments were "very moderate," though much greater than in the prewar years. If the "general impression" of the war period that there had been overreduction was correct, they "cannot be too large now." But if the revenue did not increase, Congress would have to face cutting expenses again. He feared that an "executive reduction" would be preceded by much diversity of opinion but did not doubt such a recommendation would be made if the revenue was inadequate.[28] Crawford seemed to have no desire to retrench for the sake of retrenchment; he wanted the government to operate as nearly as possible within its means and to proceed with the payment of the public debt as soon as circumstances permitted.

The secretary believed, however, that the "visionary reports" of the ways and means committee would not be realized, that his own calculation might be "too sanguine," and that he might again be charged with misrepresentations in order to break down the army. Should expenditures exceed income, Crawford would

calculated on the reduction of estimates rather than on the appropriations of the preceding year, and unexpended balances seem not always to have been handled in the same way. The appropriation figures used in this chapter are taken directly from the appropriation laws, and the pension and gradual increase funds are deducted from what might be called the ordinary expenditures. Many writers have been careless about determining the actual appropriations. Total appropriations for 1821 were $15,457,000.

27 Crawford to Tait, April 1, 1821, Tait. All of the $5 million loan was taken by the BUS at an average premium of 5.59 percent on 5 percent stock redeemable at the option of the government after January 1, 1835.

28 Crawford to Thomas Spalding, July 9, 1821, Crawford, NYH. During and after the retrenchment period there was much cabinet, congressional, and newspaper discussion of army and defense contracts, commitments, and obligations.

propose measures to increase the revenue, but the responsibility for deciding whether the revenue should be increased or the expenses reduced rested with Congress. There was no indication that the revenue for the next year would be greater than that of the current one, and he thought an excise of "considerable extent, accompanied by the prohibition of foreign spirits" would be one of the measures adopted. He detailed some other possible internal taxes and noted the probability that woolen stuffs, worsted, and blankets would be placed in the same duty category as cotton goods. Such an alteration of the tariff, he said, would promote the growth of domestic manufactures without "nurturing them in a hotbed." Industries would be indirectly encouraged while Congress would confine itself—as many believed it should —to levying duties for the raising of revenue. But if Congress should take a different view, its measures would be fairly executed and tested by experience.[29]

The revenue had taken an upswing in the second and third quarters of 1821, and in October Calhoun had indicated he would exercise every possible economy, feeling it was of the highest importance that no loan be authorized at the next session of Congress. The estimates, he said, would be regulated by the state of the treasury.[30]

Monroe, who had told Crawford he would recommend internal taxes if the state of the revenue demanded such, reported on December 5 that the "extreme point of depression" of the revenue had occurred in the first quarter of 1821; since that time income from duties had exceeded that of the corresponding quarters of the preceding year, and the improvement was expected to continue. The existing tariff, he believed, afforded sufficient protection to strengthen the bonds of union by promoting manufactures. He did not advocate internal taxation, and his remarks that a moderate additional duty on certain articles would increase the revenue "without being liable to any serious objection" were an echo of Crawford's of the previous month.[31]

By December Crawford's pessimism had changed to closely reined optimism. His report of December 10 reviewed the

29 Crawford to Charles Jared Ingersoll, Nov. 3, 1821, Ingersoll.
30 Calhoun to Monroe, Oct. 14, 1821, AHA *Annual Report*, 1899, 2:199-201.
31 Adams, *Memoirs*, 5:452, says that at Monroe's request the paragraph in the President's message dealing with economic matters had been drafted by Crawford.

receipts of 1819, 1820, and 1821, showed the substantial improvement of the revenue, and indicated that the treasury on January 1, 1822, would have $490,000 more than had been anticipated. The income for 1822 was estimated at $16,110,000 and expenditures at $14,947,000; after satisfying existing charges the balance on January 1, 1823, should be slightly more than $671,000. The $300,000 deficiency in the appropriation for the gradual increase of the navy would be provided by the more than $300,000 in the War Department estimates for arrearages of revolutionary pensions and of the Indian department estimates which would not be included in the projected expenditures for 1823.[32]

Much attention was devoted to the public debt, which was estimated at $93,400,000 on January 1, 1822. No part (except for interest and reimbursement on the 6 percent deferred stock) of the annual $10,000,000 for the sinking fund was included in the estimates. On January 1, 1825, and the three succeeding years sums due would greatly exceed the amount in the fund applicable to redemption. Since the 5 percent stock was higher than the 6 and 7 percent, he proposed a stock conversion plan for the $24,000,000 redeemable in 1825 and 1826 which would save more than $2,000,000 in interest. If this was thought inexpedient or impractical, an equal or greater saving could be effected from 1825 to 1828 by borrowing on the first of each of those years a sum equal to the difference between the amount redeemable and the portion of the sinking fund applicable to redemption. The 5 percent stock so created would be redeemable as would the 5 percent "exchange" stock, and if it was—as at present—5 percent above par there would be an additional saving.

If the expected revenue increase did not materialize and expenses should exceed income, then existing impositions should be increased or the sinking fund should be reduced. Many articles which paid 15 percent ad valorem duty ought, in justice as well as policy, to pay 25 percent—the cotton duty. The change would probably add $1,000,000 to the customs duties. If the

---

[32] He pointed out that his previous report had estimated revenue for 1821 from land sales at $1,600,000, while the ways and means committee had thought only half that amount would come in from that source. The relief act had cut the amount, which in the first three quarters reached $900,000 and was estimated at $1,300,000 for the year. *ASPF*, 3:682-84. The factory system of trading with the Indians was abolished on May 6, 1822. 3 *Stat.* 679-80.

sinking fund was cut, it might be satisfactory to know that an annual appropriation of $8,000,000 would extinguish all but a very small fraction of the debt by 1839. If the fund was reduced, an exchange of the $36,000,000 of 6 percent stock for 5 percent might be effected in 1822—if the current price continued. This exchange would mean an annual saving in interest of $360,000.[33]

The ways and means committee considered the proposed stock exchange advantageous to the government and to stockholders; the act of April 20, 1822, authorized the exchange of $12,000,000 of the 7 percent and $14,000,000 of the 6 percent. But hopes for exchange were far too sanguine: by December only $56,705 of the sixes and sevens had been exchanged for fives. Crawford thought the increased demands for capital for commercial enterprise and the rise in interest rates had prevented success of the project. He doubted, correctly, that the program would be any more successful the next year.[34]

The secretary's estimate of military expenditures for 1822 was $5,108,000; those for the navy would amount to $2,452,000. The Senate was in a drawn-out controversy with the President over appointment problems stemming from the army reduction of 1821, and the original appropriation for the military was $3,642,000 plus an unexpended balance of $419,000. Nearly $220,000 of the balance was in the pension item, and the total pension money amounted to $2,174,000, leaving only $1,887,000 for ordinary army allocation. The total naval appropriation was increased about $50,000 to $2,265,000.[35] Almost immediately after the appointment squabble was ended Congress voted an additional $1,286,000 for the military, bringing the total for 1822 to $3,173,000 or about $669,000 less than for 1821.[36]

The revenue improved far beyond expectations, and Crawford, giving his annual report on December 23, 1822, reviewed the revenue and expenses for 1821 and 1822 and made his estimates for 1823. In this instance he projected the estimates into 1824,

---

33 *ASPF*, 3:684-85; *Niles' Weekly Register* 21 (Dec. 15, 1821):249-52.

34 *House Doc.*, No. 12 (serial 76), 17th Cong., 2d sess.; 3 *Stat.* 663-65.

35 *ASPF*, 3:684, 807, 808; 3 *Stat.* 652-53, 676-77. As often happened, the inaccuracy of revenue estimates received some attention. The chairman of the House ways and means committee said no secretary had been accurate but that Crawford had come closer than his immediate predecessors. Crawford was, however, less accurate than the committee estimates of 1821. *ASPF*, 3:809.

36 3 *Stat.* 686-88 (May 7, 1822). The army appointments are discussed in the following chapter.

1825, and 1826.[37] The actual receipts for 1821, including the $5,000,000 loan, had been $19,574,000; for the first three quarters of 1822 they had been $14,700,000; with the expected receipts of the last quarter the total would be $19,745,000 or $3,600,000 more than anticipated. With the balance carryover and expenses at $18,279,000 the treasury would have $3,148,000 on January 1, 1823. Commitments would reduce this to $1,916,000. The estimated expenditures of $15,060,000 for 1823 were $7,957,000 less than the estimated income. The expenditures included $5,602,000 for the public debt (interest), $2,723,000 for the navy, $5,134,000 for the military, and $1,599,000 for the civil list.[38]

The projections for the succeeding three years showed there would be small deficits for 1825 and 1826. To meet these extraordinary demands on the treasury it was believed "expedient that the revenue should be increased." This could be done by a "judicious revision" of the tariff. Present difficulties resulting from different duties on woolen, cotton, flax, and hemp articles might be overcome by making those articles (and those of silk) or articles "of which any of these materials is a component part" subject to a 25 percent ad valorem duty. In addition, the duties on glass, paper, iron, lead, and articles of iron and lead could be increased. Crawford believed such an increase would lead to ample domestic production of those articles, except silken goods. These increased duties should be continued until the public debt of $91,000,000 was paid; then, in time of peace, the revenue should be decreased by $10,000,000, the amount that went annually to the sinking fund.[39]

The receipts for 1822 and the treasury balance of January 1 of that year had meant $21,914,000 for use in 1822; the expenses of $17,677,000 had left a $4,327,000 balance on January 1, 1823. The report of the last day of the year showed almost identical receipts for 1823 ($20,444,000), expenditures of only $15,317,000, and a balance after commitments yet to be met of $6,467,000. Projected expenses for 1824 were approximately those of 1823,

[37] There had been some discussion of making this projection in the financial portion of the President's message, but it was thought to be more appropriate to the secretary's report. Adams, *Memoirs*, 6:107-9 (Nov. 27, 1822).

[38] *ASPF*, 4:6-8. Actual appropriations were: $3,009,000 for the military (plus $1,874,000 for pensions) and $2,317,000 for the navy. 3 *Stat.* 748-49, 749-50, 783-84, 763-64.

[39] *ASPF*, 4:9; *House Doc.*, No. 12 (serial 76), 17th Cong., 2d sess.

thus permitting an anticipated balance of $9,793,000 on January 1, 1825. Authorization to purchase the 7 percent stock was requested, and all estimates assumed no extraordinary expenses. If Congress deemed it advisable to give increased expansion to the navy or to aid in internal improvement projects, means to that end could be found by carrying out a "judicious revision" of the tariff which had been recommended by the preceding annual report. Crawford said that further consideration of that proposal had strengthened his opinion that such duties would not be "onerous to the community, would be advantageous to the revenue, salutary to commerce, and beneficial to the manufactures of the country."[40]

In 1824 Crawford again made his report on the last day of the year. Normal receipts for 1824 remained about the same as those of 1823, but the total income had been greatly increased by the $5,000,000 loan to satisfy demands stemming from the Adams-Onis treaty and another $5,000,000 authorization for purchasing 6 percent 1812 stocks.[41] Ordinary expenditures were reasonably stationary and the treasury could once again carry out the program, established just after Crawford took office, for retiring the debt. Crawford thought the tariff of May 22, 1824, would increase the revenue and his projection for the 1825 income was close to the mark. He recommended for 1825 nearly $12,000,000 (including more than $7,650,000 for payment of the principal) for retiring the debt and noted that with a continued annual payment of $10,000,000 the nation would be debt free by the end of 1835. In this last report as secretary Crawford reviewed the treasury's handling of the debt since he took office. On January 1, 1817, the nation owed $123,492,000 of which $115,258,000 was funded at an average interest rate of 5.565 percent. On January 1, 1825, the debt would be $86,045,000 and the average interest rate 5.2325 percent. The principal had been reduced $37,447,000 and the interest rate 0.3325 percent—an

---

[40] *ASPF*, 4:374-77 (quotation on p. 377). Funds allocated to the army were no longer the subject of controversy. Appropriations for 1824 were: military, $3,114,000 (plus $1,505,000 for pensions), and navy, $2,469,000. 4 *Stat.* 8-9, 22, 36-37, 20-22. The tariff was changed by the act of May 22, 1824. Ibid., 25-30.

[41] The first loan was sanctioned on May 24, 1824, the second two days later. 4 *Stat.* 33-34, 73-75. Slightly more than half of the second loan was receivable by the treasury in 1824. Both loans were taken by the BUS at par and 4.5 percent interest.

annual saving of more than $275,000 based on the existing debt.[42]

Crawford also summarized the monetary income and outlay for the eight years since January 1, 1817. In that time, he said, the treasury had a "total means" of $210,276,000 (including the January 1, 1817, balance of $22,000,000 and subsequent loans of a little more than $16,000,000) and total expenditures had been $205,769,000. Major categories of expenses had been: public debt, $101,366,000; revolutionary pensions, $9,400,000; fortifications, $4,200,000; navy increase, $6,000,000; claims from the War of 1812, $4,500,000; Florida treaty claims, $4,891,000; and all others—the temporary expenses—$75,400,000 or $9,425,000 per year.[43]

Most of the eight years had been troublesome ones, troubled either by a scarcity of revenue or political acrimony. Crawford's record in "getting and spending" operations was a creditable one, but it perhaps lacked the distinction of his administrative and organizational efforts. Whether his occasional lack of forcefulness was rooted in a deep-seated belief of the coordinate nature of the three branches of the government or whether alleged primacy of Congress in monetary matters was rationalization for his unwillingness to assume stronger leadership cannot be definitely determined. This might well be the dilemma of many politicians—and the wellspring of much political philosophy—but statements by Crawford prior to his tenure as secretary of treasury indicate his actions were shaped by his beliefs, not his beliefs by his actions.

Three of the most important issues before the country during Crawford's secretaryship were the BUS, the tariff, and internal improvements, all of which touched rather directly the intake and outgo of the treasury or the conduct of the fiscal operations of the government. There is no disagreement concerning Crawford's favorable attitude toward the BUS, but most writers on the period seem uncertain about Crawford's position on the tariff and internal improvements or declare him opposed to both.

---

42 *ASPF*, 5:151-55. Military appropriations for 1825 were $3,386,000 (plus $1,248,000 for pensions and $549,000 for carrying out treaties with the Indians); the navy received $2,585,000. 4 *Stat.* 82-83, 92, 92-94, 83-85. Joseph Nourse, in one of the documents accompanying Richard Rush's first report as secretary of treasury, indicated the public debt on January 1, 1825, was $83,711,000. *ASPF*, 5:255-56. For Rush's report, dated December 22, 1825, see ibid., 240-47.

43 *ASPF*, 5:156.

Crawford's annual and special reports as secretary of treasury, his recommendations, and his letters indicate that he did not look with disfavor on the tariff as a means of revenue—though he and many others recognized the uncertainty of the source and the consequent difficulty of making reasonably accurate estimates of the return from such duties. Nor did he object to a degree of protection, incidental or otherwise, which would permit and promote the development of domestic manufacturing. On several occasions he recommended a change in the duties both for revenue and protection purposes. He was later vigorously opposed to protectionism for its own sake, but while he was in the national government he would classify as an economic nationalist.[44]

Crawford did, however, oppose the system of drawbacks, or the refunding of import duties on goods which were later re-exported, and as a senator he had prevailed on a colleague to introduce a bill for the repeal of drawbacks. Crawford's opposition was based on the relationship of drawbacks to wartime commerce; he thought they provided an increased incentive to engage in such trade and that the trade jeopardized the United States' chances of remaining free of European entanglements.[45] Jefferson agreed with Crawford, denounced the American transplantation of the British system, attached great importance to repeal as a means of preserving peace, and hoped Crawford might be able to effect repeal.[46] But the system continued, and the sums payable fluctuated rather erratically, from 12 percent of the accrued duties in 1822 to 20 percent in 1823 and 16 percent in 1824.[47] Such variations simply added to the problem of making accurate estimates of the amount of revenue available from the customs.

That Crawford was opposed to internal improvements at

[44] Crawford had written in 1816 to the consul at Bordeaux that he thought the manufacturing interests were sufficiently protected to secure their growth and ultimate maturity. "Perhaps," he said, "we have gone too far but it was erring on the safe side." Crawford to William Lee, May 19, 1816, Gallatin.

[46] Crawford to Jefferson, May 31, 1816, Jefferson, MDLC.

[46] Jefferson to Crawford, June 20, 1816, ibid. In correspondence with Crawford concerning Virginia claims growing out of the War of 1812 Jefferson said the money was needed to carry on the work at the University of Virginia. Jefferson to Crawford, April 8, 1821, ibid.; Crawford to Jefferson, April 16, 1821, Jefferson (University of Virginia).

[47] Richard Rush to Speaker of the House, March 15, 1826, *House Doc.*, No. 132 (serial 138), 19th Cong., 1st sess.

national expense is open to serious question, if not outright denial. He believed that the question might be "easily settled by precedent" and that a system would be introduced "gradually, if not directly at once."[48] During his tenure as secretary he thought it the function of the administrative branch to execute the will of Congress in this matter, showed keen awareness of Monroe's sensitivity on the issue, and was fully cognizant of the political maneuvering involved even in the locating of any important improvement.

Crawford's reference to precedent doubtless concerned the activities of the government in connection with the National Road. Most of the decisions on the road as far as Wheeling, Virginia, were made before Crawford took office. However, he did have some discretionary authority, and the location, building, and maintenance of the section between Cumberland, Maryland, and Wheeling presented some lingering problems. Crawford himself rode over alternate routes for the road between Brownsville on the Monongahela River and Washington, Pennsylvania, and established a three-stage procedure for resolving the differences between the superintendents east and west of the river; he ordered expenditures for sidewalls and masonry work reduced or eliminated; he directed steps be taken to prevent people from damaging the road by dragging logs, pulling down sidewalls over bridges, digging down banks, stopping drainage ditches, leaving parts of trees on the road, and building fences and houses on the right of way. After considerable delay contracts for the Brownsville-Washington segment were let for approximately two thirds of the estimated $9,500 per mile. Half of the costs were to be paid in western funds; if Congress at the next session should provide for an extension of the road, "western funds may be applied with the utmost propriety to that great object," thus affording relief to the public debtors in that area. The secretary indicated it was already difficult for Monroe to avoid giving approval to any law appropriating money for a road or canal, but it might be more difficult to induce him to sign a bill embracing a system. No matter, he said, "a few years in the age of nations is nothing. A system will be introduced gradually, if not directly at once."[49]

48 Crawford to James Tallmadge, July 12, 1819, enclosure in Tallmadge to John W. Taylor, July 17, 1819, John W. Taylor Papers (NYH).

The next session of Congress did provide for an extension of the road, granting authority to proceed with the location of the main road and some branches as far as the capital of Illinois. Crawford believed location of the road would probably increase the value of the lands in the area by an amount equal to the cost of the road and would make possible government reservation of the land necessary for the road without collision with individual rights. Though the law required the road to be run as straight as possible, Crawford said "he would see to make it run so as to pass through the seats of government of the three States of Ohio, Indiana, and Illinois."[50] A year later Crawford suggested to Monroe that the road not be located beyond Zanesville even if the appropriation was available; a bill directing that the road pass through the three capitals had passed the last session of the Senate but had not been acted on by the House because of lack of time. Then, too, the people of Kentucky, Tennessee, and Mississippi favored giving the road a southerly direction from Zanesville; pressures for the western and southern directions he thought "nearly in equipoise." If he was right, would it not be better to ask no funds for location beyond Zanesville? The measure had originated with Congress without any recommendation from the executive; would it not be prudent to avoid all interference with the legislative will? He was inclined to this opinion on general principles and the "particular relation in which you stand to the subject, furnishes an additional motive in its favor."[51]

Crawford apparently had no difficulty persuading the President, for five days later he informed Abner Lacock that even though the commissioners had the authority to proceed with the location of the road the President did not see any point in continuing

---

49 Crawford to Thomas Worthington, Nov. 23, 1816, Worthington; Crawford to Henry St. George Tucker (House Committee on Roads and Canals), March 20, 1818, Series E, Vol. 6; Crawford to David Shriver, June 22, 1819, Read; Crawford to Monroe, July 2, 1819, Monroe, MDLC; Crawford to James Tallmadge, July 12, 1819; *ASPM*, 2:586, 798. Henry Clay, in keeping with his promise, wrote Crawford a detailed letter about construction and other problems connected with the road after he had traveled over it on his way home. Clay to Crawford, May 15, 1818, Golding.

50 Crawford to Henry Storrs (House Committee on Roads and Canals), April 6, 1820, Series E, Vol. 6; Adams, *Memoirs*, 5:155-56 (June 20, 1820). Crawford noted that the exemption from toll of carriages with broad tires might be useful in reducing the expense of repair and tend to the gradual reduction of the cost of transportation on the National Road.

51 Crawford to Monroe, Aug. 3, 1821, Gratz.

the location to Zanesville—if this meant asking Congress for an
additional appropriation for work already done. The propriety
of making the three state capitals fixed points in the location was
"so manifest" that no reasonable doubt could be entertained of
its being done at the next session of Congress. Thus, location
should certainly not proceed beyond Zanesville. He emphasized
Monroe's previous indisposition toward appropriations for internal improvements, thought it better to avoid the necessity
of asking Congress for such money, and felt the appropriation
would be made with "better grace" if left entirely to Congress.
Although the President had "convinced himself" of the constitutionality of such appropriations, there was still no doubt
that he would rather avoid the necessity of asking for the money.[52]

Crawford may not have been an advocate of internal improvements, but nothing indicates he was opposed to using federal
funds for the building of roads and canals. He would throw all
the initiative for such projects on Congress; he saw the significant
political implications of the problem; he recognized the economic
value of the roads; he expected a system of internal improvements to come; and he was well attuned to Monroe's sensitivities
on the subject—and at times he may have attuned Monroe to
his position.

On April 4, 1818, House resolutions had called on the secretary
of war and the secretary of treasury to prepare a plan of opening
and improving roads and making canals, to submit a statement
of works that had been begun by states, private companies, and
corporations to which government aid might be subscribed, and
to supply all pertinent information that might be valuable in
the determination of congressional policy. Wide publicity was
given to the resolutions so that materials could be sent to the
treasury for preparing the report. And Crawford asked Gallatin,
when selecting books in France for the treasury library, to include
books on canals. Such works might be useful when a "system of
internal improvements shall be commenced upon national
principles." He expected nothing of the kind from the present
Congress but thought such action was not distant: "Every new
State will add to the number of advocates of the measure."[53]

52 Crawford to Abner Lacock, Aug. 8, 1821, Miscellaneous, HSP.
53 *Annals,* 15th Cong., 1st sess., 1649-50, 1678-79; *Niles' Weekly Register* 14 (May
30, 1818):240 (for treasury communication of May 26, 1818); Crawford to Joseph
Brooks, Jan. 21, 1819, Autograph File, Houghton; Edward Tiffin to Secretary of

Apparently Calhoun drafted the report, and when Crawford returned it to Monroe he noted that Calhoun had used "very strong expressions." Further, when the delicacy of the President's position on internal improvements was considered, the general tenor of the report might be termed "exceptionable." The resolutions required a plan—a designation of roads and canals, already begun or which would be useful to begin—not arguments proving any duty of the government or the usefulness of internal improvements generally. These grounds, said Crawford, were assumed in the resolutions and needed no argument in their favor. The offending remarks were removed before the final report (January 7, 1819) was sent to the House, though the secretary of war did discuss the general utility of a good system of military roads and canals—they were militarily indispensable as well as being important to commerce, manufacturing, agriculture, and "political prosperity." He thought discussion of the constitutional question improper under the resolution but suggested Congress direct that a survey and estimate be made.[54]

The survey bill did not come until 1824, and Crawford seems to have been little involved with the question after 1819. Besides, the government already had too many financial problems. Whether an abundance of funds would have led Crawford to increasingly stronger support of internal improvements can only be conjectured, but at no time did he actively oppose the federal government's participation in this area. He never raised—in this period—the question of constitutionality; he accepted the congressional sentiment on the issue and felt certain that a national system would be instituted. After he left Washington he thought the Constitution should be amended, either to deny the power or to expressly grant it. He did not wish powers to be usurped, for there was no limit to usurped powers.[55]

Crawford's record in connection with national finances is indeed creditable, particularly in light of the unprecedented problems faced by the federal government, and in the performance of his primary duties his stand on the major issues before the nation became reasonably clear and he seemed to act so as not

Treasury, June 25, 1818 (draft), ISH; Crawford to Gallatin, May 2, 1818, Adams, *Gallatin Writings*, 2:65-66.
54 Crawford to Monroe, [Dec. 1818], Monroe Microfilm, Series 2; *ASPM*, 2:533-37. The report bore only Calhoun's name.
55 See final chapter.

to injure unnecessarily the sensibilities of his chief, Monroe. The fifth President used his department heads, individually and collectively, more effectively than any of his predecessors to hammer out decisions of the executive branch. There was no strict departmentalization of advisory functions—or even administrative functions, since one secretary might act for one or two others during the summer months—and cabinet discussions might be long and sometimes heated. Monroe always made and assumed responsibility for the decisions, and it was not always easy to reconcile the views of such able and strong-willed men as John Quincy Adams, John C. Calhoun, William H. Crawford, and William Wirt. The so-called major issues led to little difficulty; lesser matters—often correctly or incorrectly linked to the political ambitions of the cabinet members—brought division and acrimony among the presidential advisers.

9

Presidential Adviser

CRAWFORD HAD been uncertain about remaining in the government beyond Madison's term until Monroe visited him in January 1817. The President-elect wanted Crawford to continue in the treasury and advanced political reasons (unspecified by Monroe or Crawford) for not moving the Georgian to the State Department, which was then thought of as the heir-apparent position. Crawford decided then to sacrifice personal interests, but he conditioned his remaining as secretary of treasury on congressional acceptance of the recommendations of the four secretaries concerning accounts and accounting procedures and on compensation to Georgia for claims connected with cession of her western lands under the 1802 agreement with the central government. There is no doubt that Monroe was anxious for Crawford to be in the cabinet; on March 3 he expressed to James Barbour the hope that the legislation would be approved and noted, "You know that the continuation of Mr. C. in the admn. depends upon it. I trust you will not fail to carry it through. Intimate this to Mr Macon & other friends." The following day he informed Crawford of the passage of the law; this, he said, will "avail your country of your services in the administration to which I shall nominate you tomorrow."[1]

Monroe sent Crawford's nomination to the Senate on March 5, and, in keeping with his expressed desire to make the government more national than it had been under Madison, he nominated John Quincy Adams (then minister to England) as secretary of state and Isaac Shelby (Kentucky) as secretary of war. Henry Clay, no more interested in the secretaryship of war than he had been earlier, could not be considered for secretary of state without the loss of Crawford's services, for as Crawford said "every reason assigned against my going into the State Department operated stronger against Mr. Clay than against me." The Senate approved all nominations, but Crawford was the only regular cabinet member in Washington for several months, and he thought Monroe was "not likely to repose on a bed of roses" during his presidential term.[2]

Filling the cabinet was a slow process. There were serious doubts about Shelby's acceptance, but Crawford had said nothing when Richard M. Johnson, also of Kentucky, was mentioned for the war post. Near the end of April Crawford knew nothing about progress toward making that appointment, though he thought George W. Campbell (former secretary of treasury) would be a better choice than Johnson, William Henry Harrison, Return J. Meigs, or Lewis Cass, all westerners. He had determined, however, never to obtrude his sentiments upon any matter unconnected with the treasury and had avoided introducing any subject that might cause Monroe to express his views on the principal appointments still to be made. But on May 26 Monroe called at Crawford's office and they discussed appointments. Shelby had declined the War Department, John Quincy Adams had agreed to become secretary of state, and Harrison would be appointed secretary of war—if that official was to come from the West. Crawford, when asked, said the people of the country were unconcerned about the place of residence of cabinet members; they expected the President to appoint men qualified to discharge the duties assigned to them. Already the War Department had been offered to two westerners, and certainly Crawford would not appoint Harrison. With the hero of Tippecanoe as secretary, "excessive vanity and inordinate love of noisy, empty popularity" would influence every action of the office. Flatterers would be favored and "every meritorious and independent officer" would be driven from the service. Monroe assented to Crawford's views; he would lay aside geographical considerations. Crawford then mentioned David R.

1 Crawford to Gallatin, March 12, 1817, Adams, *Gallatin Writings*, 2:23-25; Monroe to Barbour, March 3, 1817, Barbour; Monroe to Crawford, March 4, 1817, Golding. The laws are both dated March 3, 1817; the one on organization and accounts is discussed in chapter 6. The other, 3 *Stat.* 359-60, provided for paying Georgia a sum equal to the amount of the Mississippi stock sold or received in payment for public lands in Mississippi until payment totaled $1,250,000. Not more than $335,000 was to be paid until some Mississippi stock was redeemed. Payments to Georgia began the next month. William Rabun to Legislature of Georgia, Nov. 3, 1817, *Niles' Weekly Register* 13 (Nov. 29, Dec. 13, 1817):217, 243.

2 Monroe to Jackson, March 1, 1817, Hamilton, *Monroe Writings*, 6:4-5; Crawford to Gallatin, March 12, 1817, Adams, *Gallatin Writings*, 2:26-27; Senate *Executive Journal*, 3:89, 91; Crawford to Gallatin, Oct. 27, 1817, Gallatin.

Williams, William Lowndes, and John C. Calhoun—all South Carolinians. While all of these might decline the post, offers to them would remove any blame from Monroe if the office was not filled by a good man. Crawford hoped the offer would be made first to Williams and then to Calhoun, but he did not know the order Monroe might decide upon.[3] Whether Monroe consulted further with Crawford is not known; Lowndes declined, but Calhoun accepted. Ten years later Monroe did not remember the conversations with members of the administration concerning Calhoun's choice, but "It is probable that I conferred with all of them, and my impression is strong that none made any objection to it. I am satisfied that Mr. Crawford made none."[4]

In November, a month after Calhoun's appointment, the cabinet was completed with William Wirt's acceptance of the attorney generalship. Wirt, who had a large family, found it difficult to live in Washington on his salary—government service meant a great decrease of income from his private practice. Wirt's hints of resigning led Monroe to ask Crawford and Adams whether he should, by special message, recommend an increase for all heads of departments. Both agreed he should not; any such measure should be spontaneous on the part of Congress. Wirt remained and seems to have had a high regard for his fellow cabinet members; especially did he praise Crawford and President Monroe.[5]

Monroe had not nationalized his cabinet, but he had secured an extremely able group of advisers and administrators. Only the secretaryship of navy was held by a man of second-rate abilities, and only that position changed hands during Monroe's presidency. Benjamin W. Crowninshield (Massachusetts), appointed by Madison in 1814, was replaced by Smith Thompson of New York in 1818. Samuel L. Southard (New Jersey) accepted

[3] Crawford to Gallatin, April 23, 1817, Adams, *Gallatin Writings*, 2:35; Crawford to Bartlett Yancey, May 27, 1817, Bartlett Yancey Papers (UNC). Crawford had no objection to Richard Rush succeeding Adams as minister to England.

[4] Monroe to Calhoun, Dec. 16, 1827, Hamilton, *Monroe Writings*, 7:137.

[5] Adams, *Memoirs*, 4:83 (April 28, 1818); Wirt to Dabney Carr, Oct. 12, 1819, John P. Kennedy, *Memoirs of the Life of William Wirt* . . . , 2 vols. in 1 (Philadelphia, 1860), 2:84. By the act of February 20, 1819 (3 *Stat.* 484), salaries were set as follows: each of the four secretaries, $6,000; attorney general, $3,500; postmaster general, $4,000; chief justice, $5,000; and each associate justice, $4,500. The raises were retroactive to January 1.

the post after Thompson's elevation to the Supreme Court in 1823. Thompson was the most able of the three, but his role as presidential adviser was far less important than those of Adams, Calhoun, Crawford, and Wirt.

The President and department heads often left Washington during the hot summer season, and nearly every year one of the secretaries would fill in for another who was away from the city. In 1818 Crawford acted for Calhoun, and the following summer Adams doubled for the South Carolinian. No problems seem to have stemmed from this arrangement, since each secretary availed himself of the counsel of other members of the government whenever they were available. In consulting others, they were simply following Monroe's practice; he made unprecedented collective use of his department heads. Naturally there were differences of opinion and maneuvering for political advantage, but not even the dispute over Jackson's invasion of Florida generated, at the time, any real animosity among the cabinet members.

Relations with other nations were the most frequently discussed topics of cabinet deliberations; continental and hemispheric matters were first priority, with problems arising from the revolt of the Spanish American colonies and from ineffectiveness of Spanish administration in Florida being most persistent and in the final analysis most disruptive of party solidarity. By 1817 adventurers, freebooters, pirates, slave traders, and others of numerous nationalities were using the flags of the revolting colonies—as well as those of other countries—to shield their extralegal and illegal actions under the pretext of helping the "patriots" to discard Spanish rule. In 1817 a filibustering group, under the leadership of Gregor MacGregor, seized Amelia Island, a move that appeared preliminary to the occupation of Florida. To prevent Fernandina, the island port, from becoming a center for smuggling slaves into the United States, to protect the apprehensive citizens of southern Georgia, and to secure the southern border of the country, United States naval forces were sent to the island in the latter part of the year.[6] The action was

6 Many contemporary letters dealing with this incident are no longer available in the originals, but a rather large number of them are in *Niles' Weekly Register* 13, esp. July 16, Dec. 27, 1817; Jan. 3, 17, 1818. In this chapter, since primary emphasis is upon positions of the cabinet members (especially those of Crawford),

justified by the provisions of the act prohibiting the slave trade and by the joint resolution of the Senate and House of January 5, 1811 (and the act of the same date) authorizing the President to occupy any part or the whole of the territory east of the Perdido River and south of Georgia to counteract any attempted occupation by a foreign power.

Don Luis de Onis, Spanish minister to the United States, protested the Amelia Island action in a style which Monroe termed "outrageously insulting" and which seemed to countenance the idea that Spain was desirous of pushing a quarrel with the United States in hope of drawing the European allies into it on the Spanish side. Crawford feared the United States would be charged with duplicity, since the MacGregor "army" had been organized in Baltimore, and in December he agreed with the President that the United States should withdraw from the island. But he soon moved to the position, originally held by Adams and Calhoun, which Monroe stated in a special message to Congress on January 13, 1818: the island will be held, subject to negotiations with Spain. The cabinet unanimously rejected the British offer of mediation on the grounds, suggested by Crawford and Monroe, that differences between the United States and Spain did not threaten war. Meanwhile, Henry Clay —who seemed to want to embarrass the administration whenever possible—was goading John Forsyth (Georgia), chairman of the House Committee on Foreign Affairs, to sponsor a motion authorizing Monroe to take possession of East Florida. Crawford thought the possibility of Forsyth's proposing a resolution "contrary to the policy of the nation" was "so ridiculous" that he had dismissed it until Monroe asked him to confer with Forsyth. He was unable to dissuade Forsyth from presenting the motion; he then talked with committee member James Barbour—also at Monroe's request—and estimated correctly that the committee would not support its chairman.[7]

<hr/>

few references will be given to the presidential messages, treaties, laws, and congressional action. Documentation on these matters may be found at the appropriate places in James D. Richardson, ed., *A Compilation of the Messages and Papers of the Presidents, 1789-1902*, 10 vols. (Washington, D.C., 1903); Hunter Miller, ed., *Treaties and Other International Acts of the United States*, 8 vols. (Washington, D.C., 1931-1948); *ASPFA; Annals; Statutes;* and the congressional documents series.

7 Adams, *Memoirs*, 4:31-32, 51, 57-60, 66-67; Monroe to Crawford, Jan. 29, 1818, Crawford, MDLC; Crawford to Monroe, March 23, 1818, Monroe, MDLC.

The seizure of Amelia Island was but prelude. Several times, in December 1817, the cabinet had discussed the border situation, and on the day after Christmas it was decided to order Major General Edmund P. Gaines to assemble all the regular troops he could gather, as well as the Georgia militia, for the purpose of reducing the Seminole, pursuing them into East Florida if they should take refuge there. Andrew Jackson was then ordered to move immediately to the seat of war and take command. By early March 1818 Jackson had pursued the Indians into Florida and before the end of April he had taken Pensacola and put to death two British citizens. Cabinet discussions of Jackson's actions—especially the taking of Pensacola—began in July, with all except Adams thinking the general had acted not only without instructions, but against them. Adams thought Jackson's actions justified by the necessity of the case: he had been authorized to cross into Spanish Florida in pursuit of the Indians; all other matters were incidental, for the object of the military operation was termination of Indian warfare, not hostility to Spain. Crawford believed that if Pensacola were not returned to Spain the administration would be held responsible for Jackson's actions and for having started a war in violation of the Constitution. The people, he said, would not support such a war, United States shipping and commerce would be destroyed by privateers from all parts of the world, and the administration would "sink under it." Calhoun insisted that Jackson's actions were a violation of the Constitution and an act of war against Spain, that Jackson had really resolved beforehand to take Pensacola, that he had violated his orders, and upon his own arbitrary will set all authority at defiance. And in private correspondence the war secretary wrote of the diversity of opinion in the cabinet, the misconduct of the Spanish authority in Florida, and the popularity of Jackson as factors contributing to the conclusion that no proceedings should be instituted against the general.[8] Craw-

8 Adams, *Memoirs*, 4:108-9, 113; Calhoun to Dear Sir [Charles Tait], July 20, Sept. 5, 1818, Tait. There are few Calhoun-Tait letters. If, as Charles H. Wiltse, *John C. Calhoun*, 3 vols. (New York, 1944-1951), 1:115, says, Calhoun's influence had been important in nominating Monroe in 1816 and Crawford could not easily overlook the fact, it seems strange that the secretary of war should write these letters disclosing supposedly secret cabinet discussions to a man who had been an intimate friend of Crawford for more than twenty years. Wiltse's statement and its implications are totally unacceptable.

ford apparently talked, in August 1818, with a Georgia editor about cabinet discussions and division and later was denounced for revealing secret conversations.

It was October 1818 before an official communication went to Jackson, and certainly Monroe's letter shaded the truth about the attitudes of some of his advisers. He was sorry Jackson had understood his orders differently from what was intended; since he had, "it remains only to do justice to you on that ground." The general should state his position to the War Department, and he would be answered in a "friendly manner" by Calhoun "who has very just and liberal sentiments on the subject." Jackson, in his reply of November 15, said he was convinced of the "honorable and liberal sentiments" of Calhoun, but he was not "insensible to the implacable hostility" of Crawford. Whatever Jackson may have heard concerning Crawford's view of the Florida invasion, the relations between the general and Crawford when the latter was secretary of war seem to have created in him a lasting dislike for the Georgian: "I have for several years viewed him as a base and unprincipled man," whose desire to injure Monroe and Jackson was so strong that the "injury nay the *ruin* of his country would interpose no barrier."[9]

Jackson and his friends soon began concerted action against Crawford, apparently feeling Crawford was the general's enemy in the administration. Adams, however, said Crawford had "been less so in appearance" than Wirt or Calhoun, but the Georgian's attitude was not improved by a letter, printed in a Nashville paper, which violently attacked him. And when Congress discussed the Florida affair in the winter of 1818-1819 Jackson imputed all actions concerning this incident to Crawford's resentment of Jackson's support of Monroe for the presidency in 1816, said the matter had become a party question and must become the touchstone of the election of the next President, and saw numerous political combinations involving Crawford. Especially did he denounce the supposed coalition of Crawford and Clay whom he "despised" and castigated for his "hypocrisy and baseness."[10] Jackson, in Washington during this time, was told

9 Monroe to Jackson, Oct. 20, 1818, Hamilton, *Monroe Writings,* 6:74-75; Jackson to Monroe, Nov. 15, 1818, Monroe, NYP.

10 Adams, *Memoirs,* 4:194 (Dec. 17, 1818); Jackson to William B. Lewis, Jan. 30, 1819, Jackson-Lewis Correspondence (NYP).

by Adams that Crawford had never said a word indicating "any feeling" against Jackson (though less than a month before the secretary of state had recorded that Crawford had shown hostility to the general), but Jackson seemed in a "great passion" because of the attack made upon him by Representative Thomas W. Cobb, a Crawford supporter whose actions apparently were neither influenced nor determined by anyone but himself. Crawford thought the general had "conjured up other causes of animosity, which had no existence but in his own imagination."[11]

The defense in Congress of Jackson had been as vigorous as the attack on him, but nothing happened to let Jackson know that he had chosen the wrong target for his hostility. Crawford was well aware of this, and he was concerned about the meetings that would take place between Jackson and Monroe on the latter's southern tour in the spring and summer of 1819. Various problems, stemming primarily from economic conditions, kept Crawford from joining Monroe at Augusta. He said he had no enmity for Jackson, thought the general's services should "shield him from attack" but "ought not to serve as a shield for unjustly attacking others," and said he especially wanted to prevent Jackson from doing injury to Monroe. Crawford listed several of his friends the President would be meeting.

Monroe assured Crawford that Jackson knew (when he was in Washington) of the President's entire confidence in the integrity, honor, and friendship of his secretary, and after the conference with Monroe he had never attempted to shake it—nor did he again mention the subject. He knew Jackson would be attentive to his intercourse with Crawford's friends, and it was probable that the natural ardor of the general's feelings would lead him by "light circumstance to draw hasty and improper conclusions." The President would, therefore, confine his relations with Crawford's friends to their own neighborhoods, and he hoped to control all meetings for the good of all involved, of the country and

11 Adams, *Memoirs,* 4:207, 213-14, 239-42; Crawford to John O'Connor, April 24, 1819, John O'Connor Papers (Clements). It was at this time that Adams recorded that the success or failure of the administration would be most conspicuous in foreign relations and that Crawford, perhaps unconscious of his motives, would create obstacles to bring public dissatisfaction with the state department. It is difficult to follow Adams' "logic" that Crawford—such an important member of the executive branch—would reap gain from the failures of the Monroe administration, no matter what the area of deficiency.

government, and his own "personal fame and satisfaction."[12] He seems to have done so.

Crawford's correspondence contains only occasional reference to the Florida affair and the enmity of Jackson, but Jackson's avoiding unfavorable mention of Crawford was short-lived. Several times later in 1819 Jackson, in letters to Monroe, denounced Crawford; the following year communications of this kind were less frequent. The general accepted the governorship of Florida for a short, stormy period and seemed almost in a hurry to make recommendations to Monroe for appointive positions, which positions—even those connected with the Treasury Department—Crawford said were filled without his consent or even knowledge of his wishes.[13] The Crawford-Jackson feud grew less intense after 1820-1821 and was nearly over by 1825. After that date the two men seemed more or less to ignore each other, but Jackson could not ignore the Crawford wing of the party.

In the two years after January 1818 nearly all the major participants in the controversy over Jackson's Florida actions were guilty of some indiscretion or fabrication. Monroe's October 20, 1818, letter to Jackson was not an accurate description of Calhoun's position; both Calhoun and Crawford seem to have been guilty of divulging the cabinet division—but division had been revealed before, especially in connection with Robert Smith during Madison's first term; Jackson seized upon rumor and half-truth to seek revenge against one whom he mistakenly thought had tried to injure him; the general schemed with John Clark of Georgia to seek incriminating evidence against Crawford; Adams' own words indict him with falsehood; and Calhoun, the chief prosecutor of Jackson in the cabinet—and probably justifiably so—remained relatively silent and reaped the political rewards of Jackson's misplaced hatred. The extant materials give much support to the assertion that Jackson was the chief instigator of party dissension; in his actions he used Crawford quite effectively as a whipping boy.

[12] Crawford to Monroe, April 27, 1819, Monroe, NYP; Monroe to Crawford, May 19, 1819, Golding. Crawford hoped to meet Monroe in Ohio (perhaps Cincinnati) on his return, but he had to go west in connection with problems of the national road and said he could not stand the trip twice in so short a time.

[13] See, for example, Crawford to Gallatin, July 24, 1819, May 13, 1822, Adams, *Gallatin Writings,* 2:116-17, 241-43; Jackson to Monroe, Sept. 29, Nov. 22, 29, 1819; Jan. 15, 1820; Feb. 11, 1821, Monroe, NYP.

Meanwhile, Adams and the Spanish minister Onis had finally concluded, in February 1819, the treaty for the cession of Florida to the United States and the settlement of the boundaries of the Louisiana Purchase. Crawford continued to show the strong interest for the acquisition of Florida which he had revealed by his role before, and during the early days of, the War of 1812, and all other members of the government were in favor of acquiring the area. The presence of United States troops in Florida, inadequate geographical knowledge, the validity of Spanish land grants in Florida, and personality clashes between the two chief negotiators were troublesome factors during the negotiating period, but cabinet discussions were amicable, generally constructive, and all clearly pointed toward the achievement of the goal.[14]

The Spanish king withheld approval of the treaty (in large measure to forestall United States recognition of the new governments in South America), and the secretaries differed as to the best method of forcing Spanish ratification. Crawford thought John Forsyth, appointed minister to Spain just before the treaty was concluded, should be instructed to demand immediate ratification, but neither he nor Calhoun was prepared to support the "strict measures" Adams advocated. It was decided, however, that Forsyth should simply offer to receive and transmit the Spanish approval; if favorable action had not been taken by the fall of 1819, the President should make a full communication to Congress.[15]

Crawford considered the Spanish failure to ratify to be an act of bad faith and hoped his friend, Baron Hyde de Neuville, the French minister whose tact had done much to smooth the relations between Adams and Onis and who was returning to France, could convince his own government that Onis had not exceeded his instructions by agreeing to cede Florida and that Spain had no reasonable grounds for withholding ratification. Speaking as an individual rather than as a member of the government, Crawford believed the administration would hear what the new Spanish minister, Francisco Dionisio Vives, had to say about

---

[14] See Adams, *Memoirs,* 4: passim, esp. 145-46, 171-73, 204-7, 251-52.

[15] Ibid., 405-7 (Aug. 5, 8, 1819). For an account of Forsyth's ministership see Alvin Laroy Duckett, *John Forsyth: Political Tactician* (Athens, Ga., 1962), 42-64. See also Crawford to Jacob Brown, Aug. 4, 1819, Brown, MHS.

his government's position, but no new negotiations on the treaty would be opened. He thought Congress would grant the President's expected request for authorization to occupy Florida with the declaration that nothing would be done that would not have been done had the treaty been ratified.[16]

A few weeks later, at a cabinet meeting, Crawford recommended the action which he told Neuville he expected and then temporarily backed away from this position. Perhaps he thought it left no room for maneuvering or that it would so antagonize the Spanish minister that nothing could be accomplished amicably. At any rate, he said that in all discussions and communications concerning the treaty he preferred the "general expression." He illustrated his point by telling a story about Governor Edward Telfair of Georgia: the governor had engaged in a sharp correspondence with some officer; looking over a secretary's draft of a letter to the officer, Telfair pointed to a high-toned paragraph and said he would thank his secretary to make it a "little more mysterious."[17] Before the end of November Crawford was decidedly in favor of taking possession of Florida, whereas Adams—the only other department head then in Washington—thought they should recommend to Congress that action be delayed and explanations demanded of the new minister. Crawford thought the government would "lose character" by delay, and the enemies of the administration would charge it with lack of vigor and energy; Adams believed there would be dissatisfaction with the government's course, no matter what it was. The President was hesitant, expressing the belief that occupation would be an act of war. The next day Crawford was more inclined to concur in the plan for delaying occupation.[18]

16 Crawford to Neuville, Oct. 18, 1819, Crawford, Duke. Crawford hoped Neuville would return to the United States and "give his friends in this place the pleasure once more of enjoying your society."

17 Adams, *Memoirs*, 4:437-38 (Nov. 13, 1819). All present had laughed very heartily at the story, and a pleased Crawford repeated it in detail. But, said Adams, it was good upon repetition. Earlier that year Crawford had told the story of the Georgian who was much dissatisfied with his sons. Upon hearing that a court case was to be referred to two indifferent men, this man said it ought to be referred to his sons, for they were two of the "d--dest indifferent men in the state." Ibid., 244 (Feb. 5, 1819). Arthur Styron, *The Last of the Cocked Hats: James Monroe & the Virginia Dynasty* (Norman, Okla., 1945), 347, describes Crawford as a "shrewd and witty man."

18 Adams, *Memoirs*, 4:448-50 (Nov. 25, 26, 1819).

Monroe, patient and cautious, in March 1819 presented to the cabinet a draft of a special message to Congress recommending postponement of proceedings relative to Florida until the next session. He noted, among other things, favorable developments indicated by the dispatches of United States ministers in Europe and the good offices of the French and the British to induce Spain to ratify. Only Calhoun objected to delay. Crawford, maintaining that it was not good policy to set the opinions and wishes of other nations at defiance, thought the condition of the Spanish government—which had just experienced revolution—urged forbearance on the part of the United States, and he knew this to be the feeling of a number of congressmen. There was general agreement with this point of view. Another factor against asking Congress to sanction occupation, Crawford thought, was apprehension among department heads that Congress might not favor such a policy. Should this be the case, the expression of such a congressional posture would disarm the executive in any future efforts.[19]

A message was not to go to Congress for two months, though the cabinet was frequently concerned with the Florida treaty. When the draft of a communication to Vives was under consideration, Crawford objected to some of the language because it assented to Vives' proposal for a new negotiation, which would be fruitless and endless. His suggestion that the communication preclude any such possibility was approved. Adams was to inquire if Vives had authority—if the United States gave satisfactory explanations—to consent to the occupation of Florida as a pledge for the ratification of the treaty. The offer to give explanations would involve no discussion of them. Gallatin (minister to France) said Vives had such authority, but the Spaniard denied it. There were various speculations as to what had happened, recognition of the new republics became more ticklish, and the question of legality of Spanish grants continued

19 Ibid., 5:28-30 (March 21, 1820); Crawford to C. A. Rodney, March 27, 1820, Miscellaneous, Clements. On March 29 Monroe presented a proposal from Manuel Torres that 20,000 stands of arms be sold on credit to Colombia to assist in spreading the revolution to Peru and Mexico. Crawford supported the proposal, Calhoun and Smith Thompson were favorably inclined toward it, but Adams thought such a sale would be unneutral, impolitic, and an act of war. Crawford intimated that he did not think it would be an act of war, but when asked by Thompson what he would say to the same application if made by Spain, "he replied, laughing, that he should certainly reject it." Adams, Memoirs, 5:46-47.

as a major issue for several months. Smith Thompson (secretary of navy) and Crawford definitely differed on this matter, but Adams noted that "Crawford did not press his observations in reply to Mr. Thompson. He presses nothing further than it will bear." It was agreed that all grants made after January 24, 1818, be declared null and void.[20]

On May 2, 1820, the portion of the letter to Vives dealing with grants—he had been shown the unsigned letter and wanted to know why all grants prior to January 24, 1818, had not been confirmed[21]—received cabinet approval, but Crawford expressed apprehension that the removal of so many of the differences between the two countries might incline Congress to less vigorous measures and feared that unless the "present moment were seized" Florida would be secured only by war. With this Adams agreed, but he thought that there could no longer be any grounds for charging the United States with "precipitate and premeditated aggression" and that by reducing differences to a single point the best case could be made for Congress to act with energy.[22]

Crawford, in correspondence, had written "If we get the Floridas we must take them," and at the cabinet meeting of May 6 he maintained that immediate occupation was the last chance to obtain the ratification of the treaty. If delay occurred, the provision of the Spanish constitution—to which the king had now sworn—prohibiting alienation of any portion of the Spanish territory would prevent getting the region except by war. However, if the United States was in possession of Florida when the Cortes met, that body would be glad to seize upon occupancy to decide the whole matter settled and out of their competency. If the Cortes felt otherwise, they would be too much engaged in affairs of more interest to them to go to war over Florida. The United States could indulge Spain's scruples as to the right of negotiation as long as they pleased—meanwhile holding the area. Adams believed it indispensable that Congress authorize the President to occupy Florida. Calhoun recommended postponement until the next session of Congress and thought the message should say something favorable about the revolution

---

20 Adams, *Memoirs*, 5:73, 84-86 (April 20, May 1, 1820).
21 Some grants had been falsely predated before January 24, 1818. The Cortes annulled the grants in the fall of 1820 and opened the road to ratification.
22 Adams, *Memoirs*, 5:92.

which would bespeak the good will of those newly come to power. This immediately became a leading idea, which the President said he would take into consideration.[23] Two days later Monroe read the draft of his message, closing with the recommendation that action be delayed until the next session. No objections were made, but Crawford and Adams reiterated their beliefs that such delay was giving up the last chance for ratification. The former still thought occupancy best and the latter believed Congress should authorize occupation and give Spain a chance to ratify during the summer.[24]

In the fifteen months following the signing of the treaty the cabinet members had shifted positions a number of times. Such shifts seem in no way to have been determined by the position of a colleague; each department head appeared to advocate what he considered the best means of acquiring Florida in light of changing domestic, Spanish, and international politics. Crawford appeared the most frequent advocate of the bolder action, but the patience and the waiting policy of the President were finally rewarded. In February 1821 Spain ratified the Adams-Onis treaty. Unfortunately, a gap in Adams' diary removes the most fruitful source for determining the stands of the cabinet members during the preceding fall and winter months.

The question of United States recognition of the new governments in the former Spanish American colonies was present from the beginning of the Monroe administration and very early Crawford had recommended sending two commissioners to Buenos Aires to investigate the capacity and determination of that region for independence. He was unhappy in September 1817 that the commissioners had not departed the United States; he felt it important that the administration have full information in this area since Clay seemed determined to raise the issue of recognition at the next session of Congress. He regretted that the speaker should so involve the House, which he would "rather see . . . employed upon subjects which are strictly within their constitutional powers." Crawford believed there was a difference between recognition of a change of government in an already established nation and recognition of a new nation, and even

---

[23] Crawford to Cheves, April 25, 1820, Cheves; Adams, *Memoirs*, 5:99-101 (May 6, 1820).
[24] Adams, *Memoirs*, 5:105.

though he thought the power of recognition rested exclusively with the executive,[25] he would involve the Senate in the recognition of new governments.

His position became clear in early 1819 when the recognition of Buenos Aires was before the cabinet. He maintained there was no reason for further delay since the commissioners had returned with full and favorable information. He would send a minister, rather than grant an exequatur to a consul, because the Senate would have to consent to the nomination of a minister. Their granting or withholding of consent would commit them on the issue of recognition.[26] After February 1821 recognition was discussed several times, with Crawford again advocating the bolder action. He favored appointing ministers without an agreement for reciprocal exchange.[27] In May 1822 Congress responded favorably to Monroe's suggestion by appropriating $100,000 for diplomatic missions to five Latin American countries.

When the Monroe Doctrine was in the process of formulation Crawford was convalescing from his most serious illness. He had been confined at the home of James Barbour in Virginia for eight weeks with what he called the "most distressing attack of inflammatory rheumatism." Soon after his return to Washington on November 14, 1823, he feared there was "danger of some embarrassment" in foreign affairs from the activities of the Russian naval squadron in the Pacific and from the possible attempt of France to restore the former Spanish colonies to the control of the mother country. His apprehensions regarding Russia were nearly dissipated, and he believed England would oppose French action in Latin America. The United States might be compelled to cooperate in defeating the measures of France, for he believed it "our duty, if practicable, to arrest the iniquitous career of the holy alliance on this side of the Atlantic."[28] Crawford was obviously behind in his knowledge of events—he had not attended a cabinet meeting for more than two months—but it appears that he would have offered no opposition to the Monroe Doctrine. Whether he would have

25 Crawford to Bartlett Yancey, May 27, 1817, Yancey; Crawford to Gallatin, Oct. 27, 1817, Gallatin; Adams, *Memoirs*, 4:11 (Sept. 29, 1817), 204-7 (Jan. 2, 1819).
26 Adams, *Memoirs*, 4:204-7.
27 Ibid., 5:492-93; 6:23-26, 63.
28 Crawford to Tait, Nov. 23, 1823, Tait.

originally decided with Adams on a unilateral declaration cannot be determined. One other bit of evidence on Latin American affairs affords an insight into Crawford's thinking—and perhaps his espousal of the Monroe Doctrine. The issue was the reception of Silvestro Rebello as chargé d'affaires from the emperor of Brazil, who was reputed to have taken an oath to support the constitution. Wirt, principal objector earlier, was absent; Crawford, absent earlier, was for immediate reception. He said, "we had nothing to do with their forms of government. It is our principle not to intermeddle with them, and we could not justify delaying the recognition of the Brazilian government on that account." But Adams thought it "might be well to reflect upon the most prudent course of proceeding in this case."[29]

Many other matters of foreign relations, including such relatively insignificant items as the conduct of individuals during Adams' ministership to Russia and the appointment of a secret agent to Cuba, were discussed, but only those dealing with the slave trade and trade with Britain and France will be treated here.

On March 3, 1819, Congress passed the slave trade act, and soon section 2 became the subject of much discussion. At issue was the extent of the President's authority in connection with Africans who were to be removed from the country after being taken from persons attempting illegally to import them as slaves. Initially the cabinet agreed that the chief executive had no authority to purchase territory or establish a colony in Africa, though the act "did authorize him to take measures for removing beyond the limits of the United States the negroes who may be taken, as imported contrary to law, and to appoint an agent to receive them in Africa."[30]

Crawford, a vice president and a member of the Board of Managers of the American Colonization Society from its organization in January 1817, played a major role in reinterpreting the act to permit much greater authority to the President. Georgia legislation stipulated that slaves illegally imported and captured would be sold at auction, or they could be turned over to the colonization society if that group would agree to transport them

29 Adams, *Memoirs*, 6:328-29 (May 13, 1824).

30 Early Lee Fox, *The American Colonization Society, 1817-1840* (Baltimore, Md., 1919), 53; 3 *Stat.* 532-34; Adams, *Memoirs*, 4:298-99 (March 16, 1819).

to a foreign colony. Presiding over the Board of Managers in April 1819, Crawford called attention to an advertisement in a Georgia paper for the auction of illegally imported Africans. The Reverend William Meade, the first important general agent of the society, was sent to Georgia to "make an effort to save the negroes from slavery." Crawford informed the Georgia governor of the act of Congress, which he said provided for the establishment of a colony of free blacks on the coast of Africa and noted that the society was to make the first attempt to carry this act into effect by receiving from the agent of Georgia the Africans advertised for sale at Milledgeville on May 4. The governor agreed to postpone sale of the Africans, and by June arrangements had been made for the Negroes to be turned over to the society.[31]

Attorney General Wirt, however, said no part of the $100,000 appropriated to carry out the act of 1819 could be used to purchase land on the coast of Africa or anywhere else for settlement purposes, to transport either freedmen or illegally imported persons, to buy carpenter's tools or other materials for making a settlement, or to transport or pay the salary of an agent because the second section limits the appointment expressly to a "proper person or persons *residing* on the coast of Africa." But a conference with Crawford apparently changed Wirt's view. Crawford thought the President, from the general grant of the act, had power to provide a place to which the persons were to be removed, to send over carpenters and tools to prepare a shelter against the weather, to provide for support and safety of the persons removed, to organize a government for them, and—if deemed essential—to send over and intermix with them a portion of the more intelligent free population of color of this country (though Crawford seemed not to think this expedient). Wirt said that Crawford felt the grant of power to *remove* would "pass" all the incidental powers to give it effect; but the incidental powers were also so expressly granted—to make all arrangements

31 Fox, *Colonization Society*, 50-51, 57-58; P. J. Staudenraus, *The African Colonization Movement, 1815-1865* (New York, 1961), 30; Adams, *Memoirs*, 4:356 (April 20, 1819); Crawford to William Rabun, April 15, 1819, Georgia Portfolio, Vol. 2, Duke. Staudenraus, 174, says that after 1825 Clay succeeded Crawford as the Colonization Society's most influential friend in Washington. Some of the other vice presidents were Andrew Jackson, Richard Rush, John Taylor (of Caroline), Samuel Smith, and Robert Finley. Crawford contributed fifty dollars to the society in 1819.

deemed expedient to removal, to appoint an agent on the coast of Africa to receive them, and so on—that the issue seemed beyond doubt. Congress could never have intended so barbarous a procedure as receiving the immigrants and turning them loose; if the act were interpreted so as to limit action to mere removal, it could not be carried into effect. So large a grant of power forbids so narrow a construction; since the language of the act permits, the construction that would give the law effect should be preferred to one that would defeat it. Wirt said Crawford's is a "very strong view of the case, and is, very probably, the correct one." He regretted that this was so, for he thought Congress could have made things clear and that Congress passed the law under the impression the colonization society would have taken all the preparatory steps.

Crawford also thought the agent could be appointed here and sent to Africa, for Congress "could not but have known" there was no person already there who was qualified to act as agent. "Residing" was unguardedly used in the haste accompanying the close of Congress. "This has great force in it, too," said Wirt, "but I fear it would be rather too bold a construction, to execute what we may conjecture they intended, and not what they said. This difficulty, however, Mr. Crawford suggests, may be surmounted by the colonization society sending out an agent to be there commissioned by the President."[32]

Adams termed the colonization society indefatigable in its efforts to get hold of the funds appropriated by the act; it had secured the ear of the President and Crawford (for "purposes of his own") and had its fingers in the purse. He indicated that Crawford, who was "ready to make a colony" out of the act, had won Wirt over to his interpretation and had urged the "most liberal construction, because the object of the Act is beneficent and affects no rights." The President decided to pay $1,500 for half the freight of a vessel about to go to Africa. He would inform Congress of the interpretation of the law; if that body made no explanation of the law, "it will give the sanction of their tacit assent to the liberal construction and the discretionary

32 Wirt to Benjamin Homans, Oct. 14, 16, 1819, *House Doc.*, No. 123 (serial 387), 26th Cong., 2d sess. This document contains the opinions of the attorneys general from the beginning of the federal government to March 1, 1841. The second letter by Wirt was shown to Crawford and to the President before being sent to Homans, who was in the navy department.

expenditure."[33] Wirt apparently was not particularly interested in the legislative intent, but Crawford was. And perhaps Liberia owes more to Crawford than seems to be realized.

Little else is known of Crawford's activities with the society, but he was present at the June 2, 1823, meeting in Washington when the decision was made to establish a periodical publication. Five days later he presided over the session of the board of officers and managers who engaged in several hours of "serious debate on the interest" of the Liberian colony.[34] The rising heat of the presidential contest and Crawford's serious illness a few months later probably brought to an end his active participation in society matters, but some of his actions as a Georgia judge indicate that he perhaps continued to subscribe to its aims.[35]

The slave trade act of 1819 also permitted the use of armed vessels on the coasts of the United States and Africa for suppression of this trade, and the following year anyone convicted of engaging in this traffic was declared guilty of piracy.[36] England was aggressively involved in suppressing commerce in human beings, but it was more than two decades before the United States reached an agreement with England to make the acts of 1819 and 1820 effective. During negotiations with Britain in 1823 Crawford objected to the arguments against the right of search in Adams' proposed letter to the British minister as a "mere declamation against the practice which the projet essentially conceded," while Adams believed them justified by the traditional position of the United States against search. Much of the letter was struck in accord with Crawford's objection. Crawford had no general objection to the convention but suggested several detailed alterations, some of which Monroe approved. All members of the cabinet favored the convention, but the following summer—when the instrument was before the Senate—Crawford said he had not seen the paper. His memory probably had been affected by his illness, and Senate objections to granting the right of search may have been partially responsible for the Georgian's position in the fall of 1824. He spoke against

[33] Adams, *Memoirs*, 4:475-77 (Dec. 10, 1819).
[34] *National Intelligencer*, June 7, 1823; *Montgomery Advertiser*, July 21, 1823. The position of vice president was considered honorary and few vice presidents attended meetings.
[35] See final chapter.
[36] 3 *Stat.* 532-34, 600-601.

conceding the right: the very proposal of doing so was an insult because it implied that the United States was not competent or trustworthy to execute its own laws.[37] Though the Senate made several important amendments before ratifying the agreement, the United States would not agree to a new negotiation, and cooperation between Britain and the United States in forcefully suppressing the slave traffic was not achieved until the Webster-Ashburton Treaty of 1842.

An agreement with Britain regarding the important West Indian trade was not reached until the 1830s, but the matter was often under discussion. Crawford believed that if independence of Spanish America did not break up Britain's ambitious, monopolizing, and "huckstering West Indian empire," it will "at least serve to render *us* more independent of it." He thought that intercourse with Bermuda and the Bahamas should have been cut off in the winter of 1818-1819 so that the United States system of countervailing duties could be fairly tried.[38] More important, in trade matters, than the cabinet talks which did not bring results were the secretary's interpretations—for administrative purposes—of acts of navigation, tonnage, trade, and revenue, and the implementing of decisions which were reached on treaties of commerce. In arriving at his interpretations Crawford often conferred with members of the congressional committees which had considered the measures, with members of the cabinet, the President, and the United States minister to England. Crawford endeavored to determine the intent of Congress, thought the laws should be liberally executed, believed in removing as many restrictions on commerce as possible, and sought the best possible arrangements for American shippers and traders.[39]

As a former minister to France, Crawford was well acquainted with the difficulties between the United States and France over commerce and shipping. He favored the provisions of the act of

37 Adams, *Memoirs*, 6:148-49, 165, 328, 345, 426-28; Martin Van Buren to [Rufus King], May 26, 1824 (draft); King to Van Buren, May 30, 1824, Van Buren.

38 Richard Rush to Crawford, Nov. 24, 1818, Crawford, MDLC; Adams, *Memoirs*, 4:322-23 (April 2, 1819). See also F. Lee Benns, *The American Struggle for the British West India Carrying-Trade, 1815-1830* (Bloomington, Ind., 1923).

39 See, for example, Samuel Smith to Crawford, July 3, 1817, May 7, 1818, Smith Letter Book (film), MdHS; Crawford to Monroe, Oct. 1, 1817, Monroe, MDLC; Monroe to Crawford, Oct. 3, 1817, Golding; Treasury Circulars, May 25, July 24, Aug. 31, Oct. 1, 1818; Sept. 14, 1822; March 26, 1823.

May 3, 1815, which contemplated extending reciprocity on proof of nonexistence of discriminating duties in the ports of a foreign nation, and France maintained that Article VIII of the Louisiana Purchase Treaty (guaranteeing most-favored-nation treatment) was inseparable from the discussion of discriminating duties.[40] Gallatin, minister to France, gave qualified support to the French proposal of unequal duties—heavier on United States vessels in French ports than on French vessels in American ports—but he could reach no agreement by the summer of 1820.

All relations with France were somewhat colored by the failure of Spain to ratify the Florida treaty and were strained by American seizure of the *Apollon* and *Jeune Eugénie* for alleged involvement in the slave trade. Crawford, keenly aware of the role Neuville had played in smoothing negotiations between Adams and Onis and personally acquainted with several members of the French government, in January 1820 declared a "strong aversion" to any act of Congress which would further damage relations with France. Congress, however, passed the discriminatory French Tonnage Act of May 15, 1820; the French retaliated with an ordinance of July 26, and commerce between the two nations was virtually interdicted.[41]

Negotiations to restore "amicable" commerce were transferred to the United States in the fall of 1820. Crawford soon came to favor discriminating duties which would operate unequally on the United States, said France would agree to nothing else, and thought more restrictive laws would be necessary if the existing commercial situation were not corrected. Adams could see neither reason nor justice in the French position, and the cabinet decided to propose mutual abolition of all discriminating duties. Two days later, April 14, 1821, they decided to "agree" to the principle of unequal discrimination at least to the point of determining the degree of disproportion that France would insist upon.[42]

Crawford feared the effort to remove the commercial difficulties would fail and that an extremely embarrassing commercial warfare might result. He was concerned that a personal altercation between the negotiators might develop a spirit of hostility and

40 A good discussion of reciprocity is in Setser, *Commercial Reciprocity*, 184-206.
41 Adams, *Memoirs*, 4:505 (Jan. 15, 1820): Setser, *Commercial Reciprocity*, 200.
42 Adams, *Memoirs*, 5:287, 337, 344-45, 353-54.

widen the breach produced by each individual's efforts to protect the navigation interests of his country,[43] but he was especially perturbed by Adams' draft letter to Neuville on the *Apollon* and *Jeune Eugénie.* He wrote Monroe at Oak Hill that if the letter were sent in the form in which he had received it from Adams, a rupture between the two countries would be inevitable —if the influence of Neuville could effect it. There were many specific points to which objection might be taken, but Crawford thought that the sarcastic vein of the entire communication would make it difficult to infuse into it the conciliatory spirit that should be preserved in such correspondence. No acrimony should be manifested in refusing redress for an alleged wrong. "The refusal when clothed in decorous, or even soothing, & conciliatory language, can hardly fail to produce dissatisfaction. What then will be the reception it will meet with, when, a sneer, a sarcasm, an insult is met with in every paragraph?" Monroe agreed there should be infused into the communication the "greatest degree of moderation" and the means of conciliating the French government through its minister. He had so written to Adams.[44]

The rewritten letter caused no offense, and Adams' proposals of early 1822 were accepted by Neuville, who made some alternative suggestions that seemed to look to an ultimate abandonment of all discriminating duties. A pleased Crawford explicitly concurred with Adams that an exception should be made for articles imported for reexportation, and it was agreed that an alternative duty of $4.00 per laden ton be accepted. Later there was a warm discussion between Adams and Crawford, particularly on Neuville's proposals to repeal the May 15, 1820, and the French July 1820 acts and for refunding of duties. Crawford favored such action as conciliatory, but Adams thought it would give the appearance of retreat. Later they discussed which country should do the "first retreating" and how far the two nations should "retreat," but Crawford believed they should not lose the opportunity to put an end to discrimination.

[43] Crawford to G. W. Campbell, May 16, 1821, Campbell, MDLC; Crawford to Lowndes, June 18, 1821, Lowndes; Crawford to James Barbour, July 25, 1821, Barbour. Setser, *Commercial Reciprocity,* 204, says Adams was "extremely unconciliatory" during the discussions.
[44] Crawford to Monroe, July 20, 1821, Monroe, MDLC; Monroe to Crawford, July 24, 1821, Crawford, MDLC. Monroe approved the "delicate manner" in which Crawford proposed to handle an appointment.

Actually the decision to accept as much as $4.00 per ton duty was the crucial one, and only details remained to be settled. Perhaps Adams was not happy about this, for Crawford noted near the end of May that Adams "has certainly not been very sane when I have been with him since the adjournment of Congress. He is still in a passion about something. Nothing has been effected with the French minister tho I presume the negotiation can hardly fail. It might have been concluded a fortnight ago, as well as a fortnight hence."[45] The last obstacle to the treaty was removed by federal court decisions, satisfactory to France, on the *Apollon* and *Jeune Eugénie,* and the convention was concluded on June 24, 1822. It not only repealed the discriminatory duties imposed in 1820 but reduced those levied and collected in the ports of the two nations prior to that time. Literal interpretation in some instances would have increased some of those duties, so it was agreed that administrative interpretation should avoid doing this. As a climax to these long discussions and final agreement the act of March 3, 1823, for carrying the convention into effect permitted the refunding of the discriminatory duties collected from French vessels between May 15, 1820, and June 24, 1822.[46]

Crawford's influence in the diplomatic sphere seems to have been greatest in the areas where he had the most experience and interest—the French and Spanish Florida. He was unflagging in his determination to secure Florida and advised a tougher course there than he did in connection with the French. However, it is worthy of note that Crawford, often described as outspoken, brusque, and tactless, was quite sensitive to the feelings of nations with whom negotiations were being conducted and on a number of occasions counseled the softening of language and lowering of tone of diplomatic communications. He was firm in his convictions, but he did not wish uselessly to irritate. Crawford's attitude toward France seems not to have been adversely affected by the failure of his ministry to France from 1813 to 1815, and it is possible that he was more conciliatory toward that country than toward England because he saw in France a

[45] Crawford to Monroe, Aug. 1, 1821, Monroe, MDLC; Adams, *Memoirs,* 5:511, 529-32 (May 1, 21, 1822); Crawford to John O'Connor, May 28, 1822, Crawford, Rice. It is possible that Adams was still brooding about the Senate rejection of the military appointments.

[46] Setser, *Commercial Reciprocity,* 206; Treasury Circulars, March 23, May 12, 1823.

less serious competitor in commercial activities in Latin America. Be that as it may, he must have gained considerable satisfaction in playing a rather significant role in restoring Franco-American commerce to a friendly and mutually beneficial course.

Cabinet discussions prior to the reelection of Monroe had revealed sharp differences of opinion among the members, but a prevailing spirit of mutual confidence and respect permitted a harmonious resolution of those differences. After 1820 a growing suspicion and mistrust, a side effect perhaps of presidential fever, strained the relations among the department heads, and by the summer of 1821 Crawford was thinking of retiring from the government. A year later there was a possibility that he would be dismissed.

Congressional discussion in 1820-1821 of retrenchment, involving primarily reduction of the peacetime army, seems to have been the foundation cause of the tension between Crawford and Calhoun. Partisans of each, probably without the sanction of either, bitterly attacked the other, and many soon believed that an unfriendly, even hostile, feeling existed between the two secretaries. Crawford, troubled by this development, talked with Calhoun. He did not believe the secretary of war had any role in the attack on Crawford, but Calhoun was not explicit in his reply about Crawford's role in the attack on Calhoun. The South Carolinian denied presidential ambitions, could not understand why Crawford's friends were hostile to him, and implied that unless he was assailed by Crawford's friends or a difference on great political questions should arise between them (and he saw little possibility of this) he favored Crawford's candidacy. Shortly thereafter, in conversation with others, Calhoun seemed to say the opposite of the above.[47]

Crawford was not pleased with the congressional attacks on the executive departments, seemed astonished by some of the political combinations (unspecified) which had been formed, believed the remainder of Monroe's term would be "stormy and excessively disagreeable," and in August 1821 was "strongly tempted" to "retire at once from the scenes of turmoil and cabal, which will fill up the next three years." He would make a decision before the end of the next session of Congress; if he did quit, he would leave office in September 1822. Before Con-

47 Crawford to Tait, Aug. 11, Nov. 13, 1821, Tait.

gress met again, Crawford was "strongly disposed" to resign his post at the end of the next session and "leave to those who have more talents, more claim to the public confidence, or more confidence in themselves and stronger desire to govern, whether for their own or the public good the road to promotion entirely unobstructed."[48]

During the next session of Congress controversy over removals and appointments necessitated by the army reduction act of March 2, 1821, caused serious division in the cabinet, brought charges that Crawford was sabotaging the administration, and almost led to a break between Monroe and his secretary.[49] The act provided for four regiments of artillery and seven of infantry (plus various services), with no rank higher than lieutenant colonel in the artillery units except for the colonel of the light artillery regiment. On June 1, 1821, while Congress was not in session, Monroe had appointed Brigadier General Daniel Parker (whose office of adjutant and inspector general had been abolished) to be paymaster general, vice Nathan Towson, who was nominated to be colonel of light artillery. Several supernumerary officers had to be discharged, but by the provisions of the act they received three months' pay. On January 17, 1822, Monroe communicated with the Senate, noting that three of the four places in the artillery regiments were considered original vacancies to be filled, as the good of the service might dictate, from the army corps. The paymaster department he considered one of the corps, so Towson, formerly in artillery, was appointed. To limit his choice to officers of the line, said Monroe, would have excluded all other branches of the service, as well as the paymaster department. Several officers of distinction had to be reduced in grade, but Monroe had nominated them to brevet in their old ranks.[50]

Towson, brevet lieutenant colonel of light artillery with a

48 Ibid.

49 Before these appointments were sent to the Senate, the opportunity for frayed tempers had been afforded by the selection of Solomon Van Rensselaer to replace Solomon Southwick, delinquent in his postmaster accounts at Albany, New York. See Adams, *Memoirs*, 5:479, 480-82 (Jan. 4, 5, 1822); Solomon Van Rensselaer to William Bay, Jan. 7, 1822; R. J. Meigs to Solomon Southwick, Jan. 7, 1822; Van Buren to Charles E. Dudley, Jan. 10, 1822, Catharina V[an] R[ensselaer] Bonney, comp., *A Legacy of Historical Gleanings* . . . , 2 vols. (Albany, N.Y., 1875), 1:378-79, 383-84; Nathan Ulshoeffer to Van Buren, Jan. 13, 1822, Van Buren; King, *King*, 6, early Jan. 1822; Crawford to Thomas Worthington, Jan. 17, 1822, Worthington.

50 Senate *Executive Journal*, 3:265-66.

permanent rank of captain, had been paymaster general since August 1819; his nomination as colonel of light artillery—to the prejudice of officers who outranked him—probably provides the root answer to the difficulties between the President and the Senate. The Committee on Military Affairs reported that Towson's appointment was not authorized by law and the Senate rejected him, 25-19.[51]

Monroe, on March 26, withdrew all nominations on which the Senate had not acted until he could make a fuller communication and explanation of his views of the law and the principles on which he had acted.[52] On April 8 the President discussed with the cabinet a message he proposed to send to both houses. Crawford was decidedly against sending it while the matter was in the balance; he maintained doing so would be a breach of privilege and would be offensive to the legislative branch. Besides, he believed the appointment of Towson not warranted and had so told Wirt in the summer of 1821. Crawford thought the Constitution authorized the President to fill by temporary appointment vacancies that "happened" during the recess of Congress but not to fill newly created positions or those which occurred while Congress was in session. Adams recorded that Crawford maintained his position with "great pertinacity" against the President and Calhoun, and at the end of two hours the cabinet had reached no decision. Four days later Monroe decided to send a modified message to the Senate only; he considered this proper since Towson and James Gadsden were to be renominated. Crawford, however, expressed doubts of the expediency of the action, fearing it might cause irritation which would bring a second disapproval. He had communicated with no member of the Senate and did not know the grounds on which the nominees had been rejected.[53]

51 Ibid., 193, 197, 267, 269, 276-77, 278, 279; *Annals,* 17th Cong., 1st sess., 475. Members of the Senate Committee on Military Affairs were John Williams (Tenn.), Waller Taylor (Ind.), Richard Johnson (Ky.), John Elliott (Ga.), and John Chandler (Me.). In January the committee chairman had written that the "difficulties created by the Executive are almost insurmountable. . . . If embarrassment & confusion grow out of it, the President must blame himself and take more care hereafter." Williams to [Samuel] Dana, Jan. 27, 1822, C. E. French Papers (MHS).

52 Senate *Executive Journal,* 3:283. James Gadsden had been turned down as adjutant general by a vote of 23-20 on March 21; the following day a reconsideration resulted in his approval, 23-21. His name, however, was also withdrawn. The House had passed a resolution to censure the appointments as not conformable to law.

53 Adams, *Memoirs,* 5:487, 488 (April 8, 12, 1822). See also Wirt to Monroe, Oct.

Monroe's renominations were accompanied by a longer and more detailed analysis of his interpretation of the act of March 2, 1821. This message, the message of withdrawal, and the one of January were referred to the Committee on Military Affairs, which called for the proceedings and all correspondence of the Board of General Officers responsible for the reduction and called for other materials. All were sent, and on April 25 the committee report emphasized that the law forbade an individual being transferred into a regiment to the prejudice of the officers of that regiment. Towson's appointment was considered to be in violation of that prohibition. The Senate again rejected Towson and Gadsden—as Crawford had feared. The vote in each case was 25-17.[54] Parker was then removed from consideration, and on May 4 Towson was renominated to his earlier position. He and the other appointees were approved a few days later, but the Senate did not consent to the proposed brevet ranks of three of the artillery lieutenants.[55]

The appointments controversy, in and of itself, probably would not have engendered much animosity, but those opposing Crawford's presidential candidacy—and this included partisans of nearly all aspirants since Crawford was front runner at the time—seized upon the incident as another indication of Crawford's direct and indirect efforts to embarrass and sabotage the administration for his own political advantage. Especially did they emphasize the attack by his partisans in the spring of 1821 on the War Department and the unfavorable contrast of the Monroe with the Jefferson administration by "Trio" in July 1821. Other factors that probably tended to "blow up" the appointments controversy were the nomination for the presidency of William Lowndes (not Calhoun) by the South Carolina legislature, the newspaper quarrel between Adams and Jonathan Russell over the "duplicate letters,"[56] and the unpleasantness resulting from the attempts to ameliorate the Franco-American commercial difficulties.

22, 1823, Gratz. On April 22, 1822, Adams recorded Calhoun's "great bitterness" toward Crawford, and on July 8 he noted that his own personal intercourse with Calhoun had become one of "civility and not of confidence." *Memoirs,* 5:498; 6:43.

54 Senate *Executive Journal,* 3:286-92, 293, 295-96, 297-98; *Annals,* 17th Cong., 1st sess., 489-503. The votes were identical except that Talbot voted for Towson and against Gadsden, while Williams of Mississippi switched the other way.

55 Senate *Executive Journal,* 3:304, 305, 308, 309.

56 For treatment of several of these issues see the following chapter.

It is not at all clear how any presidential candidate—especially one who was a member of the government—would profit by the Senate rejection of the military nominations, and nothing has been discovered to contradict Crawford's statement that he had contacted no member of the Senate on them. He certainly sought to dissuade Monroe from sending his second message to the Senate. He had disavowed any connection with the 1821 attack on the War Department and he also had shown Monroe a letter replying to his communication disapproving the articles by "Trio." It is true that there were more Crawford supporters than followers of any other candidate among the nay voters, but Crawford had a larger congressional following than any other candidate. Actually, both the yea and nay votes contain the names of uncommitted senators as well as partisans of every presidential hopeful.

Crawford, by May 1822, seemed indifferent about remaining in office. He did not like and was discouraged by the tenor of negotiations in foreign affairs, and he was sensitive to the embarrassment to Monroe caused by the rejection of the nominations. For these rejections and the embarrassment he blamed Calhoun, but he had done nothing to counteract the impression that his own influence had been responsible for the rejection. It would not be injurious to him, he thought, to leave matters as they were or even be removed from office—but he did not solicit the latter.[57]

Crawford's removal was indeed predicted by some, and by others advocated, although it was thought that his dismissal would improve his chances for the presidency. Joel R. Poinsett of South Carolina urged that course on the President. It might result in the "elevation of the man," but it would be honorable to Monroe. In Poinsett's view, it did not matter whether Crawford encouraged the systematic opposition of his friends or whether he was unable to control them; either circumstance made him equally unfit for the office he held. If the opposition had originated in the current session, it might be a "more doubtful policy," but he had no hesitation in assuring Monroe that Crawford's friends, in and out of the House, had systematically opposed the administration.[58]

57 Crawford to Gallatin, May 13, 1822, Adams, *Gallatin Writings*, 2:241-43.
58 Poinsett to Monroe, May 12, 1822, Monroe, MDLC. See also Rufus King to Christopher Gore, June 5, 1822, King, *King*, 6:474-75.

It is rather strange that Crawford and Monroe did not discuss the dissension, but apparently Crawford was unwilling to take the initiative because he had no direct evidence of charges concerning his actions. Monroe was greatly embarrassed by the Senate rejection of his appointments, and in the spring he was worried about the growing division among his advisers.[59] On July 4, the day before he left for Georgia, Crawford wrote Monroe concerning some appointments and enclosed a letter from the collector at Pensacola, dealing with affairs of the Florida Territory, in which the hostility of Jackson and his associates in Florida to Crawford was said to be "without bounds." Further, a recent arrival in Florida had "delighted" the Crawford opponents with the "absurd story" that the Georgian was about to be removed from the treasury. Crawford thought the information on Florida might be useful to Monroe and said of the portion of the letter dealing with himself, "I have no comments to offer, except to assure you, that as my principal object in consenting to become a member of your administration was to be useful to you, I have no inducement to continue in it, after it is ascertained, that, that object, cannot be effected."[60]

Monroe received the letter at Albemarle on July 24 but delayed answering for almost a month. All members of the executive branch, he said, had been asked to serve in their respective positions in the full confidence that so long as they remained in office they would give their fullest support to the administration —as the most effectual way of promoting the public welfare. The President had been friends with them all and had asked of them nothing incompatible with what they owed themselves and their country. But toward Crawford he said he had "motives of a personal nature, to indulge this feeling, which I am not conscious of having departed from in a single instance." He refuted the idea (not mentioned in Crawford's letter) that there was a difference between the principles and policies of the administration in 1802 and his own—none in principle, and in policy only in the measures of the latter intended to provide for the common defense at the end of the war with Britain. Even if the present policy was questionable, and allowing the heads of the departments that "freedom of sentiment without

<hr/>

59 See Hamilton, *Monroe Writings*, 6, esp. May 1822.
60 Crawford to Monroe, July 4, 1822; Alexander Scott to Crawford, June 10, 1822 (copy), Monroe, NYP.

which their advice would be useless," he pointed out the necessity of support by all once the policy had been determined. He owed it to the country and to himself that the powers of his office "should not be paralized in my hands, but be preserved in their full force" to the last day of his term. A "painful" reference to Crawford's comment on the Scott letter said that had he "formed the resolution therein stated it would not have been so long suppressed." Monroe concluded, "Knowing as you do, the embarrassment to which, I have been, & may continue to be exposed, you can best decide, whether it comports with your own view to render me, the aid, which is desired and expected, and I refer it to your own candour to take the course which may be the most consistent with the sentiment, which you have expressed in your letter."[61]

The sensations excited by Monroe's letter were of the "most painful character," for Crawford had hoped his conduct toward Monroe for nearly fifteen years would have shielded him from the misrepresentations of men wholly unworthy of the President's confidence. Toward the latter part of the last session of Congress he had frequently heard of efforts to injure him in Monroe's estimation, but the only means he had of counteracting them was the "faithful discharge of my duty to you, both as an officer and a friend." Without evidence of misrepresentations, Crawford could not talk with Monroe about the matter, and since the President had not been impressed by the charge that Crawford's influence was responsible for the Senate rejection of the nominations, the secretary saw no need to mention it. "Your letter however convinces me that you were then either mistaken as to the state of your feelings or that the same efforts have been continued since that time, & with better success." Crawford was aware that the newspapers and perhaps the retrenchment committee of the House in the last session of Congress had attempted to make unfavorable comparisons of the Monroe administration with the Jefferson administration, but he knew of no attempt in or out of Congress to "take advantage of my standing . . . to promote that object." He then accused (without naming) Calhoun and his partisans of laboring for two or three years, by letters and publications, to produce the impression that Crawford was unfriendly to the Monroe administration. He

61 Monroe to Crawford, Aug. 22, 1822 (copy), ibid.

went into some detail, insisted he had given (and still gave) full support to the policy of fortifying the maritime and war islands, and noted that the fortification system then in a "state of progressive execution was devised before the present administration came in."

Crawford agreed that when the President had decided upon a measure the department heads were duty bound to carry it out. However, once the administration's reasons for adopting a measure had been revealed to Congress, any further interference or any attempt to "bias its decision by any other appeal than to the understanding of the members, ought to be considered an attack upon its independence." After such counsel, he said, he had made no efforts to obtain legislative approval unless invited to do so by the committee considering the proposal. He had never declined to reveal to individual members (who brought the subject into conversation) the administration's reasons for a measure—whether connected with the treasury or not; nor had he failed to try to "remove such objections as were made by them." He thought these were Monroe's ideas on the proper relations between the executive and legislative branches.

The army nominations had never been the occasion for the interchange of an idea between Crawford and any member of the Senate until long after they had been acted on. He claimed ignorance of the reasons that governed Monroe's actions until the publication of the secretary of war's letter to the Committee on Military Affairs; he could not have explained them if the opportunity had occurred. He did not even know the opinion of the Georgia senators until after they had voted; consequently, any insinuation that he had any influence on Senate rejection was utterly false.

Crawford knew embarrassments had occurred, but he maintained they had not resulted from either his action or inaction. Should he remain a member of the administration, it would "comport strictly not only with my views, but my feelings, to render you the aid which you desire & expect, if I have distinctly understood what is expected by you." But, he added, if it were expected that he be responsible for the imputation his enemies think the interest of their favorites requires them to cast upon him, then it "will be impossible for me to remain in the adminis-

tration with advantage to you, or reputation to myself." At the
moment, if he understood the spirit of Monroe's letter, he might
by implication be subject to the charge of "having been deficient
in my duty towards the President, & of practically declaring, that
if I should continue in the administration, the aid which is
desired & expected of me would not be rendered." To neither
of these would he consent to subject himself because such an
admission would be "wholly inconsistent with my past conduct,
& future intentions." He would leave Georgia about October 1
unless a communication from the President would make the
journey with his family unnecessary. But whatever the President's
decision, Crawford would continue to cherish the recollections
of the long friendship between them and should always regret if
the "intrigues of unprincipled men" have deprived him of that
friendship without his having the means or the opportunity of
defending himself against their attacks.[62]

On September 14 Crawford indicated he would not leave
Georgia until October 9; the delay would allow ample time for
him to receive the President's reply. Monroe found great satisfaction in Crawford's remarks about support of the administration,
but he denied intimating that any of Crawford's actions had been
incompatible with the conduct expected of department heads.
Crawford was mistaken about the conduct of "certain persons
to whom I presume you allude." In one case there had been
"uninterrupted silence"; in the other there had been no allusion
to Crawford except casually in conversation and always in the
"most delicate and guarded" manner. But Monroe would not
deal in minor matters since there was agreement on principle
and assurance of Crawford's friendly feeling. The President had
full confidence in his secretary's integrity and expressed the desire
for Crawford to continue in the administration.[63]

Crawford was writing to the President when he received
Monroe's letter; he found its sentiments highly gratifying. He
told the President of a number of deaths in central Georgia
from the fever, the fatal burning of his eldest brother in a "most
distressing accident," and the recovery of his family, all of whom
had been ill when they left Washington. They planned to leave
Georgia on October 9 and arrive in Washington about the end

62 Crawford to Monroe, Sept. 3, 1822, ibid.
63 Crawford to Monroe, Sept. 14, 1822; Monroe to Crawford, Sept. 17, 1822, ibid.

of the month.[64] The following day he told a friend that Monroe's letter was "entirely conciliatory and satisfactory." Though touching lightly upon the relations of others, the President's remarks were calculated to remove existing impressions and to quiet suspicions about those persons.[65] The summer had probably seemed unusually long to both Crawford and Monroe.

Crawford was to remain in the treasury post, but from this time on he had increasing reason to doubt his influence in the administration, particularly in the matter of appointments. After the summer of 1822 Crawford's recommendations for appointments seemed almost always designed simply to bring the person "into view." Upon hearing of the death of Josiah Meigs, commissioner of the General Land Office, Crawford wrote Samuel Harrison Smith that he had recommended him as Meigs' successor. Crawford was not sure his support would be useful, but he thought it proper for Smith to know what he had done, and Smith could then advance his cause as he thought best. By the time Crawford wrote, the position had been filled, but Crawford had not received Monroe's letter telling him of the choice of John McLean.[66]

The General Land Office was under the supervision of Crawford, and there is some indication that McLean was not happy in his position,[67] which was probably gained primarily through the influence of Calhoun. But McLean's term as commissioner was short. On June 10, 1823, Crawford informed Thomas Worthington that Return J. Meigs had tendered his resignation as postmaster general, indicated that Richard M. Johnson had been mentioned as his successor, and believed that the statement in the *New York Advocate* sanctioning the possible appointment of McLean was inserted to sound public opinion. But Crawford was going to see Monroe that day and tell him Worthington had his support for any office to which he might be appointed. This contact would probably be of no help to Worthington; it might

[64] Crawford to Monroe, Sept. 28, 1822, Gratz.

[65] Crawford to David B. Mitchell, Sept. 29, 1822, Moses Tyler Pyne-Joseph Henry Collection (Princeton University).

[66] Crawford to Smith, Sept. 19, 1822, J. Henley Smith Papers (MDLC); Monroe to Crawford, Sept. 7, 1822, Monroe, MDLC. Monroe said he would have been glad to have had Crawford's counsel if he had been near enough to promise early arrival.

[67] Thomas L. M'Kenney, *Memoirs, Official and Personal . . .* , 2 vols. in 1 (New York, 1846), 1:50, 52.

even be to his disadvantage. Crawford was not indifferent about the matter, but he confessed that "in my position I can do very little." His letter was prompted by friendship and public interest, and he thought Worthington might have some means of promoting his own interest. Within two weeks McLean was appointed.[68]

At this very time an appointment of far greater political implications was under consideration. There were several aspirants, including Martin Van Buren, for the associate justiceship of the Supreme Court, a vacancy caused by the death of Brockholst Livingston. Benjamin F. Butler, long associated with Van Buren in New York and visiting in Washington in May 1823, apparently in connection with this appointment, met with the secretaries of navy and treasury and the commissioner of the General Land Office; he was to see three or four others, including Joseph Anderson, who he had discovered was Crawford's righthand man. Crawford was described as a "plain *giant* of a man—very affable and talkative—seems to be a man of good sense & sound judgment, though I should not think, (and his friends do not present him as such) a man of brilliant talents. He was (of course) very civil &c &c." Butler reported that Van Buren probably would not be appointed to the Court.[69]

Butler had discovered something that Crawford, apparently, did not know, for the latter said he had no clue by which he could "offer a rational conjecture" of the decision the President would make. The only mention of the appointment in Crawford's presence had been Monroe's statement that "motives of delicacy" had induced him not to consult any of the department heads in this case. In denying a report that he had advocated the appointment of Nathan Sanford, Crawford said he was so well aware of his position relative to appointments that he had made it a rule to "manifest no preference for any individual applicant." When Monroe had introduced the Supreme Court vacancy into a conversation, Crawford had indicated his belief that Sanford would be as acceptable to New York as any other person—unless Van Buren was disposed to accept the position. He was neither recommending Sanford nor attempting to secure his appointment; if he were interested in securing the appointment of any person,

---

68 Crawford to Worthington, June 10, 1823, Worthington; J. B. Mower to C. K. Gardner, June 25, 1823, Charles K. Gardner Papers (New York State Library); White, *Jeffersonians*, 315.

69 Butler to Harriet [Mrs. Butler], May 7, 1823, Benjamin F. Butler Papers (NYS).

he would act by "indirect means, i.e. thro' other persons."[70]
There seems to have been general agreement that the President
would not elevate the political friends of the secretary of the
treasury.[71]

Monroe played well his role of impartiality toward all the
presidential candidates by choosing Smith Thompson, secretary
of the navy, for the Court vacancy. Crawford was surprised by
the choice and thought there must be a secret history of the case.[72]
Certainly Crawford had no influence in this appointment. After
the latter part of 1822 Monroe considered appointments his own
province. His determination to control nominations was admittedly influenced by the "scramble for office," but the keen embarrassment from the rejection of the army nominations was also
probably a factor in setting this course.

Crawford's participation in cabinet discussions and affairs of
government other than those of the treasury was very limited
after the Thompson elevation. His serious illness of September
1823 was followed by a relapse in May 1824, at which time
Monroe raised the possibility of appointing a temporary replace-
ment for him. In a June 22 cabinet session, lasting from 8 a.m.
until 9:30 p.m. and devoted primarily to discussing whether
Ninian Edwards should relinquish his ministership to Mexico,[73]
Adams was asked if he would assume Crawford's duties. The
secretary of state thought it would be found that the business of
the treasury had been transacted with as "much accuracy and
fidelity as was compatible with Mr. Crawford's indisposition"; if
no material inconvenience had occurred or was likely to occur,
he felt it best not to make a temporary appointment. Discussion
ranged over the whole history of the Monroe administration and
the opposition of Crawford partisans from the Seminole debate to
the slave trade convention. Monroe thought Crawford had not
"sufficiently discountenanced" the activity of his partisans but
the treasury secretary had shown Monroe Thomas W. Cobb's
reply to Crawford's letter disapproving the "Trio" attack of 1821.
Several months later the President noted that Crawford had
often spoken severely of Jackson's character and Jackson had done

[70] Crawford to Van Buren, May 9, 1823, Van Buren.
[71] Jacob Brown to C. K. Gardner, May 22, 1823, Gardner; Calhoun to J. D.
Erben, June 29, 1823, Andre DeCoppett Collection (Princeton University).
[72] Crawford to Van Buren, Aug. 1, 1823 (confidential), Van Buren.
[73] See following chapter.

the same of Crawford. Jackson had urged the removal of Crawford, but he was told that Crawford had claims on Monroe's
forbearance and friendship which probably no other man had.
These were explained to Jackson, who admitted the force of
them and had not mentioned the subject since.[74] One can only
conjecture what "claims" Crawford had, for at no place are
they spelled out. Perhaps they related to their long friendship, to
Crawford's support of Monroe in 1808, to Monroe's secretaryship
of war and state, to their membership in Madison's cabinet, to
Crawford's declining to be a candidate for the presidency against
Monroe in 1816, to Crawford's opposition to any presidential
nominating caucus in 1820, or to all these things collectively.

Crawford had refused to enter the Monroe cabinet unless the
government provided payment for some of Georgia's claims; this
was done, but the problems arising from the Indians remaining
in Georgia obtruded into the national councils throughout the
Monroe administration—and for many years after. Crawford
believed the government was bound by the compact of 1802 to
obtain cession of the Indian lands as soon as possible, and by
1823 the Indians had given up vast stretches of their holdings in
Georgia. In that year, however, the Creek and Cherokee indicated
that the several million acres they still held were not subject to
further cession. The Georgians considered the Indians dependent
tenants and were embittered that the central government had
not fully executed the 1802 agreement. Governor George M.
Troup, sharply critical of the national government, wanted the
compact carried out immediately; the legislature drafted a "memorial and remonstrance," which was forwarded to Monroe on December 20, 1823, and to the Georgia senators and representatives,
who were urged to carry out the purpose of the remonstrance.
Senator John Forsyth became very active, as did Thomas W.
Cobb, but the latter (a representative) pointed out that he derived
the right to his seat directly from the people of Georgia and thus
doubted the power of any department of the state government
to instruct him on how to discharge his duty. At the same time
he expressed hearty concurrence in the sentiments of the memorial and the governor's letter and assured Troup he would do
everything possible to obtain the object of the memorial.[75]

[74] Adams, *Memoirs*, 6:391-95, 485-86 (June 22, 1824; Jan. 31, 1825).
[75] Cobb to George M. Troup, Jan. 14, 1824, Cobb Folder (GDAH).

Forsyth and Senator John Elliott saw Monroe; he had received the memorial, but he would make no recommendation to Congress—he had already made his views known and all he would do was sign whatever measure Congress might pass. At Monroe's request the two called later; they were read materials that would serve as a basis for negotiations with the Cherokee. Shortly thereafter they were angered and surprised by the correspondence between the War Department and the Cherokee chiefs, which Monroe sent in accord with his earlier promise. Forsyth then drafted the communication (generally called the "protest") of the Georgia delegation in Congress to Monroe. This letter, signed by the two senators and six representatives from Georgia, blamed the government for the refusal of the Indians to migrate, criticized the methods of negotiating with the Indians, and demanded government use of force against the Indians if peaceful removal could not be immediately effected.

The more Monroe reflected on the "extraordinary character" of the paper the greater surprise it excited. He had pressed for cessions from the Indians since he had come into office, but this paper caused him to change his mind about sending a special message to Congress on March 15. He was satisfied Crawford knew nothing of the proceedings, but since the character of the state as well as the nation was involved he would not send the document to Congress without the secretary's having seen it. He had given the letter to Crawford, and he asked James Barbour to call on Crawford (whose eyesight was then severely impaired) and read the papers with him. Monroe did not think it proper for him to propose withdrawing the unprovoked and unexpected protest, but if it were not withdrawn he would communicate it to Congress with the other materials. Two days later Monroe again wrote Barbour and emphasized that the letter to Crawford stated explicitly that if the paper were withdrawn it would be by action of the Georgians and not by "any suggestion of mine other than to permit it." Monroe, convinced the matter was a "painful subject" to Crawford, wished to trouble the indisposed secretary as little as possible. He asked Barbour to see Crawford and then communicate with the President.[76]

[76] Monroe to Barbour, March 14, 16, 1824, Barbour. Monroe later described the letter as "Such an one as I never received either in my public or private character." Monroe to Madison, April [n.d.] 1824, Hamilton, *Monroe Writings*, 7:18.

Adams thought the letter would be withdrawn through Crawford's intercession, and he suspected it had been written with that intention. Crawford, much mortified by the letter, saw Elliott, indicated his disapproval, and intimated his wish that the communication be withdrawn. The delegation decided they would not withdraw the letter nor "communicate with him on the subject."[77] In a special message transmitting the materials to Congress Monroe reviewed the actions of the government. He noted the unwillingness of the Indians to exchange their Georgia lands for land west of the Mississippi, said the Indians could be removed immediately only by force, and asserted that under the compact of 1802 the government was not obliged to force their removal. The special committee report was followed by an appropriation on May 26 of only $50,000 for extinguishing Creek titles to land in Georgia.[78] It is interesting, but in character, that Adams should suspect a contrived plot to permit Crawford's influence to be felt. Crawford, in this instance, as in several others, obviously had no control over the actions of Cobb and some of his other followers—though their actions were often ascribed to his promptings.

During the period from the selection of the presidential electors in November 1824 and the choice of the President by the House in February 1825 there was much visiting between and among the partisans of the candidates and some among the candidates themselves. Much earlier in the Monroe administration the cabinet had several times discussed the etiquette of visiting; their practices varied considerably, and they were unable to standardize them. But the dinners, balls, and social gatherings continued. Some were gala events; others rather routine, and at times the President and Crawford (or one of the other secretaries) would exchange guest lists in order to avoid duplication of invitations.[79]

[77] Monroe to Jefferson, April [n.d.] 1824, Hamilton, *Monroe Writings*, 7:20-21; Adams, *Memoirs*, 6:258, 262 (March 15, 1824). Barbour thought the letter had been written by Forsyth and copied by Cobb. Monroe thought the act of the Georgians was motivated by eagerness for popularity in their state, the passion of the people for land, and party ambition of the Crawford faction to outdo the Clark faction.
[78] *Annals*, 18th Cong., 1st sess., 462-64, 469-71, 2348-57; *ASPIA*, 2:495-98; *House Doc.*, No. 115 (serial 98), 18th Cong., 1st sess.; 4 *Stat.* 36. This story, with emphasis on Forsyth's role, may be followed in Duckett, *Forsyth*, 105-8.
[79] Adams, *Memoirs*, 4:311, 480-81, 483-86, 487-91; Crawford to Madison, Feb. 20, 1816, Madison Papers (University of Virginia); Rufus King to Christopher Gore, Feb. 19, 1818, King, *King*, 6:59; Crawford to Monroe, Jan. 4, 1818, Monroe, MDLC.

Not a great deal of information is available on the social and family life of the Crawfords, but one would infer from Adams' comments that Mrs. Crawford was sufficiently active in the social sphere. And an occasional glimpse is given by others. Margaret Bayard (Mrs. Samuel Harrison) Smith paints a warm picture of the Crawford family life—with an infrequent touch of the social —and Crawford seems to have become a favorite of the Smiths after Jefferson retired from the presidency.[80] Louis McLane of Delaware, often in Washington without his family, attended many social affairs and frequently wrote rather frankly about them to his wife. In one instance he told of a Sunday at the Crawfords'. Crawford was exceedingly fond of his children and in the "old style had them playing about us all day." Mrs. Crawford had "none of the aire" of Mrs. Adams, but she was a kind, excellent woman whom he hoped one day to see "receiving bows at the palace." McLane was delighted with and complimentary of the children, noted especially the brightness of Macon, and said his day with the Crawfords was the most pleasant since he came to Washington. Reporting on a dinner at the President's on December 11, 1822, McLane said that Calhoun and his wife looked "as if they hoped to be settled there soon themselves." Crawford, who sat next to McLane, was no longer wearing a wig and "looks much better than I ever saw him."[81]

McLane's is the only discovered mention of Crawford's wig, and until recently the only published picture of Crawford—from the portrait by John Wesley Jarvis—shows him wigless, with only a few wisps of hair on the top of his head but with a plentiful supply elsewhere. In 1959 the portrait done by Charles Willson Peale in 1818 was discovered in Washington; it shows Crawford with a wig. The portrait was begun on December 8 and finished five days later, with Mrs. Crawford and the children present during the last sitting. Though the Crawfords were pleased with

[80] Gaillard Hunt, ed., *The First Forty Years of Washington Society* . . . (New York, 1906), 170-205 passim. It will be recalled that there are no extant letters from Crawford to his family, and no letter by Mrs. Crawford is known to exist. The Hunt item consists of letters to and from Margaret Bayard (Mrs. Samuel H.) Smith and members of her family. Mrs. Smith said, on January 14, 1825, Crawford's happiness "depends chiefly if not entirely on his family—he is the fondest father and one of the best husbands I ever knew." Ibid., 171.

[81] McLane to Dear Kitty, n.d.: McLane to Col. Allen M'Lane, Dec. 12, 1822, McLane Papers (University of Delaware). Most of the McLane papers are on microfilm.

the work, they must not have bought a copy, for there is no evidence that the artist made one.[82]

The "wigless" cabinet years must have been much less satisfying to Crawford than the earlier ones. Congenial atmosphere gave way to considerable suspicion and discord, nurtured in large measure by presidential ambitions of the cabinet members. Monroe, in an effort to preserve his neutrality in the presidential contest and probably also to try to avoid embarrassment such as he had suffered in the spring of 1822, reduced the influence of all department heads by assuming almost exclusive control over appointments. Crawford's role was further reduced by his serious illness in the fall of 1823 and his relapse in May 1824. By the latter date the presidential campaign had long been in full swing and the Georgian had been nominated by the congressional caucus.

[82] *Washington Post,* July 15, 1959; Peale to Rembrandt Peale, Dec. 5, 1818; Peale to Rubens Peale, Dec. 9, 1818, Charles Willson Peale Letter Book XV; Charles Willson Peale Diary, Dec. 13, 1818 (American Philosophical Society Library). Peale did not part with originals. On December 7 Crawford remarked that he thought Peale was pursuing a "very unprofitable business." Peale answered that he "did not think so, as I expected to carry great treasure with me."

10

One-Party
Presidential Politics

CRAWFORD'S RECORD as senator from 1807 to 1813 had placed him high in the party hierarchy, and his appointment as secretary of war, upon his return from France, had again called him to public attention. Few people, however, thought of him in 1815 as Madison's successor, though he was sometimes linked, as the vice-presidential candidate, with Governor Daniel Tompkins of New York. James Monroe, secretary of state since 1811 and also secretary of war at the end of the conflict with England, was most often mentioned as heir apparent. Though Monroe had opposed Madison's election in 1808, the key Republican leaders quickly forgave his temporary disaffection and quietly gave support to his selection in 1816. His Revolutionary service and long, though not always illustrious, career were factors in his favor.[1] Crawford favored Monroe's candidacy, but he hoped to use the nominating caucus of 1816 to improve his chances for succeeding Monroe in 1825.

By early 1816, when the presidential election became a topic of general discussion,[2] many were advocating the election of the Georgian, but extant materials reveal nothing as to Crawford's presidential hopes and ambition until he took steps to withdraw his name from caucus consideration. Support for Crawford appears to have been rooted to a considerable degree in a deep-seated resentment—in the New England area, in New York, and to a lesser degree in the South—against Virginia's continued domination of the presidential office. This might well have resulted in party division in 1816 had Crawford been willing to be a candidate for the congressional caucus nomination. He probably would have been successful, but it is by no means sure that he would have defeated Monroe—who most certainly would have been his opponent in the election. But Crawford was not a candidate and the reemergence of parties was delayed until after the election of 1824.

The feeling prevailed among many politicians that Virginia, in maintaining her supremacy, "bought off" serious challengers from Massachusetts and New York by giving them the second place on the tickets. New York had seen its earlier favorites, Aaron Burr and George Clinton, relegated to the vice presidency under the Virginia dynasty; in 1816 New York had another favorite son, Governor Tompkins, and the major maneuvering on the caucus nomination was centered in the New York congressional delegation and among prominent persons in New York state. There was some confusion as to the exact purpose of their actions, and there remains some difference of interpretation as to who was responsible for what.

The New York dilemma is revealed in a letter from Jabez D. Hammond to Martin Van Buren on January 23, 1816. Hammond, unable to see Van Buren when the latter visited Washington, wanted the "little fox" to know that the New York delegation intended to support Tompkins for the presidential nomination. The way to achieve their goal was not so easily determined, but it was clearly necessary to divide the southern interests if Tompkins were to be successful. Hammond had thought the "true policy" was to support the pretensions of Crawford in preference to Monroe if Crawford and his friends could be persuaded to pit themselves against Monroe and his friends. Then a situation might be produced that would bring the nomination of Tompkins. If not, then the next best thing—nomination of Crawford—might be achieved.[3]

Samuel R. Betts, another member of the New York congressional delegation, reported that some of those opposed to another President from Virginia had a high regard for Tompkins and acknowledged the weight of the New York claims, but they believed Tompkins was not sufficiently well known by people of

---

1 See Josiah Meigs to Oliver Wolcott, Nov. 13, 1813, Oliver Wolcott Papers (Connecticut Historical Society); Nathaniel Macon to Crawford, Jan. 30, 1814, Crawford, MDLC; John Norvelle to George W. Campbell, Feb. 18, March 3, 1815, Campbell, MDLC· Christopher Gore to Rufus King, Aug. 20, 1815, King, *King*, 5:486; Jabez D. Hammond, *The History of Political Parties in the State of New York,* 2 vols. (Cooperstown, N.Y., 1847), 1:395.

2 See, for example, *Buffalo Gazette,* Jan. 30, 1816; *Boston Patriot,* Jan. 13, 20, Feb. 7, 21, 24, 1816.

3 Van Buren Papers.

other states. If the New York claims were pressed, other anti-Virginians would make common cause with the Virginians. Betts knew this to be the case with members from North Carolina and Georgia, two from South Carolina and Tennessee, and a majority of the Kentucky delegation. The last group, maintaining the impossibility of nominating Tompkins, expressed a willingness to join New York in support of some candidate against Monroe.

Further, Betts said the statement in the *New York National Advocate* that Crawford did not wish to be a candidate was published without Crawford's knowledge; he would serve as President if elected. However, Crawford's closest friends said he would not permit his name to be presented unless he was certain of New York's support. These friends believed Crawford's career would be injured greatly if he were proposed for the nomination without a strong possibility of success—or enough votes to make his failure respectable. Only Crawford, Betts thought, could be a real competitor against Monroe, but unity among the anti-Monroe people was necessary to bring about nomination of the Georgian. If there was no possibility of carrying Tompkins in Washington, Betts suggested that Van Buren might prefer to nominate Crawford for President and Tompkins (if he would consent) for Vice President in "your legislature" thus starting the ticket with a "high character."[4]

The statement, derived apparently from conversations, that Crawford did not wish to be a candidate had been widely disseminated, though he intended it for circulation only among his partisans who should prevent his name from being placed in candidacy against Monroe. But Van Buren wanted to know definitely whether Crawford was a candidate. Van Buren had accepted the word of William W. Bibb, Crawford's successor in the Senate and spokesman for the former minister, that Crawford's name would not be presented to the caucus, and Van Buren had so informed his friends in Albany. However, "numerous letters" had indicated that the declaration in one of the papers was not authorized, and if New York would support Crawford his friends would bring him out against Monroe. Would Bibb enlighten him?[5]

[4] Betts to Van Buren, Jan. 19, 1816, ibid. See also Robert V. Remini, "New York and the Presidential Election of 1816," *New York History* 31 (1950):316.
[5] Van Buren to Bibb, Jan. 29, 1816, Van Buren.

Bibb then took "official" action designed to withdraw Crawford's name from further consideration. On February 1, 1816, he wrote the *National Intelligencer:* "In consequence of repeated enquiries . . . whether Mr. Crawford was to be considered among the competitors, accompanied with the desire that his views should be ascertained, I communicated to him what had passed. He replied, without reserve, that he did not consider himself among the number of those from whom the selection ought to be made, and that he was unwilling to be held up as a competitor for that office."[6] Not even the wide republication of this statement deterred many Crawford supporters from continuing to advocate his nomination.

The Monroe papers contain an eight-page memo, apparently written about this time, which shows that he was fully aware of events and that he was determined to be a candidate for the presidency. In this paper, which may well have served as a guide for his followers, Monroe noted the opposition to him because he was a Virginian and because of the friendship of some for Clay, Crawford, and Tompkins. He detailed the possible combinations that involved Crawford as presidential nominee and Tompkins as second choice (and the reverse), spoke of the Bibb declaration and the "denial," and hinted at Federalist machinations. The Monroe supporters, he maintained, had a right to ask whether Crawford was a candidate, and his answer should decide the matter. For him to say he was not a candidate and for his friends to continue to advance his candidacy would be absurd, since everyone would believe that he could stop the negotiations if he chose. If Crawford's friends proposed a caucus, it might be inferred that they had ascertained how the Republican members of Congress would vote and on which side the majority was. Monroe's friends, he concluded, should not attend the caucus; they should say that the great republican body of voters should decide.[7]

This paper could have been written before the publication of Bibb's letter of February 1, with the denial reference being to

[6] *National Intelligencer*, Feb. 3, 1816. Remini, "New York and the Presidential Election of 1816," 316, maintains that Crawford made "one of the greatest mistakes of his life. Beset with doubts as to his own adequacy, of the possibility of Monroe's victory and its effect upon his future career, to say nothing of the timidity he found elsewhere displayed by his supposedly ardent partisans, he unsuccessfully attempted to withdraw from the race. Foolish though it was, he authorized his close friend and advisor . . . to make his decision known."

[7] Monroe Papers, MDLC.

the assertion that Crawford had not authorized the first notice, which appeared in the *National Advocate* and other papers. Such probably was the case. There is no indication that Monroe sent this piece to anyone; perhaps he was just thinking things through so that he could better plan with his followers. However, it is possible—and even probable—that there is a connection between Monroe's memo and a communication of February 9, 1816. In the latter, several Monroe stalwarts noted that when Congress assembled they thought Monroe had the undivided support of the Republican party; the caucus had been delayed, and now the friends of Crawford were claiming a congressional majority for their favorite. The function of the caucus, the writers held, was merely to "give concert to public opinion" and not to attempt to influence it—if the people were left to themselves they would be disposed to elect Monroe. If Crawford's claims were pressed, and unless circumstances dictated a change in the "course agreed upon," Monroe's friends would refuse a caucus lest a majority be procured against what was considered the public sentiment. It was a "delicate business"; as little "eclat" as possible should be given to the communication which was intended for the use of "our republican friends only."[8]

Meanwhile, Bibb had informed Van Buren that from the beginning of the presidential discussions he had been convinced that Crawford did not wish to have his name presented to the caucus, and Bibb continued to oppose Crawford's candidacy.[9] Some, however, thought Crawford not especially sincere in his withdrawal; others took direct steps to remove their uncertainty. Among the latter was Abner Lacock, senator from Pennsylvania, who talked with Bibb and then with Crawford, who confirmed what Bibb had said. Crawford had asked Bibb to assure every man (who asked) that he was not a candidate; he never intended there should be any public notice of this action and regretted that a declaration, "made in the sincerity of my heart," had not been sufficient to end discussion of his possible candidacy. To Lacock's statement that Monroe's claims to the nomination were stronger than Crawford's and that Crawford could be President after Monroe's death, the Georgian responded, "True. If Monroe be-

---

8 James Barbour, A. T. Mason, James Pleasants, Thomas Newton, William Roane, and Hugh Nelson to Gentlemen, Feb. 9, 1816, Barbour.
9 Bibb to Van Buren, Feb. 5, 1816, Van Buren.

longed to any other state . . . there would be no other candidate spoken of." The day before the meeting with Lacock, Crawford told Erastus Root of New York that he would not serve if elected. He had authorized Bibb to say that he was not a candidate; how could he act now with such duplicity as to say that he was? Further, his feelings would not permit him to oppose Monroe: their friendship, the manner of Crawford's coming into the cabinet, the effect on that body, and "every principle of honor, justice and propriety forbid me, if I can help it, allowing my name to be entered in opposition to him."[10]

Nevertheless, Crawford's "candidacy" continued to be discussed. Editors and individuals who accepted his withdrawal often praised him for his fine qualities and his unwillingness to promote party dissension; others insisted that he must be a candidate, for only he could overcome the effects of the sectional differences shown during the War of 1812; still others, especially those favoring Monroe, saw Federalist influence behind Crawford's support and compared Crawford unfavorably with Monroe.[11]

Crawford remained the chief pivot of the maneuvers going on among New Yorkers. Betts informed Van Buren on February 5 that some of the New York congressional delegation, seeing no chance to nominate Tompkins, would vote for Monroe rather than Crawford. The uncertainty of the goal of the New Yorkers was again revealed. If Van Buren wished Crawford pushed, he would have to be nominated at Albany; the division in the New York delegation would destroy the practicability of nominating him in caucus.[12]

The Van Buren-Tompkins forces controlled the New York legislature, and even though it was obvious by the second week of February that Tompkins had no chance for the nomination, Van Buren was not willing to risk his control at Albany by making an all-out effort to nominate Crawford. Then, too, the "vindictive

[10] Abner Lacock to John Binns, Feb. 7, 8, 1816, in *Savannah Republican*, Jan. 10, 1824. The originals of these letters have not been located.

[11] See, for example, *Athens Journal*, Feb. 22, 1816; *Albany Register*, Feb. 20, March 12, 1816; *New Hampshire Patriot*, Feb. 20, 1816; *National Intelligencer*, Feb. 6, 22, 1816; *Richmond Enquirer*, Feb. 10, 15, 1816; *Philadelphia Democratic Press*, Feb. 8, 1816; *Baltimore Patriot*, Feb. 14, 1816; Spencer Roane to James Barbour, Feb. 12, 1816, Barbour; Jeremiah Morrow to Thomas Worthington, Feb. 12, 1816, Worthington; John McLean to Ethan A. Brown, March 4, 1816, Ethan A. Brown Papers (OHS); Ambrose Spencer to Jacob Brown, March 2, 1816, Brown, MHS; "No. 3—The Next President and Public Opinion," by "An Independent Citizen," Monroe, NYP.

[12] Betts to Van Buren, Feb. 5, 1816, Van Buren.

and arrogant" Judge Ambrose Spencer was strongly in favor of Crawford; if Van Buren supported Crawford this meant "submitting" to Spencer—and the possible undermining of Van Buren in New York. It is entirely possible that after the trip to Washington in January Van Buren worked secretly for the choice of Monroe—a choice that would be ensured by adhering to Tompkins. The result was that on February 14 the New York legislature resolved that the state's congressional delegation be instructed to support Tompkins, and the resolutions warned that the ascendency of the Republican party would be jeopardized by the nomination of another Virginian.[13]

The Albany action did not end the disagreement in the New York delegation. On February 23 and 26 they met to consider their instructions. Neither the friends of Monroe nor the friends of Crawford would yield, so it was concluded the nomination of Tompkins was impossible. The delegation could not unite on one man, and the meeting was broken up before a motion for unanimous support of the candidate of the majority could be adopted.[14]

Anonymously, the friends of Crawford called for a caucus to meet on March 12, but this caucus did nothing more than authorize another. The friends of Monroe were said to be in "great consternation," and those who pretended to know believed the votes for Crawford and Tompkins would exceed those for Monroe and all or nearly all of Tompkins' friends would unite against Monroe. On March 15 the Monroe partisans met and decided to attend the caucus and attempt to prevent a nomination.

As soon as the meeting organized the next evening, Henry Clay moved that it was inexpedient to make a nomination. After much discussion the motion was lost. Balloting proceeded, with Monroe defeating Crawford 65-54 and Tompkins defeating Simon Snyder 85-30 for the vice-presidential post. According to Betts,

13 Among the writers on the New York scene there is not complete agreement as to what happened and who supported whom. For accounts see DeAlva Stanwood Alexander, *A Political History of New York*, 3 vols. (New York, 1906-1909), 1:237-40; Hammond, *Political Parties*, 1:405-12; Remini, "New York and the Presidential Election of 1816," 311-17. A copy of the resolutions of the New York assembly is in the Taylor Papers.

14 Samuel R. Betts to Van Buren, Feb. 24, 1816, Van Buren; Hammond, *Political Parties*, 1:409; Remini, "New York and the Presidential Election of 1816," 318-19; John W. Taylor to John Tayler, Feb. 28, 1816, Taylor. Peter B. Porter, John W. Taylor, and Enos T. Throop were said to have been responsible for the hasty adjournment.

Monroe's friends had had cause for alarm, for William T. Barry and Micah Taul of Kentucky, Bennett H. Henderson, Samuel Powell, and Isaac Thomas of Tennessee, James J. Wilson and one other from New Jersey, Thomas Wilson of Pennsylvania, and one (Bartlett Yancey?) from North Carolina who had always declared their decided preference for Crawford voted for Monroe. Four sick members voted by proxy for Monroe; four of Crawford's friends refused to attend, as did two of Monroe's. Four, said Betts, of the New York delegation voted for Monroe.[15]

Crawford certainly was not pleased with the caucus action. He felt he had "serious cause of complaint against my particular friends. They would not consent, when the declarations of Dr. Bibb were not sufficient, that I should put an end to the contest by declaring that I would not serve if elected." Their plan, as Crawford understood it, was to attend the caucus, vote for Monroe, and state their position in a communication to the *National Intelligencer*. This procedure, they believed, would "place me on higher ground than could be occupied in any other way, as I did not wish to be elected. This plan was eventually abandoned, without any explanation ever having been given. Bibb, Tait, Macon, and Hall all absented themselves, with several others, and of course, deprived themselves of the right to make the proposed statement." He foresaw charges of intrigue and double-dealing.[16]

Crawford declined Madison's offer to shift to the treasury,

---

[15] Jabez D. Hammond to Van Buren, March 10, 1816, Otis Norcross Collection (MHS): Nathan Sanford to Van Buren, March 14, 1816; Betts to Van Buren, March 17, 1816, Van Buren: *Baltimore American & Commercial Daily Advertiser*, March 19, 1816; *National Intelligencer*, March 19, 1816. Of the twenty-four Republican members of Congress absent, nine were out of the city and fifteen were "scrupulous in regard to the propriety" of such meetings or for other reasons were not disposed to attend. *Niles' Weekly Register* 10 (March 23, 1816):59-60. Certainly three of the New York delegation voted for Monroe. Ibid., 25 (Dec. 20, 1823): 245; Hammond, *Political Parties*, 1:412. Hammond believed that only William Irving, Enos Throop, and Victory Birdseye voted for Monroe. Earlier he had thought Taylor was in this group, but Taylor told Hammond this was not the case. Betts probably included Taylor in his count. Van Buren's brief account of the 1816 nomination is somewhat less than candid. John C. Fitzpatrick, ed., *The Autobiography of Martin Van Buren*, vol. 2 of *Annual Report* of the American Historical Association for 1918 (Washington, D.C., 1920), 122.

[16] William W. Bibb, Charles Tait, and Bolling Hall of Georgia and Nathaniel Macon of North Carolina. Crawford should probably have known that Macon would not attend. Macon had an abiding hatred of caucuses; sustained and almost desperate efforts could not persuade him to attend the one in 1824 in spite of his enduring and devoted support of Crawford.

indicating that it might be better to have the next President "less shackled" in forming his cabinet. He did not know what would be the best course: "I have some doubts whether, under the particular circumstances in which I have been placed, it will not be my duty to remain some time as a member of his [Monroe's] Cabinet, if he should wish it, and at least give him an opportunity of manifesting his displeasure, if I have incurred it." That he had temporarily lost faith in the judgment of his friends is clear; in deciding whether to remain in the government, he would not consult them, "as the chances are two to one that their advice will be wrong."[17]

In late October Crawford did move to the treasury in "obedience to the earnest solicitations of the President," but he remained unhappy about what he called the obstinacy of a part of the Republican party in running his name at the caucus *"in opposition to my wishes"* and those of his friends. This had resulted in his being subjected to "torrents of abuse" from all parts of the country. He indicated he might retire at the end of Madison's term; he would leave public service with more relish than he entered it, hoping he would take with him the esteem of all good men who were acquainted with him.[18]

Crawford and his supporters certainly were denounced for the caucus actions, but the sharpest criticism was prompted by the *Exposition,* a pamphlet of undetermined authorship which purported to explain the motives of those who opposed Monroe, and which praised Crawford.[19] The *Exposition,* which seems to have been distributed in the latter part of May, attacked Monroe as the representative of the dominant Virginia group which seemed to have a "systematic design of perpetually governing the country." Further, the pamphlet asserted, Monroe was not especially qualified for the presidency; even his friends considered him of but moderate talents and "slow of comprehension." Admittedly, he was urbane, but this quality simply made him more accessible and more open to "artifices of imposture." Such a man would

[17] Crawford to Albert Gallatin, May 10, 1816, Gallatin; Adams, *Gallatin Writings,* 1:702-4.

[18] Crawford to Thomas Worthington, Nov. 23, 1816, Worthington.

[19] Copies of the pamphlet, *Exposition of Motives for Opposing the Nomination of Mr. Monroe for the Office of President of the United States* (Washington, D.C., 1816) are in the New York State Library and in the Alderman Library of the University of Virginia.

keep talent at a distance and surround himself with "compliant mediocrity, and hypocritical dullness"—an estimate made absurd by the caliber of Monroe's cabinet. Monroe's "blunders" in France were recounted, his opposition to Madison's election recalled, and his stockjobbing, government by patronage, and "entangling intercommunications with Europe" denounced.

Even at the time of its publication, no one seemed to know who the authors of the *Exposition* were. There is no indication that Crawford had foreknowledge of, sanctioned, or had any hand in it. Papers still supporting him printed it in full or in part, while others took uncomplimentary notice of it or said the owner might have all copies back by letting the editors know where to send them. The *Exposition* was one of several such items, said the *National Intelligencer;* the paper believed the *Exposition* as unauthorized as it was ill advised. The *Intelligencer* supported Monroe and maintained that the measures of Crawford's department and his own political views were fair subjects for discussion, but it entertained too high a respect for Crawford's personal and public character to suppose him capable of submitting the public interest to personal or interested feelings.[20]

Crawford's report on Indian affairs was made the subject of a systematic attack by "Americanus" of Washington, D.C., between April 10 and the end of the month. The five letters, each beginning with the quotation dealing with intermarriage of whites and Indians and the "volunteered" comment on immigrants, appeared in several papers and later were printed as *Strictures Addressed to James Madison on the Celebrated Report of William H. Crawford Recommending the Intermarriage of Americans with the Indian Tribes. . . .*[21] In his remarks about foreigners Crawford was said to exhibit a spirit of aristocracy, bigotry, and proscription that was in keeping with the principles and opinions which impelled him in 1798 to "mount the Black cockade, and volunteer in the proscription of Democracy, and the denunciation of the Rights of Man."[22] The letters rambled from one topic to

20 *Albany Register*, May 28, 1816; *National Intelligencer*, May 23, July 16, 1816.
21 Jasper Harding of Philadelphia printed the pamphlet in 1824. It seems, though it is not certain, that these may be the letters which Crawford, in his letter to Gallatin on May 10, 1816, said "are remarkable only for the grossest ignorance of the subject which they treat, and asperity of abuse."
22 *Strictures*, iii. This is a reference to Crawford's signing the letter from the young men of Augusta to President John Adams.

the other, but in their course they charged that Crawford despised the French as a "capering nation" whose language it was beneath his dignity to learn; that the gravity with which his proposals were made was a "coverslut"; that Crawford was a "mere theorist, and a very wild one"; and that it was not surprising that Crawford, who lived so long in the neighborhood of the Creek and other Indians, should make the suggestion of intermarriage. The government, however, had no means of encouraging his proposal except by some direct or indirect methods of paying the males and females who prostitute themselves to the wild schemes, and by comparison the prostitution of white women to white men was "virtue itself." Crawford was termed a "bigoted calumniator" of more than half the American people and nine tenths of their ancestors; it was implied that he was a British tool; and his return from France was ascribed to "total unfitness."

The *Philadelphia Democratic Press* carried the letters in April and continued to copy from other papers or make comments of its own until the end of July. From the *Baltimore Patriot* it reprinted a story maintaining that intermarriage would not civilize the Indians; rather it would tend to render the Americans more savage. A few issues later the *Democratic Press* asserted that Crawford had displayed in his report a "most illiberal" disposition and put the most offensive opinions in the most offensive words; he had thus forfeited whatever portion he possessed of the confidence of the great Republican family of the nation and placed himself in the "bosom of faction."[23]

The degree of Federalist involvement in denouncing Crawford —and in supporting him in order to create division to their own benefit—is impossible to ascertain; such tactics were not alien to American political parties.[24] The Federalists did not nominate a candidate in 1816, but Rufus King received the thirty-four votes from Massachusetts, Connecticut, and Delaware; the other 183 went to Monroe. Whatever the schismatic efforts of the Federalists and others, Crawford in 1816 had no desire to split the Republican party. It seems clear that he genuinely did not want to be a candidate for the nomination—and certainly not a candidate for

---

[23] *Democratic Press,* June 15, July 2, 19, 1816.
[24] *New Hampshire Patriot,* April 16, 1816. Crawford observed that the Federalists were too weak to put up a candidate and were unable to produce a schism in the Republican ranks. Crawford to William Lee, May 19, 1816, Gallatin.

election. He was well known, his abilities were well respected until political faction began to berate them, and he did want to stand on "higher ground" so far as the succession is concerned. He became a victim of his "friends"; he was the most logical rallying point for the anti-Virginia group; and his failure to take a completely unambiguous and unequivocal stand—either for or against securing the nomination—probably cost him his chance to be President. But the events surrounding the caucus action and the election of 1816 foretold the splitting of the party, and all too soon the "bosom of faction" was evident.[25]

The election of 1820 was the subject of practically no comment in the years following the election of 1816, though there was some discussion—and apparently some difference of opinion—on the propriety of a caucus to nominate Monroe for reelection. Crawford's attitude—that the call for a caucus was unfriendly to Monroe—prevailed; no nomination was made, and Monroe's election without opposition was assured.[26]

By that time several men had shown a desire to succeed Monroe in 1825. Three of his cabinet members, Adams, Calhoun, and Crawford, had presidential hopes; DeWitt Clinton of New York cherished lingering ambitions; Henry Clay was encouraged by the lack of united support for a cabinet member; Andrew Jackson had been "pushed" into the national picture before 1820; and William L. Lowndes was in strong contention until his death in 1822. Crawford, choice of a large minority in 1816, stood as the most prominent candidate to succeed Monroe, and as a native Virginian he might expect the support of that state, which for the first time in the history of the republic had no candidate for the office. Some expected Monroe to favor him, but the President maintained a strict neutrality among his cabinet mem-

---

25 No evidence whatever has been found to support the statement of Wiltse, *Calhoun*, 1:115, that "Monroe's margin of victory was in no small degree attributable to the efforts of Calhoun, a point the unsuccessful contestant was not likely to overlook." Calhoun, riding with John Quincy Adams on May 22, 1820, asked about transactions at Ghent and the project said to have been formed there, or immediately after at Paris, to have Crawford run for the presidency in 1816. Adams told him, "I have never heard anything of this either at Ghent or at Paris; and if any projects upon the Presidency had been there formed, I had not been privy to them." *Memoirs*, 5:129.

26 Crawford to Charles Tait, Sept. 15, 1820, Tait. See also William Plumer, Jr. to William Plumer, Sr., April 24, 1820, Everett S. Brown, ed., *The Missouri Compromises and Presidential Politics, 1820-1825* (St. Louis, 1926), 49, 51, 54. Cited hereafter as Brown, *Missouri Compromises*.

bers.[27] At the same time, Crawford realized the importance of the support of New York; he followed closely, and revealed an intimate knowledge of, events in that state, and by 1820 it was clear he still had many followers there.[28]

Before the reelection of Monroe some newspapers had begun to discuss the election of 1824, but most of them were fighting local battles that might or might not relate to the national campaign. There had also been anti-Crawford activity, much of which seems to have been inspired by Andrew Jackson, who had mistakenly judged Crawford as his chief "prosecutor" in connection with his Florida invasion. The publication of *Considerations* by John Clark, dueling opponent and long political rival in Georgia of Crawford, and the attempt to link Crawford directly with the alleged illegal introduction and David B. Mitchell's subsequent sale of Africans as slaves in Georgia represent the first peak of the efforts of the Crawford opponents to bring down the "king of the mountain."[29] These activities seem to have temporarily hurt Crawford within his state,[30] but their effect on the presidential election of 1824 cannot be assessed with any assurance.

By 1820 the activities of the presidential hopefuls increased, and Crawford, as the frontrunner until his serious illness in the fall of 1823, was more frequently attacked than was any other candidate. Between 1821 and 1823 Calhoun and his partisans replaced the Jackson forces as the most persistent Crawford detractors, and at the same time the abusiveness of the entire campaign became more noticeable. The sentiment against a "Virginia" candidate increased; the caucus was subjected to bitter attack; and possible coalition between various candidates was frequently discussed, with Clay's partisans usually being careful not to create irreparable breaches between their favorite and the other aspirants.

27 Adams, *Memoirs*, 4:239-43, 297-98 (Feb. 3, March 13, 1819).

28 Ibid., 359, 361 (May 6, 1819); Ambrose Spencer to Jacob Brown, Nov. 15, 1819; Brown to Crawford, Nov. 28, 1819; [Spencer] to [Brown], Jan. 27, 1820, Brown, MHS.

29 See chapter 1; Clark, *Considerations*, esp. 130-54; Thomas Henry Rentz, "The Public Life of David B. Mitchell" (M.A. thesis, University of Georgia, 1955), 87-113; David B. Mitchell file (GDAH); *House Doc.*, No. 123 (serial 387), 26th Cong., 2d sess.; *Senate Doc.*, No. 93 (serial 60), 17th Cong., 1st sess.; [David B. Mitchell], *An Exposition of the Case of the Africans, taken to the Creek Agency by Captain William Bowen on or about the 1st December 1817* (Milledgeville, Ga., 1822); *ASPM*, 2:957-75.

30 Thomas W. Cobb to Charles Tait, Oct. 20, 1820, Tait.

The political campaign gained momentum as the economic problems stemming from the Panic of 1819 increased. Crawford's mistake in the treasury estimates gave ammunition to his opponents; the paper money deposits in the western banks became a divisive issue; the acrimonious debate between Crawford and Calhoun partisans over the retrenchment legislation strained relations between the two secretaries and led some to charge that Crawford was responsible for enfilading the administration; and an event in the latter part of 1821 was viewed as little less than a clash between Crawford and Calhoun.

In July 1821 a Georgia paper, the *Milledgeville Gazette,* published a series of articles by "Trio" championing Crawford and state rights and comparing the Monroe administration unfavorably with the first Jefferson administration. In answering these in the *Augusta Advertiser* George McDuffie, a South Carolina partisan of Calhoun, charged that the denunciation of the Monroe administration resulted from Trio's being the "humble instruments of a certain magician, who stands behind the curtain and moves you by wires." Crawford was identified as the magician. On demand of William Cumming, one of Trio, McDuffie was identified by the editor and a challenge was issued. The affair dragged for some time: McDuffie was wounded in the first meeting; Cumming assumed a stooped or crouched position in the second and McDuffie refused to fire; a board of honor was held; and a final meeting on November 30, 1821, left McDuffie with a broken left arm.[31] Certainly honor must have been hard put to find satisfaction in these encounters.

Whether the Trio attack might have been inspired by a warning that Crawford's friends were not sufficiently active, that the Georgian's supporters were not increasing as were his opponents, and that his opponents were becoming better known and more active in their efforts to prevent Crawford's rise is not known.[32] But editors and others thought it "highly inexpedient" and "disrespectful" to the incumbent that the presidential question should be so much discussed; they feared the public

[31] Columns of newspapers were filled with this farcical episode. For a brief account see Edwin L. Green, *George McDuffie* (Columbia, S.C., 1936), 28, 33-36. Perhaps this was another instance in which Crawford supporters did not exercise proper discretion. Crawford said he was glad the duel was over without loss of life. Crawford to John O'Connor, June 25, 1822, Crawford, Rice.

[32] Nathaniel Macon to Charles Tait, Jan. 7, 1821, Tait.

interest might suffer from differences among the cabinet members
and from the partisans carrying their animosities into the councils
of the nation.[33]

Nor did Crawford appear pleased with the growing factionalism
and attacks. Though he expected his qualifications for office to
be reviewed—to "run the gaunlet"—Crawford said, "I shall not
degrade myself by importunity, or suffer it to be done by others.
I shall avoid the contamination of faction and intrigue. If I am
placed in office, I will be free to follow the dictates of my own
conscience and judgment. I am, however, under no more apprehensions now of being forced into office, than I was in 1816,
when office was clearly in my reach if I had been ambitious for
it." He felt that all aspirants, or at least the ones in Washington,
would unite in any attack on him under the imputation that
when he was out of the way "each one believes that his address,
or that of his friends, will enable him to put down his present
coadjutors in the work of detraction." He thought if a south-
erner were not elected in 1824, Adams would be. Crawford's
estimate of the campaign is given much support by newspaper
materials, but Hezekiah Niles analyzed things quite differently:
Adams and Crawford were "running at" Calhoun, Adams and
Calhoun were "running at" Crawford, and Crawford and Calhoun
were "running at" Adams.[34]

Whereas Crawford felt that some of his supporters in Congress
did not always act discreetly and one partisan wished that Crawford had some "prudent men" of his own party to provide leadership, one of the Georgian's most devoted followers, Representative
Thomas W. Cobb, thought Crawford did "much to injure himself with his friends" and would not wonder if Crawford's exertions in this regard were "crowned with success." Cobb seemed
piqued; he attributed his failure to be chosen senator from
Georgia to portions of a Crawford letter that had been interpreted
as disapproving his seeking that office. He was far from sanguine
about Crawford's success in the presidential race, but he had
succeeded in bringing all but two of the Georgia papers to Crawford's side. As a Southron and Republican the Georgia repre-

33 See, for example, Alexander Smyth to Dear Sir, Jan. 18, 1822, Alexander Smyth
Papers (Duke); *Montgomery Republican,* Jan. 26, March 2, 1822; *Huntsville Republican,* Feb. 8, 1822.

34 Crawford to Tait, Sept. 4, 1821, Tait; Crawford to Thomas Worthington, Jan. 17,
1822, Worthington; *Niles' Weekly Register* 22 (June 1, 1822): 220.

sentative had "determined to suffer much from his forgetfulness, his pride, his irritability, (and shall I say) *dictatorial inclination,* before I will lose the advantages of his *really splendid mind.* In truth he has 'many winning ways to make me hate him.' "[35]

The heat engendered in Congress and in the cabinet over the army appointments brought an intensification of newspaper discussion of the candidates and affairs of government. Either supporting Crawford or attacking the administration, and thus thought by opponents of Crawford to be Crawford supporters, were the *National Intelligencer, Richmond Enquirer, Boston Statesman, Portland Argus, New York National Advocate, Philadelphia Free Press,* and *Washington Gazette.* Before the summer of 1822 was over the "warfare" between Crawford and Calhoun raged, and several newspapers had been established in various parts of the country to support one or another aspirant to the presidency. Perhaps the warmest battle took place in the capital city between the *Gazette,* published by Jonathan Elliot, and the *Republican,* which began publication under the editorship of Thomas L. McKenney on August 7.[36]

The *Gazette* did not declare for Crawford until the latter part of 1822, but the paper left little doubt about the position it would take. It discussed the problems the War Department was having with contracts and contractors, protested against the political persecution of Crawford for appointing Senator Jesse B. Thomas to inspect the land offices and charged (correctly) this persecution to the friends of Calhoun. It also carried articles from other papers in support of the various candidates, but could not see the case for elevating Calhoun to the presidency. Accused by others of supporting Crawford, the *Gazette* said in September it had no candidate, but it did pay tribute to Crawford's services. On November 1 the paper began a series of articles on the qualifications of the various candidates which ran for the better part of the next two weeks. Before this series ended the *Gazette* made its position clear: it had opposed the nomination of Monroe in 1816, had favored Crawford at that time, and supported him for the presidency in 1824.[37]

---

35 Louis McLane to Dear Kitty, April 21, 1822, McLane; Cobb to Tait, March 8, 1822, Tait. Cobb was chosen senator in December 1824 (replacing Nicholas Ware, deceased); he resigned his seat in 1828 and died on February 1, 1830.

36 McKenney had been head of the United States establishment for trading with the Indians. He strongly opposed abolition of that office on May 6, 1822.

The *Republican* was not shrinking from the fray. Its opposition to Crawford was at first indirect,[38] but it became explicit about the middle of September when nearly every issue denounced the secretary of treasury. Among other things it said that on the grounds of public services or political merit Crawford's claims would not bear examination. It contended that the cost of collecting the revenue was greater than in 1802, maintained Crawford had built a patronage machine, examined the question of a political leader's responsibility for the attacks of his friends, and declared Crawford unqualified to be the reform candidate.

The *Gazette,* wondering who had heard of hostility between Crawford and Monroe before the establishment of the *Republican,* asserted the founding of its capital city rival was rooted in the friendship between Calhoun and McKenney and the desire to injure Crawford's chances for the presidency. Calhoun and his friends had tried to prevent the abolition of the Indian trading system (which McKenney headed) in May 1822, but they had not even been able to save McKenney from the "disgrace" of being barred from participating in the final adjustment of the affairs of his superintendency. The paper was then established to attack Crawford, some of whose followers had approved the change in the conduct of Indian affairs as well as much of the retrenchment legislation.[39] It should not be forgotten that the army appointments controversy occurred during this same session of Congress.

While the *Republican* and the *Gazette* were vigorously engaged, other papers throughout the country timidly or boldly declared their preferences, vowed they had none, objected to the national issue being inserted into the local ones, continued to bemoan the early agitation of the contest, or recorded varying degrees of praise for one or another candidate.[40] And the activities of the other candidates varied. Adams, seemingly agreeing with the belief of Crawford and others that the election of 1824 would be decided in the House, observed in early 1821 that a single repre-

37 *Washington Gazette,* Feb. 11, March 20, May 15, June 5, Sept. 22, Nov. 1, 6, 1822.

38 See esp. issues of Aug. 17, 24, Sept. 4, 1822.

39 *Gazette,* Nov. 22, 1822. See also Hunt, *First Forty Years,* 160-61.

40 For examples see the *Augusta Chronicle and State Gazette,* Jan. 14, 22, 31, Aug. 29, 1822; *Frankfort* (Ky.) *Commentator,* March 6, Sept. 25, Oct. 9, 1822; *Vandalia* (Ill.) *Intelligencer,* Sept. 14, 1822; *Natchez* (Miss.) *Republican,* Dec. 12, 1822; *Niles' Weekly Register* 23 (Oct. 5, 1822):80.

sentative from Illinois would balance the whole delegation from New York or Pennsylvania and subsequently recorded an increasing number of visitors from one-representative states.[41] Clay still held to his "conciliatory" position. His friends were active in the several states, counseling first one course and then another, advising that his cause be advanced by "*manly* support" of the Kentuckian rather than by attacking his competitors and their friends, indicating that the contest was between him, Crawford, and Adams but wishing him success, or agreeing with or attempting to correct Clay's estimate of the situation in a given area.[42]

One of Clay's friends, Jonathan Russell, broke out of the nonantagonizing mold by making public materials purporting to show that Adams, in contrast to Clay's position in the Ghent negotiations, would have bargained away the right to navigate the Mississippi River in order to retain Atlantic fishing rights. Adams vigorously refuted the charges, and the "duplicate letters" controversy attracted much attention in the late spring and summer of 1822. Crawford took no part in the skirmish, though correspondence indicates that Russell may have tried to involve him. Russell's primary purpose seems to have been injury to Adams, but he also hoped to advance Clay's standing. By year's end he was pointing out that Crawford and Clay were personal friends, that eventually they might join forces, and that only they among the candidates had the great common objective of preserving the old Republican party and true republican principles. In light of what finally happened, Adams' evaluation of the incident is more interesting. He thought Clay was "behind" Russell's attack and that it was a part of Clay's plan to get support wherever he could, prevent a choice by the electors, and make his bargain in the House. If Clay had nine western states, he would either make Crawford's friends join him and thus become President, or, if Crawford should be strongest in the House, he would consent to Crawford's becoming President on condition that Clay be appointed secretary of state and thus become heir apparent.[43]

41 Adams, *Memoirs*, 5:303-4, passim; ibid., 6: passim.
42 See, for example, letters in *Clay Papers*, 3:185, 196-98, 200, 202, 290-91, 292, 314-17, 321, 325, 335, 337.
43 *House Doc.*, Nos. 75 (serial 67) and 131 (serial 69), 17th Cong., 1st sess.; Russell to Crawford, June 2, 1822, Golding: Hezekiah Niles to John Bailey, June 4, 1822, Mellen Chamberlain Collection (BPL); Clay to Russell, Sept. 4, 1822; Russell to

Crawford, who said in the summer of 1821 that he had "never been so silly as to expect anything in relation to myself" from New York, continued to keep in close touch with events in that state. There seemed to be a partial understanding and commitment to Crawford in the summer of 1821, but by early 1822 even some of the more zealous Crawford supporters were willing to remain silent and await clearer indications of public sentiment. By that time Crawford had seen Van Buren several times; they were on friendly terms, but he thought Van Buren would endeavor to "make a New York President. When he finds that impracticable he will then be governed by circumstance."[44] This was probably a fair estimate of the position of the key figure in New York politics, but many other powerful persons in that state were jockeying to improve their political stature. At the end of 1822, Crawford's support in New York was probably less than it had been a year earlier.[45]

The year 1823 was one of almost frantic maneuvering, and the situation in New York was perhaps more frenzied than that in any other state. Van Buren seems to have made up his mind— some of his intimates were sure he had—but he had not definitely committed himself to Crawford. He was told by coadjutors that the responsibility for pursuing a course leading to the election of a Republican President was his, but only Crawford, among the candidates from the eastern part of the country, could rightfully be called a "democrat." The fact that Crawford had been called radical by the same sort of people who called Jefferson the democratic or jacobinical candidate was not disturbing. Continued

James Fenner, Dec. 26, 1822, Russell; Rich O'Brien to John Bailey, Aug. 22, 1822, John Bailey Papers (NYH); William Plumer, Jr. to William Plumer, Sr., Dec. 21, 1822, Brown, *Missouri Compromises*, 81 (Adams' evaluation). Russell apparently was a peevish, petulant, pestering, carping type who never seemed satisfied with the actions of an individual against whom he had a pique.

44 Crawford to John O'Connor, Aug. 21, 1821, Jan. 11, 1822, Crawford, Rice; Peter B. Porter to Clay, Jan. 29, 1822, Calvin E. Colton, *The Life, Correspondence and Speeches of Henry Clay*, 6 vols. (New York, 1857), 4:62-63. Hereafter cited as Colton, *Works*.

45 For comments on the New York scene, see Porter to Clay, Sept. 30, 1822, Henry Clay Papers (Lilly Library, Indiana University): Rufus King to J. A. King, Jan. 1, 1822; Robert Goldsborough to Rufus King, April 7, 1822; Van Buren to Rufus King, Sept. 21, 1822; memo by Rufus King, Feb. 2, 1823, King, *King*, 6:435, 468-69, 481-82, 509-10; Goldsborough to King, Jan. 31, April 17, 1822; Nathan Ulshoeffer to John A. King, Feb. 6, 1822, Rufus King Papers (NYH): Sam A. Talcott to Van Buren, Feb. 7, 1822; Rufus King to Van Buren, Sept. 24, 1822; Jesse Hoyt to Van Buren, Dec. 5, 1822, Van Buren; R. H. Walworth to A. C. Flagg, Jan. 27, 1822, Azariah C. Flagg Papers (NYH).

use of the term might make it as popular an epithet as yankee, democrat, and bucktail.[46] Many wanted to know where Van Buren stood, but he kept his own counsel.

Anti-Virginia sentiment was soon sacrificed on the altar of party unity. New York had vigorously objected in 1816 to Virginia influence, but two elections later the near monopoly of the presidency by the Old Dominion was of less import. There was some discussion of the slavery influence, but this also was held lightly by most, for the parties had not realigned on slavery and antislavery as Adams thought in 1820 would be the case. Among others, Smith Thompson, Azariah C. Flagg, and Silas Wright stressed that New York should not bind or pledge the party to any man, but it would be "fit and proper" to express an opinion in favor of a congressional caucus nomination. New York should then support the person "fairly nominated." The new President would thus feel indebted to New York and the state's interests would be served, no matter what section of the country the candidate came from.[47]

Almost immediately the *Albany Argus,* mouthpiece of the Regency, began to deprecate premature committals and asserted that New York Republicans would give undivided and effectual support to the candidate regularly nominated by the congressional caucus. It also lamented the gross personal abuse of the candidates: "The candidates for the presidency are the property of the nation, and they are identified with its character. It is degrading to us as a people, to obtrude our petty feelings and resentments, into the consideration of a question of the highest import and concern."[48] Van Buren, before leaving Washington, may have committed himself to Crawford, but apparently some members of the famed Richmond Junto were not aware of this.[49]

46 Erastus Root to Van Buren, Jan. 3, 1823; Nathan Ulshoeffer to Van Buren, Jan. 27, 31, 1823, Van Buren.

47 Rufus King to Harrison Gray Otis, Jan. 24, 1823, Harrison Gray Otis Papers (MHS); memos by Rufus King, Feb. 2, 24, [n.d.], 1823, King, *King*, 6:507-8, 509, 510; Thompson to Van Buren, March 17, 21, 1823; Flagg to Van Buren, Nov. 12, 1823, Van Buren; Flagg to Wright, Oct. 28, 1823; Wright to Flagg, Nov. 12, 1823, Flagg.

48 *Albany Argus,* March 25, April 11, 1823.

49 Memo by Rufus King, April 7, 1823; King to John A. King, April 20, 1823, King, *King*, 6:518, 521. Various New Yorkers expressed preferences or denounced individuals they opposed, but one New Yorker was quite indifferent: "In short I care not a d—n what party is in power, for I find the leaders are all scoundrels at bottom." J. W. Clark to Thurlow Weed, June 6, 1823, Thurlow Weed Papers (University of Rochester).

The *Argus* had prepared the way, and Van Buren, staunch advocate of party discipline and unity and fully aware of the division that would result from any nomination by the New York legislature or caucus, moved according to advice. On April 22 the Republicans at Albany unanimously approved, and called for support of, a congressional nomination. Admitting there were objections to this method of selection, the New Yorkers maintained that a national meeting was less susceptible to sectional jealousies than state caucuses and state legislatures whose nominations were condemned for their "tendency to disturb the harmony" of the great Republican family.[50]

Almost as if it were footnoting the caucus action, the *Argus* on that very day took notice of the newspaper controversy that had been raging for some time over Crawford's part in the Augusta address of 1798. Following a vigorous and lengthy defense of Crawford's action and his unswerving Republicanism, the editor said that had Crawford been a real supporter of the Federalists the *Argus* would have been content to "whistle him off, and let him down to the wind of fortune"; it owed him nothing and had nothing to expect from him.[51]

Opponents of Crawford realized the power of the Crawford press in New York; as one of them put it, for one man to expose himself to their "battery without any press to which he could resort for protection would be madness." This person, Charles K. Gardner, in cooperation with Winfield Scott, Samuel Gouverneur, Henry Wheaton, and John C. Calhoun, was at the time attempting to set up a paper in New York City to combat the denunciation

[50] Erastus Root was one of the drafters of the resolution, and on the copy he sent to Samuel Smith he underlined the portion "one who is not only a sound Democratic Republican in principle and practice" and wrote in the margin "This is against Adams." Root to Smith, April 24, 1823, Carter-Smith. Ambrose Spencer, whose support shifted from Crawford to Calhoun to advocacy of the reelection of Adams, said New York would throw her weight to the side that would be victorious with that added weight, for "politics here use a trade, not matters of principle." He thought Crawford had a majority in the legislative caucus, but his partisans did not nominate him because they realized the "general odium" that legislature had incurred. Governor Joseph C. Yates, a Crawford supporter, was said to have lost all respect and consideration. Spencer to Jacob Brown, April 2, 22, May 5, 1823, Jacob Brown Papers (Clements).

[51] The *Baltimore American & Commercial Daily Advertiser* on June 10, 1823, took note of the New York caucus action, indicated that the large states dreaded the possibility of the election going to the House, and said a congressional nomination might make election by the people certain and prevent the great evil of election by the House. See also Van Buren to Thompson, May 16, 1823, DeCoppett; John Taylor (of Caroline) to Van Buren, May 12, 1823, Van Buren.

of various Republicans by Mordecai M. Noah's *National Advocate,* to try to destroy the Van Buren influence, and to prevent the choice of Crawford by New York. The *Patriot* began publication in May 1823; Selleck Osborn was associated with Gardner in the editorial capacity, but much of the most trenchant writing was done by Henry Wheaton. The *Patriot* gained subscribers at Noah's expense, but the enthusiastic support of Gardner's paper was short-lived. The subscribers did not return to Noah, whom many felt had done much injury to the Republican cause by his vanity and want of judgment.[52]

Crawford kept in close touch with his long-time correspondents, especially O'Connor, Tait, and Van Buren. He believed the New York support of a national caucus would have a "permanent influence upon the general question," and in the summer of 1823 he again observed that all aspirants to the presidency seemed to think it necessary to assail him. Calhoun appeared to think that "success can be secured by importunity, as heaven itself can be obtained by violence," but Crawford thought the secretary of war had made little progress toward his goal. Calhoun's calculation that he would be the "general residuary legatee of the others who may become politically defunct" Crawford termed without foundation except in Calhoun's imagination, which is "as fervid as Etna, and as wild as the storms of winter." He did believe Adams had gained strength in the preceding twelve months and considered the secretary of state the only one whose conduct during that period had been such as to "deserve commendation, or rather to be exempt from censure."[53]

Throughout the remainder of 1823 the *Argus* shrewdly avoided a commitment to Crawford, but its preference was clear. It spoke of the absurdity of the charge that Crawford was going to be forced upon the Republicans of the state, of the "common

[52] Scott to Gardner, April 8, May 2, Aug. 7, 1823; Gardner to Noah, July [n.d.], 1823, Gardner; Calhoun to Gouverneur, April 28, May 25, June 6, 1823; Scott to Gouverneur, April 8, 1823, Samuel Gouverneur Papers (NYP); G. W. Erving to Crawford, July 14-15, 1823, Crawford, MDLC; Robert V. Remini, *Martin Van Buren and the Making of the Democratic Party* (New York, 1959), 39; Hammond, *History,* 2:130; Elizabeth Feaster Baker, *Henry Wheaton, 1785-1848* (Philadelphia, 1937), 44-54. Samuel Gouverneur was Monroe's son-in-law. For other information on Calhoun's maneuvering in New York in 1823 see Thomas R. Hay, ed., "John C. Calhoun and the Presidential Campaign of 1824: Some Unpublished Calhoun Letters," *American Historical Review* 40 (1934-1935):82-96, 286-300.

[53] Crawford to Van Buren, May 9, 1823, Van Buren; Crawford to O'Connor, May 16, 1823, Crawford, Rice; Crawford to Tait, July 12, 1823, Tait.

privilege" of Crawford's friends to believe him fitted by talent and experience for the presidency, of its lack of concern about Virginia influence and southern domination—those "phantoms" that "political jugglers have conjured up to subserve their temporary purposes," and asked why the calumnies, slanders, and venom had been directed against Crawford almost exclusively. It copied with approval material from non-Crawford papers that spoke of the binding nature of the nomination and a free discussion of the presidential question. Some of these other papers could see no excuse for the slander and said the discussion would not be "less free, if some slight regard were paid to truth and decency."[54]

Beginning in 1820 the selection of a certain person as speaker of the House was considered by some as favorable or unfavorable to the candidacy of a particular presidential aspirant, but congressional alignments shifted so rapidly and so many representatives and senators changed their allegiances by 1824 that most claims concerning these selections must be viewed as little more than political rhetoric.[55] Especially in 1823 did many relate the choice of the speaker to the presidential contest, since they expected the election to be decided by the House of Representatives. Philip P. Barbour, friend of Crawford and speaker during the Seventeenth Congress, was to oppose Henry Clay for the position, but it was said that many of Crawford's friends would vote for Clay. After the election of Clay by a vote of 139 to 42, some of the Kentuckian's friends thought the defeat of Crawford's supporter had made the Georgian's friends realize Crawford was not as strong as they had supposed, whereas some of Crawford's partisans were pleased that the election had not been placed on presidential grounds and thought Clay's friends would join with Crawford if Clay could not win the presidency.[56]

54 See esp. issues of July 1, Sept. 16, Oct. 24, Nov. 18, 25, Dec. 2, 23, 1823. On September 9 subscribers were informed that copies of the "splendid" engraving of Crawford had been left at the *Argus* office for delivery. On northern resentment and southern influence see also William P. Duval to James Barbour, Aug. 12, 1823, Barbour.

55 See, for example, *Annals*, 16th Cong., 2d sess., 437-38; ibid., 17th Cong., 1st sess., 514-17; Adams, *Memoirs*, 5:201-3, 429, 431-32, 437-40, 450, 451: M. P. Follett, *The Speaker of the House of Representatives* (New York, 1896), 50, 51, 83; Plumer, Jr. to Plumer, Sr., Dec. 3, 1821, Brown, *Missouri Compromises*, 65: *Niles' Weekly Register* 21 (Dec. 15, 1821):242-43; John Taylor to William D. Ford, Jan. 18, 1822, Taylor.

56 See Lewis Williams to Bartlett Yancey, Nov. 30, 1823, James G. deRoulhac

Partisans of the candidates often interpreted state election results as they did the contest for House speaker; if those elected
favored their candidate, there was a direct association between
the local and national contests; if the elections were against them,
there was little or no relationship.[57] The elections for congressmen and senators in 1822 and 1823 were of significance for the
presidential hopefuls, for they would have a bearing on the caucus
nomination and—if the election went to the House—on the choice
of the President. In retrospect, the close gubernatorial contest in
Georgia and the selection of a Tennessee senator might be viewed
as indicators of Crawford's chances. In Georgia it took the
legislature three days to choose Crawford supporter George M.
Troup over Matthew Talbot by a vote of 83 to 81, and in Tennessee John Williams, ardent Crawford follower and senator until
March 4, 1823, was defeated for reelection by Andrew Jackson.
Williams believed that the weight of Monroe, Adams, and Calhoun had been exerted against him. He also thought the "advance
object" of Jackson's friends in sending him to Washington was
to place him on the same footing with the other presidential
candidates and to give him an opportunity for testing his civil
qualifications for the office.[58]

Williams may have had to contend with an unusual combination
of forces—as well as the general's popularity—but his defeat was
a localized manifestation of Crawford's lack of widespread support
in any of the country west of the mountains. Nathaniel Macon,
much earlier that year, had pointed out that events in the
assemblies of several of the western states showing a preference
for Clay and the presence of a party in Illinois recommending
the election of Adams were indications unfavorable to Crawford.
Exertion by Crawford's supporters was necessary; the Georgian's

---

Hamilton, ed., "Letters to Bartlett Yancey," *James Sprunt Historical Publications*
10 (2): 36 (hereafter cited as Hamilton, "Letters to Yancey"); W. B. Rochester to
Clay, Dec. 20, 1823, Colton, *Works*, 4:85-86; Jonathan Russell to Jonas Sibley, Dec.
23, 1823; Samuel Smith to Russell, Dec. 15, 1823, Russell.

57 For comments by several newspapers and by Niles on these elections see *Niles'
Weekly Register* 25 (Oct. 25, Nov. 22, 29, 1823):114, 178, 195, 203.

58 Williams to Jesse B. Thomas, Nov. 2, 1823, Thomas. Earlier another Tennessean
had noted Crawford's weakness in Tennessee and Alabama and stressed the objections of the Alabamans to the influence of the Georgia group in that state. He
called the government of Georgia "provincial" and said the state was a "hot bed
of faction and violence of the most damnable mobocracy that ever cursed any state
in the union." James Campbell to David Campbell, April 21, 1823, David Campbell
Papers (Duke).

chances seemed best at the beginning of the session of Congress, but he had probably not gained any support during the session. The outcome had become more uncertain.[59]

Clay was aware of his and Adams' strength in the upper west and of his weakness in the southeast, where Crawford appeared strong. The long friendship of Clay and Crawford and the moderateness of the attacks by Clay partisans on Crawford led some to believe that the two would ultimately join forces. Others thought Clay's popularity may have suffered in some areas because of a belief that an understanding existed between the two. Clay, who either honestly or for political reasons thought there was little difference among his, Adams', and Crawford's views on the tariff and internal improvements, considered it highly important to impress on Crawford's friends the sentiment of the western states. Even if only Adams were matched against Crawford in that area, Clay believed Adams would receive all, or nearly all, the electoral votes. Clay's popular support was somewhat offset by the "active and managing politicians" who favored Crawford, but the Kentuckian thought Crawford's chances were declining in 1823. There might be "other phases exhibited before the question is settled," Clay said, and he cautioned that his friends maintain "respectful relations with the other gentlemen and their friends. That is the best course under all circumstances."[60]

Newspaper comment became more heated and unreasonable in 1823. The *Washington Gazette* continued its support of Crawford, and the *Republican* continued its unconditional condemnation. When the matter of the Augusta address was before the public—and the *Republican* had denounced Crawford as a Federalist—the paper said if he were not a Federalist and in "good faith and sincerity a supporter" of the Adams administration, then he must be viewed as a "shameless parasite, a base dissembler." Crawford was said to have blundered and failed in public business of importance and was in fact a *"giant in intrigue, but a dwarf in public service."* The *Republican* was single-minded in denouncing the Georgian but did not print anything

59 Macon to Bartlett Yancey, Jan. 27, 1823, Yancey.
60 See Clay to Charles Hammond, Oct. 29, 1823, Clay, Lilly; *Washington Republican*, July 5, 1823, citing *Louisville Advertiser, Nashville Advocate, Florence (Ala.) Gazette*; William Carroll to Clay, Feb. 1, 1823; Clay to Peter B. Porter, Feb. 2, 1823; Clay to Amos Kendall, Feb. 16, 1823; Porter to Clay, May 26, 1823; Clay to Francis T. Brooke, Aug. 28, 1823, *Clay Papers*, 3:361, 365, 382, 421, 480.

uncomplimentary about any of the other presidential hopefuls.[61]

Perhaps the cleverest bit of political writing of 1823 was called "Political Horse Racing and Presidential Contest," which appeared originally in the *Nashville Gazette* and was copied, frequently with some variations, by many papers. In this piece all the horses were given the names of the candidates. The Crawford was a

> tall, majestic figure, with wonderful bone, muscle, and sinew. His tread was *firm* and indicative of great strength and activity. He sprung from the old Virginia stock of racers; one of the best strains in these United States. . . . When young, he was taken to Georgia and occasionally run a few cider races successfully, when his owners emboldened by his success, ventured to enter him in the *State* jockey club, where he defeated the favorite horse of Georgia, although often opposed by that scare-devil, John Clark, a nag of some distinction in that quarter, who had lately, however, become *spavined, splintered and stringhalted*. It is singular that supporters of all the other nags vied in their abuse of this horse and his performances.

He was first managed by some Georgians but was then taken to the Old Dominion and again looked after by some of the "old grooms of ninety-eight." In the Crawford "dress" were blended the fashions of the white man and the Indian; his flag bore in capital letters the words "states rights," "economy," and "republicanism of ninety-eight." In the background the bow of cupid overcame the scalping knife of the savage, an emblem of the "new mode of inculcating civilization by means of the pleasant process of intermarriage." Neither goad nor scourge was carried, but the enemies had thrust under the saddle large bundles of suppressed documents which the rider "with the slight [*sic*] of hocus pocus" got rid of. A speck of federalism was bedizened by the "resplendent dapples of Republicanism which pervaded the whole body."

The race began in Maine where there was a Missouri Tract and a Maine Tract; the Crawford selected the Missouri and at first ran far ahead of the Adams but lost ground by temporizing. The race was run through all the eastern states in this manner until the Calhoun was turned back at Georgia by a Colonel

[61] *Republican*, April 5, May 14, July 2, Aug. 9, Oct. 25, Dec. 23, 1823.

Cumming. The Crawford had great support in going from Georgia to the west for there he crossed the Indian territory and was greeted with "yells of victory." The judges awarded the prize to the Crawford and in "all due form" he was installed as President.[62]

On a different level and characterized by better writing was the Nashville Whig sketch of several distinguished members of the Woodbee family, published on July 28, 1823. William H. Woodbee received favorable treatment though obviously some of the phrases were worded to cut two ways. It was said that as a financier his talents were known and deservedly celebrated: his fame depended upon mathematical niceties; it rises "superior to ordinary calculation; lives in the aggregate, and soars above and beyond the addition or disposition of a cypher." He affected the "tribune rather than the consul" and emulated the Gracchi rather than the Caesars, and in domestic policy he presented a new and fertile field for conjecture and experiment. Though this may have been an error and in opposition to public sentiment, it should be remembered that the proposition was "humane, practicable and full of gallantry. It was but for substituting the torch of Hymen for that of Mars, and the syren song of love for that of savage war, of victory and of death." This essay was followed by similar ones on John Q., Henry, and John C. In addition brief attention was given to the Hasbeens, the Cantbees, the Mightbees, and the Woodabeens.[63]

Many of the papers withheld endorsement of any single candidate and opened their columns to communications from Tell, A Farmer, A Friend of the People, Publius, Cato, Consistency,

---

[62] The five-column original has not been located. Among the many copies are those in the *Illinois Intelligencer*, June 14, 1823; *Kentucky Gazette*, July 10, 1823; *Mobile Commercial Advertiser*, July 17, 1823; *Pittsburgh Gazette*, July 18, 1823; *Washington Gazette*, June 19, 1823. The Washington paper concluded with a paragraph saying that some would think it strange that a horse should reign over intellectual beings. "Reader, rather rejoice that it is not our fate to be governed by an *Ass!* It is the lot of hundreds of nations to be ruled by the latter." The *Boston Galaxy* had earlier run a horse race. There was a $25,000 purse (the President's salary) and the race ended differently. The paper said this contest might "serve to render those who have the direction of *colts* and *half bloods* to be more cautious how they hazard their reputation, against steeds of tried, approved, and established character." *Montgomery Republican*, Feb. 1, 1823.

[63] There were also boat races, balloon races, and accounts of the "singular woman" who according to the laws of the land was entitled to a new husband every four years. For examples see *Montgomery Republican*, Nov. 22, 29, 1823; *Nashville Whig*, Dec. 29, 1823.

Truth, A Militia Man, and dozens of others. As in comparable communications of later years, passion and bias far outweighed reason and balance, and opinion was far more in evidence than fact. Independence Day celebrations were cluttered with toasts to the favorites of those assembled and frequently were more extravagant in their claims than the letter writers.[64]

Two of the papers outstanding in their support of Crawford late in 1823 and in 1824 were not absolutely committed in early 1823. The *Richmond Enquirer,* under Thomas Ritchie, published much pro-Crawford material in 1823, but its columns remained open for anti-Crawford matter, including the "Pendleton" and "Roanoke" series by Winfield Scott. The *National Intelligencer* aided the *Washington Gazette* in the running battle with the *Republican* in 1822 and 1823, and in the latter part of the campaign it definitely was the front line.

Mahlon Dickerson of New Jersey wrote an anti-Calhoun pamphlet, *Economy, Mister Calhoun,* which was reprinted in the *Raleigh Register;* letters appeared against the Richmond Junto which created a great deal of contemporary excitement; George Hay (Monroe's son-in-law) published materials against Crawford that led some to charge that Monroe opposed Crawford's election; and before the end of the year some of Crawford's closest supporters decided that if the election went to the House of Representatives Crawford had no chance.[65]

None of these political battles, however, had as much effect on the election of 1824 as did Crawford's prolonged illness, which began in September 1823. In May Crawford planned to remain in the district throughout the summer, but should fever return to the capital city, he might take a short excursion into the mountains of Virginia. He sarcastically noted that perhaps he could visit his relatives without being suspected of electioneering

[64] See *Albany Argus,* July 11, 1823, and *Savannah Republican,* Aug. 2, 1823, for toasts from parts of New York and from Georgia, North Carolina, and Virginia.

[65] For the planting of some of these materials and contemporary speculation on authorship and effects, see David Campbell to James Campbell, Dec. 5, 1823, Jan. 27, 1824; David Campbell to Edward Campbell, Dec. 10, 1823, Campbell, Duke: Lewis Williams to Bartlett Yancey, Dec. 15, 1823, Hamilton, "Letters to Yancey," 38-39; Romulus Saunders to Yancey, Dec. 7, 1823, Clark. Adams continued to write for the papers, and Jonathan Russell continued to gratify his pique by dragging out the John Adams-Cunningham letters. He wrote several long letters, private and confidential, to Crawford on this matter, but Crawford's only known reply was very circumspect. Russell to Crawford, June 23, July 20, Nov. 30, 1823; Crawford to Russell, Aug. 7, 1823, Russell.

maneuvers. By early August Mrs. Crawford had a "pretty severe attack of bilious fever," the fourth Crawford son was confined to bed, and President Monroe was recovering from a violent attack of "spasms in his stomach." Crawford hoped to leave soon for Virginia, where *en passant* he would visit with Jefferson and Madison and "breathe a little of my native mountain air."[66]

But Crawford did not leave the capital until September 2. Three weeks later he was desperately ill at the home of James Barbour in Orange County. Crawford called his illness "inflammatory rheumatism"; others have termed it bilious fever and erysipelas; he may well have suffered a stroke, but the major problems seem to have developed from the improper ministration of medicines—digitalis (foxglove), perhaps laudanum and calomel, and maybe lobeline. For nearly eight weeks he remained at Barbour's home in a virtually helpless condition: practically blind, hands and feet paralyzed, tongue thickened, and speech stumbling and nearly inarticulate. He was bled more than twenty times—"a depletion an ignoramus like myself wd think nearly sufficient to kill a giant." A much reduced Crawford returned to Washington on November 14 and imprudently devoted all the next ten days to business. The left, and then the right, eye became painfully inflamed. An application of leeches on December 30 brought some relief, but for nearly three months his vision was seriously impaired. He remained in a darkened room and conducted treasury business with the aid of his daughter Caroline and clerk Asbury Dickins, who came daily to his home. He returned to cabinet meetings in April 1824, suffered a relapse the next month, and did not attend another cabinet meeting until after the election in November.[67]

[66] Crawford to John O'Connor, May 16, 1823, Crawford, Rice; Crawford to Russell, Aug. 7, 1823, Russell. Jefferson expressed great pleasure when he learned of the possibility of seeing Crawford. Jefferson to Crawford, Aug. 23, 1823, Jefferson, MDLC. On September 18, 1823, the *Washington Republican* termed Crawford's trip to Virginia and his proposed visits to Madison and Jefferson a part of the management and intrigue to secure the presidency.

[67] *National Intelligencer*, Sept. 3, Oct. 8, 20, 1823; *Baltimore American & Commercial Daily Advertiser*, Sept. 29, Oct. 21, 1823; [James Lloyd] to William Eustis, Nov. 19, 1823, Autograph File, Houghton; Romulus Saunders to Yancey, Dec. 31, 1823, Clark (quote); Crawford to Tait, Nov. 23, 1823, Tait; Crawford third person note to Monroe, Nov. 17, 1823, Monroe, NYP; Margaret Bayard Smith to Mrs. Samuel Boyd, Dec. 19, [1823], Hunt, *First Forty Years*, 162-63; John Forsyth to John O'Connor, Dec. 31, 1823, O'Connor, Clements. On October 14 Jefferson arrived at Barbour's for a visit with Crawford. John Floyd attributed Crawford's eye difficulties to an overdose of digitalis. Floyd to O'Connor, Jan. 6, 1824, ibid.

Crawford wrote little during his serious illness, but just over a week after his return to Washington he took note of some of the newspaper writing of General Winfield Scott and George Hay and said that Scott was about to be sent to the West. Whether he was going to "marshall the white allies or chastise the red enemies of the army candidate cannot at this time be ascertained, except by the initiated." This remark is especially interesting in light of a letter from General Jacob Brown to General Edmund P. Gaines in which there is reference to the "extreme political excitement" and the "strenuous exertion" that would probably be made at the next session of Congress to break down Calhoun's increasing influence. One of the instruments for this would be the rising Indian wars. It was important, therefore, to throw the "whole burden of censure on the savages by manifesting toward them all the lenity which is consistent with the outrages which it is our business to redress." The matter was mentioned only because of the "personal political relations of our secretary."[68]

Illness lost for Crawford such advantage as he may have enjoyed over his rivals, and his health was much discussed until the day Adams was chosen by the House.[69] Crawford's friends were continually disturbed by his physical condition, but in the summer of 1824 some maintained his affliction was not as great as that of Madison in 1813-1814 when he discharged the duties of the presidency. One of his most ardent journalistic supporters noted almost a year after the onset of his illness that when one remembered that Crawford had been for twelve months in the hands of doctors, "bled to the verge of death, digitalized into fits, and ptyialized to infantine helplessness, we have reason to be more than satisfied with his recovery."[70]

Crawford had been assailed on many fronts, but perhaps the most politically damaging attack on him opened in the columns of the *Republican* in January 1823. Between January and April fifteen letters signed "A.B." accused Crawford of mismanaging the public funds and of suppressing information damaging to himself when he sent to Congress on February 15, 1822, a report and documents concerning the relations between the treasury and the western banks. The "A.B." letters raised an immediate

68 Crawford to Tait, Nov. 23, 1823, Tait; Brown to Gaines, Sept. 24, 1823 (private), Brown, MHS.
69 See following chapter for additional discussion.
70 Joseph Gales to Van Buren, Sept. 14, 1824, Van Buren.

public storm, and it was more than a year later that their authorship was publicly admitted by Ninian Edwards—a revelation that
shed considerable light on the political motivation of the attack.[71]

Edwards, former governor of the Illinois Territory, a director
of the Edwardsville, Illinois, bank in which deposits of "unsound"
money had been made as payment to the United States government
for land purchases, and one of the first senators from that state,
was opposed in Illinois by Jesse B. Thomas, the other senator
and a Crawford partisan. Tied by marriage to John Pope, for
several years the chief rival of Clay in Kentucky, Edwards was
an early supporter of Adams' candidacy, switched to Calhoun,
and later returned to Adams' camp when Calhoun withdrew
from the presidential race. Edwards' son-in-law, Representative
Daniel Pope Cook of Illinois, was deeply involved in the machinations of Edwards and in 1825 cast the vote of Illinois for Adams.

Following the first letter, which was addressed to Joseph Gales
and William W. Seaton, printers to Congress and publishers
of the National Intelligencer, a special committee of the House
made an investigation. Crawford partisans on the committee,
though directing many questions to Cook, were unsuccessful
in determining the authorship of the letters. Crawford himself
was certain that an "insidious conspiracy" had been formed
against him by "Ninian Edwards & Co. of which Cook has again
been made the cat's paw." He listed Hugh Nelson, confidential
friend of the President, as among "this reputable group of con-
spirators" and others as "working coadjutors." The committee's
report satisfied no one and a new committee was appointed.[72]

---

71 *House Doc.*, No. 66 (serial 66), 17th Cong., 1st sess. Some of the materials
dealing with Edwards may be found in Washburne, *Edwards*, but many more—often
less favorable to Edwards' image—are in the Ninian Edwards Papers and the
Daniel P. Cook Papers, both in the Chicago Historical Society. The latest scholarly
treatment of the episode, perhaps minimizing too much the complicity of Calhoun, is
Charles M. Wiltse, "John C. Calhoun and the 'A.B. Plot,' " *Journal of Southern
History* 13 (Feb. 1947):46-61. Wiltse gives no evidence of having used the unpublished Edwards and Cook papers or any other unpublished materials. Wayne Cutler,
"The A.B. Controversy," *Mid-America* 51 (Jan. 1969):24-37, uses only printed
materials and makes no mention of Wiltse's article.

72 Crawford to Tait, Feb. 16, 1823, Tait; *Niles' Weekly Register* 23 (Feb. 8, 1823):
esp. 360-62 (report). Perhaps one of the most interesting comments of the period
came from the pen of Samuel L. Southard, a Calhoun supporter and soon to
succeed Smith Thompson as secretary of navy. He said, "I look, with some
curiosity, for A.B. He is a troublesome fellow. I wish we could find him out. I
would write more, but am pressed for time. Write frequently; I shall be pleased
to hear from you often and freely." Southard to Ninian Edwards, March 26, 1823,
Washburne, *Edwards*, 206.

Crawford, indicating that when he prepared his report of February 1822 he thought the House wanted the correspondence he considered relevant (not the entire correspondence), supplied twenty-eight additional documents to the committee, which took testimony from a number of individuals, including Cook, Dickins, and Edwards, who continued to write the letters during the investigation. The committee report did not establish authorship of the letters or attach guilt to anyone. The committee seemed to accept Crawford's statements that treasury practices and policies toward the western banks were justified because—among other things—they prevented an increase of the already great distress of the western country. There was never any question but that the government lost money and that the western country was "indulged."[73]

The "A.B." letters were designed to injure Crawford—and apparently they did adversely affect his popularity—not to recover money due the government. But in late March the fifth auditor transmitted the letter of the secretary of treasury to the district attorney in Illinois requesting him forthwith to institute suit against the Bank of Edwardsville for the public monies deposited there. The suit should be for the sum due on January 31, 1821, and for a later deposit, a total of $141,238.90.[74]

The suppressed documents were repeatedly referred to by the newspapers, but before the issue was rejoined Calhoun had withdrawn from the presidential race, Crawford had been nominated by the congressional caucus, and Edwards had been appointed minister to Mexico. The animosity between Edwards and Crawford seethed in the background, and apparently Monroe got little help from his cabinet in the matter of selecting the minister. Edwards was approved by a large vote of the Senate on March 4, 1824, and less than three weeks later he departed for Mexico. Almost on the eve of his departure, Crawford sent to the House a detailed report of the correspondence between the treasury and the banks in which public monies were deposited. The lateness of the report, called for by Cook's resolution of May 8, 1822, can be partially explained by its length (more than 1,200 printed

73 *House Doc.*, No. 119 (serial 69), 17th Cong., 1st sess. See also *National Intelligencer*, March 8, 1823.

74 Stephen Pleasanton to Jepthah Hardin, March 24, 1823, Jepthah Hardin Papers (ISH). The bank had not kept current on its reports to the treasury. Crawford to Benjamin Stephenson, Nov. 19, 1821, Edwards.

pages) and Crawford's illness, but its transmittal on March 22, 1824, seems to have been deliberately timed to interfere with Edwards' departure. Crawford reopened the "A.B." matter by reference to Edwards' testimony of February 1823 in connection with a letter from the Edwardsville bank to the treasury in 1819.[75]

Edwards delayed his departure by one day to collect some documents, wrote his reply while enroute to Wheeling, and on April 6 addressed it to Clay, speaker of the House. It was sent, however, in care of Calhoun, from whom Cook got it on April 17. Cook also secured from Calhoun's files those "A.B." letters which had appeared between March 29 and April 9 of the previous year. He planned to show the papers to some of his friends before giving them to Clay and noted that Calhoun thought they should not be printed in the *Republican* until the committee had released them through its report.[76]

Edwards' communication, sent to the House on April 19, specifically charged that Crawford had mismanaged the national funds, had received a large amount of uncurrent notes from certain banks in partial discharge of their debts to the United States contrary to a resolution of Congress in 1816, had misstated the amount of such notes in a communication to the House, had acted illegally in a variety of instances by making and continuing deposits of public money in certain banks without reporting thereon to Congress, and had withheld information and letters called for by the House. Edwards admitted writing the "A.B." letters, said he would not charge Crawford with bad intentions in any of the acts mentioned, and would not ask for an investigation. "Such a request ought more naturally to be looked for from himself."[77]

Monroe was "highly exasperated" by Edwards' memorial, which he thought might give the impression—because it followed so closely on the President's nomination of Edwards as minister—

---

[75] Senate *Executive Journal*, 3:364; *House Doc.*, No. 140 (serial 102), 18th Cong., 1st sess., 3. Edwards was all but accused of perjury. Evidence about the letter from Benjamin Stephenson to Crawford is conflicting, and it is possible the letter was not sent to the Treasury Department. See Edward Coles to Crawford, July 1, 1824, Edward Coles Papers (Chicago Historical Society).

[76] Cook to Edwards, April 17, 1824, Edwards; Washburne, *Edwards*, 223-24; Duckett, *Forsyth*, 29-31.

[77] *House Doc.*, No. 139 (serial 102), 18th Cong., 1st sess., 21-22. There were fifty pages of supporting documents. For the charges, testimony, Crawford's answer, and the committee report see also *ASPF*, 5:1-146.

that he was acting in concert with Edwards against Crawford.[78] Apparently he was dissuaded from immediately suspending Edwards' trip only by the unanimous opinion of the cabinet that such action should await the report of the investigating committee. This committee, appointed by Clay, consisted of John Floyd (Virginia), John Randolph (Virginia), John W. Taylor (New York), Daniel Webster (Massachusetts), Duncan McArthur (Ohio), George W. Owen (Alabama), and Edward Livingston (Louisiana). The first two were Crawford supporters; Taylor favored Adams; Webster was uncommitted; McArthur was for Clay; and the last two supported Jackson. Taylor thought Edwards should be sent for, and so did Adams. Crawford's friends seemed anxious that this be done and thought postponement of an investigation would be unfavorable to Crawford's presidential ambitions.[79] The House sent its sergeant at arms to bring Edwards back to Washington.

Excitement was widespread and the opinion prevailed that Crawford or Edwards must "go down." Some non-Crawford men thought Edwards' conduct was "strongly marked with knavery" and that his memorial was a "plausible, Jesuitical impudent production." It was argued that the men of the West—and Edwards was one of them—not only claimed but urged the aid to the western banks; it was possible to reason that the government gained rather than lost by these arrangements, for otherwise the sale of public lands would have come to a standstill, thousands would have been ruined, the paper money would have perished in the hands of the community, and the debt to the government would have remained unpaid; impoverishment would have fallen on all.[80]

Crawford's reply to Edwards was prepared by Asbury Dickins and sent to the committee on May 11. Two weeks later a committee report, written by Livingston and revised by Webster,

---

[78] In a report of March 1823 Crawford claimed Monroe had sanctioned the measures taken in connection with the western banks. Monroe admitted this and since that time had considered any attack on Crawford for these actions as an attack on him also. Therefore, he had not viewed his appointment of Edwards as unfriendly to Crawford. Adams, *Memoirs*, 6:299 (April 20, 1824); Monroe to Wirt, Sept. 27, 1824, Hamilton, *Monroe Writings*, 7:36-40.

[79] Adams, *Memoirs*, 6:297-98 (April 20, 1824).

[80] D. P. Cook to Henry Eddy, April 24, 1824 (typescript), Henry Eddy Papers (ISH); James Strong to William Woodbridge, April 5, 1824; Duncan McArthur to Woodbridge, April 23, 1824, Woodbridge; Charles Hammond to J. C. Wright, May 3, 7, 9, 1824, Charles Hammond Papers (OHS); Adams, *Memoirs*, 6:309-10.

admitted the facts charged by Edwards but acquitted Crawford of any evil intentions. Nor did it express any opinion against Edwards. Just a day or two before, Crawford had suffered a relapse and was confined to bed.[81]

With the return of Edwards to Washington on May 31 the investigation was resumed by a partial committee.[82] The examination and cross-examination continued for three weeks, with Cook questioning for Edwards and Forsyth for Crawford. Testimony damaging to Edwards was given by Senator James Noble of Indiana, who steadfastly maintained that on February 21 or 22, 1824, he had heard Edwards deny authorship of the "A.B." letters and believed Edwards' purpose in doing so was to overcome the opposition of Crawford's friends to his appointment as minister. Noble's testimony had nothing to do with the charges themselves, but it threw a cloud over Edwards' character—and Edwards had no satisfactory reply. The committee thought nothing had been proved to "impeach the integrity of the secretary" or cast doubt on the "general correctness and ability of his administration of the public finances." The Crawford papers and partisans rejoiced in the report, and some of the opposition papers were also pleased—they thought the attack on Crawford had been unfair.[83]

The cabinet on June 21 again discussed the matter at length; Monroe had already drafted a revocation of Edwards' commission, and all thought Edwards should be removed if he did not resign.[84]

81 Draft of an answer prepared by A[sbury] D[ickins], May 8, 1824, Asbury Dickins Papers (MDLC); *House Doc.*, No. 145 (serial 102), 18th Cong., 1st sess.; *ASPF*, 5:41-67, 69-74. Crawford's reply was accompanied by forty-six documents.

82 Randolph had left for England on May 13; McArthur and Owen were no longer in attendance. Before leaving, Randolph informed the "Freeholders of the Counties of Charlotte, Buckingham, Prince Edward, and Cumberland, and the Commonwealth of Virginia" that it was at his instance that the committee had given Crawford the chance to answer Edwards' charges. Until Crawford's answer, Randolph said he had little interest in the election of 1824, but he now had a keen desire that Crawford be elected. *Baltimore American & Commercial Daily Advertiser*, May 29, 1824, citing *Richmond Enquirer*.

83 *ASPF*, 5:80-146 (testimony), 79-80 (report); *Nashville Whig*, July 19, Aug. 30, 1824 (quoting *Boston Statesman*); *Argus of Western America*, July 7, 1824; Joseph Gibson to Louis McLane, July 25, 1824, McLane; Van Buren to Jefferson, July 13, 1824 (draft), Van Buren; Richard Rush to Crawford, Aug. 4, 1824, Crawford, MDLC. The *Boston Statesman* noted, "It is said that the degree of A.B. i.e. *Absolutely Bad*, has been conferred on *Ninian Edwards* by the Committee of Investigation at Washington." A duel between Cook and Forsyth, expected by many, did not take place.

84 Adams kept in close touch with the hearings, saw Edwards and some of the committee members several times during the hearings, said Taylor and Livingston moderated Webster's proposed panegyric on Crawford's management of the treasury,

The following day the cabinet resumed their discussion at 8 a.m. and continued until 9:30 p.m. Edwards' resignation was submitted, and Wirt, who the day before had thought Edwards should resign, said that if there was no reason to remove the minister there was no sufficient reason to accept the resignation. They decided to wait on this decision until the next day, but the issue was resolved in the evening by the *Republican*'s announcement of the resignation.[85]

This episode of the campaign faded away, but Edwards' national career was ended. He was elected governor of Illinois by a small margin in 1826, but Cook was not returned to the House. For several years Edwards seemed to be trying to play against Crawford the role Crawford later played against Calhoun. The coalescing of the Crawford and Jackson forces in Illinois was too much for Edwards to overcome.[86]

In the second phase of the "A.B." affair Crawford regained some of the ground he had lost in the first, but this gain was probably offset by increasing opposition to a caucus-nominated candidate and by Crawford's protracted illness after his relapse in May 1824.

---

and was concerned that his own candidacy might be hurt by cabinet involvement in the affair. *Memoirs,* 6: esp. 371, 374, 384, 387, 388-91.

[85] Edwards to Monroe, June 22, 1824, Edwards; Adams, *Memoirs,* 6:391-94. Edwards said that Crawford knew all the accusations made against him were true, but he was resigning because he did not want to cause Monroe any embarrassment.

[86] Theodore Calvin Pease, *The Story of Illinois* (Chicago, 1925), 114-15; Duff Green to Edwards, Sept. 6, 1826; Hugh Nelson to Edwards, Oct. 8, 1828, Washburne, *Edwards,* 256-58, 372-74; Green to Edwards, July 14, 1828, Duff Green Letter Book (MDLC).

11

The Last Congressional
Nominating Caucus

IN THE LATTER stages of the campaign of 1824 Crawford's candidacy was adversely affected by the rather general revolt against the caucus method of nomination, by the allegation that he was the candidate of the "managing" politicians rather than the candidate of the people, and by contradictory reports concerning the state of his health. The emphasis placed upon the will and the sovereignty of the people indicated widespread dissatisfaction with existing political processes and methods, and the caucus had for years been denounced as an infringement on the people's rights and as an attempt to lead rather than reflect public opinion. Though most politicians would not hesitate to use the caucus if they felt it beneficial to their political fortunes, there was anything but unanimity on how the will of the people should be expressed. Crawford-oriented politicians preferred retention and use of time-honored machinery, believing this would be advantageous to their favorite, but many others advocated the type of political organization that became prevalent in the 1830s, the popular and democratized party.

This difference in orientation doubtless helps to account for Crawford's lack of popularity, an impression which was assiduously disseminated by those who courted the sovereigns. The caucus bore the brunt of the attack, but the procedure by which some states chose the presidential electors was also sharply criticized as being inconsistent with the democratic principles of the country. The cleavage between proponents of the old and advocates of the new was sometimes narrowed, sometimes widened, by reports or rumors about the health of the candidate from Georgia.

The congressional caucus (sometimes also referred to as convention) had been under severe indictment since 1816 and was generally discredited by 1824. Numerous charges were made against the caucus, but perhaps the remark of William Plumer, Sr., expressed the basic dissatisfaction of many. He said there had been too much management and intrigue in the caucuses with "too much regard for *private* & too little respect for the public interest."[1] In various parts of the republic the use of the caucus at any level was attacked,[2] but it was not until 1822 that Hezekiah Niles opened his "final war." When principle was involved, he said, the caucus could be tolerated as a means of extinguishing personal views and promoting union. But in caucuses where only personality, management, intrigue, and bargain were concerned, "truth is kicked out of doors and decency trampled under foot." He would rather the halls of Congress be "converted into common brothels" than be used for such caucus meetings and vowed to oppose the reelection or future advancement of any member of Congress who participated in such gatherings. Niles periodically continued his opposition, but in the fall of 1823 he devoted much space to this subject and seemed to delight in reminding caucus supporters Gales and Seaton of the *National Intelligencer* and Ritchie of the *Richmond Enquirer* that they had opposed the caucus in 1816.[3]

Niles was definitely captain of the anticaucus writers and Ritchie, Gales, and Seaton were co-captains of the procaucus group; by early 1823 many had already taken up their positions. The *Washington Gazette* thought that nomination by the states was not a good thing, that the necessity of a national caucus was more apparent each day, that it was requisite to adjust the "opposite *state claims*" set up for the presidency and to prevent the election from going to the House, and indispensably requisite to prevent intrigue in the electoral college. On the other hand, the *Maryland Republican* held the claim of necessity was only a pretext for the caucus supporters. Niles continued to say that the choice must be left to the people.[4]

---

1 Plumer, Sr., to Plumer, Jr., April 24, 1820, Brown, *Missouri Compromises*, 51.

2 See for early examples the *Pittsburgh Gazette*, which in the summer of 1818 carried numerous condemnations of caucus nominations of candidates for Congress.

3 *Niles' Weekly Register* 21 (Jan. 22, 1822):339; 25 (Sept. 20, Oct. 18, Dec. 27, 1823): 40-41, 99-101, 257; *Richmond Enquirer*, Nov. 7, 1823.

4 *Washington Gazette*, Jan. 27, 1823; *Maryland Republican . . .* , Jan. 7, Feb. 1, March 15, 29, 1823; *Niles' Weekly Register* 24 (June 28, 1823):258. See also *National Republican and Ohio Political Register* (Cincinnati) during 1823, especially the

Newspapers, through editorial comment, news stories, and communications were the major antagonists, but on occasion others committed their opinions to writing. Calhoun seemed to approve a caucus among those holding similar principles and policies but thought a caucus unnatural and to a "great degree indefensible" if it involved compromise or if it was held to elevate a candidate who must be governed by men "wholly opposed to our views" of the nation's interest. Adams was unequivocally opposed to his being nominated by a caucus, while Clay felt he had nothing to fear from a caucus of all Republican congressmen. Another observer believed a caucus would help to keep the Federalists "in their holes."[5]

Jonathan Russell, who had carried on his vendetta against Adams and had transferred his support from Clay to Crawford, defended the caucus at great length. Such a meeting, he maintained, was neither provided for nor prohibited by the Constitution; at a congressional caucus there was no self-constituted cabal; every member admitted to the meeting had been constitutionally elected; all sections of the country were represented; and a caucus was essential to bring about compromise. He ridiculed the newer methods of nomination by state legislatures and mass meetings. The President should be the President of the whole people and not just a part of the United States.[6]

Hugh Lawson White of Tennessee, long a supporter of Jackson, thought the general's nomination by the Tennessee legislature "highly improper" and a precedent "dangerous in the extreme." He had been opposed to a nomination by a congressional caucus but had no doubt that nominations by state legislatures were "much worse." The making of a President was the business of the whole people through the medium of the electors: the state legislature had nothing to do with it; nor was it the concern of Congress. It was the people's business to select electors, and

---

October 24 issue which carried a quite lucid condemnation of the caucus and reprinted the resolutions of the Tennessee legislature against that method of nomination.

5 Calhoun to J. D. Erben, June 25, 1823, DeCoppett; Adams, *Memoirs*, 6:235-37, 241-44; Clay to Charles Hammond, Jan. 3, 1824, Clay, Lilly; H. G. Balch to N. G. Howard, Jan. 25, 1824, N. G. Howard Papers (Mississippi State Library and Archives). Calhoun's remarks seem to indicate that he thought he could not be the nominee of a caucus.

6 Congressional Caucus, 18-page manuscript, Russell. This 1823 paper was published in the *Boston Statesman* over the name Hancock.

the legislative nomination was an unwarranted usurpation of power which should not be countenanced.[7]

Several states followed the example of Tennessee—and of South Carolina—by placing their favorites in nomination, but the Tennessee resolutions against a congressional caucus nomination as a violation of the principles of the Constitution perhaps caused more discussion than any other single item. These resolutions were sent to the various states and were widely reprinted in the papers. New York rejected the proposals; Rhode Island tabled them; a committee of the Virginia legislature reported that it was both "politic and expedient" to have a caucus which was the only practicable means whereby the wishes of the majority of the nation were likely to be obtained. This report was indefinitely postponed, 77-76, but about two weeks later 157 of the 236 members of the legislature, acting in their "individual capacities," approved the action of the New York caucus and recommended that the Republican members from Virginia in Congress endeavor to procure the nomination of fit persons to fill the offices of President and Vice President.[8]

In North Carolina, incorrectly thought to be certain for Crawford, sentiment against Virginia domination brought a heated three-day debate on the caucus and on the postponement, 82-46, of the anticaucus resolution introduced in the House of Commons by Charles Fisher, former congressman. In the discussion, Fisher verbalized North Carolinians' dissatisfaction with the number of appointments to office the state had received during thirty-six years of following Virginia, and thought it "time for North-Carolina to stand alone—time to break the charm of Virginia influence—and think and act for ourselves."[9]

When Georgia Governor George M. Troup, Crawford partisan, submitted the Tennessee anticaucus resolutions to his assembly, he could not conceive what precise and definite meaning the legislature intended to attach to "caucus," a word not in the dictionary or in the constitution or laws of Tennessee. Appar-

7 White to David Campbell, June 10, 1823, Campbell, Duke.

8 *Niles' Weekly Register* 25 (Jan. 3, 10, 24, 31, 1824):281-84 288, 292, 323, 340. The Tennessee resolutions are conveniently available in ibid., 137-39.

9 Ibid. (Dec. 20, 1823):243; Raleigh *Register and North-Carolina Gazette*, May 21, 1824. A Crawford supporter thought (incorrectly) the defeat of the resolutions by so decisive a vote had blasted the hopes of the Calhoun group in North Carolina. Romulus Saunders to Bartlett Yancey, Dec. 17, 1823, Hamilton, "Letters to Yancey," 39.

ently, the Tennessee body was referring to a contemplated meeting of members of Congress to influence a decision on a "certain question," over which a state legislature had no jurisdiction. Although the members of Congress stood in both a public and private relation to society, they forfeited none of their rights as individuals by assuming public duties. The

> most arbitrary despotism could not prevent their assembly for purposes not inhibited by the laws. Such an assembly for convivial or social purposes might intermingle with its amusements the gravest discussions, and among those the very question, the discussion of which, by that assembly, the Legislature of Tennessee so ardently denounces:—it would give to itself a name other than that of Caucus, and then the vain unprofitable resolution of the Legislature of Tennessee would not have even a shadow on which to fix itself.[10]

The resolutions were tabled for the remainder of the session.

Not all state legislatures acted on the Tennessee resolutions, but of those that did only Maryland (with eleven electoral votes) approved them; Maine, New York, Virginia, and Georgia (with seventy-six votes) specifically approved a caucus nomination; North Carolina, Rhode Island, Pennsylvania, and Ohio (with sixty-eight votes) postponed action; and one house of the South Carolina legislature concurred in the Tennessee statement. Thus, legislatures of states with 144 electoral votes, or a majority of the 261 total, had declared for a caucus nomination or postponed action on a statement against such a nomination.

Discussion of a caucus quickened as the time approached for the convening of Congress. At the end of the last session of Congress many Crawford supporters had expected a caucus in the early days of the next session, but Crawford's illness made them hesitant to commit themselves until the recovery of their candidate seemed more certain, and the caucus was delayed. Jonathan Russell, however, was not deterred from his unremitting advocacy of a caucus nomination. Without a caucus, he said, the Republican party would be fragmented, love of persons or districts would predominate over love of republic and destroy the sentiments of freedom and patriotism, and delay of a caucus would provide time for disciplining and rendering more formi-

10 Troup to Senate of Georgia, Dec. 16, 1823, Cuyler.

dable its adversaries, since all other candidates seemed to think Crawford their most serious rival. Other Crawford friends, such as Jesse B. Thomas, continued to support a congressional caucus, as did some of the established and newly founded papers. Other papers, as well as county and local meetings, did not lessen their opposition.[11]

In late 1823 Adams believed Crawford's friends intended to precipitate a caucus to forestall the movements of the state legislatures and of the people in Adams' favor. He expected a caucus to be held and apparently thought Crawford would be elected, for he said "if his Administration should prove an unpopular one, the caucus appointment will eventually recoil upon him." Former Secretary of Navy Crowninshield did not see how the caucus would be held, since only Crawford's friends favored it. Each candidate, though, was doing all he could to make friends: Jackson was patching up private quarrels, the friends of Crawford were similarly engaged, Calhoun and his followers were playing "deep and rather impudently" and laughing at Adams, and Adams alone was "still & firm as Atlas, waiting the result of public movement." Jackson felt opinion in Washington was against a caucus—there were not more than forty-two people in favor of it—and without a caucus the treasury candidate had but little chance.[12]

The Crawfordites' support of a caucus brought accusations that Crawford had Federalist backers, but his friends vigorously maintained that he trod the beaten Republican path of Jefferson, Madison, and Monroe, that he did not seek to elevate himself by "new-fangled inventions," and that he left it to the people alone to judge him. Some pro-Crawford papers said a comparison of those favoring and opposing the caucus showed the former held "old republican standards" and had invited confidence by their steadfast adherence to principle, while the latter were a "new race of politicians, in a great measure unknown, or not long known, to the nation; and if known, remarkable only for their

---

11 Russell to Samuel Eddy, Nov. 24, 1823, Russell: Thomas to Gov. S[hadrack] Bond, Dec. 8, 1823, Thomas. See also *Albany Argus* and *Taunton* (Mass.) *Free Press* for November and December 1823; *Niles' Weekly Register* 25 (Nov. 15, 29, Dec. 20, 1823):166, 194, 242.

12 Adams, *Memoirs*, 6:191 (Nov. 19, 1823); B. W. Crowninshield to Genl [H. A. Dearborn ?], Dec. 19, 1823, Crowninshield Personal Miscellany (MDLC): Jackson to William B. Lewis, Dec. 22, 1823, Jackson-Lewis. Jackson said he was clear of both intrigue and caucus mongers and intended to stay that way. Philip Barbour had received forty-two votes in his contest with Clay for the speakership of the House.

abandonment of principle and pursuit of office and emolument, by attaching themselves to the skirts of other candidates." Excepted from this evaluation were those who had always declined attending a caucus; their consistency attested their principles. The voice of the Republican party and the national interest called for a caucus; if a majority was against a nomination after a fair trial, something would be gained by ascertaining that fact. Rather than hold an anticaucus meeting, opponents of this method of nomination should go into caucus and vote down the "radicals"— thus making the country safe. If they were not sure of their ability to do this, they should stay away and let it die a natural death. On the other hand, why should they voluntarily absent themselves and "suffer the scheme of such tremendous wickedness to be carried on in open defiance of them?"[13]

It was apparent the friends of Crawford wanted a caucus in the hope that endorsement by such a gathering would give a boost to their candidate. The friends of the other candidates did not want a caucus: no two groups (including Crawford's) had been able to effect a coalition, and no other single group had the congressional strength and cohesion of the Crawford forces. Crawford's illness and the known anticaucus attitude of some of his staunchest supporters constituted problems of some magnitude, but James Barbour and Thomas W. Cobb worked valiantly for his nomination and election. Early in 1824 Cobb wrote that the "precarious" state of Crawford's health had been a "great drawback," but arrangements for a caucus were being speedily made. Crawford, he thought, would receive the votes of 70 to 80 of the 100 to 120 who would attend. New York was described as firm, but he believed they would lose Pennsylvania and that Calhoun was throwing his weight to Jackson, whose prospects were improving more rapidly than those of any other candidate. A few days later Cobb was not so sanguine about the caucus prospects: if all Crawford friends would attend, there would be about ninety, but probably only about eighty would go into caucus. No other candidate had more than twenty or thirty, and they were trying to unite in an anticaucus association. He thought he saw some signs of a coalition between Clay and Calhoun; Jackson had

13 *Washington Gazette*, Feb. 4, 11, 1824: *Savannah Republican*, Feb. 20, 1824; CW to Samuel Gouverneur, Feb. 3, 1824, Gouverneur; *Milledgeville Georgia Journal*, Feb. 17, 24, 1824.

reconciled himself with all but Crawford; and Adams had "also conducted himself like a gentleman at last." He named ten Crawford men who he thought would not caucus; there were others he did not remember. At the moment he thought they could count on the votes of seven states but indicated that no doubt "great changes will be made by circumstances."[14]

Crawford supporters, hoping to substantiate the assertion that Crawford trod the path of Jefferson and other illustrious Republicans, tried to devise some way to persuade Jefferson to declare himself, but apparently they never got beyond the "planning" stage. They did, however, make special efforts to get Nathaniel Macon to attend a caucus and to induce Gallatin to come to Washington to use his influence with the Pennsylvania delegation. Macon, more than thirty years a member of the House and Senate, a strong supporter of Crawford, and considered one of the few remaining Old Republicans, had not attended a caucus since 1800. He thought nomination by a congressional caucus preferable to nomination by state legislatures, but he objected to a caucus because it was not provided for by the Constitution, produced electioneering among members of Congress that bordered on intrigue and bargain, and forced the minority to yield their opinion.

Macon was convinced his attending a caucus would do no good to Crawford's cause and might do harm. He was not in favor of the new tariff, he did not advocate internal improvements, and he was not a member of the colonization society. His stand— opposite to that of Crawford—on each of these would have weight in the election, and his attendance would raise the suspicion of bargain. These differences did not trouble Macon, who had a high regard for Crawford's abilities and remembered only Crawford's vote on the first Bank of the United States as being at variance with Republican principles. By the end of January 1824

14 Cobb to Dear Sir, Jan. 24, 1824, Gratz; Cobb to Charles Tait, Feb. 2, 1824, Tait. Among the persons named were Willie P. Mangum and Nathaniel Macon of North Carolina, John Randolph of Virginia, Joseph McKim of Maryland, and Louis McLane of Delaware. In his "Dear Sir" letter Cobb said the doctors indicated the quantities of digitalis administered in Virginia had caused Crawford's eye trouble. Recently there had been improvement in one eye but very little change in the other. See also Willie Mangum to Seth Jones, Feb. 11, 1824, Henry Thomas Shanks, ed., *The Papers of Willie Person Mangum*, 6 vols. (Raleigh, N.C., 1950-1956), 1:115-16 (hereafter cited as Shanks, *Mangum*); Benjamin Ruggles to Thomas Worthington, Feb. 5, 1824, Worthington. Ruggles was the only Ohio representative to go into caucus.

he had "not decided to attend." (It would appear from the context and from all previous statements of his position that Macon really meant "decided not to attend.") However, he advised caucus advocates to convene—if they intended to do so. The meeting should have been held in December, since the strong side rarely gains by delay.[15]

Crawford and his friends wanted Gallatin to come to Washington, for they believed he could unite the Pennsylvania delegation in support of a caucus. In the course of their efforts Macon sent Gallatin a note he had received from Cobb, in which Cobb relayed Crawford's request for Macon to write Gallatin that it was necessary for him to come to the capital for "his interests and interests of others were suffering in consequence of his absence." Macon's comment was: "I know not to what it relates."[16] Macon's influence did not get Gallatin to Washington, nor was Gallatin's to persuade Macon to go into caucus. Several letters were exchanged. Macon thought he did not have the influence Gallatin supposed, reported he had vowed in 1800 never again to attend a caucus, and said "I cannot go." Should he attend, the charge of intrigue would be renewed against Crawford who would be said to be the only man who could "touch the chord that moved me," and probably the wicked and false adage that every man has his price would be revived. Time would prove them false, but the election would be over and the injury done.[17]

On February 7 caucus advocates had agreed to a meeting on February 14, the obvious purpose of which was nomination of Crawford. The *Baltimore Morning Chronicle* derided the action:

> *The Question Settled.*—The poor little political bird of ominous note and plumage, denominated a CAUCUS, was hatched at Washington on Saturday last. It is now running around like a pullet, in a forlorn and sickly state. Reader, have you ever seen

15 Macon to Van Buren, May 9, 1823, Van Buren; Macon to Bartlett Yancey, Dec. 12, 1823, Yancey; Macon to Yancey, Jan. 31, Feb. 1, 1824, Hamilton, "Letters to Yancey," 42, 43.

16 Jesse B. Thomas to Gallatin, Jan. 5, 1824; Macon to Gallatin, Jan. 16, 1824, Gallatin. This could well be a bit of Macon humor; he sometimes ribbed and teased his correspondents and displayed a disarming boyishness. On other occasions Macon does appear surprisingly naive.

17 Walter Lowrie to Gallatin, Feb. 10, 1824; Macon to Gallatin, Feb. 13, 14, 1824, ibid. Macon would have preferred to talk with Gallatin about the caucus. Lowrie later said of Macon: he is "an honest & good man; but he is so entirely made up of negatives, that we can expect nothing positively active from him." Lowrie to Gallatin, Feb. 20, 1824, ibid.

a chicken directly after it was hatched, creeping about with a bit of egg shell sticking to its back? This is a just representation of this poor forlorn Congressional caucus. The sickly thing is to be fed, cherished, pampered for a week, when it is fondly hoped it will be enabled to cry the name of Crawford, Crawford, Crawford.[18]

Benjamin Ruggles was chairman and Ela Collins of New York was secretary of the caucus meeting. An attempt to postpone action until March 20, when a "more full assemblage of members might be expected," was opposed by Martin Van Buren and failed. Van Buren thought it impossible to fix a time convenient and agreeable for all to attend and asserted that the people were anxiously awaiting the nomination. Sixty-six—just more than one third of the Republicans in Congress—attended and two others voted by proxy. The result was not unexpected: Crawford 64, Adams 2, Macon 1, and Jackson 1. Tompkins, Van Buren told the gathering, had declined reelection; Albert Gallatin received 57 votes for the vice-presidential nomination, and eight others garnered a total of nine votes.[19]

The sixty-six attending consisted of eight (of nine) from Georgia, ten (of fifteen) from North Carolina, fourteen (of twenty-five) from Virginia, sixteen (of thirty-six) from New York, three each from Connecticut, Pennsylvania, and Maryland, two from Maine and South Carolina, and one each from Rhode Island, New Jersey, Ohio, Indiana, and Illinois. Thus, only Georgia, North Carolina, and Virginia showed a majority of their delegations in caucus, and only three people from west of the mountains attended.

The maneuverings of the anti-Crawfordites had not prevented the caucus, but the Crawford supporters were not able to lure to the meeting some of the Old Republicans. And the attendance fell some dozen or more short of the estimates of the "managers." For some time the supporters and opponents of the caucus played a numbers game, with the opponents having a little better of the

---

[18] Quoted in *National Journal*, Feb. 11, 1824.

[19] *Baltimore American & Commercial Daily Advertiser*, Feb. 16, 1824. A thousand or more spectators attended the meeting; on the "annunciation of the name of Mr. Crawford for President, some approbation was expressed from the galleries, which was followed by a slight murmur or hiss, proceeding, among others, from a clerk in the War Department." With this "trifling exception," the "utmost harmony" was said to have prevailed.

contest since a smaller percentage of Republicans in Congress attended the 1824 gathering than had attended any previous caucus. Crawford's opponents never let the public forget that the Georgian had been nominated by a minority of the Republicans in Congress.[20]

The caucus nomination certainly seems not to have advanced Crawford in the standings, and it is highly probable that the caucus apologia, "Address to the Republicans in the United States," was a serious political mistake. The Address justified the meeting by the usual reasoning of the caucus advocates and called attention to the twenty-four years of Republican control of the central government, the danger of division within the party, and the disruptive mischief that might have been done by the Tennessee resolutions.[21] The absence of so many Republicans was regrettable, but it was said to be "neither our privilege nor disposition to exercise any right of judgment on their conduct." The caucus participants did not conceal their anxiety that the "course of recent events points to the entire dismemberment of the party to which it is our pride to be attached" and spoke of the "unalleviated mischiefs" of an election by the House of Representatives. The conclusion was a reference to Crawford's refusal to stand for caucus nomination in 1816:

> Without intending to derogate from the merits of others, for whom your confidence might be solicited, it is just to remind you that the candidate we recommend for the first office in your government, has established a peculiar claim to the esteem of the republican party, by his manly and disinterested conduct upon a former occasion, under the strongest temptation to become the instrument of compromising his integrity.[22]

The statement was accusing in tone, partisan in approach, and pessimistic in outlook.

If the Address was intended to placate the anticaucus people

---

20 Barnabas [?] to John Holmes, March 4, 1824, John Holmes Papers (Maine Historical Society). For examples of the numbers game and comments thereon see *Raleigh Register and North-Carolina Gazette*, Feb. 17, March 5, 1824; *Constitutional Whig*, Feb. 20, 1824; *Washington Gazette*, March 4, 1824; *Niles' Weekly Register* 25 (Dec. 20, 1823):244, and many subsequent issues.

21 Since only Maryland had approved the Tennessee resolutions, the Address was creating its own straw man to tear down.

22 *Niles' Weekly Register* 25 (Feb. 21, 1824):390-91; *Nashville Whig*, March 15, 1824.

and to soothe the feelings of various factions of the party, it was apparently couched in the wrong terms. William King, governor of Maine, was "greatly chagrined" by the paper and said it was all the work of John Holmes of his state and of Van Buren, was against the opinions and wishes of a great majority of Crawford's best friends and supporters in and out of the caucus, and misrepresented the sentiments of the one it was intended to serve. It had placed King in the most unpleasant predicament since his administration had known no distinction in politics and he had consistently asserted that Crawford would be tolerant of all sects and parties in the conduct of the government. He believed that only New York and Pennsylvania would respond to the doctrine of party contained in the Address.[23] Many others felt that no statement should have been made. The Address recalls the *Exposition* published by Crawford supporters in 1816; the 1824 statement might well have been another case where Crawford's best friends were his worst enemies.

The journalistic war over the caucus did not subside. Opponents thought the Crawfordites' "forcing" the caucus would have a fatal reaction, Crawford would not be the next President, and there would be no more caucuses. Some "reflective and candid" friends of Crawford were said to review the caucus with chagrin and regret, but the friends of Clay viewed the meeting as the herald of Crawford's fall and the harbinger of Clay's elevation. Clay himself thought the nomination would destroy whatever prospects Crawford ever had. At least one Crawford paper saw an insidious design in the continued opposition to the caucus nomination: all the hue and cry came from those who were determined that no election should be made by the people.[24]

That a selection might be made by the people—or that greater control be given to the people—seems to have been the major

---

23 John A. King to Rufus King, March 5, 1824, King, *King*, 6:353. The publisher of the *Boston Statesman* thought the caucus would help in "this quarter" and those New England Republicans who were afraid to attend would have much to repent of later. Nathaniel Greene to John Holmes, March 2, 1824, Holmes.

24 For example see *Augusta Chronicle and Georgia Advertiser*, Feb. 28, March 10, 13, April 3, 14, 24, 1824; *Kentucky Gazette*. Feb. 26, March 18, 1824; *Pittsburgh Gazette*, Feb. 27, 1824; *Portsmouth Journal*, Feb. 14, 28, 1824; *Columbian Centinel*, Feb. 18, 1824; Charles Hammond to [J. C. Wright?], Feb. 23, 1824, Hammond, OHS; *Constitutional Whig*, Feb. 20, 1824; Clay to Francis Brooke, Feb. 23, 1824, Henry Clay Papers (University of Kentucky Library); *Western Argus* reprinted in *Albany Argus*, Feb. 17, 1824.

objective of numerous proposals to change the manner of choosing the electors and to establish a new procedure for selecting the President. A measure introduced by Senator John Taylor of Virginia provided that the states should choose, by districts, as many electors as they had representatives; those electors should then choose an additional two to represent the senators. If, in the electoral college, no candidate received a majority, the electors would vote again. As reported by one committee, the second vote would be between the two highest candidates; if no majority was attained, the matter would be referred to the representatives and senators, meeting jointly but voting individually. A majority of the whole number present would elect, but in case two candidates had the same number of votes the person having the highest number at the earlier meeting should be declared President. If tied both times, the balloting should continue until a choice was made. The same procedure would be followed in choosing a Vice President. This measure was twice read to the Senate committee of the whole on December 22, 1823. A similar proposal by Thomas Hart Benton was also before the Senate, and on January 8, 1824, a select committee recommended that the senators and representatives should choose among the three candidates with the highest number of votes, and a majority would be necessary for a choice on the first ballot. Thereafter only a plurality would be required for election. Further, no person twice elected to the office should again be eligible. No change was recommended in the manner of choosing the Vice President.[25] Neither of these measures—nor any of the others—so much as passed the house in which they were introduced.

The Taylor bill would have required choice of presidential electors by the congressional districts, thus bringing the election considerably closer to the people, but giving the individual voter less "power" than he would have if all the electors of a state were chosen by the general ticket. Actually, in the spring of 1823 the district method was used by five states with a total of sixty electoral votes. Electors were also chosen by the general ticket (nine states with 114 votes) and by the legislature (ten states with 87 votes). Criticism of the last method was sharp, and especially was the

25 See *Annals* of appropriate dates and *Niles' Weekly Register* 25 (Dec. 13, 27, 1823, Jan. 3, 17, 1824):240, 270-71, 273, 317.

practice denounced because it too often involved managing, intrigue, manipulation, and usurpation of the people's rights. Many newspapers and letter writers attacked this method of selecting the electors who would choose the President, but one article reprinted by Hezekiah Niles will suffice to indicate the tenor of the discussion.

The lengthy article, originally published in the *New York Patriot* and probably written by Henry Wheaton, was obviously opposed to the legislative choice of electors in New York. The people, it said, were not merely the "source of power" but were the "sovereignty of the country": there was no political authority above or beside them, no bound or limit to their power except natural right, justice, and the fundamental principles on which the government was founded. "State," as used in the constitutional provision that the state appoint electors, by common sense and usage means the people, not the land, the trees, the court, the legislature, or the executive. Further, the fact that "elect," "appoint," and "choose" were and had been used indiscriminately was substantiated by examples drawn from the Federalist papers and from discussions in the conventions called to consider ratification of the Constitution. James Monroe, George Mason, Edmund Randolph, and James Madison were cited, and the conviction was expressed that the Constitution would never have been ratified if it had been believed or imagined that the legislatures of the states would take the appointment of the electors from the people.[26]

The group in power were most often the advocates of existing practice. On occasion they openly defended the status quo; at other times they resorted to delaying tactics or sanctioned a new system that would have made matters worse (as in New York), but between the spring of 1823 and the fall of 1824 five states in which the legislatures had chosen the electors had transferred that power to the voters. Only in Vermont, New York, Delaware, Georgia, and Louisiana (60 votes total) did the legislatures still choose the electors, and Georgia had authorized the polling of the voters to see whether they wanted the choice of electors transferred to them. Three of the five states that abandoned the choice-by-legislature method adopted the general ticket, bringing

26 *Niles' Weekly Register* 24 (July 19, 1823): 317-20.

to thirteen (with 150 votes) the number using the means many considered the fairest and best. The other two states joined the four already using the district system; the electoral vote of those six was 51.[27] Clearly, a democratizing process had been operative; in all but one of the states retaining the choice of electors in the legislature, the legislators were chosen only a short time before the presidential elections. In New York the time span was twelve months, and there the infighting was bitter.[28]

Crawford's poor health and the lack of completely reassuring statements on his degree of recovery was a most important factor in the presidential campaign from September 1823 to February 1825. The Georgian's illness unquestionably delayed the caucus, prevented or curtailed personal contact with new members of Congress, precluded his keeping in close touch with electioneering activities, permitted a greater freedom of action for some of his not-always-discreet partisans, and—because of confinement to his home—gave greater credence to the stories that the secretary was near death or at least would be withdrawn from the race. On the other hand, uncertainty about Crawford's condition seemed to induce many to assume a noncommittal position on a caucus nomination and might well have contributed to softening some of the acerbities of the campaign, for no matter what happened to Crawford, his wing of the party was a powerful force in national politics.

Unlike some other prominent public figures, Adams seemed genuinely to wish for the recovery of Crawford and several times addressed his diary in this vein. In the early spring of 1824 Crawford seemed well on the road to recovery; he returned to cabinet meetings, walked over the grounds of his new place in the country, appeared to be regaining his strength, and was in "fine spirits." He could not yet use his "own eyes & pen" for writing.[29] By this time his friends had decided he would regain

---

[27] For convenient tabulations of the methods of choosing electors see *Illinois Intelligencer*, Sept. 24, 1824; *Niles' Weekly Register* 24 (May 17, 1823):161. See also ibid., 25 (Dec. 20, 1823):242; 26 (June 5, 1824):221; 27 (Sept. 4, 1824):3. Niles thought (June 5, 1824, p. 221) the general ticket "may prevent much dirty intrigue by the people-mongers." In 1842 Congress provided that all electors be chosen by the general-ticket method.

[28] The choice of the New York electors is discussed in the following chapter.

[29] Adams, *Memoirs*, 6:267, 275; Crawford to Richard Rush, April 26, 1824, Rush Family Papers (Princeton University); Mrs. S. H. Smith to Mrs. Boyd, April 11, 1824, Hunt, *First Forty Years*, 164. On June 28, a little more than a month after Craw-

his health, the long-delayed nominating caucus had been held, and Crawford had reopened the "A.B." affair when he presented his lengthy report to the House. Then near the end of May he suffered a relapse. He was distressed that he could not confer with his friends during the questioning of Edwards and later wrote that he was "deranged" just after the adjournment of Congress and that he spoke of Edwards' "stealing" his horses and of his "shooting" Edwards.[30]

In late May and early June 1824 death or incapacitation for office seemed probable. Troup expressed the fear of "our friends" that Crawford's illness might prove fatal or otherwise disqualify him, and Clay thought the Georgian's friends "begin to own that his death is now but too probable, and that in any event he can no longer be held up" for the presidency. Clay reported that Crawford had suffered a paralytic stroke and conjectured that a proposed visit to Virginia by Van Buren and Dickerson involved measures for a new campaign.[31] The *Washington Gazette,* whose attacks on the administration had prompted Crawford to withdraw the federal patronage from it only two months before, was not so pessimistic: Crawford was "progressing" and his bodily affliction was not "near so great" as that of Madison in 1813-1814. And an ardent Adams paper reported Crawford's improving health, noting that as Adams' prospects of election increased daily "his friends, in addition to their sympathies as men, are gratified in hearing the above tidings. The triumph over a sound and healthy rival will be augmented."[32]

There were many other reports and rumors, favorable and unfavorable. Niles took note of the irreconcilability of these, said he could not discover the truth, but could find no reason why there should be any misrepresentation of Crawford's true state. He thought it probable that Crawford was much better,

ford's relapse, Mrs. Smith noted that Crawford proposed walking to their home to spend part of the day, but her husband had persuaded him to ride. She thought Crawford "so venturesome that he will make himself sick again." Ibid., 166. The Crawfords had lived at the corner of Massachusetts Avenue and 14th Street; their new rented home, to which they moved in May or June, was a Captain Doughty's farm, which was separated from the Smith place "only by the road." Catholic University is situated on land that formerly was a part of the Smith place.

30 Romulus Saunders to Bartlett Yancey, Dec. 10, 1824, Clark.

31 George M. Troup to John Randolph, June 15, 1824 (typed copy), John Randolph Letter Book (UVa); Clay to Francis Brooke, May 24, 1824, Clay, UKy.

32 *Washington Gazette* as quoted by *Albany Argus,* June 8, 1824; *Columbian Centinel,* June 12, 1824.

and the restoration of his health and reestablishment of all his faculties must be the wish of every liberal-minded man—even though he might utterly reject the arguments advanced for Crawford's elevation to the presidency. Apparently Crawford was much improved by the end of June, and the *Albany Argus* said readers were not likely to forget that the editor of the *Columbian Observer* had said Crawford's illness was the *"retributive justice of Providence"* for his crimes.[33]

Crawford, still weak, was advised by his physicians to avoid the seacoast and take a journey into the interior of Pennsylvania and New Jersey. Near the end of July Adams found him "convalescent, in cheerful spirits," and intending to start on his trip the next week. He noted that Crawford's articulation was still affected, "but he appears otherwise quite well." On August 4 Crawford spent about an hour with Monroe and five days later left the city.[34]

Crawford did not go into Pennsylvania and New Jersey; instead he took part of his family with him to Berkeley Springs (or Bath), Virginia, where he arrived on August 13. He described himself as "at least as well as when I set out from Home" and asked that he be written to three times a week while he was away.[35] Whether the faithful Dickins met this request is not known; little correspondence for this period remains. It can only be guessed that Crawford made such contacts as were possible at the Springs. He remained there for the entire period of his absence from Washington, to which he returned on September 12.[36]

33 *Niles' Weekly Register* 26 (June 12, 1824):240; *Albany Argus*, July 2, 1824.

34 Crawford to Mahlon Dickerson, July 6, 1824, Dickerson; Adams, *Memoirs*, 6: 402, 405, 408 (July 29, Aug. 4, 9, 1824). Two days before Crawford's departure Joseph Anderson said he would send Monroe a copy of the attending and consulting physicians' report on Crawford's health. Apparently at least three doctors were involved and they declared that from the standpoint of physical as well as mental health Crawford was fully competent to discharge the duties of his official station. Anderson to Monroe, Aug. 7, 1824, Monroe, MDLC; *Richmond Enquirer*, Aug. 10, 1824.

35 *National Intelligencer*, Aug. 10, 1824; Crawford to [Dickins?], Aug. 15, 1824, Alexander Calvin Washburn Papers (MHS). It was reported that before Crawford left for his trip he walked about, took a long ride, and saw all who came to visit him each day—sometimes as many as twenty. Also it was stated that Calhoun and Crawford were in the same neighborhood while Crawford was in the "upper country," that Calhoun condescended to visit Crawford, and that the visit was returned. *Federal Gazette and Baltimore Daily Advertiser*, Aug. 13, 1824, citing *National Advocate; Richmond Enquirer*, Sept. 17, 1824.

36 Henry St. George Tucker to David Campbell, Aug. 29, 1824, Campbell, Duke; *National Intelligencer*, Sept. 14, 1824.

Two days after his return Gales and Seaton wrote Van Buren fully about Crawford's condition. The "prostration" of his system had been so extreme that "without a personal knowledge of it, no one can properly even judge his present condition." They had not seen him at his worst; but when they did see him, every function of his body—except perhaps his hearing—was impaired. After a week they could see a visible improvement, and there had not been the slightest retrogradation. On his return to Washington he traveled through rain over the "worst roads in the world" at the rate of thirty miles a day. A half-hour interview on September 13 (the day after his return) had convinced the editors that in all essentials Crawford was his former self. The distortion of his mouth had wholly disappeared; this had been the most distressing to look at, "though the effect merely of mercurial affection." They had seen Crawford at his office and considered him competent for any "description of Executive business." His eyesight and the use of his pen hand were not perfect, but "sufficiently so." Using glasses he was able to read the small print of a newspaper. "His *mind & memory* are perfectly *sound, vigorous, & active.*" Considering the change that had taken place in six weeks, it was thought that by or before the meeting of Congress he "will be in a fit state to be exhibited with pride as the President of the United States." In frankness, they thought they should state what was unfavorable about Crawford's condition: his limbs had not "regained all their flexibility, nor his speech all its distinctness." He walked for miles with firmness. He spoke intelligibly enough, but his utterance was not as clear as it usually had been. But there had been so much improvement in his speech that "we trust the impediment will soon altogether disappear." A few days later John Forsyth, who saw Crawford on September 18, said he "looks uncommonly well. The only difficulty with him now is a *thick tongue.*"[37]

His friends continued to say that he was recovering and his political opponents continued to represent him as incapacitated. Just before the election an anti-Crawford journal published a letter saying information obtained from medical gentlemen, from others, and from the writer's observations indicated Crawford's "disease" had "entirely disqualified him from adequate attention

[37] Gales and Seaton to Van Buren, Sept. 14, 1824; Forsyth to Van Buren, Sept. 20, 1824, Van Buren.

to any business that requires ordinary mental and bodily exertion."
The physicians considered his last attack apoplectic rather than
paralytic. Soon after the election a pro-Crawford paper thought
no well-informed man could believe that Crawford would not
have received a majority—or at least the largest number—of the
electoral votes if he had not been ill, and it charged that if his
health had not been misrepresented with the "most assiduous
industry" he would have gained a plurality of the votes.[38]

Perhaps the most accurate statement of Crawford's health in
late 1824 came from Thomas W. Cobb, as frank and outspoken
as the man he supported. He said Crawford's cheeks were full
and florid and his spirits admirable. The speech impediment
remained and gave him considerable trouble with articulation.
His imperfect vision was improving: he could read about half a
page and then the letters became indistinct and he had to stop.
His doctors had prohibited his reading. He could easily distinguish those with whom he had been acquainted but had
difficulty recognizing those whom he seldom saw. His feet and
hands were in a "state of great debility," and the stiffness and
"extreme weakness" of his fingers was the cause of his bad writing.
Cobb had never known his mind to be more active or strong; his
memory appeared as correct as ever; and he reasoned with the
same rapidity. Another partisan corroborated the view that
Crawford's health in general was restored but indicated he was
no longer the "commanding man" he once was in conversation.[39]

This then was probably Crawford's condition on the eve of the
casting of the electoral votes. His mind was functioning well
and clearly, but his stammering or defective articulation might
have led some to believe otherwise. He had not regained his

[38] *Constitutional Whig,* Oct. 29, 1824; *National Intelligencer,* Nov. 23, 1824.
Slightly later an Adams supporter said that since there was no chance for Crawford's
election his friends began to confess his mind was affected by disease. He said Crawford
put his hat on when Lafayette was at the President's, would not drink wine at the
dinner because it "injured" him, and then drank freely after inviting others to drink
with him. There were many other "proofs" of "mental alienation" which he had
heard in such a way that he would not doubt them. George Tichnor to George
Bancroft, Dec. 1, 1824, George Bancroft Papers (MHS). Tichnor wanted to see
Jackson and Mrs. Jackson; if what he had heard was true, "she has few compeers
for vulgarity and ignorance."
[39] Cobb to Bartlett Yancey, Dec. 8, 1824, Yancey; Saunders to Yancey, Dec. 10,
1824, Clark. Saunders had seen Crawford on December 9. Lewis Williams wrote
Yancey on December 2 (Yancey) that Crawford looked as well in the face as he ever
saw him, but his "strength is not yet perfectly regained."

weight, and this deficiency—coupled with the feebleness of his hands and feet—must have created an impression that contrasted sharply with the Crawford image prior to September 1823. He was on the road to recovery, but he was not yet a really healthy man.[40]

[40] That Crawford had been very ill and that his recovery was rather slow no one should deny, but Parton, *Jackson*, 3:24, 58, is not quite fair when he says, "Piteous attempts were made to *show* the afflicted man, by driving him, propped with cushions, about the streets of Washington" and describes Crawford as a "tottering, imbecile old man—old prematurely."

12

The Election of 1824

LONG BEFORE Crawford was nominated by the caucus it was apparent that each of the candidates had a sectional backing corresponding to his place of residence, but since there were two hopefuls from the Southeast and two from the West, support was divided in those areas. The middle area was uncommitted, with "managing," continued control of state political machinery, personalities, and the slight divergencies of the candidates' views on the supposed issues playing roles in the outcome. Crawford's greatest strength was known to be in the Southeast, and the long established political machinery was expected to bring him rewards in the middle area, especially in the key state of New York.

Only the most sanguine supporters held much hope for Crawford in New England, where his active workers were primarily people who had been associated with him in public service. The most vigorous of these in Rhode Island was Jonathan Russell. He had fenced for Clay in 1822 and against Adams in 1823; for the rest of the campaign he dipped his pen where he could find the most vitriol, not hesitating to touch upon what he called Monroe's double-dealing.[1] James Fenner also supported Crawford in Rhode Island; he and his co-workers were unable to postpone legislative action, and Adams was nominated prior to the meeting of the congressional caucus.[2]

In Massachusetts the Georgian's backers were numerous; some were Federalists, and others were accused of being such. They were assisted in their efforts by several newspapers, notably the *Taunton Free Press* and the *Boston Courier*. The latter paper carried pro-Crawford articles by the old Federalist Timothy Pickering, brought out the "connection" between John Quincy Adams and John Bailey's election as representative from Massachusetts, emphasized the relation between Benjamin W. Crowninshield and political patronage, praised Crawford for reducing the salaries of weighers, gaugers, and inspectors, said Adams had long lived in Europe where "frauds and corruptions are countenanced and protected by the governments," and gave encouragement to the unsuccessful move to choose an unpledged set of electors.[3]

The *New Hampshire Patriot* supported Crawford, and C. P. Van Ness, elected governor of Vermont in the fall of 1824, seems not to have been impaired in popularity by his imputed Crawfordism, but in those two states the Crawford loyalists were few. In Maine, Crawford partisans stressed the division of sentiment among the legislators, proposed that John Holmes send frequent messages to influential friends, and suggested that the Methodists and the Baptists be courted. The optimism of Holmes, most ardent in the Crawford cause, far outstripped his ability at political analysis (he thought it probable that Crawford would carry nine states), but he said "We must engage this summer with all zeal." Engage they did, but zeal was not enough. All fifty-one New England votes went to Adams.[4]

New York was the key state in the election of 1824. Van Buren, taking no chances in 1823 and waiting for the congressional caucus to act, might well have lost the opportunity for New York to play the decisive role in the election. While the Clay, Adams, Clinton, Crawford, Regency, and anti-Regency factions were maneuvering for advantage, there was a great ground swell in favor of the electors being chosen by the people rather than by the legislature. Clinton would be the chief beneficiary of such a change, but many members of the assembly thought refusal to yield to the people's wishes would expose the party to overthrow.[5]

The three leading presidential candidates in New York—Adams, Clay, and Crawford—appeared to have little or nothing to gain by giving the choice of electors to the people, but in early

---

1 See, for example, Russell to Smith, May 3, 1824, Russell.

2 Wheeler Martin to John Bailey, Jan. 24, 1824; D. J. Pearce to Bailey, Jan. 31, 1824 (copy), Bailey; John Adams to Bailey, March 18, 1824, Washburn.

3 *Boston Courier*, Sept. 8, 9, 14, 22; Oct. 7, 12, 19, 20, 21, 23, 25, 27, 29, 1824; *Columbian Centinel*, Aug. 28, 1824. Bailey, a clerk in the State Department, was not seated by the House.

4 See for some aspects of Maine activity, Barnabas [?] to Holmes, March 4, 1824, B. Johnson to Holmes, March 9, 1824, Holmes; Holmes to N. G. Howard, April 4, 1824, Chamberlain. It should be noted that New England was setting something of a voting pattern for a favorite son or the candidate of the Northeast.

5 William L. Marcy to Van Buren, Jan. 11, 1824, Van Buren. Marcy had received four letters saying Van Buren had abandoned Crawford for Clay, and according to a letter read to him Crawford must lose his eyes or his life.

February the lower house made its gesture toward public demand and opinion by passing a bill giving the people this right. The bill required the electors to have a majority of the votes cast, an impossibility given the number of slates and the division in the state. The senate, however, accepted the report of its nine-man committee that it was not expedient to consider the bill from the lower house, or any other bill, until efforts in Congress to establish a uniform mode of selection had either failed or succeeded. The measure was postponed until the first Monday in November.[6]

Just at this time the Regency was having problems with its mouthpiece, the *Albany Argus*. Marcy complained that Isaac Q. Leake, then running the paper, had for some time been hostile, had mutilated many articles, favored the election law, opposed a national caucus, regaled visitors with anticaucus and pro-Clay sentiments, and had lately discovered it was "highly improper" for the state paper to be a party paper. Van Buren related the circumstances of his treating for the purchase of the *Argus,* indicating that Leake, a "millstone around our necks good for nothing . . . except to excite prejudice agt. the establishment," had not been in his original plans. Van Buren hoped his correspondent would open Leake's eyes to the disgrace his course would cause him.[7] Leake soon withdrew and harmony was restored.

Van Buren thought he saw the way to get Clay to retire from the contest in New York and throw his support to Crawford. If the electoral law was not changed, and the caucus nomination was supported, and if Clay could not secure the vote of Pennsylvania and thus be excluded from consideration by the House, he would make an "early and comparatively honorable retreat"

6 The proposal for a committee to study the question was a Regency move to forestall a stated intention of a People's party member. The committee was 6-3 in favor of Crawford. Hammond, *Political Parties,* 2:142-47, 153. On activities in the New York legislature in 1824 and the election in New York see also Harriet A. Weed, ed., *Autobiography of Thurlow Weed,* 2 vols. (Boston, 1884), 1:102-38; Alexander, *Political History,* 1:323-43; Hay, "John C. Calhoun and the Presidential Election of 1824," 83-96, 287-300; C. H. Rammelkamp, "The Campaign of 1824 in New York," *Annual Report* of the American Historical Association, 1904 (Washington, D.C., 1905), 177-201; Remini, *Van Buren,* 30-92, esp. 58-92. Remini, 72-84, deals with the choice of the presidential electors in November; for Weed's account of the same event see *Autobiography,* 1:123-28.

7 Marcy to Van Buren, Feb. 15, 1824; Van Buren to G. A. Worth, Feb. 22, 1824, Van Buren. In 1820 Moses Cantine (Van Buren's brother-in-law) and Leake acquired Jesse Buel's interest in the *Argus.* Upon Cantine's death Edwin Croswell had become editor.

unless letters from New York raised his hopes for the vote of that state. Van Buren said such hopes could never be realized and advised his correspondent to "Get some of the most prudent & confidential men together at your home & read them this letter— *But for Strong reasons enjoin upon them not to speak of my name in connection with it.*"[8]

But Clay was receiving letters that raised his hopes, and some of them he sent on to friends in other states. These indicated that Crawford could not get the vote of New York, that there was much dissatisfaction with the caucus and especially with the nomination of Gallatin, and that the contest was between Clay and Adams. Clay believed Pennsylvania would go to Jackson, and Crawford would not come before the House because he had nothing to add to the votes of Virginia, North Carolina, and Georgia. If the Georgian should get into the House with Jackson and Adams, Adams would be chosen; if the House had to choose among Crawford, Adams, and Clay, Crawford would not be chosen. Slightly later Clay thought the defeat of the electoral bill had removed Clinton, the "principal object of the majority," as a candidate: the Kentuckian would be relieved of "collision" with him in Ohio.[9]

Failure to act on the bill for popular choice of electors was followed by two other serious miscalculations by the Regency men. Late in March it seemed doubtful that the legislature would endorse the caucus nomination or renominate Joseph C. Yates for governor. It was believed that election of the Regency candidate as governor would make the state "safe" for Crawford; "present interests" would be best promoted by the nomination of Yates, but the "ultimate safety of the party" called for other action.[10] The other action, nomination of Samuel Young for governor and Erastus Root as lieutenant governor, was taken by legislative caucus on April 6.[11]

8 Van Buren to Benjamin F. Butler, Feb. 17, 1824, Van Buren.
9 Clay to Francis Brooke, Feb. 26, March 16, 1824, Clay, UKy.
10 Benjamin F. Butler to Van Buren, March 27, 1824, Van Buren. Butler mistakenly thought Nathan Sanford would be the gubernatorial nominee.
11 There were various speculations on the significance and possible effects of this action. Adams thought it an indication of the decay of Van Buren's influence; John W. Taylor said Adams' friends might be compelled to support Young (said to be friendly to Clay) and Crawford to keep Jackson out; Clinton thought Jackson might ultimately prevail in the legislature. Adams, *Memoirs*, 6:284, 290, 340 (April 8, 11, May 19, 1824); *Niles' Weekly Register* 26 (April 10, 1824):85.

The nomination of Young was doubtless in keeping with the time-honored doctrine of equivalents which was basic to New York politics. But the removal of Clinton from the board of canal commissioners seems to have been Roger Skinner's scheme for embarrassing the People's party and venting his spleen on Clinton. Clinton was politically dead in early 1824; he had no intention of offering himself for governor that year, and served with efficiency on the board. In its last meeting the legislature removed him; public indignation was quick and widespread, and Clinton was politically revived, much to the detriment of the Regency group.

Yates, apparently stung by not being renominated, decided to call the legislature into special session to consider the electoral law. A Van Buren lieutenant thought such a meeting might "induce doubt whether our state is settled for Crawford," but John Quincy Adams felt the call and recommendation of a new electoral law would "instantly kill" Crawford and Clay.[12] The special session met on August 3 with the galleries and lobbies overflowing. The next day the senate resolved that the call was unconstitutional and it would entertain no measure from the lower house—not even the one saying that it was not expedient to pass a law giving the choice of electors to the people. After its resolution, the conduct of any business would have been out of order for the senate. The three-day session accomplished nothing.[13]

Although partisans of every major candidate were involved in the choice-of-electors farce, with anti-Clintonism as the common denominator, the control of the senate by the pro-Crawford forces brought on that group a large share of public indignation. The Regency had made too many mistakes and flouted too strongly the popular will; the key to the errors probably lies in Van Buren's belief in the efficacy of a firm centralized party control. The people showed him otherwise: the "popular" convention, mentioned as a possibility in April, met at Utica on September 22 and nominated Clinton for governor and James Tallmadge (who had voted for Clinton's removal from the canal board) as lieutenant

12 J. A. Hamilton to Van Buren, May 19, 1824 (two letters), Van Buren; Adams, *Memoirs*, 6:340 (May 19, 1824). Ambrose Spencer, in late April, thought the contest to be between Adams and Jackson. He had never seen a party so ruined by its own acts of desperation. Spencer to Jacob Brown, April 24, 1824, Brown, Clements.

13 Rammelkamp, "The Campaign of 1824," 193-94.

governor. Both were elected by large majorities in November.[14]

The newspapers throughout the state continued their partisan activities, and the *Microscope* and *Argus* conducted their own logomachy in Albany. In late June the *Microscope* said, "Since the Governor had turned People's man, and the People have hauled around into *Bucktailism,* or something like it, and all the Crawfordites, by some 'secret process,' have become real *prime-bang-up* Republicans, we have . . . been . . . at a *stand*, not knowing exactly where to strike or what to say; and at one time we had so far lost our reckoning as to entertain serious doubts of which side we were on." The paper also directed frequent gibes at the *Argus* editor, Edwin Croswell.[15] The two Albany papers reflected in full measure the name-calling going on throughout the country, but with special vigor in the mid-Atlantic and New England states.

The *Microscope* rebuked the *Argus* and other Crawford papers for calling Crawford opponents Federalists, while the *Argus* questioned the assertion that the "ultra Federalists" and "ultra democrats" were the supporters of Crawford. It contended the *Post* was the only Federalist paper in the state favoring Crawford and asked if the *New York Daily Advertiser,* edited by the secretary of the Hartford Convention was not ultra? And the *Commercial Advertiser?* the *American?* These and twenty-four others, equally ultra, were all supporters of Adams. In Vermont every Federalist paper supported the New Englander. Further, the *Microscope* was asked if it would designate Jefferson, Madison, Langdon, Macon, Gallatin, Gerry, and others ultra democrats. In distributing the stigma of Federalist support the *Argus* was in effect extending its earlier efforts to relieve Crawford of the stigma of sectionalism. It contended his claims to the presidency had been built on neither a southern nor northern ground.[16]

In September and October the *Argus* published six articles on the life of Crawford. These seemed designed to counteract the efforts of the opposition to condemn the Georgian for certain actions during his career. They dealt, among other things, with the Augusta Address, Crawford's duels, the embargo, the BUS,

14 Hammond, *History,* 2:173-75. Before adjournment the convention passed resolutions declaring legislative caucuses improper.

15 *Albany Microscope,* June 26, July 31, Aug. 6, Oct. 9, 1824.

16 *Albany Argus,* Aug. 27, July 9, 1824: July 11, 29, 1823. It is only fair to state that every candidate had some ardent supporters among Federalists or former Federalists.

the report in which Crawford proposed intermarriage of whites and Indians, and the charge that Crawford was a radical. The treatment of each topic was systematic and dispassionate and took less liberty with the facts than most of the other campaign literature.[17]

The New York leaders, especially Van Buren, were deeply involved in the removal of Gallatin from the Crawford ticket and in seeking an understanding with one of the other candidates, meaning, of course, agreement by that candidate to replace Gallatin. Individuals from North Carolina, Virginia, and especially Pennsylvania also played important parts in pushing Gallatin out. Crawfordites had initially pulled Gallatin in on the assumption that his presence on the ticket might turn pivotal Pennsylvania to the support of Crawford. Apparently only Gallatin's friendship and high regard for Crawford and his deep devotion to republicanism induced him to accept. Almost immediately after the caucus nomination Gallatin's eligibility was questioned because of his Swiss birth (with the anti-Crawfordites who had attacked the Georgian's 1816 remark on foreigners playing into the hands of the pro-Crawford men); within less than a month the Harrisburg convention had declared for Jackson, and Calhoun cast his lot with the general; Gallatin's candidacy engendered no enthusiasm in New York, and there was talk of his withdrawal.[18]

17 Ibid., Sept. 3, 14, 28, Oct. 5, 19, 22, 1824. The widely reprinted articles were also published as a pamphlet: Americanus [Benjamin F. Butler], *Sketches of the Life and Character of William H. Crawford* (Albany, N.Y., 1824).

18 Gallatin had written his wife on January 24, 1824, that he did not want the office but would dislike to be proposed and not elected. Adams, *Gallatin*, 594. Correspondence on his citizenship and his statement of February 19, 1824, are in the Gallatin Papers. An account of the Harrisburg convention, including the resolutions, is in *Niles' Weekly Register* 26 (March 13, 1824):19-20. On July 29, 1824, Gallatin wrote his life-long friend John Badollet (Gallatin) his estimate of the candidates. During his twelve years in the treasury he had looked for someone to take his place and to take "general direction" of national concerns—to replace Jefferson, Madison, and himself. At last one man appeared who filled Gallatin's expectations. This was Crawford who "united to a powerful mind a most correct judgment and inflexible integrity; which last quality, not sufficiently tempered by indulgence and civility, has prevented his acquiring general popularity; but notwithstanding this defect (for it is one), I know so well his vast superiority over the other candidates for the office of President that I was anxious for his election and openly expressed my opinion." Jefferson and Madison felt as Gallatin did about Crawford, but they too were aware that he was not popular. Gallatin thought his nomination as Vice President was a mistake; but the bonds of party were nearly dismissed, none of the candidates for President would withdraw, and they were at a loss whom to nominate.

Walter Lowrie of Pennsylvania, primary contact with Gallatin, sought without success to secure from Jefferson, via Gallatin, support for his conviction that the Harrisburg convention did not represent the democracy of Pennsylvania. He did the Crawford cause more harm than good by foolishly becoming involved in a newspaper controversy with the President about Jackson's 1816 letter encouraging Monroe to disregard party affiliation when making appointments. Lowrie wrote that Crawford had a "deep cordial and sincere" regard for Gallatin, but Lowrie would act on Gallatin's authorization for withdrawal, if such would aid the cause. He did not expect a situation that would make this necessary, and he optimistically thought the vice-presidential contest might be decided by the Senate, where twenty-one senators would vote for Gallatin in preference to anyone else, thirteen were doubtful, and twelve against. Four, perhaps six, of the doubtful would vote for him in opposition to Calhoun or if Crawford were successful.[19]

After Crawford's relapse in May and while his recovery still seemed uncertain, less attention was given to Gallatin's possible withdrawal; in August, while Crawford was at Berkeley Springs, Joseph Gales indicated he was anxious for Gallatin's election because Crawford's health, though improved, was not certain. Another, however, took a different view and asked whether the people were prepared to see Gallatin the acting President, an occurrence he knew some of the caucus men had calculated on.[20]

Apparently Crawford's improvement at the Springs removed any possibility of withdrawing him from the race and revitalized the desire to remove Gallatin. In early September word from Richmond indicated Gallatin could not be elected and was a "weight" on Crawford; his withdrawal in a "proper manner" would help the cause and make possible the move to get Clay

[19] Lowrie to Gallatin, March 10, April 29, 1824, Gallatin. Lowrie used an X to denote senators opposed to Gallatin; Rufus King of New York was marked XXXXXX. On May 22 Gallatin wrote that Jackson was due a debt of gratitude for his military successes but had "most dangerous opinions on the subject of military and Executive power" and was unfit to be president of a republic. Lowrie had these remarks copied and gave them to a paper for publication. He hoped Gallatin would review the correspondence and conduct of Jackson and send it to him for publication. Gallatin to Lowrie, May 22, 1824; Lowrie to Gallatin, June 17, 1824, ibid.

[20] Gales to Gallatin, Aug. 24, 1824, ibid.; *Niles' Weekly Register* 27 (Sept. 4, 1824): 4. Niles' comments were in the first of a series called "The Sovereignty of the People."

to take the vice presidency. It was thought injudicious to consult Clay on the matter; rather the New York electors for Crawford (the writer seemed sure New York would be for Crawford) should nominate Clay for Vice President. A plan, apparently outlined by Van Buren, called for Lowrie and Abner Lacock of Pennsylvania to meet with Gallatin at New Geneva and for Lacock then to go to Tennessee to contact Clay. There would be no more than twenty days between the Lacock-Clay interview and the selection of the New York electors. Lowrie, who had earlier expressed displeasure over Van Buren's silence, felt a "miscalculation has been made somewhere" and chafed at the burden placed on him and Lacock.[21]

The original plan was modified in several ways: only Lacock saw Gallatin, Gallatin did not condition his withdrawal on Clay's acceptance of the vice-presidential nomination, and—in keeping with Gallatin's opinion (supported by C. W. Gooch of the Richmond Junto) that direct negotiation with Clay would encourage him to advise his friends in New York to make no compromise— Lacock did not visit Clay. On September 25 Lacock delivered Lowrie's letter, written with the "greatest pain of embarrassment," indicating to Gallatin that his chances for election were "almost hopeless" and expressing the desire for an "arrangement" with Clay. Gallatin was perplexed by a lack of information but thought withdrawal proper if his remaining a candidate would be injurious to Crawford or prevent the choice of a proper person as Vice President. He preferred Nathan Sanford of New York, who had already been nominated by Clay's friends in the West. Gallatin was satisfied that his nomination was a "misfortune founded on miscalculation" and he was "anxious to do no act that might aggravate the evil, to omit none that might have a tendency to remedy it." He was most disturbed by the growing Jackson mania in North Carolina and Pennsylvania and required that publication of his withdrawal take place before choice of the New York electors.[22]

Gales and Seaton of the *National Intelligencer*, in the front

21 C. W. Gooch to Van Buren, Sept. 11, 1824; Lowrie to Van Buren, Sept. 14, 24, 1824, Van Buren.
22 Lowrie to Gallatin, Sept. 25, 1824; Gallatin to Lowrie, to Stevenson, to Van Buren, Oct. 2, 1824; Gallatin to Gooch, to Lowrie, Oct. 7, 1824, Gallatin. Several of these letters are also in Adams, *Gallatin Writings*, 2:294-300, and the Van Buren letter is in the Van Buren Papers.

rank of Crawford supporters, wrote Van Buren that Gallatin's letter of withdrawal had "every appearance of having been distorted [sic] from him." Gales, who like Gallatin favored Sanford for the vice presidency, let Van Buren know that whereas his views of party discipline might be correct for state politics, they did not appear applicable to the national scene; Gales "must be allowed to follow as far as it is practicable the dictates of my own judgment with respect and deference to the opinions of others, but obedience to none."[23] The *Intelligencer* planned to withdraw Gallatin's name as soon as they heard from Richmond on the subject of a substitute. But Richmond exercised the discretion allowed by Gallatin, and on October 19 the *Enquirer* published Gallatin's statement of withdrawal, the object of which, it said, was "to promote union among the friends of the republican cause." An accompanying statement by the Central Corresponding Committee, formed for the express purpose of promoting the election of Crawford and Gallatin, disclaimed the right to substitute another as vice-presidential candidate.

Some Crawford supporters were not sure Gallatin's resignation would produce much good or much harm. They had no confidence in Clay, feared the whole scheme might be turned to Crawford's disadvantage, favored Van Buren as Vice President but considered it unwise to risk the attempt to elect anyone other than Clay, and thought the vice-presidential nomination could be acted on after the choice of electors. They emphasized to Van Buren that the selection of a Vice President was entirely secondary and should be "regulated" by the major objective, the election of Crawford. Since Clay and Crawford were both born in Virginia, a nomination of Clay by New York would be preferable to one by Virginia. Virginia might follow suit, but the electors were free to act for themselves. One Virginian thought the best chance to prevent the election of Calhoun, who had the support of the friends of Adams and Jackson, was to support Clay—a stance that might help Van Buren in New York and took cognizance of the importance of Clay's strength in the House. If Crawford's friends in New York favored such a plan, they should

23 Lowrie to Gallatin, Oct. 8, 1824, Gallatin; Gales and Seaton to Van Buren, Oct. 14, 1824; Gales to Van Buren, Oct. 17, 1824, Van Buren. Gales said he had acquainted Crawford with the substance of his letter and thought their judgments corresponded on the matter.

let it be known immediately.[24] What happened in New York was not worth communicating to Crawford's supporters in Virginia; the Old Dominion electors acted for themselves, casting a unanimous vote for Crawford and Nathaniel Macon.[25]

Van Buren and his Bucktails bungled matters almost beyond belief in the legislature, which met on November 2 to choose New York's thirty-six electors. Decisively beaten in the elections, they caucused on November 5 to make their choices. A number of Clay partisans who were leaning toward Crawford as their second choice participated. On November 10 the senate nominated the Crawford ticket—with seven places reserved for the Clay people—as it had been drawn up in caucus. The Crawford-Adams-Clay division in the lower house prevented a majority, so Van Buren advised the Bucktails to vote for the Adams ticket, thinking that if the candidates for each electoral position were reduced to two the Clay people would vote for the Crawford men—this they had assured him they would do once Clay was excluded. For this support he was prepared to give the Clay men as many as fifteen votes. The Clay men, uninformed of Van Buren's contemplated "generosity," were shocked on November 12 by Azariah C. Flagg's announcement that the Crawfordites would support the Adams slate. They moved adjournment. That evening the promise of fifteen votes was conveyed, and the next day the Adams ticket was nominated, the Clay and Crawford men voting with the majority.

The joint session, however, was delayed until after the weekend. The Clay men, feeling betrayed, met with the Adams supporters and formed a third slate on which Clay people replaced seven of the Adams men on the house ticket. Regulations prevented voting for anyone not on one of the tickets, but the Regency knew nothing of this extralegal third slate (printed by Thurlow Weed) until after the beginning of the joint session on November 15. Much controversy ensued, Root and some of the Regency group walked out, but it was decided that seven Clay and twenty-five Adams electors had been chosen. The next day the Clay men crossed back to help elect four Crawford electors, supposedly as

24 McLane to Van Buren, n.d. and Oct. 27, 1824; Asbury Dickins to Van Buren, Oct. 28, 1824, Van Buren; Gales and Seaton to James Barbour, Oct. 17, 1824, Barbour; P. N. Nicholas to Van Buren, Oct. 19, 31, 1824, Van Buren.
25 Barbour to Gales and Seaton, Dec. 1, 1824, Barbour.

insurance that the election would go to the House of Representatives. The Van Buren tactics had been faulty and poorly communicated; mistake after mistake had followed on the heels of miscalculation; the results could scarcely be interpreted as effecting a Crawford-Clay coalition, for the Bucktails had taken an almost unbelievable beating.[26]

Van Buren—in not quite complete candor—wrote Crawford of these events, insisting that the Clay men had deceived them. He regretted only the results but said if a different course had been adopted "our men" would in the end have gone over to Clay. If Clay had been accepted as the antagonist, the Adams men would have gone against the Crawfordites and the sixteen "honest" Clayites would not have gone with the Crawfordites.[27] In whatever way Van Buren might interpret events in New York, Crawford's cause had suffered a severe setback: he needed a greater number of the New York votes to ensure getting into the House and to improve his chances of having the New York delegation vote for him once he got there. That he might get more of the votes in the electoral college appeared possible; there seemed little expectation that the New York vote would be the same as the joint ticket would indicate: Adams twenty-five, Clay seven, and Crawford four.[28]

The Crawford-Clay combination was the one most talked about before and after the congressional caucus, and in some areas the friendliness of the favorites of these two was apparent. In the West the support for Crawford was slim—in Ohio there was not even a Crawford ticket—and his supporters generally joined the Clay cause. They were welcome, but it led to the charge that this

26 See Remini, *Van Buren,* 72-81; Hammond, *Political Parties,* 2:176-79; T. S. Smith to Samuel Gouverneur, Nov. 15, 1824, Gouverneur.

27 Van Buren to Crawford, Nov. 17, 1824 (draft), Van Buren. Van Buren thought his letter should be shown only to friends and that he should not be quoted. James Tallmadge and Henry Wheaton had been among the chief manipulators against Van Buren. See also Jacob Barker to Van Buren, Nov. 7, 1824, Van Buren; Henry Baldwin to James Tallmadge, Nov. 14, 1824, Chamberlain; John C. Spencer to Albert Tracy, Nov. 15, 21, 1824, Albert Tracy Papers (NYS).

28 McLane to James A. Bayard, Nov. 18, 20, 1824, McLane; Gales to Van Buren, Nov. 22, 1824, Van Buren; *National Intelligencer,* Nov. 23, 1824. Van Buren led some Crawford people to believe Clay would get no votes, and though Gales thought "everything was done for the best" and hoped it would turn out that way, he was critical. He said if Crawford had not been ill and his recovery misrepresented he would have received at least the largest number of votes. Further, if "an imposition had not been practised upon the country by the decision in the Legislature of New York, he would now be second in the list of candidates."

union was part of the general plan whereby in the end one or the other was to receive the combined support. This was most often taken to mean that Clay's support from the West would be thrown to Crawford. But since Crawford was considered less enthusiastic in his advocacy of internal improvements than some of the other candidates, the Adams and Jackson followers circulated the charge of coalition industriously. The westerners were often told that a vote for Clay would really mean a vote for Crawford.[29]

Ruggles of Ohio, one of the most zealous Crawfordites in the West, was anxious to promote a coalition with Clay and was encouraged by Van Buren, whose comments of July and August on Crawford's strength and the sureness of the New York vote appear absurd in light of the early November events in that state. In early October, when Gallatin's possible withdrawal was being much talked about, Ruggles broached the matter to Charles Hammond, editor of the *Cincinnati Gazette* and Clay partisan, painting a rather bright picture of Crawford's chances and a gloomy one of Clay's. Hammond, noting no marked differences between the two that would make union impracticable, had always kept the possibility of such a coalition in view and believed most other Clay friends had done likewise. Friends of the other candidates had been so attentive to the activities of the Clay people that no effective cooperative measures could be taken. It had even been necessary for Hammond to deny publicly the existence of a Clay-Crawford coalition; he could, therefore, not become a party to the arrangement suggested by Ruggles. He disagreed with Ruggles on several points: Clay's friends did not concede New York to Crawford; he did not think the votes of the western states would go directly to Crawford, and was not sure the Ohio electors would vote for Crawford even if Clay withdrew, for the Adams and Jackson men working together would resort to any arrangement to defeat Clay and Crawford. Even if Clay should turn to Crawford, Hammond believed he should stay in the House rather than become Vice President. Some Clay men did not overlook the possibility that the death of Crawford, if elected, would elevate the Vice President, but

29 For a discussion of the election in Ohio and some observations on the West in general, see Eugene H. Roseboom, "Ohio in the Presidential Election of 1824," *Ohio Archaeological and Historical Publications* 26 (1917):153-224, esp. 196-200.

most Clay supporters held firm to their choice.[30] Clay would not commit himself, and the managers continued to maneuver.

Every possible combination was considered, but the probability of a Crawford-Adams ticket had died early. Adams had said he could not accept the second position without "inverting the natural order of things and placing the North in a position of inferiority to the South."[31] Apparently Crawford partisans realized that Adams was firm in this conviction. At various times, however, there was speculation of the Adams vote going to Crawford, and vice versa. Much of this seemed occasioned by the belief that Crawford was the second choice in New England and that Adams was the second choice of Virginia.[32]

The first combination consisted of all the other hopefuls running against Crawford. Some felt this necessary to stop Crawford, but they noted the several noncaucus candidates were "remarkably obstinate" and "refuse all overtures from one another each expecting to profit by the confusion their conduct has created in the Union."[33] After Crawford's illness the other candidates engaged in less anti-Crawford activity, and the fusion of the Jackson-Calhoun forces in early 1824 decreased enormously the number of combinations spoken of. Actually, any possibility of union between Adams and Calhoun backers had ended long before; in 1822 Adams had terminated confidential intercourse with the South Carolinian. However, the possibility of an Adams-Jackson ticket, spoken of early in 1824, persisted until the eve of voting in the electoral college. Adams thought his friends' support of

30 Ruggles to Van Buren, July 31, 1824; Van Buren to Ruggles, Aug. 26, 1824, Van Buren; Ruggles to Hammond, Oct. 5, 1824; Hammond to Ruggles, Oct. 11, 1824, Hammond, OHS; Johnston to Clay, Aug. 9, 25, 30, Sept. 4, 11, 1824, Clay, Lilly; *Clay Papers,* 3:819ff. The statement in the *Gazette,* denying a coalition, was signed by Hammond and Jacob Burnet; in the same issue William Henry Harrison had a note to the same effect. Both are reproduced in *Niles' Weekly Register* 27 (Oct. 23, 1824):113. See also Elijah Hayward to John Larwill, Aug. 30, Sept. 29, Oct. 4, 1824, John Larwill Collection (OHS); Romulus M. Saunders to Bartlett Yancey, Dec. 4, 1823, Clark; Hammond to J. C. Wright, Aug. 30, 1824; Wright to Hammond, Sept. 10, 1824, Charles Hammond Papers (OSL); *Clay Papers,* 3, for the latter part of 1824 and early 1825.

31 Adams, *Memoirs,* 6:245-47 (Feb. 4, 1824).

32 See, for example, *National Journal,* April 21, 1824, citing *Charleston Courier;* Ruggles to Worthington, Feb. 23, 1824, Worthington; Benjamin Crowninshield to John Crowninshield, Dec. 13, 1824, J. C. Warren Papers (MHS).

33 Joseph E. Sprague to John Bailey, Feb. 2, 1824, Bailey; George A. Shufeldt to William Wilson, Feb. 15, 1824, William Wilson Papers (Clements); Benjamin Crowninshield to Henry A. Dearborn, April 10, 1824, Crowninshield Miscellany, MDLC.

Jackson advisable until something from the general's friends indicated his unwillingness to take that post.[34]

Not even the pooling of the Jackson-Calhoun interests after the Pennsylvania "commitment" seems to have cooled the ardor of a number of the proponents of the Adams-Jackson combination. In several of the western states the Adams and Jackson forces operated almost in tandem, and in North Carolina the People's ticket, supposedly uncommitted, was a combination of Adams and Jackson men. As late as October Jacob Brown noted that as long as it was possible that Jackson would accept the vice presidency the Adams people felt the place should be reserved for him; that hope had now been abandoned and he urged support of Calhoun. But even at the end of November some Adams people considered it "highly important" that all states supporting Adams for the presidency should vote for Jackson for second choice. Jackson's age and geographical residence would give strength and influence to the Adams administration.[35] After about April 1824 only a Crawford-Clay combination had remained possible for Crawford; Clay was the pivot between Crawford and Adams.

Crawford's chances in New England were always regarded as slight, and his setbacks in Pennsylvania and New York had seriously jeopardized the chances of his election, but his friends worked valiantly in other areas. In New Jersey Mahlon Dickerson and others sought to elect Crawford, but they could not overcome Jackson's popularity. Although the New Jersey congressional delegation was said to prefer Crawford, they felt bound to reflect the will of the people, if that will were expressed decisively at the polls.[36] It was so expressed: Jackson received the eight electoral votes, and the congressional delegation favored him 5-1.

The key to Crawford's chances in Delaware was Louis McLane, who in 1823 yielded to entreaties of friends and refused election to the Senate. In January 1824 he had second thoughts about this sacrifice but decided in April to stay in the House. Delaware chose one Adams and two Crawford electors, and McLane as the

---

34 Adams, *Memoirs*, 6:284-85 (April 9, 1824). If Jackson was not willing to accept the vice-presidential post, Adams would be personally satisfied if his friends supported Nathaniel Macon.

35 Jacob Brown to Oliver Wolcott, Oct. 16, 1824; Henry Dearborn to Wolcott, Nov. 27, 1824; D. Peavie and William Richmond to Wolcott, Nov. 27, 1824, Wolcott. There are several other letters in the Wolcott Papers which express the same idea.

36 A. Dodd to C. K. Gardner, Oct. 23, 1824, Gardner.

state's only representative controlled the state's vote in February 1825.[37]

Samuel Smith was in the forefront of Crawford partisans in Maryland. Crawford and Adams had full slates of electors by the middle of July; Jackson was lacking only in the seventh district, but Clay had only two of a possible nine. The newspapers of Baltimore and other areas were almost taken over by the contest, which Smith noted "engages all the attention of the politicians." Crawford's health had been injurious to his expectations, but Smith still believed he could be elected.[38]

Virginia was the southern anchor of the Richmond-Albany axis, with Thomas Ritchie's and C. W. Gooch's *Enquirer* the chief propaganda agent and the Central Corresponding Committee —or Richmond Junto—the chief campaign managers and manipulators. But the *Constitutional Whig,* under John H. Pleasants, was established in January 1824 to oppose Crawford, indicating in its first issue that it preferred Adams "as a choice of evils." He united a "greater number of qualifications" and was the candidate most likely to harmonize the sectional feelings of the North and South. The newspaper campaign was vigorous and the "managing" of the election—as well as the earlier caucus nomination— was severely criticized by many. Quite often the principles of Crawford's supporters, rather than Crawford himself, bore the brunt of the criticism.[39]

North Carolina, considered by many as sure for Crawford, was heatedly contested. Though it was the native state of some veteran and ardent Crawford men, the revolt against the caucus system and Virginia domination, as well as active campaigning by the other groups, put the state in the Jackson column. The Jackson and Adams men combined to support a People's ticket

37 McLane to James A. Bayard, Dec. 16, 22, 1823; Jan. 4, Feb. 1, 22, April 12, 1824; McLane to [Bayard], Jan. 14, 1824; McLane to Asbury Dickins, Dec. 3, 1824, McLane.

38 Smith to daughter, June 6, 1824, Carter-Smith. See also *Baltimore American & Commercial Daily Advertiser,* April 10, 16, June 15, July 3, 15, 29, Aug. 19, 1824. Smith corresponded frequently with Jonathan Russell in 1824 and early 1825; there are eighteen letters from him during this period in the Russell Papers. Correspondence between Crawford opponents in Maryland and Rufus King may be found in the published King material and in the Rufus King Papers.

39 For some details of the Virginia events see John Tyler to James Barbour, Jan. 5, 1824, Barbour; Charles Henry Ambler, *Thomas Ritchie: A Study in Virginia Politics* (Richmond, Va., 1913), 89-98; *Richmond Enquirer; Baltimore American & Commercial Daily Advertiser; Constitutional Whig,* Jan. 27, 1824; *Niles' Weekly Register,* esp. Sept. 4, Oct. 16, 1824.

of electors, which was officially not committed; this practice was considered by the Crawford men to be unfair. Gallatin was said to "clog" the Crawford machinery, and it was difficult to electioneer against Jackson. The general's service and character were of the kind people could appreciate, and "one cup of *generous whiskey* produces more literary ardor, than can be allayed by a month of reflection and reason." The opposition to Virginia domination was best exemplified in the Fisher resolutions and the attitudes of Fisher and Archibald Murphey. Fisher emphasized that Virginia had been followed so long that her politicians "fancy we do not part from her; tell her that North-Carolina will not vote for her candidate, and they will laugh you to scorn." And North Carolina had received practically no offices in the thirty-six years she had supported Virginia. No better could be expected from Crawford. Murphey felt so strongly on the matter of North Carolina subordination to Virginia that though he thought Crawford the best man among the candidates he opposed him and rejoiced in his defeat.[40]

South Carolina was never in doubt, and Crawford backers were few. Among them was William Smith, who accused Calhoun of being a "master spirit" in the art of intrigue, of shifting from one candidate to another, and of trying to prevent the election of a President so that he, as Vice President elect, might assume that office.[41]

The contest in South Carolina brought forth two of the better campaign pamphlets. "Southron" thought it only natural that zeal had been aroused by the Carolinian Calhoun, but since he had withdrawn from the race a "causeless spirit of revenge" should not "lead you to throw yourselves into the arms of those who are either unfit for your confidence, or whose interests are not common with yours; or what is still worse, whose interests are essentially at war with yours." Several pages are devoted to examining Jackson's qualifications, but most of the pamphlet is

40 On North Carolina activities see Albert Ray Newsome, *The Presidential Election of 1824 in North Carolina* (Chapel Hill, N.C., 1939); Shanks, *Mangum*, 1: esp. 97, 105, 111, 130, 137-38; William Henry Hoyt, ed., *The Papers of Archibald D. Murphey*, 2 vols. (Raleigh, N.C., 1914), 1:290, 293; 2:32; Hamilton, "Letters to Yancey," 18, 46-49; *Raleigh Star and North-Carolina Gazette*; *Raleigh Register and North-Carolina Gazette* (May 21, 1824, for Fisher); Letters to Peter Force, esp. Sept. 1824, Peter Force Group, Emil Hurja Collection (Tennessee Historical Society); John Owen to Bartlett Yancey, July 21, 1824, Miscellaneous 2, NCDAH.
41 William Smith to Samuel Smith, Oct. 17, 1824, Van Buren.

devoted to Crawford. Praise for some of Crawford's characteristics is sparing and Southron notes his disagreement with some of Crawford's positions. He reviewed the Georgian's public career and reached the conclusion that if the people wanted economy, curtailment of useless establishments, strict subordination of the military to the civil power, a scrupulous regard for the Constitution, freedom from burdensome taxes in time of peace, rapid extinction of the national debt, and salvation from the effects of the protection of domestic industry by the new school of politicians, their votes should go to Crawford. The final appeal was sectional: if the *"southern people* wish *restrictions* upon State sovereignty, and other measures, whose end shall be the *abolition of slavery,* by *emancipation among us,* then, of course, Mr. Adams should be preferred."[42]

"South-Carolinian" denied the people of the state had been unduly and unfairly excited and prejudiced against Crawford. The excitement against Crawford, he maintained, arose from the circumstance that a man against whom there were so many and weighty objections should persevere against the wishes of the people. Fifteen objections were presented. None was new; many had no basis in fact; but they were effectively couched in such terms as *"negative, hidden or doubtful, weak, illegal* and *unconstitutional"* (Crawford's course as secretary of treasury) and a *"Radical, creeping policy"* which he would pursue as chief executive. The writer thought it would be a master stroke in the game Crawford was playing to get the "irresistibly increasing popularity" of Jackson out of his way so he would have the "easier task of prostrating Adams by an unfounded jealousy upon the Missouri question." Southron's statement that Crawford was "amiable, honest, and intelligent" was conceived to apply to his private life. "If it be so, let him enjoy the full benefit of such a reputation."[43] South Carolina was overwhelmingly for Jackson, while Georgia threw her full force behind Crawford for President and Van Buren for Vice President.

The newspaper campaign continued through 1824 in the same

42 *To the People of South-Carolina. An Address on the subject of the approaching Presidential Election, in which the claims of William H. Crawford are impartially canvassed* ([Columbia, S.C.?], 1824).

43 *Some Objections to Mr. Crawford as a Candidate for the Presidential Chair, with a few remarks on the charges preferred against South Carolina as being "in error, and uncertain in her Politics"* [Columbia, S.C. (?), 1824], esp. 3, 11, 23, 38.

vigorous vein of the year before; its unfairness, one-sidedness, and intensity drew the disapproval of many. Ruggles objected to the indiscriminate praise and eulogy by the friends of the candidates and the indiscriminate censure and reproach by opponents. He thought this morally and politically wrong and a practice no man could justify to his own conscience. He asked: "Is the thief who steals his neighbor's goods, to be ignominiously punished, and the murderer of reputation to escape unhurt?" And a non-Crawford man wrote that if one took the "calumnies of the most abandoned newspapers for the moral standard of this nation," it would be "supposed, that our Presidents, Secretaries, Senators, and Representatives, are all traitors and pirates, and the government of this people, had been committed to the hands of public robbers."[44]

A much used and much criticized new device of the campaign might be termed the abbreviated public opinion poll. This practice began before the caucus and was first applied to the members of Congress by a "sort of inquisitorial committee" of the friends of each candidate who were appointed to go around and count the members opposed to Crawford. The purpose was to make a publication to Crawford's disadvantage.[45] As soon as the caucus nomination was made, great play and emphasis were placed on the small number who had engaged in this meeting; such counting continued until Adams was chosen. Throughout the spring, summer, and early fall counts were taken at public sales, militia musters, meetings to consider the tariff and internal improvements, grand juries, on steamboats, and apparently at any kind of actual or fancied meeting. They nearly always showed that Jackson was in the lead—often overwhelmingly—though occasionally Clay or Adams was the favorite. There were also private polls.[46] Whatever the accuracy of the polls might have been, the frequent and repeated use of them seems to have been designed to show that Crawford was the candidate of the minority and that he did not have a broad-based support. It is true that Crawford

44 Ruggles to Hammond, Jan. 5, 1824, Hammond, OSL: *Federal Gazette & Baltimore Daily Advertiser*, June 7, 1824. These are given only as examples; literally dozens of similar sentiments were expressed.
45 Ruggles to Hammond, March 10, 1824, Hammond, OSL.
46 For examples see *Niles' Weekly Register* 26 (May 22, June 5, 1824):194, 221; *Federal Gazette & Baltimore Daily Advertiser*, Feb. 16, March 30, 1824; *Mississippi Republican and Literary Messenger*, March 26, 1824; *Daily National Journal*, Oct. 11, 1824; D. Reinhardt to editor of *National Journal*, Aug. 21, 1824, Force Group.

did not enjoy great popularity (he thought it wrong to court popularity) in most areas of the country, but the effect of this tactic on that already thin support can be easily conjectured.

That personal popularity of the candidates was an important factor in the election is unquestionable, and most writers have discussed the election of 1824 in terms of personalities. Obviously there were other factors—even issues on which the candidates held slightly different opinions—but the most recent study on issues raises a number of questions.[47] Should *sectionalism* as such be classified as an *issue,* or was it a manifestation of dissatisfaction with continued control of the executive branch by one state or area? Or a "normal" voter support for the candidate of his own area or region? If issues were of great import, can one reconcile the nearly identical views of Jackson and Crawford on the tariff and internal improvements with the great difference in their popular votes? Or the nearly identical popular votes of Clay and Crawford? After admitting that the importance of issues in the accepted sense varied from state to state—and even within states— is it not possible that in the first contest approximating the "typi-cal" American political election the major "issue" was the "people" versus the "managers"? It seems doubtful that the posture of the candidates on the tariff, internal improvements, or the bank had any material effect on the outcome of the election.

Crawford and his supporters were often referred to as the Radicals, a term applied so variously that it really had no meaning. In general, many of those advocating Crawford's election were perhaps more conservative than the supporters of the other candi-dates, and James Buchanan said they favored a strict construction of the Constitution and were not willing to give the central government any powers but those manifestly contained in the Constitution. But, as should be perfectly obvious, such a state-ment could not be reconciled with Crawford's stand on the bank, to say nothing of his direct statements on several of the other so-called issues. At times the term was used synonymously with Federal, to designate an opponent of "every salutary measure of government," or simply to indicate the group opposed to Calhoun and favorable to Crawford. At other times the Radicals were

---

47 Paul C. Nagel, "The Election of 1824: A Reconsideration Based on Newspaper Opinion," *Journal of Southern History* 26 (Aug. 1960):315-29. See also Curtis Wiswell Garrison, "The National Election of 1824" (Ph.D. diss., Johns Hopkins University, 1924), which concentrates on New York, Pennsylvania, and Virginia.

said to advance the same doctrine the Federalists advanced in the late 1790s: the people, their own worst enemies, are not to be trusted with the exercise of political power. Radical came to have so little meaning that some strongly anti-Crawford papers by late summer of 1824 had replaced it with ultra. They maintained that the extremes of both parties had joined to support Crawford, and that this party was tainted with unpopular principles and must finally be found in conflict with the people's rights.[48] These papers might well have been more nearly correct than those who persisted in using the term Radical.

Some Crawford supporters, in describing the desirable attributes of Crawford, used the radical designation to heighten the similarities between Jefferson and Crawford and between their principles. Jefferson and Madison did favor Crawford's election, but the Crawfordites were never able to get either man to declare his position. Nor did the Richmond Junto offend the dignity of the two former Presidents by putting them on the Crawford electoral ticket.[49]

The Crawford group would have been pleased to have the open support of Jefferson and Madison, but they did not bridle when it was not forthcoming. The attitude toward Monroe, however, was quite different. Crawford partisans seemed to feel Monroe had a special debt to repay: Crawford had refused to stand against him in the 1816 caucus—and his action was emphasized in the Address following the 1824 caucus. By the time of Monroe's second administration three of his cabinet members were obviously seeking to succeed him, and any logical and

48 Buchanan to Thomas Elder, Feb. 27, 1824, Gratz; *Charleston City Gazette and Commercial Daily Advertiser*, April 24, 1824: *Daily National Journal*, Aug. 10, 13, Sept., Oct. 19, 1824; *Albany Microscope*. The first issue of the *Daily National Journal*, Aug. 9, 1824, notified the subscribers to the *Washington Republican* that that paper had been "disposed of" to Peter Force, editor of the *Journal*.

49 Crawford's illness seriously curtailed his correspondence, but there were some exchanges with the two former Presidents. Crawford sent flax seeds to Jefferson and recommended Henry Jackson for a position at the University of Virginia. He sent Madison a volume dealing with French diplomacy and wished a copy of his note refusing the War Department, the only written evidence he knew of that would refute the charge he had sought to avoid responsibility during the war and had solicited the appointment as minister to France. Madison reassured Crawford on these points, and Jefferson delayed acknowledging receipt of the seeds in the hope that he might have added congratulations which "would have been very cordially offered." Crawford's defeat brought deep disappointment to Jefferson and "much damped" the confidence he had placed in the discretion of his fellow citizens. Crawford to Madison, April 8, 1824 (copy), Phillips: Madison to Crawford, Oct. 1, 1824, Gross: Crawford to Jefferson, Feb. 4, 1825, Jefferson, UVa; Jefferson to Crawford, April 20, 1824, Feb. 15, 1825, Jefferson, MDLC.

rational analysis of the situation seems to indicate the correctness of Monroe's impartial or neutral position. Some of Crawford's partisans attacked the administration, compared it unfavorably with that of Jefferson, and periodically accused Monroe of hoping for the succession of one of the other candidates. Less than a month after the caucus nomination the *Washington Gazette* leveled a violent attack on Monroe in connection with the money voted in 1817 and 1818 for furnishing the White House; Crawford withdrew the federal patronage from the paper. No rationalization of the action remains; doubtless simple propriety would have been sufficient reason. Patronage or no patronage, the *Gazette* continued to attack Monroe, claiming by mid-April that the entire influence of the executive was "evidently bent" on elevating Jackson to the presidency and "further concealment" by the paper would be treachery to the nation. A volunteer contributor to another paper said Monroe had thrown all his influence against Crawford—but in favor of Adams.[50]

On several occasions Monroe did admit his deep obligations to Crawford, and several times he indicated his belief that Crawford did not countenance the activities of his friends. Again, he sometimes thought Crawford did not sufficiently discountenance them, and more than a year after the election Monroe said he "could not be insensible" to these attacks and Crawford did not separate himself from his friends by "any public act, so as to shew that he did not approve their attacks." Monroe insisted that he had been impartial. Crawford seemed to understand Monroe's neutrality and, so far as has been discovered, only once (and that in 1830) did he "complain" of Monroe's lack of support.[51] One is forced to conclude that a strong sense of fairness and neutrality did attend Monroe's actions. Had Monroe thrown his support to one of the candidates about the time of his reelection in 1820,

50 *Washington Gazette*, April 6, 15, 1824; Adams, *Memoirs*, 6:285, 287-88 (April 9, 10, 1824); John Moore to Jonathan Elliott, June 1, 1824; A Maryland Planter [Daniel Jennifer?] to Elliott, [n.d.], Force Group. The volunteer and solicited articles were, of course, common to the papers of all candidates.

51 See above passim; Adams, *Memoirs*, 6:229-30 (Jan. 8, 1824); Monroe to Tench Ringgold, May 8, 1826, Hamilton, *Monroe Writings*, 7:81-82; Crawford to Dear Sir, Feb. 4, 1830, Crawford, Duke. The letter to Ringgold contains by far the strongest and most condemnatory of Monroe's statements on this matter. Only William Wirt among the long-time cabinet members was not actively involved in the campaign. For speculation as to what might happen to his position and his characterization of the candidates see Wirt to Dabney Carr, Aug. 27, 1824, William Wirt Papers (VSL).

that candidate might easily have succeeded to the presidency. On the other hand, Monroe's designation of a favorite after 1822 probably would have brought no change in the election results.

Crawford was often accused by his opponents of "management"; his supporters countered with queries on the purposes of the large parties given by others and on management of the cabal against Crawford. And they pointed out that Crawford had written no electioneering letters (as had Calhoun) to advance himself, nor had he published pamphlets (as had Adams) to court the people. This was true, but it might have been better if Crawford had written some of the newspaper material that his supporters presented to the people.[52] Of course, no presidential candidate campaigned in the present-day sense of that word.

There was much talk about patronage, especially "Treasury Pap,"[53] and its use in building a political campaign. Perhaps the most widely reproduced "pap" item was the presidential caricature, "Caucus Curs *in full* Yell, *or a* War Whoop *to saddle on the* People *a* Pappoose President," first printed in the *Baltimore Patriot.* In the background is the President's house, to the right of which stands Uncle Sam's treasury pap house with its amalgamated tool department. Jackson, with sword, is looking at the curs, which are growling and barking at him. Over the door is *"pappoose meat by* W.H.C." W.H.C. has a bowl labeled dollars; by his side is a beautiful female with a papoose, lashed upon a board in aboriginal style, in her lap. He is offering her the contents of the bowl, saying "There's a bowl full of *solid pappoose* meat, That's a good girl; better marry our wild Indians *than foreigners, good or bad."* He feeds her; she cries; it is noted that papoose is better than rum. The *Richmond Enquirer* is a pointer and has scented Old Hickory for his master to shoot at. Much comment followed.[54] It was an effective presentation of several charges against Crawford.

52 See, for example, *Washington Gazette*, Jan. 20, 27, 1824: Dickins to Russell, Sept. 8, 26, 28, 1824; Russell to Dickins, Sept. 18, 1824, Russell: [James Barbour?], *Four Letters addressed to the People of the United States By a Fellow-Citizen* (Raleigh, N.C., [1823]): Butler, *Sketches.* The *Four Letters* may be found at Duke University. They originally appeared in the *Richmond Enquirer* and apparently were in answer to Wythe, Pendleton, Roanoke, and some other writers.
53 See, for example, *Washington Gazette*, Jan. 17, 1824; *Savannah Republican*, Dec. 3, 1824.
54 *Tuscumbian*, Dec. 27, 1824. Dreams, lotteries, court cases, and presidential voyages were among the journalistic devices used to support or oppose candidates. See *Camden* (S.C.) *Southern Chronicle*, Oct. 24, 1824; *Milledgeville Georgia Journal*,

This item was one of many subjecting Crawford to sarcasm and abuse for his remarks about Indians and foreigners made eight years before. There was no real "defense" for his remarks, but his supporters did point out that Patrick Henry and Thomas Jefferson had previously made a similar recommendation concerning intermarriage of whites and Indians. "But this is not all. We have known men to be the noisy and unrelenting calumniators of Mr. Crawford, on account of his suggestion, in regard to the Indians, who could, with calm indifference, and with an undisturbed conscience, behold, on their own plantations, certain *mongrel* beings, who bore in their countenance the lineaments and their veins the blood of their masters, writhing under the scourge of an unfeeling task master."[55] Every candidate was subjected to ill-deserved abuse.

Crawford partisans saw anti-Crawford possibilities in every event—even the visit by Lafayette, who they feared might be used to the advantage of one and the disadvantage of others. G. W. Erving, rather bitter toward Monroe who, he said, had unwittingly demoralized the Republican party, attempted to delay the departure of Lafayette, who understood Erving's apprehensions and thought if they had been expressed earlier he would have postponed his sailing. But he would do everything to stay neutral, to assuage the asperity of parties, and to show the necessity of union. He pointed out that he was equally the friend of Crawford and Adams and had a high respect for Jackson though he did not know him.[56] Lafayette's visit was a triumphant one, and only the most irrational partisan could interpret it as harmful or helpful to any one of the presidential aspirants. At the reception for the French patriot in Washington Monroe was flanked on his right by the secretaries of state and treasury and on his left by the secretaries of war and navy.[57]

April 6, 1824; *National Republican and Ohio Political Register,* Feb. 27, 1824; *Nashville Whig,* Feb. 23, 1824.

[55] *National Intelligencer,* Aug. 31, 1824, citing *Georgia Journal.*

[56] Erving to Crawford, April 20, June 26, 1824, Crawford, MDLC. Erving in many respects seems to have been much like Jonathan Russell: he was a gossip, a carper, a nit-picker, and very verbose.

[57] *Richmond Enquirer,* Oct. 16, 1824, citing *National Intelligencer.* Later several stories of Crawford's "bad" behavior at the reception for Lafayette were bruited about. These are seriatim rather than simultaneous and appear to be rooted in gossip and rumor rather than fact. The following February 7 Lafayette, the President and his family, Crawford and family, Adams and family, and Clay were among the audience at the Cooper benefit. *Daily National Journal,* Feb. 9, 1825.

When the election was over, it was soon clear that no candidate had received a majority, but it was not certain whether Clay or Crawford would go into the House with Jackson and Adams. It was a month before the electoral college voted, and the Crawford supporters continued to press their case for electors to switch their votes and for union with Clay. Partisans of the other candidates also sought additional votes for their favorites. But Clay, in late October, had privately indicated that he could not accept the proposals to take the vice presidency. He thought candidates should neither seek nor agree to compromises and should avoid either giving or receiving promises. He hoped he would not have to decide what course he would take if he did not get into the House. He did wonder how they could "get over" the minority caucus nomination of Crawford, the state of his health, and the principles of administration he might adopt because of "his position and Southern support." There were, he said, strong if not decisive objections to each of the other candidates, but Clay did not enumerate them. He wanted his friends to act together, especially in Ohio and Kentucky, and he "would make great sacrifice to that object."[58]

A month later the vice presidency still did not appeal to Clay, who did not know what had happened in New York but thought cooperation between his and Crawford's friends might have given the votes of that state to the one or the other or divided them between the two. He believed he would join Adams and Jackson before the House but wondered what Crawford's friends would do in that circumstance. Without Crawford's support Clay could scarcely expect to be elected, but he saw "much probability of success" with it. He wanted to know what Virginia would do and obviously was encouraging the casting of the Virginia electoral votes for himself.[59]

Clay made no public statement about his lack of interest in the second position, and Crawford partisans continued to advocate that Crawford electors cast ballots for Clay as Vice President.

[58] Clay to Hammond, Oct. 25, 1824, Clay, Lilly. Hammond later noted Clay had stated "objections to Crawford" and this indicated to Hammond that Clay preferred Adams. He was going to write an article for the *National Intelligencer* in which he would include this letter to vindicate Clay from the accusation of uniting with Adams in a bargain. Clay requested Hammond to leave out the words "from his position and Southern support." Hammond to J. C. Wright, April 2, 1825, Hammond, OHS; Clay to Hammond, April 25, 1825, Clay, Lilly.
[59] Clay to Francis Brooke, Nov. 26, 1824, Clay, UKy.

At the same time they maneuvered to try to keep Crawford's votes from being drained away—and to try to drain away some votes from the other candidates. As an alternative, they sought vice-presidential votes for their favorite in the hope that the choice of the Vice President might be made by the Senate.[60]

Van Buren was apprehensive about what would happen to the "few electors that we have been able to save" from the wreck. Latest reports from the West indicated that if the electors "do as they ought," Crawford would come respectably into the House, where his chances were as good as those of any of his opponents. As second choice in the East, Crawford would get the vote of some of the western states in the House. Van Buren seems to have had a different standard for what the eastern and western electors "ought" to do, for he said that the casting of New York's seven Clay votes and four Crawford votes for Crawford would make some reparation for the injury done by the legislature in choosing the electors. He thought his poor opinion would not have much weight with the electors, but authorized showing his letter to "our friends" in the electoral college, that is, the eleven Republicans who were supported on "our" ticket.[61] In the first part of December some of the Crawford people were encouraged by the confidence of westerners Ruggles, Thomas, and Noble and seemed to believe that if "*Clay* behaves well, we may triumph."[62]

The final electoral college vote was not known until near the end of the year, and shifts, though not as great as Van Buren suggested, in the New York vote did put Crawford in the House and exclude Clay. For some unknown reason two of the Clay electors did not appear for the voting; the substitutes, chosen by the other electors, voted for Adams. One of the original Adams electors voted for Crawford, and one Clay elector voted for Jackson. The New York vote was: Adams 26, Crawford 5, Clay 4, and Jackson 1, or changes of + 1, + 1, − 3, and + 1, respectively.[63]

---

60 See, for example, *Washington Gazette*, Nov. 24, 1824; Asbury Dickins to Bartlett Yancey, Nov. 21, 26, 1824, Yancey. The first Dickins letter was confidential, the second in "strictest confidence."

61 Van Buren to John Lansing, Nov. 28, 1824, Lansing Miscellaneous MSS (NYH).

62 See, for example, McLane to Dear Kitty, Dec. 6, 1824, McLane; Thomas W. Cobb to Yancey, Dec. 8, 1824, Yancey; James A. Hamilton to Van Buren, Dec. 12, 1824, Van Buren.

63 Probably no one will ever know exactly what happened, but there have been several speculations and accounts. Roger Skinner, writing to Van Buren on December 1 (Van Buren), said John Taylor (who had been appointed to one of the vacancies) was active, as was Ambrose Spencer, in trying to secure six votes for

Had the original New York vote held, Clay and Crawford would have had forty votes each, and only Jackson and Adams would have been before the House.

Was a two-man contest before the House deliberately prevented, or was the three-way contest an accident of politics? If Crawford were no longer in the contest and had a greater number of congressional supporters than any other candidate (as was generally conceded), what would have been his power or influence as President-maker? With the certain election of Calhoun as Vice President and thus a Crawford-Clay combination out of the realm of possibility, Clay's influence might well have been subordinate to or at least nullified by Crawford's. But if Crawford is also before the House and "his" states adhere to him. Clay would have the "swing" power. With only Jackson and Adams before the House the result probably would have been the same, for Crawford later said he would have favored Adams in such a situation. The reason for the shift in the votes of the Clay and Adams electors in New York is unknown and apparently unknowable. Was it a calculated shift, designed to diminish the influence of the Crawford wing of the party?

In the final electoral count, Jackson had all the votes of New Jersey, Pennsylvania, North and South Carolina, Alabama, Mississippi, Tennessee, and Indiana, 7 from Maryland, 3 from Louisiana, 2 from Illinois, and 1 from New York for a total of 99. Of Adams' 84 votes, 51 came from the New England states, 26 from New York, 3 from Maryland, 2 from Louisiana, 1 from Delaware, and 1 from Illinois. Crawford's 41 votes represented the full votes of Virginia and Georgia, 5 from New York, 2 from Delaware, and 1 from Maryland, while Clay's 37 were the full votes of Kentucky, Ohio, and Missouri, and 4 from New York. Jackson's votes represented at least a majority of the vote in eleven states; Adams had a majority in seven; and Crawford and Clay had majorities in three each. The popular vote seems to have been about as follows: Jackson 152,000, Adams 103,000, and Crawford and Clay 47,000 each.[64]

Crawford. Hammond and others, according to Skinner, said the Adamsites had violated a pledge to give Clay eight votes in consideration of Clay's friends' support of the successful ticket. Jackson's friends had attended the meeting of the electors and sought to effect a division of the votes between Jackson and Adams. See also Hammond, *Political Parties,* 2:187-88; Remini, *Van Buren,* 82; Van Buren, *Autobiography,* appropriate places.

[64] Calhoun was elected Vice President with 182 votes.

Crawford still had a chance, though a slim one, in the House. In late December Jackson's prospects lessened because Illinois was understood to be for Adams. Clay was still "neutral," and a Crawford partisan believed the Kentuckian's friends would act with the Crawfordites if they "can have good reason to count upon success." With their aid, there were strong hopes for Crawford's election, but the contest would be "obstinate and protracted." McLane's calculation soon changed: if Clay should decidedly go to Crawford, the Georgian would be elected; the chances were that he would go to Adams.[65]

Friends of Crawford and Clay were reported to have approached Adams with "more or less distinct" overtures. The Virginia delegation gave assurances that, after voting two or three times for Crawford, they would vote for Adams rather than for Jackson. Clay friends said they would perhaps vote for Adams in the first instance and thus secure his election on the first ballot, but nothing definite had been promised by the end of 1824.[66] Albert H. Tracy, member of the House from New York and an Adams man, thought by year's end that Adams' election was certain. The intriguing portion of his letter is the remark, "I have *confidential* reasons for believing it to be more certain than I have expressed."[67]

In early January Clay and Kentucky still held back, the Crawford forces had no "second man," and some thought New York, "true to her character," would abandon Crawford in the House. In any event, the one-vote states were still crucial. Louis McLane controlled Delaware, Daniel P. Cook the vote of Illinois, and John Scott the vote of Missouri. McLane was avidly pro-Crawford, and there seemed to be no question about Cook's voting for Adams. Scott, formerly for Crawford, was wavering and saying that the friends of Crawford could not expect him to sacrifice himself to no purpose. Thomas Hart Benton, reported to be "warmly" in the Crawford cause, thought he could hold Scott's support. In the states with more than one representative in the House, Henry H. Gurley was the swing vote in Louisiana and George E. Mitchell in Maryland. Samuel Eddy of Rhode Island was expected to vote for Crawford and thus neutralize

65 McLane to James A. Bayard, Dec. 27, 1824, Jan. 9, 1825, McLane.
66 Plumer, Jr., to Plumer, Sr., Dec. 24, 1824, Brown, *Missouri Compromises*, 123-24.
67 Tracy to Thurlow Weed, Dec. 30, 1824, Weed.

that state. But it was thought certain that if Clay's friends went against Crawford, the contest would be between Adams and Jackson, for Crawford would have only Delaware, Virginia, North Carolina, and Georgia.[68]

Though the tone of the letters of the Crawford men long before the middle of January was far from sanguine, they never completely despaired until the vote was cast. Their hope was to prevent the election of Adams on the first ballot; they believed they could then turn the tide to Crawford. Their thin veneer of confidence was badly scratched by the announcement on January 24 of the Clay-Adams coalition. McLane said it "required no such formality to make it certain"; Adams would now get twelve and perhaps thirteen states on the first ballot. He feared Adams' election could not be prevented, but Crawford's friends would stand firm and "leave the responsibility of this infamous bargain where it ought to rest." The Jackson men, he said, were outraged; the indignation of the Crawford men was "not less, though much more composed." Clay "boasts openly" that he will elect Adams on the first ballot; "What a scoundrel he is!"[69]

Crawford said the coalition was "astonishing every person here except myself" and that the justification of the coalition was the state of his health. He thought, then, that Jefferson might be surprised by his statement that his general health was good, "but my handwriting is nearly destroyed as you will perceive by this letter." The Georgian had "long known the principal juggler" and had been "well convinced that he would [act] according to any calculation of interest that he might make." He had expected a "different calculation," but there could be no doubt that the die had been cast.[70]

The week before the election there were many statements on

[68] Lowrie to Gallatin, Jan. 3, 1825, Gallatin; Willie P. Mangum to Thomas Ruffin, Dec. 15, 1824; Mangum to Duncan Cameron, Jan. 10, 1825, Shanks, *Mangum*, 1:160, 173-74; Saunders to Yancey, Dec. 19, 1824; Jan. 11, 1825, Clark; Mangum to Yancey, Dec. 25, 1824, Hamilton, "Letters to Yancey," 51; John Forsyth to Henry Meigs, Jan. 8, 1825, John Forsyth Papers (Princeton).

[69] Saunders to Yancey, Jan. 18, 1825, Clark; McLane to [James A. Bayard], Jan. 24, 1825, McLane. One does not have to ponder long what McLane's reaction would have been if Clay had decided to support Crawford. Adams had been meeting with numerous people, said that Samuel Ingham had been trying to persuade Cook to vote for Jackson, and decided that "intriguing for votes is excessive, and the means adopted to obtain them desperate." Adams, *Memoirs*, 6:476-84 (Jan. 23, 25, 26, 30, 1825). See also *Washington Gazette*, Jan. 21, 27, Feb. 10, 1825.

[70] Crawford to Jefferson, Jan. 31, 1825, Jefferson, MDLC.

the certainty of success of a particular candidate and many others that the outcome of the voting in the House was in doubt. Hopes for Crawford's election were buoyed by the belief that in the private feeling of the members of Congress Crawford had more good will and was better esteemed than either of the other gentlemen, by the "assurance" that the New York vote would at first be divided and later go to Crawford, by the possibility of getting Scott's vote, and by McLane's "masterly appeal" in the House which was said to have rescued Crawford from the disadvantage of the low state of his health. McLane, however, would not be surprised if Adams were elected on February 9; if he were not successful on that day, then his election was doubtful.[71]

On a snowy Wednesday, February 9, only one (Robert S. Garnett of Virginia) of the 213 House members was absent. New York was the big question mark and not even the members of the delegation knew which way it would go. McLane, writing from the chamber, told of an incident that occurred at the opening of the session. Stephen Van Rensselaer, troubled for some time about the necessity of having to make a decision, had come to him in tears, desired McLane's commiseration, and confessed himself "dreadfully frightened." The New York vote depended on him; if he voted for Adams, the New Englander could be elected on the first ballot. McLane told Van Rensselaer, who he said had been firm for Crawford the night before, that no one had a right to expect him to support Adams. Van Rensselaer did vote for Adams, and later that day McLane informed Bayard that "Mitchell gave him [Adams] Maryland and I groan to say old Genl. Van Rensselaer N. York!"[72]

Crawford partisans did not expect the decision on the first ballot; they were again disappointed in New York. The fourteen held, but two went for Jackson; had Van Rensselaer cast his vote for either Jackson or Crawford, as some expected, the state would

---

71 John McLean to Henry Eddy, Feb. 3, 9, 1825 (typescript), Eddy; McLane to Dear Kitty, Feb. 8, 1825, McLane; Saunders to Yancey, Feb. 8, 1825, Clark. This John McLean of Illinois should not be confused with John McLean of Ohio who was postmaster general at this time. For McLane's speech of February 7 see *Register of Debates*, 18th Cong., 2d sess., 498-508.

72 McLane to Dear Kitty, Feb. 9, 11, 1825; McLane to Bayard, Feb. 9, 1825, McLane. McLane told Kitty he had "really loved" Van Rensselaer, but on the night of February 10 "I wiped him from my heart . . . on a sleepless pillow." See also Stephen Van Rensselaer to Solomon Van Rensselaer, Jan. 22, 1825, Bonney, *Legacy*, 1:415; Adams, *Memoirs*, 6:493 (Feb. 3, 1825).

have been divided. But, of course, Van Rensselaer's was not the single "decisive" vote. Eddy of Rhode Island hesitated for a long time and then gave that state to Adams by a 2-0 vote; Mitchell's vote gave Maryland to Adams; Gurley cast his vote for Adams and gave him Louisiana.[73] One Crawford supporter attributed the New York vote to Rufus King who was said to have persuaded Van Rensselaer the night before to go over to Adams. Another thought that if Adams was eventually to be elected, he was not sorry that the balloting had "terminated at once."[74] Some of the New Yorkers believed Clinton and his friends had deceived Jackson, and the Jackson people were bitter toward Clinton. Further, it was charged that an agreement between Clinton and Adams involved Clinton's being made minister to England.[75]

It is impossible to say what determined the outcome, but the decision was made by a very small number of people. Two one-vote states, Illinois and Missouri, went to Adams; one three-vote state, Louisiana, went to him, 2-1; two other states, New York and Maryland, went to him by one-vote majorities. From the New England states he lost only one vote in Massachusetts; he carried Kentucky 8-4 (Jackson) and Ohio 10-4 (2 Jackson, 2 Crawford). He secured single votes from New Jersey, Pennsylvania, Virginia, and North Carolina for a total of 87 votes and 13 states. Jackson's 7 states were New Jersey, Pennsylvania, South Carolina, Alabama, Tennessee, Indiana, and Mississippi (a one-vote state). His total of 71 votes included 1 from Massachusetts, 2 from New York, 3 from Maryland, 1 from Virginia, 2 from North Carolina, 1 from Louisiana, 4 from Kentucky, and 2 from

[73] Forsyth to Meigs, Feb. 9, 1825, Forsyth; Lowrie to Gallatin, Feb. 28, 1825, Gallatin; Plumer, Jr., to Plumer, Sr., Feb. 13, 1825, Brown, *Missouri Compromises*, 137-38. It was said Mitchell would have voted for Jackson had he not been afraid of his constituents who were for Adams.

[74] William Coleman to Timothy Pickering, Feb. 13, 1825, Timothy Pickering Papers (MHS); Forsyth to Meigs, Feb. 9, 1825.

[75] L. Clark to Roger Skinner, Feb. 28, 1825, Van Buren. Clinton declined the appointment, and it was given to Rufus King. Many intriguing comments may be found in the period immediately before and after the House vote. One such was made by a Clay supporter: noting that "we" were friends of internal improvements and anxious to learn the views of the different candidates, he said, "Many of us were friendly to Crawford & we desired to secure him from *sacrifice* although we did not intend to make him President." J. C. Wright to Charles Hammond, Jan. 22, 1825, Hammond, OHS. Nathaniel Macon apparently was not surprised at the outcome. A month before the voting he wrote that Crawford "might I verily believe have been elected eight years past president, but whether he ever will be now is very uncertain." Macon to Tait, Jan. 9, 1825 (copy), Nathaniel Macon Papers (Duke).

Ohio. Crawford's 4 states were Delaware (a one-vote state), Virginia, North Carolina, and Georgia. In addition he secured 14 votes in New York, 1 in Maryland, and 2 in Ohio for a total of 54. Besides the states he carried in the electoral college he took North Carolina from Jackson. In addition to North Carolina, Jackson lost Maryland, Louisiana, and Illinois to Adams. Clay delivered Missouri, Ohio, and Kentucky to Adams. In the electoral college the state count had been Adams 7, Jackson 11, and Crawford 3; in the House it was 13, 7, and 4, respectively.

Crawford, said not to have been anxious or impatient but always "mild, cheerful and affectionate" before the voting, received the news about three o'clock from Asbury Dickins, who arrived just before Thomas W. Cobb. Crawford showed no "emotion of any kind," and his first remarks were: "Is it possible! Well, I really believed from what I heard last night that Jackson would have been elected."[76] The Crawford house was crowded from eleven in the morning until eleven at night, but after tea Crawford played some whist, and Mrs. Smith believed that he forgot all about the election. The evening was cheerful and gay, and the whole family displayed so "much good humor and pleasantness" that Mrs. Smith was almost tempted to think the outcome was the one they preferred.[77] Perhaps it was.

When Adams' request that Crawford remain as secretary of treasury arrived the following day, Crawford declined the offer in a friendly note, overruling the suggestions of some that he send a "rude" answer. Among those present at the time was Louis McLane, who considered the offer an "insult." Too disturbed by Van Rensselaer's vote to go to Crawford's on Wednesday, on Thursday he found the Georgian playing whist with his children and Mrs. Smith. He observed that no one could have conjectured that Crawford had lost the election; only Mrs. Crawford "exhibited marks of mortification" and spoke of Van Rensselaer in "terms of contempt and indignation which astonished me." Mrs. Smith, however, indicated no such feelings on

76 Hunt, *First Forty Years*, 173-74. Crawford had said the night before that he would be Adams and Mrs. Samuel H. Smith could be Jackson in their "presidential" chess game, "for of the two I would wish him [Adams] to succeed." Each game they called one ballot, and Adams won three of the five "hardly contested" games. Ibid., 175. Mrs. Smith, who was at the Crawford home most of the week of the election, said Crawford was "excessively fond of chess."

77 Ibid., 177, 179.

Mrs. Crawford's part, said that her only wish was to return to Georgia as quickly as possible (this was necessary to her husband's health), and reported little condemnation of Van Rensselaer but numerous comments (including Crawford's) expressing pity for him and attributing his action to "weakness" alone. As on some other occasions in his career, Crawford showed less perturbation than his close friends and supporters. Though he did not seem unhappy about the results of the election, he was buoyed in spirit by a three-hour visit from Lafayette the following day.[78]

The longest presidential campaign in United States political history was finally over; Virginia domination was at last overthrown; the bases for the reestablishment of the two-party system were laid; Adams had his prize; Clay had his reward; Crawford had his memories and perhaps some regrets that he had not run in 1816—but he never expressed any. He showed no bitterness toward Clay, Adams, or Jackson, and apparently he had no regrets. In 1830 he wrote that he did not consider his defeat unfortunate, for "I then verily believed, and I do now believe, that had I been elected, my remains would now be reposing in the national burial ground, near the eastern branch of the Potomac."[79]

[78] McLane to Dear Kitty, Feb. 11, 1825; Hunt, *First Forty Years*, 177-78, 181-96. Jackson visited on February 11, and Robert Owen was among the many visitors on February 12. Crawford resigned his secretaryship on March 3, 1825. Crawford to Monroe, Monroe Microfilm, Series 2.

[79] Crawford to Calhoun, Oct. 2, 1830, Shipp, *Crawford*, 241.

13

The Last Georgia Years

MOST HISTORIANS have either said nothing about Crawford after the choice of Adams as President or have contented themselves with the statement that he returned to Georgia to die. One recent scholar of the period, writing of Van Buren's visit to Crawford in early 1827, states that "at the bedside of the dying Crawford it had been agreed that, in return for Crawford's influence, Van Buren would accomplish the ruin of John Caldwell Calhoun."[1] Crawford by 1827 was quite well restored to health; he lived to witness, and to participate in, the ruin of Calhoun; he retained a hard core of influential followers in the party; and he remained active in Georgia educational, political, and judicial circles until his sudden death in 1834.

There seems little doubt, however, that Crawford was not a well person in 1825 and for some time thereafter. He was bitter toward no one except Calhoun, whom he thought most responsible for keeping him from the presidency, but he was reluctant to discuss what had happened in the election—a reluctance he never seems to have lost. In February, he agreed with John O'Connor that the "untoward events" in New York were "unfathomable upon any other ground than imbecility in the principal actors," but those events were now history, and further discussion of them was not required. He described his health as good, though he said he was still feeble, and he indicated that he considered his retirement temporary by saying that he would probably return to the Senate as soon as his strength was recovered.[2]

Crawford, his family, Senator Thomas W. Cobb of Georgia, and Lewis Williams of North Carolina left Washington about the middle of March in the Crawford carriage. He refused several invitations to public dinners along the way, noting that he had declined dining in public since his first indisposition, for the regimen prescribed by his physicians made it inconvenient to eat at any other than a private table. His itinerary took him through Fredericksburg and Charlottesville, Virginia, Milton and Salisbury, North Carolina, and Pendleton, South Carolina—seemingly the most direct and certainly the most passable route at that time of year. Not as an exile but as a hero he returned to Georgia. People gathered at the borders of Oglethorpe County to welcome him, and a few miles from Lexington they formed a procession to lead him into town, where he was entertained at the home of his friend Judge John Moore.[3]

He then proceeded the three miles to Woodlawn, his pleasing, comfortable, and unostentatious home to which in happier circumstances he had wished to return ten years earlier. There he piddled about his orchards, puttered at some agricultural experiments, and busied himself with other chores for the remainder of the spring and early summer. The latter part of July he went to Madison Springs—presumably to take the waters—where he stayed until going to Athens for the University of Georgia commencement in early August. In the fall he attended several public dinners in his honor, and the winter of 1825-1826 he spent "on the sea coast."[4]

Apparently during 1825 and most of 1826 Crawford was physically unable to supervise carefully the activities of his plantation, but he did continue to carry out some agricultural experiments. He regretted he could not do more along this line when he later wrote of his experiments with sugar cane and fertilizers and of his up-coming test of "Indian or corn-field" peas as a possible substitute for red clover and "plaister" of Paris, notably successful in the northern states.[5] During those two years Crawford said he wrote with such difficulty and so illegibly that he had an almost "invincible aversion" to writing. His script, which bore not a "single trait of resemblance" to his earlier hand, and his imperfect articulation were by 1828 the only remaining "visible" effects of

1 George Dangerfield, *The Awakening of American Nationality, 1815-1828* (New York, 1965), 278.
2 Crawford to O'Connor, Feb. 24 or 26, 1825, Crawford, Yale.
3 *National Intelligencer,* March 19, 29, 31, 1825, copying in first two instances from the *Virginia Herald* and the *Raleigh Observer;* Shipp, *Crawford,* 196: Cobb, *Leisure Labors,* 233. Cobb says Crawford's friends were distressed by Crawford's difficulty of speech, his unsure walk, and his debilitated condition.
4 Crawford to Margaret [Mrs. Samuel H.] Smith, July 20, 1825, J. Henley Smith; Crawford to Samuel H. Smith, Nov. 21, 1826, Autograph File, Houghton; Shipp, *Crawford,* 199-201.
5 Crawford to John D. Legaré, April 4, 1829 (copy), Phillips. Legaré, editor of the *Southern Agriculturist,* had inquired about Crawford's experiments.

his affliction. Though he was nearsighted, his vision was slowly improving, and he had enjoyed uninterrupted good health after early 1827. He was not, however, as active and as strong as he had been before his first affliction.[6] Crawford's writing was actually reasonably good by 1828, but he had a tendency to omit words and apparently did not give the same attention to his composition as formerly. There is no indication that he ever overcame the articulation difficulty.

Crawford quickly resumed his active participation in the affairs of the state college, in which he had long been keenly interested. He and his wife attended the senior examinations on June 20, 1825, and on the following day dined with President Moses Waddel at Judge Augustin S. Clayton's.[7] In August he took part in the commencement exercises and attended the meetings of the board of trustees, of which he had been a member since 1812.

After the trustees' meetings of July and September 1812, Crawford's mission to France had prevented his attendance until July 1816,[8] when the board accepted the resignation of William Greene, professor of mathematics and astronomy, and of President John Brown. Crawford, Peter Early, and David B. Mitchell were the committee to find a new president.[9] Their choice, Robert Finley of New Jersey, died before he had served a full year. Crawford, though not present at the board meeting, was again appointed to the search committee. After Nathan Berman, presi-

6 Crawford to Samuel H. Smith, May 30, 1828, J. Henley Smith. See also Crawford to Col. George Bomford, Jan. 24, 1829, Baldwin Family Collection (Huntington); Lafayette to James Barbour, Lafayette Letters (UVa). In the letter to Smith Crawford wrote about his children: John had been admitted to the bar; Macon was in college at Athens; William was at the academy in Lexington; Robert, Susan, and Bibb were in the plantation school, about a half mile from the mansion house, taught by the seventy-year old Virginian who had been Caroline's first teacher. He was an excellent instructor; he knew Latin, but William had to go to Lexington to study Greek.

7 Moses Waddel Diary (MDLC). Crawford and George M. Troup "supped" with Waddel on August 1 and on November 15 Waddel dined with "Crawford &c."

8 Manuscript minutes of the meetings of the board of trustees are in the University of Georgia library; a microfilm copy is in the Georgia Department of Archives and History. Volume 1 covers the years 1794-1817; Volume 2, 1818-1834. For the history of the early years of the University of Georgia see E. Merton Coulter, *College Life in the Old South* (New York, 1928).

9 Greene and Brown apparently were unable to explain satisfactorily their reasons (called for by resolutions introduced by Crawford) for not obeying and enforcing the rules of the college. In response to Greene's request for a statement concerning his merits, the trustees resolved that "it is the opinion of the board that Mr. Professor Greene is a man of Science and Literature, and a zealous instructor of youth."

dent pro tem, and Ebenezer Porter declined appointment as president, the board in March 1819 chose Moses Waddel.[10]

Disciplinary regulations of the college pleased neither students nor faculty; problems were perennial and approached crisis proportions in 1820. Crawford, as a supporter of Pestalozzian schools, advocated considerable freedom for the pupil in the early years of schooling, but he apparently believed that disruptive influences should not be tolerated at the college. In 1821 he advised Waddel to seize the "earliest moment" to inflict punishment on or to purge from the college the "restless spirits which necessarily gain admittance." To make possible this rapid action a number of trustees sufficient to form a board should live close enough to be convened in one day. If Crawford's resignation would facilitate forming such a board, Waddel was at liberty to tender it when he thought proper.[11] Waddel never exercised the option. Problems of student conduct seem to have been less critical during the remainder of the 1820s.

Crawford, grappling with the question of continuing in the cabinet in the summer of 1822, doubtless felt warm paternal satisfaction in the successful examination of two of his sons on August 3 and 5 and their admission to the college on the latter date.[12] And he must have enjoyed other activities connected with this commencement. At the graduation ceremonies Governor John Clark, Crawford's one-time duelling opponent, almost "burst with rage" because he had to walk on the left side of Waddel, while Crawford, at the president's request, was on the right. Clark's hostility to the college was public knowledge, and he had received several "buckets"—slanderous anonymous letters— which he suspected had come from the students. He laid the letters before the board of trustees with the request that the "delinquents" be ferreted out and punished. Crawford called for the reading of the letters; he "enjoyed their satire greatly, and

10 See Minutes of Dec. 23, 1816; Dec. 10, 1817; Nov. 8, 10, 1818; March 1, 1819. Crawford conferred with Finley in Washington. Coulter, *College Life*, 31. Joel Abbot and Thomas W. Cobb served with Crawford on the second committee. In June 1817 the board requested that Crawford ask Henry Jackson, who had gone to France with Crawford as secretary of legation and had remained in the post under Gallatin, to resume his duties at the college. Jackson did so in 1818, but he resigned in 1820 because he was dissatisfied with the policing duties required of the faculty. He was rehired in 1822 (with no policing duties), again resigned in early 1825, and was once more added to the faculty on August 3, 1825.

11 Crawford to Waddel, Jan. 27, 1821, Gratz.

12 Waddel Diary. Crawford "lodged" and "sat up late" with Waddel on August 5.

continued for a long time after to repeat the expressions which were the most irritating to Clark."[13]

Crawford did not again meet with the board until 1825, but on the evening of August 3, 1824, the college had conferred on him an honorary LL.D. At the July 1826 session Crawford was put on the laws and discipline committee, and the following summer he became a member of the committee on college buildings, library, and apparatus. He continued to attend somewhat more than half of the meetings and was presiding on August 4, 1829, when the board accepted the resignation of Waddel with regrets and warm appreciation for his services. That same day Crawford's second son, (Nathaniel) Macon, delivered the valedictory and received the A.B. degree.[14]

Within the next year Crawford presented to the school the forty-five-volume *Dictionaire des Sciences*, for which the board voted its thanks on August 3, 1830.[15] In the absence of the president the next day, senior trustee Crawford presided, and the board approved his motion that the students' petition for a well on campus was reasonable. Crawford attended only one more meeting—in November 1830. On the tenth of that month, in conformity with Crawford's wishes, the board accepted his resignation. Crawford's decision to resign may have been prompted by the course of events in the legislature of 1830; the Baptists and the Clark party joined forces and increased the board from 17 to 28. All additional members were Clark men. The school thus became the "victim of political exploitation and religious bigotry—a precedent which was to plague the institution more than once thereafter."[16] For almost two decades Crawford had taken an active and significant part in the affairs of the college, and he seemed always to have the interest of the school at heart.

The commencement period was often an occasion for intense political activity: agreement upon gubernatorial and other candidates, the pronouncement of political principles, the mending of

---

13 Gilmer, *Sketches*, 203-4.

14 Macon Crawford later became president of Georgetown College in Kentucky and of Mercer College in Georgia.

15 Crawford had also given the college a cutting (presented to him by the French government) from the weeping willow tree at Napoleon's grave on St. Helena. This cutting grew into a large tree in the college's famous botanical garden, and in 1928 it still stood "weeping over the departed glories of the garden." Coulter, *College Life*, 55.

16 Ibid., 205.

fences and renewal of personal contacts, and sometimes laying the bases of animosities that brought no good to the school.[17] Crawford, no doubt, was as busy as anyone else in the political sphere, but his reference to the 1828 actions is the only one that has been discovered. He wrote the editors of the Milledgeville and Augusta papers that a congressional ticket would be agreed upon at that time, and requested that the editor urge the attendance of "our political friends" and suggest that those who had been or would be selected as candidates send their acceptance to the postmaster at Athens.[18]

Crawford by then was a judge and was on the verge of abandoning the ambition to return to the United States Senate. His close political friends and supporters looked forward to his reentry into politics, and Thomas W. Cobb had said he would resign his Senate seat at any moment Crawford and his friends thought fit. As late as October 1, 1827, Crawford confidently expected to be in the Senate that fall: Cobb was even anxious to create the vacancy, but the bar of the northern circuit had been opposed to Crawford's leaving the bench, especially since George Gilmer—the only other person they were willing to have as judge—had, without knowledge of Crawford's intention to quit the judgeship, consented to run for and been elected to Congress. It was understood, said Crawford, that Gilmer would be his successor; Gilmer's congressional seat could be filled without inconvenience at the general election the next October.[19]

By the time of the next general election Crawford had given up the idea of going back to the Senate. Writing from Sparta, amid the "bustle and confusion" of court, he noted that the low price of cotton made his salary of $2,100 "quite convenient" and more valuable to him than $6,000 would be in the capital city. He had, therefore, decided not to return to the Senate where the

17 Ibid., 187.

18 Crawford to John Stevens, June 6, 1828, Read. Crawford asked Stevens, collector of customs at Savannah, to keep as many as he wished of the twenty olive and twenty fig plants sent to Crawford by the American consul at Leghorn. The remainder should be forwarded as soon as possible to Musgrove and Wetmore at Augusta. Two years earlier G. W. Erving had written that the consul at Marseilles had sent seed to Crawford and the vine cuttings "(say 200)," were to be sent from Bordeaux at the first opportunity. Erving to Crawford, Jan. 28, 1826, Crawford, Duke.

19 Nathaniel Macon to Crawford, Dec. 16, 1825, Crawford, MDLC; Lewis Williams to Bartlett Yancey, April 14, 1825, Hamilton, "Letters to Bartlett Yancey," 52-53; Crawford to Van Buren, Aug. 15, Dec. 21, 1827, Van Buren. See also Crawford to Yancey, Dec. [Jan.] 1828, Yancey.

"defect in my articulation would prevent my holding the same rank as when I was a member of that body."[20]

Though Crawford's physical abilities were low in 1825 and 1826, his political influence was still a factor of considerable magnitude. With party realignment taking place after the 1824 election and Calhoun casting his lot with the Jacksonians in 1826, it was important to know where the Crawford wing of the party would stand. Van Buren's visit to Crawford in April 1827 probably had the double purpose of determining whether his host could again become a contender for the presidency, and—if he could not or would not—to whom he would throw his support. At the time of the visit, Crawford's presidential ambitions were near the vanishing point, and the coalition of his and Jackson's followers seemed acceptable. Later, taking note of rumors and speculations that he would be a candidate in 1828 if Adams' friends were convinced that their favorite could not be reelected, Crawford said Adams would actually have to be defeated before his friends would come to this conviction; therefore, there was a "moral impossibility that any contest can arise between Jackson and myself."[21]

Whatever might have been Crawford's desire for office, he seemed determined to do everything possible to prevent Calhoun from becoming the heir of Jackson. In the spring of 1827 he wrote Hugh Lawson White, senator from Tennessee, that only the apprehension that Jackson's election would bring Calhoun "into power" prevented the North and South from uniting behind him in 1828. He said Calhoun had only recently become a supporter of Jackson: he had favored Adams until Clay declared for the New Englander. Further, Crawford referred to letters he had received which noted that the term "military chieftain" was much bandied about at the Calhoun caucus in Columbia, South Carolina. Crawford thought Jackson should know these things. White sent a copy of the letter to Jackson, who wrote to another that it "*adds proof* that Calhoun was as much my enemy as Clay until him and Adams fell out. *Can this be.*"[22]

20 Crawford to Samuel [H.] Smith, Oct. 21 (postmark), 1828, Crawford, Duke. Cobb had resigned from the Senate earlier in 1828.

21 Crawford to Van Buren, Aug. 15, 1827, Van Buren.

22 Crawford to White, May 27, 1827 (copy); White to Jackson, June 19, 1827, John Spencer Bassett, ed., *Correspondence of Andrew Jackson*, 7 vols. (Washington, D.C., 1926-1935), 3:365; Jackson to John Coffee, July 1, 1827, Coffee Family Papers (MDLC).

Crawford also wrote Van Buren that David Williams had expressed regret that Van Buren seemed disposed to leave Calhoun in the vice presidency; Williams, he said, thought Calhoun "ought to be punished for the mischief he has done." Crawford deemed it "extremely desirable" that a candidate for the vice presidency be started against Calhoun during the present session of Congress. Jackson's frail health made it important that the Vice President be a man worthy of the highest trust. He suggested Nathaniel Macon.[23]

Ambition did not die easily, and Crawford's vanity, *amour propre,* or political ego was temporarily twitted in late 1827 by his nomination for the vice presidency by the lower house of the Georgia assembly. Crawford was privy to the action, for earlier at Milledgeville his friends had prevailed upon him not to interpose any obstacle if his name was put forward. Thomas W. Cobb, in answer to a query, had told Lewis Williams of North Carolina that Crawford would accept the nomination but indicated that he would not run as a partisan of either Jackson or Adams.[24]

Crawford, though he said that his own feelings would not have led him to seek the vice presidency, did make at least one attempt to promote his candidacy after the nomination by the Georgia house. Since his name had been put up, he wrote Yancey, he "should not like to fail," and he believed a nomination by North Carolina would have more weight than one by Georgia or Virginia, which supported him in 1824. If North Carolina should take any action he wished Virginia to be informed, and the notice might be accompanied by "such suggestions as your judgment shall dictate."[25] But the failure of the Georgia senate to support the action of the lower house had doubtless precluded any possibility of success. And Van Buren did not adopt Crawford's suggestion of nominating Macon; the fear of division of the Jackson forces and consequent encouragement of the adversary induced many reluctantly to support Calhoun, though Van Buren

23 Crawford to Van Buren, Dec. 21, 1827, Van Buren. See also Crawford to John Taylor, March 1, 1831, Crawford Letterbook.

24 Crawford to Bartlett Yancey, Dec. [Jan.] 2, 1828, Yancey; Lewis Williams to Yancey, Dec. 11, 1827, Hamilton, "Letters to Bartlett Yancey," 66-68.

25 Crawford to Yancey, Dec. [Jan.] 2, 1828. Crawford said he wrote at the suggestion of Lewis Williams; it would be too late for Williams to write after receiving Crawford's reply. Crawford was referring to the fact that if North Carolina's action was to be effective it should be known in Virginia by January 8, the day the Virginians would meet.

thought the "approbation of Georgia is hardly to be expected."[26]

By 1828 Crawford's more influential followers seemed to have decided that their interests would be best served by allying themselves with the Jackson forces. But Clay's political future was quite uncertain at the moment, Clay and Crawford remained friends, and many Crawford partisans as well as others who were backing Jackson were confused and perplexed by reports of a Crawford letter to Clay in early February 1828. In that letter Crawford expressed the hope that Clay knew him too well to "suppose that I have countenanced the charge of corruption which has been reiterated against you. The truth is, I approved your vote for Mr. Adams, when it was given; and should have voted as you did, between Jackson and Adams. But candor compels me to say, that I disapproved of you accepting office from him." He thought Clay had thus "indisputably connected" his fortune with Adams', that he must fall with him, and that only the course of the Adams administration could have driven Georgia to the Jackson banner. He singled out Adams' recommendation for building "light-houses to the sky" (observatories) for especial derogation and said the "whole of his first message to Congress is replete with doctrines which I hold to be unconstitutional."[27]

Clay did know Crawford too well to suppose he had countenanced the charge and the frank admission that he would have voted as Clay did "accords with the estimate I have always made of your intelligence, your independence, and your patriotism." Clay was neither surprised nor dissatisfied with Crawford's opinion that he had erred in taking a place in the Adams administration. He had not been inclined to accept, but he was under pressure from his friends—as well as from Louis McLane and John Forsyth, close friends of Crawford—to take the post. He had not foreseen the unpopularity of the administration, but popularity had not

26 Van Buren to Crawford, Feb. 15, 1828, Crawford, MDLC. Some interpreted the feeble efforts to nominate Crawford for the vice presidency as a serious attempt to produce dissension in the Calhoun ranks in Georgia, Virginia, North Carolina, and New York and saw a link with Clay's alleged plans to promote Governor James Pleasants of Virginia for the vice presidency and DeWitt Clinton for the presidency. Others, aided greatly by rumor, saw a carefully developed plan to run Crawford for the presidency, throw the election into the House, and by management reelect Adams. See, for example, Duff Green to [Pressley Edwards or William T. Barry], Dec. 1, 1827; Green to Ninian Edwards, Dec. 18, 1827, Duff Green Letter Book, 1827-1830; Littleton W. Tazewell to George W. Crump, Dec. 22, 1827, Littleton W. Tazewell Papers (UVa).

27 Crawford to Clay, Feb. 4, 1828, Colton, *Works*, 4:191-92.

been the deciding factor in his public conduct. Rather, he had asked was the measure right? Will it conduce to general happiness and the elevation of the national character? He thought perhaps it was Adams' metaphor rather than the observatory which had provoked Crawford's censure, for nearly every President had made such a recommendation. He then turned

> with pleasure to the recollection of our amicable relations. What-
> ever you may have thought, or may have been sought to be
> infused into your mind, my friendly feelings toward you have
> never ceased; and, although our correspondence has been inter-
> rupted four or five years, I have always entertained a lively
> solicitude for your welfare, and availed myself of every oppor-
> tunity to inquire particularly about your health and situation.
> I have heard with unaffected pleasure of the improvement of your
> health. That it may be perfectly re-established, and that you may
> be long spared for the benefit of your family, and the good of
> your country, is the sincere wish of your faithful and obedient
> servant.[28]

Four days later Clay briefly related to Francis Brooke the contents of Crawford's "curious" and "very friendly" letter, which he had answered in the most friendly terms. Soon several of Clay's friends had seen Crawford's letter, which Clay thought "does Mr. C. as much credit as it does me." Clay understood it was spoken of generally in Washington, but he would regret the subject getting into the newspapers.[29] Most people knew only the rumored contents of the letter and were troubled by its possible effect on the presidential election. Crawford's long-time friend, Nathaniel Macon, was greatly perturbed. He thought sickness must have weakened Crawford's strong mind and that Crawford's adversaries in Georgia would use the letter against him and his friends. Cobb, Gilmer, and some other friends of Crawford were concerned that the letter might so change their party in the state as to put it in the minority. Macon, who was

28 Clay to Crawford, Feb. 18, 1828, ibid., 192-95. A copy is in the Clay Papers at the University of Kentucky.

29 Clay to Brooke, Feb. 22, 27, 1828, Clay, UKy. On April 29 Clay sent Brooke copies of Crawford's letter and his reply and permitted Brooke some discretion in showing them to others. Colton, *Works*, 4:201. Brooke, writing Clay on February 25, 1828 (Clay, Lilly), was "much gratified" with Crawford's remarks about the charge of bargain and corruption and asked whether Crawford would have any objection to having this known.

not sure what was in the letter, had heard that Crawford had written other letters that some of his warm supporters thought imprudent. Before the end of the month talk about the letter had died away. The full contents apparently had begun to circulate, and Macon thought Crawford's remark that he did not approve the Adams administration and would not support Adams for reelection probably accounted for the termination of the discussion and speculation.[30]

But a month later the *Richmond Enquirer* took up the matter, commenting on accounts of other papers and letters on which those journals reportedly based their stories. The *Enquirer* concluded that Crawford did not write a letter saying he never "gave any credit" to the charges against Clay; such a letter would not "correspond with the declaration he had heretofore made." The statement by the *Raleigh Register* that Crawford not only acquitted Clay but said he would have voted as Clay did was called a "fal-tal"; the sentiments of Crawford were too well known for such a clumsy, not to say dishonest, trick to be "played off" successfully.[31] Certainly the *Enquirer* publicized its fallibility and just as certainly the incident showed that frankness and honesty could easily be considered politically imprudent.

As on several previous occasions, the person most affected was among the least agitated. Crawford explained the situation in early April. He had wanted to obtain, through Joel Poinsett in Mexico, some of the best Mexican cotton seed and thought the most certain way of conveying the request was through the secretary of state. This he did; and since "Clay and myself had always been on friendly terms," he thought his covering letter would have an "unfriendly appearance" if it took no notice of the "unpleasant situation" in which Clay had been and was then placed. Crawford gave an accurate summary of his letter, using many of the phrases he had in the original. In keeping with his habit, he had no copy, but he had requested a friend to demand its publication in order to stop the misinterpretation.[32] Nothing more on the letter was noted.

---

30 Macon to W. N. Edwards, Feb. 22, 23, 27, 1828, Nathaniel Macon Papers (NCDAH).

31 *Richmond Enquirer*, March 28, 1828. In this particular instance it is impossible at times to tell whether the remarks are from the *Raleigh Register*, the *Washington News*, or the *Washington Telegraph*.

32 Crawford to Charles Jared Ingersoll, April 4, 1828, Ingersoll. He probably

Just at the time the Crawford-to-Clay letter reached the rumor stage, the death of DeWitt Clinton (February 11, 1828) raised among Calhoun supporters the specter of Van Buren being persuaded by the Federalists to become the vice-presidential candidate and through the union of the Clintonians and the Crawfordites bring the defeat of Calhoun. It was thought certain that Van Buren would be pressed by a section of the Crawford interest, and this group would rejoice in his elevation as a means of personal advancement for themselves. But it was not believed that Van Buren would become the dupe of such a plan— the examples of Burr and George Clinton would be sufficient to guide him on the right path.[33]

Crawford's enthusiasm for his own vice-presidential candidacy was very short-lived, but until the end of 1828 he continued his efforts to elect someone other than Calhoun. In late October he wrote a number of almost identical letters in an effort to pull votes from the South Carolinian. Georgia, he said, could not "consistently with her feelings and character" vote for either Calhoun or Richard Rush, and to relieve the state from the embarrassment of voting for either he deemed it his duty to advocate the choice of Macon. Both the declared candidates had already been more than amply rewarded for any services they may have rendered or probably would ever render, but Macon, in the public service since 1791, had received no mark of the national confidence or any compensation other than the pay of a member of Congress. Crawford approved the idea of not distracting the attention of the nation from the presidential contest by discussing the vice presidency, but this should not prevent an effort in favor of a man who for nearly forty years had been a conspicuous member of the councils of the nation. Macon's advanced age probably meant this was his last chance.[34]

---

made the request for publication to Thomas W. Cobb, who replied that he had not published the letter. Cobb had been "in trouble about it"; but since Crawford did not manifest the same degree of interest, Cobb had concluded that "I need not make myself uneasy, especially as it was on *your* account and not *my* account that I felt any trouble." Cobb to Crawford, April 11, 1828, Golding.

[33] Russell Jarvis to A. Ware, Feb. 22, 1828; Duff Green to Dear Sir, Feb. 23, 1828, Duff Green Letter Book. Jarvis was Green's partner on the *Telegraph*.

[34] Crawford to Jesse B. Thomas, Oct. 25 (postmark), 1828, Thomas. He asked Thomas to advance Macon's claims before the Illinois electors and let him know as soon as possible of the probable electoral results in Illinois. It is interesting to note that in late 1827 Crawford supported Macon on grounds of his good health and the feebleness of Jackson. Macon lived until 1837.

In other letters he asked that Macon's name be brought before the New York electors in a "most impressive manner" and expressed the hope that letters written to distinguished individuals in all states except New Hampshire, Vermont, Massachusetts, Rhode Island, and Connecticut would bring success. Crawford did not think Jackson would take a defeated Calhoun into the cabinet, but said he would himself "cause representation to be made to Jackson" that would prevent it. He supposed the election of the President must be determined by party, but he saw no reason why the Vice President could not be chosen by "sober reason," without reference to party.[35]

Party prevailed over sober reason, and Crawford's efforts went for nought. The Georgia electors gave nine votes to Jackson, seven votes for the vice presidency to Senator William Smith of South Carolina, and two votes to Calhoun. Crawford voted for Jackson more "as a choice of evils, than as a matter of abstract preference," opposing the election of Adams rather than advocating the election of Jackson. He blamed no man for his choice between these two, felt it wise to soothe the disappointment of any state or section, and ascribed the rejection of Adams to his political opinions and actions rather than to any feeling of disrespect for New England.[36]

Following the election of 1828 some of the key appointments went to warm partisans of Crawford who had become Jackson and Van Buren supporters. This did not please the Calhoun followers, including Duff Green, who was much dissatisfied with and freely remonstrated against Samuel Ingham's choice of Asbury Dickins as his chief clerk. Four of the five foreign ministers were said to have been Crawford men and the fifth was originally a friend of Clay.[37] Among this group was Louis McLane, neo-

---

35 Crawford to Van Buren, Oct. 21, 1828, Van Buren; Crawford to David Daggett, Nov. 15, 1828, Crawford, Yale. Similar letters went to Samuel Smith of Maryland and Felix Grundy of Tennessee; the latter replied that he considered the Tennessee electors pledged to Calhoun. Grundy suggested to Jackson that a future split of the party was in evidence, but he thought it would be the Crawford faction that probably would break with the administration because of a dislike for Calhoun. Crawford to Smith, Oct. 21 (postmark), 1828, Crawford, Duke; Joseph Howard Parks, *Felix Grundy, Champion of Democracy* (University, La., 1940), 175.

36 Crawford to Jesse B. Thomas, Jan. 9, 1828 [1829], Thomas.

37 Virgil Maxcy to Calhoun, April 9, May 7, July 4, 1829, 2 vols. American Historical Association, *Annual Report*, 1899 (Washington, D.C., 1900), 2:795-807, 810-14. Maxcy said that Ingham cut the discussion short by plainly intimating that he would not be interfered with in appointments in his own department.

Jacksonite who had given the Delaware vote to Crawford in early
1825.[38] When Crawford informed Secretary of State Van Buren
of his pleasure with McLane's appointment as minister to England, he also gave him some advice and counsel on instructing his
ministers to England and France and expressed his unhappiness
that Stephen Olin had not been made secretary of legation. He
presumed the appointment had been made before his letter of
recommendation arrived, but Georgia would think it strange that
the present administration refused what the last had granted.
Maybe Olin could be given a position without removing another
person; but if it is necessary to replace someone, that "should not
be hard if the newspapers give us a true account of the cabinet."[39]
    Intermittently the coals of Crawford's smoldering ambition
seem to have been fanned by thoughts of Calhoun's fortunes—or
wishes for his misfortune. In early 1830 Crawford felt Jackson's
decision on a second-term candidacy would make no difference to
Calhoun's career; the South Carolinian never had any prospect
of votes except in South Carolina and Pennsylvania, but he might
take North Carolina if pitted against Van Buren. On the other
hand, Van Buren might be a powerful competitor for the
Pennsylvania vote. He speculated on the states that Clay and
Van Buren might carry and decided that in addition to the votes
the latter could command "I could certainly obtain" the votes
of North Carolina, and probably those of Tennessee and Alabama.
Again, it was probable he would lose some votes north of the
Potomac. However, Crawford would deeply regret being placed
in competition with Van Buren—the House of Representatives
would probably have to choose the President. If Crawford's name
were brought forward, it ought to be at the instance of Van Buren
and his friends. Crawford thought it within the "pale of possibility" that it would be better to postpone Van Buren's claim for

[38] In speculating and then commenting on the cabinet appointments McLane
called John Branch (the new secretary of navy) an "old woman," and he said the
new secretary of war, John H. Eaton, "has just married his mistress—& the mistress
of 11-doz. others.!!" McLane to [?], Feb. 12, 13, 1829, James Bayard Papers (University of Delaware).
[39] Crawford to Van Buren, May 12, 1829, Van Buren. Later Crawford recommended six persons to Van Buren as negotiators with the Cherokee (he himself
wanted no appointment that would make it necessary to move his family) and
repeated—as he had several times earlier—his belief that the ministers of the United
States received such low salaries that they could not, without injury to their personal
fortunes, stay abroad as long as the public interest required. Crawford to Van
Buren, July 11, Sept. 9, 1829, ibid.

another term; if Clay and Calhoun should be vanquished a second time, they will be "hors du combat in all future time, and will not be able to offer any obstacles to VB's elevation."

But Crawford said he had no personal ambition to gratify; his only ambition—if it could be called such—was to educate his five sons so as to render them useful citizens to the Republic. This he was able to do. When that goal was achieved and his daughters were "advantageously settled in Society," he would have accomplished his work in this world and "shall be ready to depart hence & be no more seen amongst men." A postscript said that Van Buren's friends may "possibly apprehend the same course of conduct from me that I experienced from Mr Monroe, but I think my character ought to be sufficient guaranty against such an event."[40]

Occasionally there was mention in the press and private correspondence of a possible Crawford-Clay coalition; to some such a union probably seemed reasonable because of Crawford's lack of enthusiasm for Jackson and his continued friendship with Clay. Crawford explored this possibility with Clay in March 1830 and appears to have done a good job of ending a friendship of twenty years. He perceived from the papers that Clay, Calhoun, and Van Buren would be the next presidential candidates—if Jackson were not a candidate. If so, Van Buren would be elected. Crawford believed Clay would not get a vote in New England: his and Adams' "manners *habits,* sentiments and *principles*" were so different that it was not probable the two could be supported by the same men. The Kentuckian's popularity in the Atlantic states south of the Potomac had been destroyed by his union with Adams, and Crawford's standing in Georgia had been injured by his defense of Clay against the charge of corrupt bargaining.

If Clay wished to become President, Crawford thought his "most likely way of success" was to avoid the next presidential contest. Some of Crawford's friends wished to place his name in nomination; if this were done and Clay, not a candidate, supported Crawford, the Georgian presumed there would be no doubt of his receiving the votes of the western and southwestern states, which with Virginia and some other states would secure his election. Clay would then be brought into the cabinet and "could hardly

40 Crawford to Dear Sir, Feb. 4, 1830, Crawford, Duke. This letter, well written and with an excellent signature, was in reply to "your first letter from Washington." Crawford presumably was referring to Monroe's neutrality in the election of 1824.

fail to succeed when I retired." Crawford thought it possible his friends would make the same proposal to Van Buren, but "I should rather it should take place with you." Really, however, it was of little concern to Crawford:

> Do not suppose that I feel any solicitude upon the subject of this letter. I feel none; but supposing from what I have seen in the public papers that you feel some, it occurred to me that the most certain mode of gratifying that feeling was to adopt the course which I have suggested. If you should be of a different opinion, let the matter rest where it is, & there no harm will have been done.

If Clay concurred in the proposal, Crawford would be happy to hear from him.[41]

Clay thought this "singular" letter indicated "some want of self-possession." He did not answer because he could not do so in terms "consistent with the friendship which I once bore to Mr. Crawford."[42] Nor did he think the letter should be published. Crawford was not—and was not likely to be—formidable; and his "friends, though few of them are mine, are generally respectable. Their feelings would be affected. He has been high in public confidence. Ought that to be shown as having been misplaced, especially as he may not be in his right mind?" Clay remained firm against publication: "It could only be justified by some public good, and I see none that it would accomplish."[43]

There is a little evidence that just at the time of this "singular" letter some friends of Crawford had announced his candidacy for the vice presidency (not the presidency), that an effort would be made in his behalf in Massachusetts, and that some supporters were boosting him in Georgia. Crawford took much the same approach he had two years before by noting that once a person's name had been announced for a public office that person could not feel "perfectly indifferent."[44]

Slightly more than a month after Crawford's letter to Clay

41 Crawford to Clay, March 31, 1830, Clay, MDLC.
42 Clay to Francis Brooke, May 23, 1830, Clay, UKy; Colton, *Works*, 4:271-72. See also Clay to J. S. Johnston, April 30, 1830, ibid., 264-65.
43 Francis Brooke to Clay, June 6, 1830, Clay, Lilly; Clay to Brooke, June 16, 1830, Clay, UKy; Clay to Brooke, April 24, 1830 [1831], Colton, *Works*, 4:263. Reference to the Crawford letter of March of the preceding year and contents of the Clay-Brooke letters indicate improper dating of this last letter. Contents, actual and supposed, of the Crawford letter circulated at least until the fall of 1831. See George W. Erving to Crawford, Sept. 7, 1831, Crawford, Duke.
44 Crawford to Edward Harden, March 21, 1830, Edward Harden Papers (Duke).

the final episode in the Jackson-Calhoun split was triggered by revelations concerning events following Jackson's Florida invasion; the possibility of Calhoun's succeeding Jackson was eliminated; Crawford's "solicitude" about the first and second offices disappeared before the election of 1832 took place. Jackson might have known the true situation in 1818 had he been willing to listen,[45] but his previous brushes with Crawford as secretary of war had preconditioned him for one conclusion only. By mid-1827 Calhoun's duplicity had been strongly intimated to Jackson, and more direct evidence was available in the letter from John Forsyth to James A. Hamilton in early 1828. Fear of endangering the election of Jackson seems to have dictated withholding this information until a more propitious time.

The sanctity of cabinet deliberations served many as sufficient moral cover for keeping the truth hidden, but both Calhoun and Crawford at the time of—or shortly after—the discussions had intimated the prevailing public belief was incorrect. Crawford believed that the cabinet deliberations belonged to history, but he thought it unnecessary to make public his feelings that Calhoun, Adams, and Wirt were hypocritical in their remarks about the confidential nature of cabinet deliberations.[46]

The story has been told many times before and will not be repeated here. The point of no return for Calhoun was reached on May 12, 1830, when Forsyth placed in Jackson's hands a copy of Crawford's letter of April 30 to Forsyth. For nearly a year everyone seemed to be corresponding and conferring with everyone else, John Quincy Adams was reading and rereading for his benefit and for others the entries in his diary, Crawford was making "deep and deadly" thrusts at Calhoun (indicating among other things that ever since Calhoun had established the *Republican* to slander and vilify Crawford's reputation Crawford had considered him a "degraded, a disgraced man"), Calhoun was publishing his version of the incident, and contemporaries were keenly aware that Calhoun was fighting for his political life.[47]

45 See Jackson to John Overton, May 13, 1830, Andrew Jackson Papers (Tennessee Historical Society); John Williams to Van Buren, March 22, 1831, Van Buren.
46 It should be noted that Wirt seemed thoroughly sincere in this matter, but nearly identical accounts—at several different times—in Adams' *Memoirs* and *Niles' Weekly Register* might lead one to wonder where Niles got his information.
47 Relevant materials and accounts may be found in *Niles' Weekly Register* 40 (March 5, 12, 19, 1831):11-24, 37-45, and at the appropriate places in Bassett, *Correspondence of Andrew Jackson;* Hamilton, *Monroe Writings;* Richard K. Crallé,

Most general accounts of the period have relied heavily on John Quincy Adams' account of events, and biographers of the principals have defended their subjects—with Crawford being accorded a full share of denunciation and condemnation for his perfidy and intrigue, his unrelenting hatred of Calhoun, and his unpatriotic disclosure of cabinet "secrets." Partial disclosure of the cabinet discussions had been made years before. That Crawford heartily and steadfastly disliked Calhoun—and sought to destroy him politically—cannot be denied. The charge of intrigue is probably not a very serious one in the political world; doubtless all the principals were guilty. Perfidy is not provable against Calhoun or Crawford, but certainly Calhoun lived for a decade under the lie that he had been the defender and Crawford the persecutor of Jackson. There seems little question—and there was none in Crawford's mind—but that Calhoun was schemingly involved in the "A.B." affair and that he had been an important factor in Crawford's not gaining the presidency in 1824. Crawford's actions prior to 1828 certainly indicated he did not want Calhoun as Vice President in that year, and surely he did not want him to become President.

But in many respects Calhoun had only himself to blame for his fate. When he cast his lot with the Jacksonians in 1826—before the Crawford wing of the party had done so—he or some of his intimates might have explained his position to Jackson or to some of Jackson's intimates. Such explanation might have been acceptable at any time before the end of 1828. However, Calhoun and his partisans apparently thought Crawford reduced to a cipher in the party and preferred not to take the risk. Even so, Crawford did not go directly to Jackson; and though the whole thing might have been a carefully conceived conspiracy to ruin Calhoun, the early actors were numerous and Crawford did not play a major role until the late scenes of the drama. The exigencies of politics probably determined the actions of the principals;

ed., *The Works of John C. Calhoun*, 6 vols. (New York, 1857-1864); Wiltse, *Calhoun;* Duckett, *Forsyth;* Adams, *Memoirs.* Among materials not generally used in discussing this episode are Crawford to Asbury Dickins, March 1, June 17, 24, 1831, Washburn; Forsyth to Crawford, Jan. 26, 1831, Golding. These do not materially alter the picture, but the Dickins letters show that Crawford made a serious effort to get his facts straight. The Forsyth letter indicates that Jackson was "entirely satisfied" with Crawford's account, regretted that he had been so long deluded, and imputed "no hostility for an opinion honestly entertained and frankly and constantly expressed."

if blame is to be attached, it should be spread among a half dozen or so. It is highly unlikely that Crawford expected personal political gain from the episode, but he doubtless derived a certain satisfaction in seeing Calhoun finally get his "punishment," which Crawford thought should have been administered some time before.[48]

Shortly after a copy of Crawford's letter to Forsyth had been given to Jackson, Crawford became keenly interested in assembling a convention to amend the Constitution of the United States. He was disturbed by what he considered unconstitutional actions of the national government and by the spirit of discontent among the people. He was not surprised that in more than forty years much "contrariety of opinion" had arisen about the construction of the Constitution and that the central government had sometimes exercised doubtful powers. But dissatisfaction had increased to such an alarming extent and the disposition to exercise doubtful if not unconstitutional powers had become so pronounced that Crawford feared civil war if something were not done to conciliate the dissidents. He was not at all sure a convention would provide an answer, but he felt it would "go farther" than any other measure to allay discontent.

His objection to the system of internal improvements contemplated by Congress was greater than to the tariff system, which he had always thought would "cure itself" before the country was ruined. Then, too, ultimately the tariff would probably do more harm to those it was intended to benefit than to those it was designed to "fleece." He believed that in a convention the "western people" would not abandon their support of internal improvements, but it was probable they would agree to a limitation of the power of the central government in that area. At present there was no limitation: all usurped powers are unlimited. It had occurred to Crawford that a "remedy" for the tariff controversy might be found in a requirement that all laws imposing duties or taxes be passed by majorities in both houses and then by a majority of the states, voting by states.[49]

48 Though Crawford had corresponded with Van Buren about electing someone other than Calhoun as Vice President in 1828, there is no evidence of direct collusion between Crawford and Van Buren in the Jackson-Calhoun matter.

49 Crawford to Van Buren, May 31, 1830, Van Buren. The preceding winter Crawford had written Cambreleng C. Churchill suggesting the New York legislature ask for a national convention.

Crawford wrote several letters seeking support for calling a convention. Replies were cordial, but no correspondent agreed to assist actively in accomplishing Crawford's purpose. One concurred that a convention might tend to compose differences, but his state (Virginia) was so absorbed with organization of the government under the new constitution and so internally agitated and divided that he thought her incapable of any vigorous action on national affairs. Another emphasized that varied interests of the country would always foster differences of opinion and believed a convention might "encourage insubordination" rather than allay discontent.[50]

At the beginning of 1831 Crawford reopened the subject with Van Buren, who had requested an opinion on the best means of carrying Jackson's views on internal improvements into effect. Van Buren was correct in supposing that the presidential veto of the Maysville Road bill would give "unpleasure," but Crawford said the best and only means of regulating internal improvements was the calling of a convention to revise the Constitution. Crawford understood Jackson's message to deny to Congress the right to make local internal improvements, but if money is distributed to the states they will use it for that purpose. He emphasized that the westerners were a great distance from ports, did not have the money to build the roads and canals, and insisted that necessary improvements be made at the expense of the entire nation. He thought, however, they would be satisfied with the distribution proposed by the President. Crawford was, and if he were a member of the proposed convention he would sponsor an amendment to make the procedure constitutional. Distribution of funds would then no longer depend on the whim or caprice of Congress and, since the United States could raise money more inexpensively than the states, this method would be financially advantageous to the states. A resolution from the New York legislature requiring the calling of a convention would have great weight with the other states.[51]

Federal involvement in internal improvements was far less than Crawford seemed to expect, and by the summer of 1832 the tariff

[50] Benjamin Watkins Leigh to Crawford, Jan. 15, 1831; [John Williams] to Crawford, June 29, 1830, Crawford, Duke. Leigh said that before receiving Crawford's letter on the convention proposal he had seen his letter on the same subject to Bartlett Yancey. Williams was replying to Crawford's letter of June 5.

[51] Crawford to Van Buren, Jan. 3, 1831, Van Buren.

LAST GEORGIA YEARS

was the major cause of his irritation. After a discussion of the amalgamation of parties following the War of 1812, the latitudinarian construction of the Constitution held by Clay and Calhoun, and Calhoun's turn to the opposite extreme of nullification, Crawford said the southern states had made up their minds that they would no longer be "filched and robbed" by the tariff. He disagreed with McDuffie's contention that the southern states paid all the duties, and he rejected the doctrine of nullification as "self-evidently absurd." The tariff, however, was unjust and oppressive; it must be abandoned or the union would be dissolved. He had fought against the nullification forces and for the calling of a national convention to consider this and other problems. If the tariff states refused to join, then the antitariff states could hold the convention, frame a constitution, and terminate the oppression. If the tariff states did unite in a convention that failed to resolve the differences, they could then peaceably form a constitution for themselves. These developments he did not wish to see; they were a "choice of evils of great magnitude."

The South, Crawford maintained, was being fleeced by the tariff; when this can no longer be done, the tariff will fall as a matter of course. He did not insist on total repeal, but he wanted a partial repeal and some assurance that the whole of the "brigandage shall ultimately and at a certain time entirely cease." He pictured some of the extremists of the tariff states as saying that dissolution of the union would be better than meeting some of the demands of the antitariff states, and the South as saying the same thing of the tariff states. Crawford hoped these extreme views would produce reflection and moderation in the deliberation upon the tariff and warned that the issue must be compromised at the current session or the opportunity of reviewing it would never arise—the question would "pass irretrievably into other hands never again to be discussed in the capital."[52] The issue was not compromised, and two months later Crawford was sorely troubled. He had hoped his earlier communication would have helped to promote a solution, but the time for reviewing the tariff had now passed. The expectations of the South had not

---

[52] Crawford to Mahlon Dickerson, July 8 (recd.), 1832, Dickerson. The first four pages of this nine-page letter are missing. The first part of the fifth page deals with Calhoun's ideas of consolidation in government. Dickerson of New Jersey, a strong Crawford supporter in 1824, was a long-time influential member of the Senate.

been realized; she would right her own wrongs and put an end to the "robbery and pillage which had been inflicted . . . under color of law." He concluded, "I shall not advocate secession myself, but it will be popular in this state."[53]

For some time Georgians had been deeply agitated about the tariff. In August 1828 Crawford was chairman of a group of more than one thousand which met in the college chapel at Athens, passed a protest against the tariff, and recommended that the state set to work to manufacture what it needed. The extent to which Crawford carried out plans for doing the manufacturing for his own "family" is not known. He was quick to make a start, however, for the next month he asked the help of a Philadelphia friend in finding a power loom "to go by hand"; spinning machines he could obtain in Georgia on short notice. He thought the tariff unconstitutional, but in the final analysis it might be productive of good: he probably would not have reached his decision concerning home manufacture but for the import duties.[54]

In 1832—again following commencement exercises at Athens— there was a call for the "friends of . . . Jackson, and those opposed to the *Protective System,* and opposed to a redress . . . by *Nullification*" to meet at the new chapel. This group, of which Crawford was leader, suspecting that the nullifiers would counter by calling a meeting at the same time and place, arrived before the appointed hour. Crawford was presiding when the group led by John M. Berrien and Augustin S. Clayton arrived in such numbers that they took complete control of the meeting, condemned the tariff, and called for the election of delegates to a convention at Milledgeville on November 12. One hundred and thirty-one delegates from sixty of the eighty counties of the state assembled on the designated day. John Forsyth, after some parliamentary maneuvering designed to show the hand of South Carolina in the movement in Georgia, led fifty delegates from the hall of the house of representatives. The actions of the rump convention were inconsequential.[55]

53 Crawford to Dickerson, Sept. 6, 1832, ibid.

54 E. Merton Coulter, "The Nullification Movement in Georgia," *Georgia Historical Quarterly* 5 (March 1921): 8; Crawford to Charles Jared Ingersoll, Sept. 11, 1828, Ingersoll. Crawford on occasion used "family" to refer to his slaves as well as to his wife and children.

55 Coulter, "The Nullification Movement in Georgia," 14, 24-25.

Between the Athens and Milledgeville meetings Crawford had been asked to dine with a group on September 22 and to "lay before the people" his views on measures that should be taken in the present crisis, particularly in relation to a southern convention. Judicial duties prevented his attendance, and he used a letter as the best available means to communicate his ideas. He favored calling a national convention to revise the Constitution; the antitariff states should pass resolutions requiring Congress, by terms of the Constitution, to call the convention. It was by no means certain, he said, that a convention would reject the changes sought by the South, for the behavior of men in convention would probably be different from the behavior of those same men in Congress. In Congress the only question was what power had been granted, and the answer was so often "abusively determined" that it is "in fact no inquiry at all." In convention the question would be what powers shall be granted. After the powers of the central government had been determined, the advantages of union and disunion could be deliberated. If it were discovered that the number and population of the states disposed to secede was not sufficient for self-protection, he deemed it unwise to separate. It would be better to submit to the evils of the tariff and even a system of internal improvements than to form a connection with a foreign state.

Crawford opposed a southern convention until a general convention had been tried and failed. And he opposed "any unconstitutional, or extra constitutional measure, until every measure of redress promised by the constitution, shall have been fruitlessly exhausted. Let us keep ourselves in the right; and put our opponents in the wrong." He made his position very clear in his closing remarks:

Any measure of resistance, whether nullification or secession, is so fraught with awful consequences, too much caution and deliberation cannot be exercised. . . . We know not to what consequence the measures now in embryo may lead. . . . I reject nullification as a peaceable, constitutional measure, for I verily believe that *no man in his senses ever believed it to be so.* I reject it as a revolutionary measure, because every constitutional measure of redress has not been tried, and because it will, in all human probability, be ineffectual, and will injure none but those who resort to it. Under this belief, I shall be sorry to see South

Carolina, or any other southern state resort to it. I should prefer
a southern convention to nullification.[56]

Crawford's letter may well have had some influence on the Forsyth
followers at Milledgeville, but nothing deterred South Carolina
from passing her nullification ordinance on November 24, 1832.

Crawford followed the deepening nullification controversy
with much interest and great concern. By early January 1833 he
had heard of only one "nullifier in this country" who found the
bill for modification of the tariff unacceptable. The more reasonable people would accept an even more gradual reduction of
rates than provided by the measure. If they could be sure that
the principle of protection was to be abandoned, they would not
"stickle" about a few years difference in its final terminal date.
Crawford's only fear was that the measure would not be passed
at the current session, and he reiterated his belief that nullification
was a "self evident absurdity" when pictured as peaceable and
constitutional. That the states must be the judges in the last
resort, the "ultima ratio regum," he had always admitted, and if
the South Carolina leaders had presented this view to the people
he would have thought better of them. But they, like "all other
hypocrites concealed its true character until they had deluded
the people into the doctrine."[57]

Commenting two weeks later on Calhoun's apparent fear of
consolidation of power in the central government, Crawford correctly pointed out that both as a member of Congress and as a
department head Calhoun had been an ardent advocate of such
consolidation. Now, in an "arbitrary" and "around" definition,
Senator Calhoun was equating consolidation with government

56 Crawford to the Committee at Alford's Cross-Roads, Sept. 13, 1832, *Niles' Weekly Register* 43 (Nov. 17, 1832): 185. The original of this letter has not been located. In early 1831 Crawford, disappointed that the South Carolina legislature had adjourned without requesting a national convention, contrasted the violent method of change in European countries with the peaceable and constitutional changes which could be made in the United States. No state which resorted to revolutionary measures without exhausting all constitutional methods of obtaining redress would "stand justified in the sight of Heaven," he said. "That nullification & seceding from the union are revolutionary measures cannot I think admit of rational doubt. The strongest objection I have to the Carolina doctrine is that its authors have deceitfully and hypocritically represented both measures to be constitutional and peaceable. They must have known better, and therefore acted dishonestly." Crawford to John Taylor, March 1, 1831, Crawford Letterbook. Taylor had been governor of South Carolina, 1826-1828.
57 Crawford to Richard Henry Wilde, Jan. 16, 1833, Crawford, MDLC.

by majority. Crawford was pleased that the nullifiers had post-poned the operation of their ordinance until the adjournment of Congress, but he was disappointed in Jackson's message and thought the movement of troops to Charleston and Augusta "imprudent."[58] This is the last known comment by Crawford on the tariff and nullification.

The above pages indicate that someone other than Calhoun had changed his views: Crawford certainly had not held the tariff and internal improvements unconstitutional when he was a department head. On another great issue of the Jackson period his views had not changed. He seems to have been little concerned with the controversy over the Second Bank of the United States and observed—in answer to a request—that his opinion was recorded in the two speeches he made in the Senate in 1811. Since then he had had no occasion to review the question and had not altered his views. No man, he believed, could preside over the treasury one year without being "deeply impressed with the expediency of the bank in conducting the finances of the union," nor did he believe the framers of the Constitution ever could have intended to prohibit the passage of a law proper to carry a power into effect because it might be carried imperfectly into effect by another law. His construction of the grant of power to pass "all laws which may be necessary to carry the enumerated powers into effect" included the power to pass all laws which are "necessary and proper to carry the enumerated powers into effect in the most perfect manner, and not in an incomplete and imperfect manner." If necessary, Crawford said his recorded speeches might be republished; he was persuaded he could not improve upon his earlier ideas, even if he had the means of investigating the subject.[59]

Jackson's veto of the bank recharter bill very probably did not meet with Crawford's approval, but Crawford's assertions concerning the powers of the secretary of the treasury over the bank and most particularly over the deposits were cited to justify Jackson's "pet bank" policy.[60] There is absolutely no evidence

58 Crawford to Wilde, Jan. 29, 1833, Norcross. Crawford's references to Calhoun by name were much more frequent after the beginning of 1830 than they had been in the preceding five years.

59 Crawford to Ingersoll, Dec. 5, 1831, ibid.

60 Jackson to Van Buren, Sept. 8, 1833, Van Buren; Francis N. Thorpe, *The Statesmanship of Andrew Jackson as told in his Writings and Speeches* (New York, 1909), 265-66.

for the statement of some writers, as well as implications of editors and politicians for several years after Crawford's death, that Crawford had changed his ideas about the constitutional right of Congress to charter a bank.

Crawford never secured a national convention, but he did serve in a state convention called to consider changing the basis of representation for the state assembly. In the early 1800s the James Jackson-Crawford (and later the Crawford-Troup) party, though Republican, was composed of more well-to-do and aristocratic elements than the opposition or Clark party. Political lines were often drawn more on men than on principles, and in a number of instances both the Georgia parties were in opposition to the dominant national party.[61] There was a growing cleavage over the matter of representation in the state legislature; and though not exactly an east-west division, it was basically a clash between the older and the newer settled areas. The constitution of 1798 provided for one to four representatives for each county, depending upon the population calculated on the federal ratio. The rapid increase in the number of counties resulted in a large and expensive legislature and an increasing dissatisfaction with the equal representation in the senate. A call for a convention to consider changes was defeated in 1821, but such a body did assemble in Milledgeville from May 6 to 15, 1833. Crawford, a delegate from Oglethorpe County, was defeated for the presidency of the gathering by James M. Wayne, candidate of the Clark faction, 151 to 88. He was one of twenty-seven, three from each judicial district, appointed by the president to present a plan for the consideration of the convention.

In the call for the convention the legislature had stipulated that all delegates must have lived seven years in the state and must take an oath "not to change, or attempt to change or alter any other section, clause or article of the constitution other than those touching the representation of the General Assembly." Many delegates thought the legislature had exceeded its authority by imposing these restrictions. On May 6 Crawford asserted that the law and the prescribed oath "reversed the order and nature

---

[61] The Clark faction drew more heavily from frontier and small farmer groups and from migrants from the Carolinas; the Crawford-Troup faction had many adherents of Virginia background and from the longer settled areas. *Niles' Weekly Register* 41 (Oct. 22, 1831):150, said, "We know not what they differ about—but they do *violently* differ."

of things": the creature had presumed to dictate to the creator. If there was any one recognized principle in the United States, it was that the people were sovereign. The legislative action he considered a "gross and palpable usurpation," and he disagreed with the delegate from Muscogee that the citizens had adopted the law of the legislature as a letter of instructions to the delegates; he thought that not one in a thousand had done so. The oath opponents lost, 102 to 132, and the delegates not meeting the residence requirements were not seated.[62]

The committee report of May 8 provided for a senate of thirty-six members and a house of 144 members, preserving the federal ratio. By May 13 the plan had been rejected, and a senate of forty-five—one from each two counties regardless of population—and a house of 144 based on white population was voted. Every county would have one representative; those fifteen counties with the greatest population would have two additional, and the next most populous twenty-five would have one additional. Each new county would increase the size of the house by one.[63]

Crawford spoke on several occasions, and at times his remarks were quite barbed. On May 8 he "cut down" a delegate who was not speaking to the point at issue by saying the "time of the committee has been spent without profit or advantage." The following day he thought the time of the convention would be "greatly economized" if the advice of President John Witherspoon to the Princeton graduates was followed. Whether they entered politics or any other field that involved discussion, Witherspoon counseled: "First, never rise to speak until you *have something to say*. Second, *be sure to sit down as soon as you have said it.*" If this advice had been followed, the convention would not have been told that Negroes created taxation (a "discovery" of the gentleman from Muscogee); they never had done such in any age in any part of the world, but they were the subject of taxation. Nor, said Crawford, was there a single point of analogy between the federal ratio and the rotten boroughs. Rotten boroughs did prevent a fair expression of public will; sparsely settled counties

---

62 *Athens Southern Banner*, May 11, 1833; *Milledgeville Georgia Journal*, June 13, 1833. A brief account of the convention is in Albert Berry Saye, *A Constitutional History of Georgia, 1732-1945* (Athens, Ga., 1948), 170-73.

63 *Athens Southern Banner*, May 25, June 8, 1833. The white population of the senate districts ranged from 1,371 to 17,851 and the "federal" population from 1,730 to 20,584. Ibid., June 8, 1833.

produce the same evil. Members of the assembly from such counties represent territory and not people; the rotten boroughs represented only some lordly aristocrat. Such boroughs may have brought much good intellect into Parliament, but in Georgia residents of the counties themselves must be sent to the legislature.

Four days later Crawford said he did not consider the federal ratio a debatable question and presumed that the convention of 1798 so viewed the matter. The ownership of slaves did not give a man votes—it mattered not whether he held five or five hundred —but the federal ratio gave to the whites of counties where slaves were owned the right of representation. He contended that every free white had a larger portion of power in the sixty-two small counties than did the whites of the twenty-seven larger counties, if federal ratios were used. He had never said nor feared that Congress would interfere with the three-fifths ratio, and he never expected Congress, except by inadvertence, to pass a palpably unconstitutional act. But—he asked the members to cast their eyes over the "interminable prairies"; their imagination was dull if they could not foresee the time when three fourths of the states would be nonslave, and then the three-fifths ratio and the right of property in slaves might be disputed. Long before this time the question of abandoning the federal ratio might be presented, and he would "blush to contend" for the right of representation in Congress which the state had discarded as unjust in state representation.[64]

The following day he returned to the matter to repel the charge that he had deserted principle. Yes, he had said earlier that as a general abstract principle free population was the correct base of representation. But this was liable to exceptions, and where a part of a community had property not generally diffused— especially if that property was taxed—the right of that property should be secured in the constitution. Slaves he considered that type of property, and the right of representation secured to the southern states for this very population increased the obligation of the convention to adhere to the federal numbers for state representation. He did not consider this a desertion of principle as the delegate from Richmond had charged. No man of "common sense" would make the charge, but he (King) in the committee of

64 *Georgia Journal*, June 13, 1833.

twenty-seven had asserted the right of a minority to govern a majority—and endeavored to prove this right. At this point Crawford was called to order and declared out of order for referring to something done in a different branch of the government. Crawford wished to know who "will assert that a committee appointed by a deliberative body is a different branch from the appointing body." He admitted being out of order but said the rule had no application to the case. Other gentlemen had amused the convention with "what they have heard, not in this house, but out of doors, in the woods, and possibly no where. No gentleman has indulged more largely in this way than the gentleman from the county of Wood. I beg his pardon, the gentleman from McIntosh, Mr. Wood."[65]

Crawford and his supporters lost 123 to 126 on May 13 in their effort to substitute federal numbers for free whites as the basis of representation in the lower house. A move to reconsider, followed by debate which lasted all the next morning, was lost 114 to 130. Names were not given but Crawford's convention statements would indicate he was with the minority on May 15 when the delegates voted 152 to 80 to submit the amendment to the electorate.[66] Some of the papers opposed to the amendment noted—as Crawford had on May 9—that the proposed representation gave influence to counties, not individuals, and insisted that population or population and taxation were the only true bases of representation in harmony with republican institutions.[67] The proposed amendment was rejected by a majority of approximately five thousand votes; in Oglethorpe, Crawford's county, the vote was 620 to 145 against adoption.[68]

Crawford apparently continued to work for reform of the legislature, and on the same day it carried the news of his death the *Southern Banner* printed the presentment of the Madison County grand jury, September term, 1834. It said, in part, that "On the subject of the call of a Convention as given in charge by his Honor, Judge Crawford, we have taken the liberty to differ from the views submitted by his Honor on that important subject." They justified their action by the recentness of the other convention and their contention that the plan rejected was

65 Ibid.
66 Ibid., May 16, 23, 1833.
67 See, for example, *Athens Southern Banner,* June 1, 8, 1833.
68 Saye, *Constitutional History,* 172-73; *Athens Southern Banner,* Oct. 19, 1833.

open to as few objections as any likely to be proposed by another convention at that time. Before going again into convention, a majority of the citizens of the state should "feel the necessity" of reducing the size of the legislature, no matter what the judges of the superior courts might recommend.[69] The next convention was held in 1839.

The tariff, nullification, and reapportionment issues had cut across the old party lines, which had never been clearly drawn. George M. Troup, co-leader with Crawford of the James Jackson party, former governor (1823-1827) who had been vigorous in his opposition to the central government, and supporter of nullification, refused the nomination for governor in 1833. Joel Crawford became the "unanimous" nominee to oppose Wilson Lumpkin in his bid for a second term. The Clark newspapers seemed to believe that the Troup party was extinct, but "responsible members" of that group asserted that parties then in the state were essentially the same as had existed for years. Crawford thought this a correct evaluation but indicated that the Milledgeville constitutional convention—where the Clark party first made an effort to assume the character of the Union administration party—showed that there were "wolves in sheep's clothing in our ranks." The Clark party, he said, had always abused power and the convention was a good example of such abuse. When the "Ethiopian changes his skin and the leopard his spots," it might be possible for the Clark party to change its political and moral character. Admittedly nullification had affected both parties, but that influence was passing and Crawford thought the most violent nullifiers in Georgia "probably never indulged a desire of making a permanent schism" in republican ranks. Joel Crawford, however, was no nullifier and might be a rallying point for the republicans. Crawford was hopeful that in a few more years things would settle down to a "proper basis," for the "college is doing much for the cause of civilization, and correct principle in politics, morals and religion. Let the people be enlightened, and we shall have a good Republican Government firmly established among us."[70]

69 *Athens Southern Banner*, Sept. 20, 1834. Sincere thanks were extended to Crawford for the impartial manner in which he presided.
70 Troup to Crawford and others, May 11, 1833; Golding; Crawford to Editor De La Motta of the *Savannah Republican*, June 3, 1833, in *Athens Southern Banner*, June 22, 1833. Crawford believed that his party had the "ascendancy in intelligence and respectability." Lumpkin was reelected.

One week after printing this letter the editor of the *Southern Banner* regretted the college reference because he anticipated the "handle that would be made of it by enemies of the college"—the *Macon Telegraph* had said that the college would be used as a party engine. On June 20 the editor of the *Federal Union,* obviously pro-Clark, apologized for publishing this "absurd letter": he realized Crawford's opinion had long ceased to be respected, but the position which he had taken against the nullifiers had made his course the object of some curiosity. Crawford's defeat for the presidency of the recent convention was attributed to the suspicion that his professed attachment to the union was only hatred for Calhoun in disguise, and the convention members knew that his "want of courteous and affable manners, the excessive irritability of his temper, and the unrestrained violence of his malevolent passions" would render him incompetent and offensive as the presiding officer. The paper was not surprised at what it called Crawford's attachment to the nullifiers and said it would have been greatly surprised if he had not made the Union party the object of his "vindictive abuse."[71]

A "friend of learning" regretted Crawford's remark and the political implication but pointed out that Crawford knew the situation at the college, was familiar with its management, and could not have intended to convey the idea attributed to him unless he wished by slander to arouse the prejudice of the community against the school. However one might feel about Crawford, this writer "would sooner suppose that all he intended was that the institution was doing much for the cause of knowledge and religion in general."[72] Even though the commencement periods had been occasions for politicking, when one considers Crawford's long connection with the board of the college, his deep respect for and devoted efforts in behalf of learning, his failure to inject politics into the school activities while on the board and his children's connections with the school, it seems reasonable to assume that "friend of learning" was close to the truth. It was one of several instances in his career when Crawford had either not spelled out his idea sufficiently or had so placed it in his text that it could be interpreted to his disadvantage.

71 Copy in Phillips Papers. The paper said Wayne received nearly all the Union party vote, while Crawford received all but one of the nullification votes.
72 *Athens Southern Banner,* Aug. 3, 1833.

As has been noted, Crawford had become a judge in June 1827. Governor Troup had appointed him judge of the superior court, northern circuit. At that time the circuit contained Franklin, Hart, Elbert, Madison, and Oglethorpe counties; by 1834 the first two counties had been removed but five others had been added, and court met twice a year in each of the county seats.[73] The superior courts were the highest in Georgia until 1845. The constitution of 1798 did not specify the method of choosing judges; in practice they were elected by a joint meeting of the two houses of the legislature, with the governor filling vacancies that occurred when the legislature was not in session. Crawford was elected without opposition in 1828, but on November 11, 1831, he defeated Nathan C. Sayre by only seven votes, 110 to 103.[74]

Crawford's opinions as judge give evidence that he used the English, American, and Georgia law books that were available to him and that he frequently was more concerned with justice than with the letter of the law. He reputedly remarked that *summus jus* is sometimes *summa injuria,* and "I must so construe the rule as to do the parties substantial justice." And in an Oglethorpe County land case of 1829 he said that when substantial justice had been done between two parties a new trial would not be granted—although the verdict might be against the evidence. Crawford's "clear and conscientious sense of right, an extraordinary recollection of what he had known in early life, kept him in the straight course,"[75] and he seems to have been a humane and rather good judge.

Crawford was, however, more excitable in temper than he had been before his illness, and he was especially impatient with what

[73] Crawford's warrant of appointment, June 1, 1827, with an attached oath that he had not engaged in a duel since January 1, 1819, and that he would faithfully execute the duties of his office, is in a display case in the Georgia Department of Archives and History. The oath is dated June 20, 1827. The court vacancy resulted from the death of John M. Dooly.

[74] The *Federal Union,* Dec. 8, 1831, charged that every possible means, including denunciation and proscription, were used by Crawford's friends to secure his election. Votes for two other judgeships were close: Charles Daugherty won the Western District (112-93) on the third ballot and William W. Holt the Middle District (108-104) on the fourth ballot. Apparently Crawford won on the first ballot.

[75] Such superior court minutes as are available are on microfilm in the Georgia Department of Archives and History. See Oglethorpe County Superior Court Minutes; Opinion on Lewis Brown and Thomas Wooten, administrators of Felix G. Hay, deceased, versus David M. Burns, Harden; Shipp, *Crawford,* 201; Gilmer, *Sketches,* 128.

he called a "silly speech." He is said to have told a lawyer who repeated his argument that he went " 'round and 'round like a blind horse in a gin." A practical and blunt judge, Crawford touched on the "right chord . . . was as tender as a woman," and he was often moved to tears by the eloquence of the future Georgia chief justice, Joseph Henry Lumpkin.[76]

The case that perhaps best shows Crawford's humanity as a judge is Reuben Jones v. Heirs and Distributees of James A. Bradley, decided at the October 1830 term of the Oglethorpe County Superior Court. Bradley's will directed that if any of his slaves wished to go to the African colony they should be permitted to do so and their expenses to the port of embarkation should be paid. In opposition to carrying out the provisions of the will the Georgia act of 1818 prohibiting emancipation was read. This act declared null and void every will or other instrument intended to give freedom to slaves. Crawford ruled that the 1818 act was designed to prevent the emancipation of "people of color" whose presence would be injurious to the slave population, but this will did not contemplate that such freed persons would remain within the state and was not calculated to "produce the mischief intended to be guarded against. . . ." The will, therefore, did not come within the "reason of the law." The fact that there was no fund from which to pay the expenses of getting the freedmen to the port ought not to be considered an insurmountable obstacle; it was probable the Colonization Society would pay the costs if necessary.

The judge was of the opinion that neither the "letter nor intention of the several statutes of the state, are in opposition to the provisions of the will. . . . Neither the laws nor the settled policy of the State impose any obstacle to its execution in relation to the slaves." He presumed the executor was as competent to determine the desires of the slaves as the court was to direct him. If placed in the situation of the executor, the court would convene the legatees of the estate and some of the most respected neighbors, proceed to interrogate the slaves as to their desires, and make a memorandum of their several answers. If any wished to go to Africa, they should immediately be disposed of according to the provisions of the will. If there was no fund to defray their expenses

[76] Garnett Andrews, *Reminiscences of an Old Georgia Lawyer* (Atlanta, Ga., 1870), 59. Other anecdotes of the bench period may be found in Shipp, *Crawford*, 202-3.

to the port of embarkation, those desiring to emigrate might be hired out until the requisite sum was obtained.[77]

For many years as a senator and cabinet member Crawford had been concerned with and about extinguishing the Indian title to lands within Georgia's borders. The long delays and perhaps his illness increased his impatience and intensified his dissatisfaction with inaction. Just before he left Washington the Treaty of Indian Springs—negotiated on behalf of the Indians by a handful of chieftains—had "taken" from the Creek all their lands in Georgia in return for an equal amount of land in the West and $400,000. One of the negotiating chieftains was William McIntosh, cousin of Governor Troup, and for his major responsibility for the treaty the Upper Creek decreed his death—and carried it out. Georgia, incensed over seeing two states (Alabama and Mississippi) carved out of her cession already in the union and the Indians still on her lands, was on the verge of armed conflict with the central government. Monroe's agents were investigating the matter at the end of his term, and the problem fell to Adams. Adams disallowed the treaty on grounds of fraud and forbade Troup to begin survey of the land. Troup proceeded —with preparations for the survey and for war. The negotiation of the new treaty of Washington involved the time-honored use of bribery and chicanery, but the negotiating chieftains were more representative of the Upper and the Lower Creek than had been the case earlier. Still dissatisfied because not all the Creek lands had been ceded, Troup openly defied the secretary of war. Hurriedly, still another treaty was negotiated in November 1827; by this instrument the Creek quit title to the last of their lands in Georgia.[78]

Crawford was not pleased with Adams' action on the Treaty of Indian Springs or with the vote of some of his friends on the renegotiated agreement. He expressed surprise that Samuel Smith of Maryland had voted for it and pointed out that the old treaty vested in Georgia fee simple title to the lands—and Georgia intended to carry the old treaty into effect. While it was expected

[77] G. M. Dudley, *Reports of Decisions Made by the Judges of the Superior Courts of Law and Chancery of the State of Georgia* (New York, 1837), 170-71.

[78] The Treaty of Indian Springs and other documents dealing with the Georgia matter may be found in *ASPIA*, 2, passim. The treaties of Indian Springs and Washington dealt with all the lands—except for a small strip along the Chattahoochee River—west of a line from Marietta to Albany.

that Adams with "accustomed perverseness" would interpose his authority, such action would cause civil war "in which I expect to have a part." He told Smith that to gratify a "few Indian savages who had no claim on your benevolence, you have probably subjected the nation to the horrors of a civil war for I assure you we will not give up the land without a struggle."[79]

Fortunately, the war did not come and the last major difficulty with the Indians in Georgia arose over the Cherokee lands in the northern part of the state. Many of the Cherokee did not wish to leave Georgia; treaties had permitted them to receive individual allotments of land; Sequoyah had invented his alphabet by 1825; and the *Cherokee Phoenix* was being published at New Echota, the capital of the Cherokee "nation." A constitution was adopted in 1826, but the Cherokee soon found that Georgia law had been made applicable to them and they were forbidden to continue with their government. The discovery of gold in the region in July 1829 made the issue more acute and brought the requirement that all whites in the Cherokee country must secure, from Georgia authorities, a permit by March 1, 1831, if they wished to continue residence there. This led to the Worcester *v.* Georgia case, with Georgia refusing once again to be bothered by the opinion of the Supreme Court.[80] It was 1838 before the Cherokee began their "trail of tears" to the West.

Crawford had no role in the final removal of the Indians from Georgia, but he was involved with the famous Tassels incident. In September 1830 Tassels (George or Corn) was indicted in Hall County for the murder of another Cherokee. The indictment was founded on the 1829 statute extending Georgia law over the Cherokee and giving to the superior courts of certain counties jurisdiction over offenses committed in the Cherokee country. A plea as to jurisdiction was filed and Judge Augustin S. Clayton reserved the question to the convention of superior court judges, which met annually and functioned as an ad hoc supreme court. The judges were unanimous in their decision, and Crawford, chairman of the convention for the seven years he was a judge, wrote the opinion.[81]

79 Crawford to Samuel Smith, Nov. 21, 1826, Autograph File, Houghton.

80 Georgia officials had refused to receive or record the decision in the Cherokee nation case. There are many accounts of these events, but a good summary is in E. Merton Coulter, *Georgia: A Short History* (Chapel Hill, N.C., 1947), 218-37.

81 An amendment to the Georgia constitution in 1835 provided for the establish-

Crawford was convinced that the "very grave question" would not have arisen but for the political, party, and fanatical feeling excited during the last session of Congress. The deputation of Cherokee attending discussions in Washington learned that the decision of Congress would be unfavorable to them and eagerly seized upon the suggestion that their case be taken before the Supreme Court. Relations with the Indians, he pointed out, had undergone many changes since the English arrived in the new world, but whatever rights the English possessed over the Indians were now vested in the state of Georgia. The correctness of this had been ably elucidated in Johnson v. McIntosh (8 Wheaton 543). He quoted at considerable length from this 1823 decision; part of the quotation stated that these "grants have been considered by all, to convey a title to the grantees, subject only to the Indian right of occupancy." Another part emphasized that the Indians were considered merely as occupants to be protected and were deemed incapable of transferring absolute title to others. The Indians were not then considered sovereign powers, and, further, the Constitution gives Congress the power to "regulate commerce with . . . the Indian tribes." When this power is exercised, said Crawford, Congress directs how the citizens of the United States shall behave; it does not have this authority in regulating relations with foreign countries. Why? Because the Indians are members of communities that are not sovereign states. And though there have been many wars against the Indians, there is not a single declaration of war against them. "They must have been judged improper objects of a declaration of war, only because they were held not to be sovereign states."[82]

Even by the decision of the Supreme Court, every acre of land in the occupancy of this *"sovereign, independent Cherokee Nation"* is vested in fee in the state of Georgia. Are the Indian tribes within the limits of the United States legal objects of the treaty-making power? They are not legal objects for war; can any other evidence be required? It seems self-evident that if not

---

ment of a supreme court, but the court did not begin to function until 1845. Crawford and Thomas P. Carnes, an earlier judge of the northern circuit were two "leading spirits" in the movement to establish a supreme court. William J. Northen, ed., *Men of Mark in Georgia*, 4 vols. (Atlanta, Ga., 1906-1908), 1:36. See also Saye, *Constitutional History*, 177-86; Ruth Blair, comp., *Georgia Official Register* (Atlanta, Ga., 1931). The opinion is in Dudley, *Reports*, 229-38.

82 Dudley, *Reports*, 233.

an object of declaration of war, they cannot be an object of treaty-making. Even if they were such at one time, the rights, position, and other factors had been unalterably fixed before the treaty-making power had been given to Congress.[83] It seemed strange that objection should be made to Georgia's exercising its jurisdiction over the Cherokee territory, for if a government is "seized in fee of a territory, and yet have no jurisdiction over that territory, [it] is an anomaly in the science of jurisprudence." To contend that a state may exercise jurisdiction over a territory but not over its inhabitants is to present a "more strange anomaly than that of a government having no jurisdiction over territory of which it is seized in fee."[84] The contentions of the counsel for the Cherokee that by the articles of treaty and cession between the United States and Georgia the United States had been given by Georgia the right to hold treaties with the Cherokee and that Georgia was bound to abstain from all efforts to extinguish the Indian right to lands within her own limits were conceived to be erroneous. He emphasized here that even when the United States made war against the Seminole residing outside the limits of the United States, there was no declaration of war.[85]

The matter was concluded as follows:

> This convention deems it a waste of time to pursue this examination. It has satisfied itself, and it is hoped the community, that independent of the provisions of the State constitution claiming jurisdiction over its chartered limits, that the State of Georgia had the right in the year 1829 to extend its laws over the territory inhabited by the Cherokee Indians, and over the Indians themselves; that said act of 1829, is neither unconstitutional, nor inconsistent with the rights of the Cherokee Indians. The plea to the jurisdiction of the court submitted to this convention is therefore overruled.[86]

One cannot help but notice the similarity of Crawford's arguments and conclusions concerning the status of the Indians and those of John Marshall in his opinion on Cherokee Nation v. Georgia only a few months later.[87]

83 Ibid., 234-35.
84 Ibid., 236.
85 Ibid., 237-38.
86 Ibid., 238. Tassels was hanged.
87 See 5 Peters 1 (1831). Of course, in Worcester v. Georgia (1832), when a mis-

During Crawford's seven years on the bench many young lawyers were admitted to practice. Perhaps the two most famous licensed by Crawford were Robert A. Toombs and Alexander H. Stephens. Toombs was admitted to the bar on March 18, 1830, in the Superior Court of Elbert County, and Crawford was said to have given him "favor from the first."[88] Stephens seems to have been the last person whose license to practice was signed by Crawford. On July 22, 1834, he was examined in Crawfordville by Joseph H. Lumpkin, William C. Dawson, and Daniel Chandler, the solicitor general for the northern circuit whom Stephens considered the most eloquent and promising of the rising young men of the state. Stephens was a bit disturbed about how he would perform but took some consolation from a remark of his lawyer-friend, Swepton C. Jeffries, that Crawford was not too exacting; after an examination to which he had paid little attention, the judge ordered, "Swear him, Mr. Clerk; if he knows nothing he will do nothing." Stephens would have been satisfied for Crawford to follow the same course with him, but the judge paid attention all the time. The young lawyer seems to have done well; the examiners favored passing him; and when it was over, Crawford said, "Take an order for admission, Mr. Solicitor, and have the oath administered. I, too, am perfectly satisfied."[89] Crawford was to hold only one court after the admission of Stephens to the bar—the one in Madison County.

All indications are that Crawford was in good health on September 1, 1834, when he wrote Andrew Jackson concerning the vacancy on the Supreme Court caused by the death of William Johnson of South Carolina, an associate justice since 1806. He thought it might be difficult for Jackson to fill the vacancy to his

---

sionary who was definitely a citizen of the United States was involved, the Court accepted jurisdiction of the case and said the Georgia law of 1829 was void. See 6 Peters 515. The decision was, however, of no effect; Georgia officials even forbade its being officially recorded.

88 Pleasant A. Stovall, *Robert Toombs* . . . (New York, 1892), 13; Ulrich B. Phillips, *The Life of Robert Toombs* (New York, 1913), 15-16.

89 Myrta Lockett Avary, ed., *Recollections of Alexander H. Stephens* . . . (New York, 1910), 363-65. Stephens and William H. Crawford, Jr., were classmates and, though no honors were given, those two and James Johnson were chosen to give the commencement orations. Crawford drew "Valedictory," but Stephens said his class standing was higher than that of the other two, who he thought "stood equal, two marks only below me." Ibid., 230-31. Stephens said he stood with the Troup-Crawford group in 1833, repudiating nullification but standing on the doctrine of state rights. Ibid., 232.

satisfaction, for in South Carolina the most prominent legal personages belonged to the "nullifying party which cherishes the most deadly hostility to the federal administration." He had heard good things of the former state attorney general, James L. Petigru, but he had held only that office and membership in the state legislature. The district judge, Lee, stood well with the late David Williams, but Crawford did not know to what party in South Carolina he had attached himself. In Georgia, John M. Berrien's abilities were thought sufficient for the station, but he too was against the administration. The character of the district judge "forbids the idea of his promotion."

For seven years, said Crawford, he had been judge in a circuit where the bar in character, intelligence, and respectability was equal to any in the state. His official conduct had given this group complete satisfaction although he had been twenty years absent from the legal profession when the judgeship was conferred without his or any other's solicitation. Parties in the state were so fluctuating that he might not be reelected next November if the party "to which I am opposed should have a majority in the next legislature." Such a view of the situation made appointment to the federal bench desirable to him at that time, and should Jackson, "upon a full survey, of the materials out of which you have to make the selection feel disposed to select me, the appointment will be thankfully received and the duties of the office discharged to the best of my understanding and with strict fidelity and impartiality."[90]

Perhaps the last letter Crawford wrote also concerned the Supreme Court position. On Saturday, September 13, he communicated to Mahlon Dickerson a number of the ideas and evaluations contained in his letter to Jackson. He indicated, however, that nullification had made considerable progress in Georgia—so much so that he had been "upon the brink of denunciation" for more than twelve months. When one considered the length of his service in the federal government, the offices he had held, and his role in public affairs, it seemed to Crawford that appointment to the Supreme Court "furnishes the proper & appropriate retreat for the decline of life; such a retreat as is

90 Crawford to Jackson, Sept. 1, 1834, Jackson, MDLC. Petigru had been state attorney general from 1822 to 1830. He was, and remained, an outstanding and eloquent spokesman against nullification and secession.

suitable to my past life & public services." He would provide testimonials if required. He understood that Levi Woodbury, secretary of the treasury, was in favor of his appointment, and he knew he need not request Dickerson to use his friendly influence. Dickerson was at liberty to show the letter to such of his colleagues as he thought proper, and Crawford asked him to give an "intimation of the probable result" as soon as practicable—the election for circuit judge took place in early November.[91]

Crawford had spent Friday, September 12, with his daughter Caroline, her family, and the newest grandchild, and on the following day had gone to the home of Valentine Meriwether, about fourteen miles from Lexington. He did not feel well; a physician prescribed for him and relieved the symptoms. He retired early but was stricken during the night. While sitting in a chair the next day he became unconscious and never recovered. He died in the early morning of Monday, September 15—the day he was to begin court in Elbert County. Cause of death was described as an "affection of the heart."[92] Crawford was buried the next day in the family plot at Woodlawn; the only other grave at the time was that of the Dudley boy who had died about fifteen months before.

A number of the newspapers had heavy black lines at the top or bottom—or used other methods to denote mourning—when they carried the notice of Crawford's death. The *National Intelligencer*, which had perhaps the longest story, noted that Crawford's Senate speeches were "remarkable for their strength, and his votes for their honesty and independence." But his "unconcealed disdain of every thing like pretense, subterfuge, or the ordinary arts and tricks of mere party-men" probably earned him "more respect and general regard" than any of his other qualities. He was bold and fearless in his course, he shunned no responsibility, he compromised no principle. "If, indeed, he had a fault as a politician, it was rather in contemning too haughtily the customs and seemings which form a part of the usages of those who mingle

91 Crawford to Dickerson, Sept. 13, 1834, Dickerson. This letter of three pages was well written and the signature is almost identical to that of the 1816-1818 period. On the back of the letter Dickerson noted the circumstances of Crawford's death and indicated this was probably the last letter he wrote. James M. Wayne of Georgia was appointed to the Supreme Court in 1835.

92 *Athens Southern Banner*, Sept. 20, 1834; Shipp, *Crawford*, 213; *Niles' Weekly Register* 47 (Sept. 27, 1834):51; *National Intelligencer*, Sept. 27, 1834.

much in public affairs; preferring downright truth, in all its simplicity, and all its nakedness too, to the circumlocution and periphaze of older and more practised statesmen." In his domestic and private relations he enjoyed no less the love of his family and affection of his friends, than in his public life he "possessed their unbounded respect and confidence."[93]

The *Intelligencer* had caught several of Crawford's characteristics and attributes; others it understandably did not mention under the circumstances. He was a man with fine native ability, though he seemed to think his talents "modest" and considered himself unqualified to handle the secretaryship of war during wartime. He honestly exercised the talents he had, was devoted to his duties, and had a great capacity for work.

He was open-minded; carefully examined available information and points of view; subordinated personal, sectional, and party interest to the national interest; stressed that public good should be the decisive factor, especially when decision rested with one person; was calm and dispassionate in speech and discussion; and though he defended his position with ability and sometimes with pertinacity, he never (according to Adams) "pressed" too far. Perhaps this was in keeping with his belief that any proposition carried to the extreme was open to suspicion. His opinions and ideas were sincere and honest, and he assumed that those who differed with him spoke from the same bases. He thought rapidly and was generally viewed as a man of good judgment.

Crawford thought he had no "claim" to any office, and his ethical standards were high. Competence, honesty, and performance of duty were prerequisites to appointment to and retention in office, where one should exercise the same economy as in his private affairs. Crawford was imaginative, efficient, and practical in his administration of the war and treasury departments, constantly seeking a stricter accountability of public officials, exercising close supervision of subordinates, and searching for better methods of conducting the public business. His contributions in the areas of inspection and accountability were indeed significant.

He was never a dilettante—in the arts of any other area—and had a deepseated distaste for hypocrisy and pretense. Justice was

93 *National Intelligencer,* Sept. 27, 1834. See also *Athens Southern Banner,* Sept. 20, 1834; *Richmond Enquirer,* Sept. 30, 1834.

more important to him than legal technicality, and verbosity troubled him. Perhaps at times he assumed too much understanding on the part of others. As a result, his ideas were sometimes too sparingly stated and caused him political difficulties.

Crawford had the ability to work with those with whom he disagreed, except with Calhoun after 1822. From that date he considered the South Carolinian unprincipled, and it might be noted that Adams terminated "confidential" relations with Calhoun at about the same time. But it seems doubtful whether Crawford hated Calhoun as he seemed to hate John Clark. Crawford seemed to see in these two men an opportunism—rather than honesty and sincerity of conviction—which he did not see in most of his other associates and political opponents.

The strict tripartite division of constitutional powers, Crawford believed, should be observed. The judiciary should exercise restraint, the executive and legislative branches should not encroach one upon the other, and in administering laws legislative intent should be considered. Power should not be usurped, but the necessary and proper clause of the Constitution should be interpreted to allow legislation that was necessary and proper to carry out the function of government in the most perfect manner. He was an unqualified supporter of the American form of government; his nationalism was ardent. His importation of seeds, plants, books, and other items was a manifestation of a desire to improve the position of the United States, and his long treasury circular to consuls in 1819, a large portion of which dealt with collecting and importing plants and seeds, has been described as among the first practical national measures for the promotion of American agriculture.[94]

Crawford could, at times (especially after his illness of 1823)

[94] Treasury Circular, March 20, 1819; Henry Barrett Learned, The *President's Cabinet* (New Haven, Conn., 1912), 309, citing Elkanah Watson, *History of the Rise, Progress, and Existing Conditions* . . . (Albany, N.Y., 1820), 205-6. The treasury circular, concerned primarily with uniform execution of the act of April 20, 1818, also dealt with the importation of inventions. Crawford encouraged Mason Locke Weems to translate and publish Le Sage's *Historical Atlas,* which he thought the "most successful effort of the age to facilitate new acquisitions of historical, genealogical, chronological, and geographical information." He sometimes sought to give publicity to the writings of his friends or was suggested as a person who "might feel an Interest and a pleasure in furthering the efforts of some intellectual." Crawford to Weems, July 18, 1824, Chamberlain; Crawford to Benjamin de Constant, April 26, 1824, Crawford Letterbook; Joseph C. Cabell to William Wirt, June 17, 1821, William Lowndes Papers (UNC).

be abrasive in personal contact, but ordinarily he seemed to be otherwise. Described by some as "commanding in conversation," he seemed to enjoy the give and take of personal interchange, had a sense of humor that was rather uncommon for the period, much enjoyed telling anecdotes, told them well, and was a "capital laugher." Apparently, he liked substance in his conversations and was not much given to idle chit-chat.

Little information on his family life remains, but what is available indicates a warm, loving, and compassionate husband and father who wished his children to develop into independent individuals strongly committed to democratic processes in all walks of life. He might be described as a permissive parent.

Independent but not a loner, firm but not rigid, modest but not unambitious, decisive but not dogmatic, principled but not doctrinaire, careful but sometimes not sufficiently cautious, forgiving but not always forgiven, Crawford truly was a free spirit who philosophically accepted what came. He refused a contest for the presidency with his close friend Monroe in 1816; eight years later the prize was beyond his reach. His enviable record of eighteen years of national service ended in 1825; after 1827 he added seven more years of service to his adopted state.

The Oglethorpe County will books bear no evidence that Crawford died testate. John, the oldest son, became administrator of the estate, and George M. Dudley, Crawford's son-in-law, was attorney for the administrator. The inferior court of the county, composed of the first five justices of the peace appointed for the county, designated freeholders B. Pope, Joseph I. Moore, and James L. Thomas to divide the slaves, horses, and mules equally among Mrs. Crawford and six of the children.[95]

The three appointees determined that the slave property subject to distribution was valued at $16,175, or a little more than $2,310 for each heir. The slaves were put into seven groupings as nearly equal in value as possible, "due respect being had to keeping families together." Mules and horses were added so that five lots were valued at $2,450 each, one at $2,445, and one at $2,470. As best can be determined there were forty slaves (eight of whom were children), six mules, and seven horses. The remain-

[95] These six children were (Nathaniel) Macon, William H., Jr., Robert, Eliza Ann, Susan, and (W.W.) Bibb. Crawford had settled a competence upon his oldest child, Caroline, at the time of her marriage to Dudley. It is presumed that John had also received a portion of the family goods.

ing personal property could not be divided without destroying its value, so it was considered expedient to have it sold. The proceeds of that sale and from the sale of the land were to be equally divided among the seven heirs at a later date. The court gave approval on May 2, 1836, for sale of the land.[96]

Though Crawford was for many years the first citizen of Georgia and among the first citizens of the nation, little has been done to collect Crawfordiana or to honor his memory. On the centennial of his death citizens of Madison, Georgia, sub scribed $106.75 of which $100 was given to Mr. and Mrs. C. H. Crawford for a gold watch that had belonged to Crawford. Three years earlier the state historian had written to William Dudley, descendant of Caroline Crawford, asking about the "uniform" Crawford had worn at the French court and about other items that might be in their possession. The watch and the cloak are on display in the Georgia Department of Archives and History.[97]

Although the parks, squares, circles, and public buildings of Georgia towns and cities are replete with plaques, statues, busts, and monuments, Crawford seems to have been completely forgotten until the 1950s. In 1955 the Georgia assembly approved the establishment of the Hall of Fame for Illustrious Georgians in the rotunda of the state capitol at Atlanta. The first six chosen for inclusion were Alexander H. Stephens, the three Georgia signers of the Declaration, and the two signers of the Constitution. Crawford was seventh. Four years later, in elaborate ceremonies, Crawford's was one of the first four busts to be presented and unveiled. A plaster bust was placed in the Washington-Wilkes Historical Museum at Washington, Georgia.[98]

The horizontal marble slab that covers Crawford's grave gives

96 Annual Returns for 1836 . . . State of Georgia, Oglethorpe County, January term, 1836; Minutes of the Court of Ordinary, May term, 1836, from copies in the Phillips papers. The only other information found on the administration of the estate shows that the "amt. left on hand" on September 15, 1834, was $553.37½, that eight bags of cotton were sold on November 6, 1834, for $339.78, and seven bags for $471.97 on November 28. Crawford Letterbook.

97 The purchase of the watch seems to have been prompted in part by a desire to help the C. H. Crawfords; he had been bedridden for four years, and his wife had suffered a degree of invalidism. Crawford Folder, GDAH. The 50-cent fractional currency, series of 1875, issued under the acts of March 3, 1863 and June 30, 1864, bore the likeness of Crawford. A piece of this currency and three photos made from the J. W. Jarvis painting of Crawford are in the Keith Read Collection.

98 The other busts were of William Few, Abraham Baldwin, and Crawford W. Long. All were the work of Bryant Parker. See Jan. 7, 1959 *Program of the Hall of Fame for Illustrious Georgians* (Atlanta, Ga., 1959).

a brief outline of his career and says he was "alike independent, energetic, fearless and able." It is broken into two almost equal pieces; the burial plot is ill kept—if at all; the iron fence is all but fallen down; and it is nearly impossible to reach the graveyard, which is just west of Crawford, Georgia, about four hundred yards north of U.S. Highway 78. One is hard put to imagine that a short distance away the mansion house stood; broad acreages were fertile and green; agricultural experiments with plants and seeds from many parts of the world were being conducted; joyous family gatherings took place on the lawn with the big, jovial, fun-loving father in the middle of the intellectual as well as the physical activity. The house has long since burned down and the historical marker (just off the highway) indicating that Crawford lived not far from its location is devoted primarily to his duelling activities. May he become better known for more important things.

Note on Sources

MORE THAN a century ago fire destroyed a large collection of Crawford letters and papers assembled by his daughter and son-in-law. However, there still exist hundreds of letters to and from Crawford in several small Crawford collections and in the papers of his contemporaries and political associates. These are scattered from Maine to California in more than two hundred collections found in almost a hundred depositories. In addition, the vast congressional and executive department materials make possible a thorough study of his ministership, his administration of the war and treasury departments, and his role as a senator and cabinet member. Most of Crawford's contemporaries who achieved national stature have been the subject of one or more scholarly biographies, but only recently did a really satisfactory biography of his closest political associate, James Monroe, appear. Many of the studies of the period give little space to Crawford, and one soon reaches the point of diminishing returns when examining the biographies, general histories, and monographic materials of the first quarter of the nineteenth century. Nevertheless, hundreds of books and articles have been studied for information on, or pertinent to, Crawford, but only a few that significantly touch on his career or are considered essential to an understanding of the topics discussed will be treated in this note. A comparable standard of selectivity is applied to manuscripts, memoirs, diaries, edited works, and newspapers.

Manuscripts

The two largest collections of Crawford materials are in the Manuscript Division, Library of Congress, and in the Duke University Library. The first includes, among other things, his Letter-book (which contains the Journal he kept during the first part of his ministership to France), letters to Crawford, and photostats of letters to Crawford. The materials at Duke are varied in nature and include jottings, calculations, a number of personal letters, and items dealing with his judgeship. Papers at Yale University deal primarily with problems of enforcing the revenue laws; those at the William Clements Library, the New-York Historical Society, and the Chicago Historical Society are wide-ranging in subject and period. Those at Rice University are chiefly correspondence with John O'Connor. Many other depositories have Crawford items, limited in some instances to a single accession. The papers in the possession of Crawford's great-great-granddaughters, Miss Fanny Golding of Columbus, Mississippi, and Mrs. E. E. (Patty) Gross of Hattiesburg, Mississippi, are especially rewarding: they seem to be in the category of cherished items, they have not heretofore been available to researchers, and they bridge a number of gaps in other Crawfordiana.

The James Monroe Papers in the Library of Congress, the New York Public Library, and the University of Virginia Library are barely second in importance to the Crawford papers, for they contain not only letters to and from Crawford and Monroe but items which Crawford had received and transmitted to Monroe in connection with various matters. The Albert Gallatin Papers, in the New-York Historical Society, and the Martin Van Buren Papers, in the Library of Congress, are indispensable. The Gallatin Papers touch upon just about every major event and facet of Crawford's national career up to 1825. The Van Buren Papers are basic to an understanding of the presidential elections of 1816 and 1824.

Papers of Langdon Cheves, the South Carolina Historical Society, and of William Jones, Historical Society of Pennsylvania, are necessary to proper treatment of the relationships between the Treasury Department and the Second Bank of the United States and of the efforts to alleviate and solve the bank and currency problems. The Charles Tait Papers in the Alabama Department of Archives and History are perhaps more intimate in nature than any other collection and reveal much of Georgia, Alabama, and national politics. The large collection of Henry Clay papers in the University of Kentucky Library and the smaller one in the Lilly Library, Indiana University, illuminate the personal and political relationships of Clay and Crawford between 1814 and 1830.

For Georgia matters the holdings of the Georgia Department of Archives and History—which include the manuscript journal of the House of Representatives, the Oglethorpe County tax and other records, the Superior Court records, the governors' files, and the individual name folders—and those of the University of Georgia Library—minutes of the meetings of the university trustees, the Henry Jackson Papers, and the Telemon Cuyler and Keith Read collections—are of paramount importance. The papers of William Lowndes and of Bartlett Yancey at the University of North Carolina and of Walter Clark at the North Carolina Department of Archives and History were the most fruitful for North Carolina; the Edward Harden, Nathaniel Macon, and David Campbell papers at Duke University deal with North Carolina and less confined matters. The Joseph Bryan Papers at the Virginia State Library were especially rewarding for the early part of Crawford's national career, and the Correspondence of John Randolph and James M. Garnett at the same depository and the Randolph Letter Book at the University of Virginia have a wider chronological range.

Materials in the Joseph Nicholson, Asbury Dickins, and J. Henley Smith papers, and the Moses Waddel Diary in the Library of Congress; the Charles Jared Ingersoll Papers and the Simon Gratz, C. W. Conarroe, and Frank M. Etting collections in the Historical Society of Pennsylvania; the John Bailey, Rufus King, John O'Connor, and John W. Taylor papers in the New-York Historical Society; the James Barbour, Samuel Gouverneur, and Azariah C. Flagg papers in the New York Public Library; the Charles K. Gardner Papers in the New York State Library; the Jacob Brown Papers and the Alexander Calvin Washburn and Otis Norcross collections in the Massachusetts Historical Society; the Charles Hammond and the Charles E. Rice papers in the Ohio Historical Society; and the Thomas Worthington and Charles Hammond papers in the Ohio State Library provided much information on the states and on the national scene. The papers of Louis McLane (University of Delaware), Mahlon Dickerson (New Jersey Historical Society), and Jesse B. Thomas (Illinois State Historical Library) were especially useful on Delaware politics and the election of 1824, appointments, and Illinois politics, respectively. Papers of Ninian Edwards and Daniel P. Cook in the Chicago Historical Society are vital to fleshing out some parts of the "A.B." affair, and the Jonathan Russell Papers at Brown University provided many useful items, especially for the years 1818 to 1825. The worth of the autograph files, notably the one at Houghton Library of Harvard University, and of the name and miscellaneous collections of many depositories can readily be determined from the documentation.

Material from the records of the State, War, and Treasury departments, in the National Archives, form the corpus of the treatment of Crawford's ministership to France and his administration of the War and Treasury departments. The Diplomatic Despatches (France, Vols. 14-16) contain not only the correspondence between the secretary of state and the minister but also many of the letters between Crawford and members of the French government. There are many routine materials in the War Department records, but the Military Books are central to policy and to the relations between the department and Congress. The quantity of the Treasury Department records is staggering; many are routine and not germane to this study. Most necessary to the functions chosen for discussion were Series E, Letters and Reports to Congress; Letters Received, Second Comptroller's Office; Letters Received from the Secretary of Treasury, First Comptroller; Treasury Circulars; Excise Letters; Revenue Letters; General Land Office, Miscellaneous Letters; and Series IV (General Land Office and Secretary of Treasury).

Government Publications

For Crawford's senatorial career the *Annals of Congress* are the most important single item. The *Senate Documents* and *House Documents,* containing communications from and to the secretary and Congress, from the President, annual reports of the secretary, reports of committees, and a variety of other information are indispensable to the study of the activities of the War and Treasury departments. Equal importance—though the yield is smaller—must be attached to the Finance, Foreign Affairs, Indian Affairs, Miscellaneous, Military Affairs, and Public Land volumes of the *American State Papers.* The Senate *Executive Journals* are necessary to a detailed analysis of the appointments controversy of 1822, and trustworthy information on appropriations can be secured only from the *Statutes.*

Edited Works

The story of cabinet discussions would sometimes be nonexistent and often meaningless without careful attention to appropriate volumes of Charles Francis Adams, ed., *Memoirs of John Quincy Adams* . . . , 12 vols. (Philadelphia, 1874-1877). Adams was rarely wrong on his facts, but his views, opinions, and evaluations of associates are too frequently strongly biased and jaundiced. The value of Henry Adams, ed., *The Writings of Albert Gallatin*, 3 vols. (Philadelphia, 1879), is diminished by the omission of large portions of letters. The total effect of a number of letters, most of which are easily accessible in the Gallatin Papers in the New-York Historical Society, is vastly different from that conveyed by the published version. Stanislaus Murray Hamilton, ed., *The Writings of James Monroe*, 7 vols. (New York, 1898-1903); Charles R. King, ed., *The Life and Correspondence of Rufus King*, 6 vols. (New York, 1894-1900); and the three volumes of James F. Hopkins, ed., Mary W. M. Hargreaves, assoc. ed., *The Papers of Henry Clay* (Lexington, Ky., 1959-   ), contributed valuable information on many topics, while Catharina Visscher (Van Rensselaer) Bonney, comp., *A Legacy of Historical Gleanings* . . . , 2 vols. (Albany, N.Y., 1875), contains a number of letters no longer available elsewhere, and Everett S. Brown, ed., *The Missouri Compromises and Presidential Politics, 1820-1825* (St. Louis, Mo., 1926), is important for ideas, opinions, and positions of several national figures during the half decade covered. Gaillard Hunt, ed., *The First Forty Years of Washington Society* . . . (New York, 1906), discloses important information on Crawford's family and social life, as well as political maneuverings and social activities in the national capital. E. B. Washburn, ed., *The Edwards Papers* . . . (Chicago, 1884); Richard K. Crallé, ed., *The Works of John C. Calhoun*, 6 vols. (New York, 1857-1864); and J. G. deRoulhac Hamilton, ed., "Letters to Bartlett Yancey," *James Sprunt Historical Studies*, Vol. 10, No. 2, also have limited significance.

Newspapers

Niles' Weekly Register occupies a unique position for any student of the second, third, fourth, and fifth decades of the nineteenth century: it is far more than a newspaper since it contains not only news but copyings from papers throughout the country, many documents, reports, letters, and other materials that are no longer available elsewhere. At least one newspaper in each state —usually more than two—was run for the lengthy 1824 campaign; more comprehensive coverage was given to the Washington, D.C., and Georgia papers for all of Crawford's career. Among the most useful were: *National Intelligencer, National Journal, Washington Gazette, Washington Republican,* Washington, D.C.; *Augusta Chronicle and Georgia Advertiser, Milledgeville Georgia Journal, Savannah Republican, Athens Southern Banner, Athens Journal, Athens Gazette,* Georgia; *Raleigh Observer, Raleigh Star,* North Carolina; *Richmond Enquirer,* Virginia; *Baltimore Patriot, Federal Gazette & Baltimore Daily Advertiser, Baltimore American & Commercial Daily Advertiser,* Maryland; *Philadelphia Democratic Press,* Pennsylvania; *Albany Argus, Albany Microscope,* New York; *Boston Patriot, Boston Columbian Centinel, Taunton Free Press,* Massachusetts; *Portsmouth Journal, New Hampshire Patriot,* New Hampshire; *Mobile Commercial Advertiser, Montgomery Republican,* Alabama; *Nashville Whig,* Tennessee; and *Illinois Intelligencer.*

Others

Most biographies, monographs, and other secondary materials make little contribution to the understanding of Crawford's career. A few of these accounts do deal extensively with the Georgian, with his contemporaries, or with problems, issues, and events that are central to a proper perspective and evaluation of Crawford's activities. J. E. D. Shipp, *Giant Days, or the Life and Times of William H. Crawford* (Americus, Ga., 1909); [George M. Dudley], "William H. Crawford," James Herring and James Barton Longacre, *The National Portrait Gallery of Distinguished Americans* (Philadelphia, 1840), vol. 4; Joseph H. Cobb, *Leisure Labors; or, Miscellanies Historical, Literary, and Political* (New York, 1858); George R. Gilmer, *Sketches of Some of the First Settlers of Upper Georgia, of the Cherokees, and the Author* (New York, 1855; rev. ed., Americus, Ga., 1926); Ulrich B. Phillips, *Georgia and State Rights* (Washington, D.C., 1902); and Alvin Laroy Duckett, *John Forsyth, Political Tactician* (Athens, Ga., 1962), contribute most to the Georgia phase of his career. Henry Adams,

History of the United States of America, 9 vols. (New York, 1909-1911); Henry Adams, *The Life of Albert Gallatin* (Philadelphia, 1880); Irving Brant, *James Madison,* 6 vols. (Indianapolis, Ind., 1941-1961); Charles M. Wiltse, *John C. Calhoun,* 3 vols. (New York, 1944-1951); Samuel Flagg Bemis, *John Quincy Adams and the Foundations of American Foreign Policy* (New York, 1949); and Harry Ammon, *James Monroe: The Quest for National Identity* (New York, 1971), provide a more general and national setting. Ralph C. H. Catterall, *The Second Bank of the United States* (Chicago, 1903), and Bray Hammond, *Banks and Banking in America from the Revolution to the Civil War* (New York, 1957), are fundamental to comprehension of the bank and currency issues. The same is true of Leonard D. White, *The Jeffersonians: A Study in Administrative History, 1801-1829* (New York, 1951), in the area of administrative practices and trends. DeAlva Stanwood Alexander, *A Political History of New York,* 3 vols. (New York, 1906-1909); Jabez D. Hammond, *The History of Political Parties in the State of New York,* 2 vols. (Cooperstown, N.Y., 1847); and Robert V. Remini, *Martin Van Buren and the Making of the Democratic Party* (New York, 1959), throw much light on political events in New York, especially during the 1816 and 1824 elections.

Index